A HISTORY OF SINO-RUSSIAN RELATIONS

A HISTORY OF SINO-RUSSIAN RELATIONS

Tien-fong Cheng

Formerly Minister of Education of the Republic of China

INTRODUCTION BY JOHN LEIGHTON STUART,
AMBASSADOR TO THE REPUBLIC OF CHINA, 1946-1952

Public Affairs Press, Washington, D. C.

419 New Jersey Ave., Southeast, Washington 3, D. C.
Printed in the United States of America
Library of Congress Catalog Card No. 57-6908

Introduction

It has given me great pleasure to write a brief introduction for Dr. Tien-fong Cheng's book on the subject of Sino-Russian relations.

Dr. Cheng has been known to me for the past thirty years as an ardent believer in Dr. Sun Yat-sen's "Three People's Principles" and a distinguished scholar, well educated both in the United States and Canada. He has also been active in various fields in promoting cultural exchange between China and the Western world. I have ample reason to believe that his democratic views and his long service in the past have been sources of inspiration to write this book as a historian more than a partisan. I doubt if there is any person whose understanding of the Sino-Russian relations and their political complications equals that of Dr. Cheng. His intensive study and pragmatic experience in government service have made his opinions more pertinent.

After all, the ideological conquest of China by the Soviet Union has been one of the greatest tragedies since the Second World War. It is hard to believe that China with so rich a cultural heritage could be ruled by Bolshevism too long. I do not think that the mainland of China is irrevocably lost. The Communists have consolidated their position on the mainland and it does indeed look now as though they are very firmly in control there. But who can say that any political regime in China is permanent? Who, if he thinks of the changes that have taken place in China and throughout the Far East since the days of Sun Yat-sen, can say that the Communist regime is in China to stay? The Communist ideology is alien to China's political philosophies. The Communist practices are violent, indifferent to human rights, and oppressive. The Communists show no regard for China's international obligations, are contemptuous of the rights and interests of other nations, and they have gone so far as to invade several neighboring states and to make war on the United Nations. I cannot believe that such a Russian dominated Chinese regime will last. I have faith that somehow and within a not very long time this Russian satellite will have run its course and will be forced to relax its grip.

JOHN LEIGHTON STUART

Washington, D. C.

Preface

Lin Tse-hsu, a famous Chinese statesman, declared in the middle of the nineteenth century that "the country which will eventually be a great menace to China is Russia". This opinion was expressed not long after the Opium War (1839-1842) when British imperialism began to be felt in China while all was quiet on the Sino-Russian frontiers. Yet it was prophetic, for from 1858 to 1917 Russia seized the Amur and Ussuri regions, penetrated into Manchuria and Sinkiang and made Outer Mongolia a Russian protectorate. Then came the Russian revolution. After its establishment the Soviet Government continued the old aggressive policy but adopted new tactics in China. Instead of applying outside pressures alone it used the tactics of "boring from within" and created fifth columnists—the Chinese Communists. Ever since 1921 there has been a gigantic struggle in China between the Chinese Communists and all anti-Communist forces led by the Kuomintang. The Communists were twice on the brink of annihilation when the Mukden incident of 1931 and the Sian incident of 1936 saved them. Then the Sino-Japanese War (1937-1945) gave them a golden opportunity to expand and the Chinese mainland fell into their hands in 1949. But the struggle is not yet over; it is being carried on by Free China, by the overseas Chinese, and by the Chinese people on the mainland in an underground way.

As a member of the Kuomintang, as a government official, as an educator, and as an advocate of democracy, the author has taken part in this struggle for more than thirty years and almost lost his life for the cause. He has thus been keenly interested in Sino-Russian relations and has given it a great deal of attention. In the spring of 1955 he was invited by the Far Eastern Institute of the University of Washington to give lectures on the history of the Kuomintang and on Communism in China and in the spring of 1956 he lectured on Sino-Russian relations at Fordham University. These lectures necessitated additional research work and resulted in the writing of this book.

In this book the author has tried his best to present all the salient facts in Sino-Russian relations as they are and not to distort them; in other words he has tried to write as a historian and not as a member of the Kuomintang. But every historian is entitled to his views and interpretation of historical events and the author has clearly expressed his views and interpretation in the book. It is anticipated that these views may not be accepted by every reader and that they will be criticized by Communists, fellow-travelers and left-wing writers as reactionary because they are anti-Communist. The author will be happy if by reading this book interest is aroused in one of the greatest problems confronting the world today.

For the convenience of the reader the author has used sources in the English language as far as possible, but sometimes it is unavoidable to use Chinese materials. To give first-hand information he has also occasionally quoted from his diary the account of events when they actually took place. As the book has been written rather in a limited time errors are bound to occur which, the author hopes, will be discovered and corrected in the future. Thanks are due to Dr. John Leighton Stuart for writing the introduction and to the Library of Congress for giving the author every facility in using its books, periodicals, newspapers and even unpublished manuscripts.

As the author is writing this preface in the shadow of the Capitol dome, symbol of a true democracy, he cannot help thinking of his compatriots on the Chinese mainland who have lost every freedom and human dignity and live directly under tyrannical Communist rule and indirectly under Soviet domination. He can only wish and pray that they will, with the help of Free China and the free world, throw off their Soviet and Communist yoke and become free men again some day.

TIEN-FONG CHENG

Washington, D. C.

Contents

CHAPTER I

Mongolian Conquest of Russian Principalities

Although China and the Soviet Union today have a common border line extending more than 5,000 miles, the longest boundary line between any two countries in the world, yet for many centuries the Chinese and Russians existed without knowing each other. It was through the Mongols that they first came into indirect contact.

The Mongols were nomadic people who emerged, towards the end of the 12th century, from complete obscurity to a prominent place in history. In 1162 a son was born to the chieftain of the Mongols, Yesukai, who had just defeated Tartar Chieftain Temuchin[1] in a fierce battle. In the clenched fist of the infant there was a clot of blood like a red stone and in the eyes of superstitious Yesukai this referred to his victory over Temuchin. So he named his son Temuchin as a rememberance of the victory. Temuchin succeeded Yesukai as chieftain at the age of thirteen. Because of his youth some tribes began to desert him but his mother, Yulun, a very able woman, kept the allegiance of half of them.

Temuchin, though uneducated, was a military genius. When he grew up he became an excellent warrior and military organizer. He defeated the Normans, Keraits, Merkits and Uighurs and subjected them to his rule. In 1206 he summoned all his tribal chieftains to Karakorum, proclaimed himself the ruler of the new Mongol empire and assumed the title Chengiz Khan[2] (Chengiz means in Mongolian "perfect warrior"). He then pursued the remnant forces of the Norman Khan, Polo, and the Merkit Khan, Toto. Polo was killed in a battle and his successor Kushlek fled with Toto to the Irtysh region. In 1208 a battle was fought on the banks of the Irtysh in which Toto was killed and Kushlek fled to the court of Khitan Tartars. Then Chengiz Khan proceeded to conquer the Kingdom of Hsia and the Empire of Chin in North China. He and his son Tule commanded the Central Army, occupied Peking and pushed as far as Shantung. The Right Wing under the command of his other sons Jugi, Jagatai and Ogotai marched southward to Honan; the Left Wing under the command of his brothers Hochar, Kwangtsin Noyen, and Chowtsteposhi entered present-day Manchuria and occupied Liaosi. At that time Kushlek usurped the power of the Khitan Khan and was preparing for an attack on the Mongols. Upon hearing this news Chengiz Khan returned to Karakorum and took the intiative to attack the Khitans first. The Khitan army was defeated and Kushlek was captured. The whole khanate was incorporated into the Mongol empire.

The invasion of Europe by Chengiz Khan was incidental rather than intentional. After conquering the Khitan khanate the Mongol empire became a neighbor of the Kharismian (or Khwarism) empire which then controlled Turkestan, Persia and North India. At first Chengiz Khan wanted to keep friendly relations with Kharismia. So he sent envoys to Shah Mohammed with a letter which read in part: "I send thee greetings; I know thy power, and the vast extent of thine empire; I regard thee as my most cherished son. On my part thou must know that I have conquered China and all the Turkish nations north of it; thou knowst that my country is a magazine of warriors, a mine of silver and that I have no need of other lands. I take it that we have an equal interest in encouraging trade between our subjects."[3] Had this friendly gesture been reciprocated by the Shah, peaceful relations would have been maintained. Unfortunately soon after the despatch of this letter a group of Mongolian traders was sent into Transoxiana and was executed by Governor Inaljuk of Otrar as spies. Chengiz Khan then demanded the expatriation of Inaljuk to Mongolia to be punished. This demand so irritated Shah Mohammed that he executed the chief envoy of Chengiz Khan and expelled other envoys after cutting off their beards. As a consequence Chengiz Khan in 1219 started an expedition from Karakorum against Kharismia.

Shah Mohammed personnally commanded an army of 400,000 to defend his empire but was crushingly defeated by the Mongol army of Tuji with 160,000 deaths. Another Mongol army commanded by Jagatai occupied Otrar after five month's seige and executed Inaljuk. A third Mongol army occupied Khogent in the Jaxantes. A fourth Mongol army commanded by Chengiz Khan and Tule, after occupying Tashkent, Nur and Bukhara, pushed on to Samarcand where Mohammed had fled. Samarcand soon surrendered. Mohammed fled to Nishapur, but before reaching it he died of pleurisy at Astara on the shore of the Caspian Sea. His son Jelaleddin succeeded him as the Shah in India. After occupying Nessa and Nishapur Chengiz Khan and Tule attacked Jelaleddin on the banks of the Indus. Although the Turkish army under Jelaleddin fought very bravely it was finally defeated by the Mongols and Jelaleddin had to flee to

Delhi. The Mongol army then razed several provinces in northern India and returned to Mongolia.

It was in the course of pursuing Jelaleddin that Chepe and Sabutai, two Mongol generals, marched their troops through Azerbaijan and entered Georgia in the spring of 1222. Thus began the Mongol invasion of Europe. They defeated the combined forces of the Lesghians, Circussins and Kipchaks and occupied Astrakhan near the mouth of the Volga. They then pushed westward to the Don river. At that time Russia was not unified and was divided into many principalities ruled by native princes. At Kiev the Russian princes were completely surprised by the news that an unheard-of enemy, the Mongols, was approaching from the east. Under the leadership of Prince Mitislaf seven princes gathered their troops on the Dnieper region to defend their territory. The Mongol generals sent envoys to the princes to talk about peace but the envoys were executed. Thus enraged the Mongols declared to the princes: "You have killed our envoys. Well, as you wish for war you shall have it. We have done you no harm; God is impartial; he will decide our quarrel."[4] A battle was fought on the banks of the Kalka for several days and the Russians were utterly defeated. Nearly all the princes and seventy bogatyns perished in the fighting. After ravaging South Russia and Great Bulgaria the Mongol army retreated to Mongolia.

In 1227 Chengiz Khan became seriously ill in Kansu and died at Halaotu on his way back to Karakorum. When Chengiz Khan succeeded his father as chieftain of the Mongols he controlled only a part of present-day Outer Mongolia. At the time of his death fifty-two years later he had built an empire extending from the Pacific to the Dnieper and from the middle of Siberia to the borders of Tibet and India.[5] Even after his death the Mongol empire continued to vigorously expand. In 1234 his son Ogotai. who succeeded him as the Grand Khan, put an end to the Chin empire and thus completely conquered North China and Manchuria. Ogotai also granted to his nephew Batu, son of Juji, all the territory from the Ural mountains to the Dnieper river. By way of expressing his appreciation Batu led a second expeditionary army of 300,000—mostly Mongols, Tartars and Turks—into Europe in 1235; it was an amazing march. In 1236 Batu conquered the kingdom of the Bolgars on the Volga; in the following year Batu crossed the river and pushed ahead toward Vladimir, which had become a new center of Russia. Vladimir was surrounded and taken and Grand Prince Yury retreated northward to raise a new army.

The Mongol army followed him and took all the Volga towns from Yaroslavl to Gatech. Moscow was also devastated. Then in March 1238 the Mongols came up with Yury on the Sit river and destroyed him and his forces. They marched westward toward Novgorod. But the marshes saved the city and the Mongols turned away southward without attacking it. After occupying Pereyaslavl and Tchernigor in 1239 they demolished Kiev.

Subsequently, Batu crossed the Carpathians and routed the Hungarians on the Sajo. In 1241 he laid Poland waste and annihilated a mixed army of Poles and Germans at the battle of Liegnitz, but he failed to take Olmütz and was repulsed by the Czechs under King Vaclar I. The Mongols then returned to Hungary and tried to enter Austria; there they were again stopped by the combined forces of King Vaclar I and the Duke of Austria, but they continued southward and reached the Adriatic. When news of the sudden death of Ogotai reached the Mongols in Europe in 1242 many generals led their troops back to Mongolia to take part in the Kuriltai or the assembly of the notables for the election of a new Grand Khan. Instead of returning to Mongolia Batu retreated to the valley of the lower Volga and established his headquarters at Saray. Thus in six years (1236-1242) the Mongols overran almost all Russia, Bulgaria, Poland, and Hungary. "Now, this story of Mongolian conquests is," in the opinion of H. G. Wells, "surely one of the most remarkable in all history. The conquests of Alexander the Great cannot compare with them in extent. Their effect in diffusing and broadening men's ideas and stimulating their imaginations was enormous."[6]

What accounts for the success of the Mongol army over the Europeans? In the first place the Mongols were brave and hardy warriors. They were absolutely obedient to their superiors and would fight to the death; proud of their record of many years of victorious war, they believed that they were destined to carry out their mission to conquer the world. As Marco Polo told us: "They could live for a month . . . on mare's milk, of which they made a kind of porridge; they could stay on horseback for two days on end, and sleep while their horses grazed. Each man took about 18 horses with him and rode them in turns; if without other food, they would draw blood from their veins. In battle they executed their cavalry maneuvers like one man with extraordinary rapidity."[7] Their victory was also due to superior strategy and intelligence work.

"It is only recently," says Bury in his notes to Gibbon's *Decline and Fall of the Roman Empire,* "that European history has begun to understand that the successes of the Mongol army which overran Poland and occupied Hungary in the spring of A.D. 1241 were won by consummate strategy and were not due to a mere overwhelming superiority of numbers... It was wonderful how punctually and effectually the arrangements of the commander were carried out in operations extending from the Lower Vistula to Transylvania. Such a campaign was quite beyond the power of any European army of the time. There was no general in Europe, from Frederick II downwards, who was not a tyro in strategy compared to Subutai. It should also be noticed that the Mongols embarked upon the enterprise with full knowledge of the political situation of Hungary and the condition of Poland—they had taken care to inform themselves by a well-organized system of spies; on the other hand, the Hungarians and the Christian powers, like childish barbarians, knew hardly anything about their enemies."[8]

The Khanate of Kipchak was now established by the Mongol empire to rule the Russian people. Its Khan was Batu and its capital was Saray. It was more widely known as the Khanate of the Golden Horde, a name derived from the magnificent golden tent used by Batu Khan. Like other empires founded by nomads the relation of this Khanate with the mass of people was simply one of taxation for the maintenance of the horde. Mongol officials went to different principalities and cities each year to collect tributes. The Russian princes kept their titles and ruled their subjects but had to make personal visits to Saray and sometimes even to Karakorum to pay their respects to the Grand Khan.

In 1247 the Mongol envoys came to Novgorod for tribute. As the city had not been conquered by the Mongols the people were stirred and there were riots which endangered the envoy's lives. Prince Alexander Nevsky of Vladimir who had visited Batu knew that it was hopeless to resist the Golden Horde and persuaded his subjects to submit. In 1263 a number of towns on the Volga refused to pay tribute and drove the Mongol tax-collectors out. A large Mongol army was on its way to punish these towns when Alexander made another journey to Saray and succeeded in begging the Khan to call off the expedition while the towns paid their tribute.

In the meantime Kuyak, who had succeeded Ogotai as the Grand Khan, died in 1251 and Mangu, son of Tule, was elected to succeed Kuyak. During his reign Mangu further extended the Mongol empire. He sent his brother Kublai to conquer South China which was still ruled by the Sung dynasty and another brother Hulagu to invade

Persia and Syria. Tibet was also invaded by Mangu's army and devastated. When Mangu died in 1259 Kublai was elected by the Kuriltai to be the Grand Khan. Kublai removed his capital from Karakorum to Peking and established the Yuan dynasty in China. In 1279 South China was completely subjected and the Sung dynasty went out of existence. At that time the Mongol empire was at the height of its expansion. There was the main empire (Yuan) which controlled China proper, Mongolia, Manchuria, and a part of eastern Siberia. Outside this main empire there were four khanates: viz., (1) the Khanate of the Golden Horde which ruled Russia and a part of Central Asia; (2) the Khanate of Sibir which ruled Altai and western Siberia; (3) the Khanate of Zagatai which ruled Chinese Turkestan and Central Asia; and (4) the Khanate of Il which ruled Persia, Arabia, Asia, and Kharismia.[9] Such a vast empire was indeed the greatest in history and was not easy to be kept together. So during the late years of Kublai's reign the ties between the khanates and the empire began to loosen. After Kublai's death in 1294 the title of the Grand Khan was abolished and the Khanates became practically independent.

For two and a half centuries the Khanate of the Golden Horde ruled the Russian principalities. The Russians, both the princes and the people, naturally resented Mongol rule but at first they were too divided, weak and helpless to shake off the yoke. Moscow grew in power and played a more and more important role in Russian history. The name of Moscow first appeared in 1147 and ten years later it was surrounded with wooden walls. It was centrally situated and with easy access to other parts of Russia through various rivers. During the Mongol invasion many Russian people in the Volga region fled to Moscow and greatly increased its population.

Alexander Nevsky, owing to his submission to the Golden Horde was bestowed the office of Grand Prince by the Khanate. This title passed later to his brothers, Yaroslav of Tver and Basil of Kostroma in succession and then to the next generation. Moscow, being then a small principality, went into the hands first of Khorobrit, younger brother of Nevsky and later of Daniel, youngest son of Nevsky from whom the permanent line of Moscow started. When his son Yury succeeded Daniel in 1319 he feuded with his cousin, Prince Michael of Tver, and murdered the latter. Yury was in turn killed by Dmitry, son of Michael. Dmitry was also killed and Alexander of Tver became Grand Prince in 1326. Next year Khan Uzbek sent his cousin and lietenant, Chol-Khan, to collect tribute in Tver. The arrogance and violence of the Mongols enraged the people of Tver who rose and killed Chol-Khan and his subordinates. Seeing his chance for revenge Ivan I of Moscow, brother and successor of Yury, went to the Golden Horde and returned with a punitive army of 50,000 Mongols. Tver was ravaged and Alexander was killed. Khan Uzbeg then appointed Ivan I Grand Prince and thereafter the title never passed out of his family.

Ivan I was very able in managing the finance of his principality and was nicknamed Ivan Kalita (moneybag). With money he could please the Khan and secured immunity from Mongol invasions. He was even entrusted by the Khan to collect tribute from other principalities and thus exercised some power over them. During his reign (1328-1340) the domains of Moscow were extended considerably. His son, Simeon, was not only confirmed as Grand Prince but the Khan "put all the other princes in his hands".[10] On Simeon's brother, Ivan II, who succeeded him in 1353 the Khan further bestowed the right of justice over other princes.

During the reign of Dmitry, son of Ivan II, the rule of the Golden Horde over Russia began to shake. The Mongols of the Golden Horde had by then become Mohammedans. There were then two rival Khans. Abdul and Murad, and the political power was in the hands of the Vizier, Mamai. In 1365 a Mongol force on its way back from a raiding mission was sharply defeated by the men of Ryazan, southeast of Moscow. Eight years later Mamai led an army into Ryazan and destroyed it. Next year Mamai's envoys and 1500 Mongols were massacred in Nizhny-Novgorod. In 1375 Nizhny was devastated. In 1378 the Mongols again surprised Nizhny and burned the town but Dmitry defeated them on the Vozha. Mamai now became the Khan himself and demanded the old tribute as Moscow was paying only a reduced one. Upon Dmitry's refusal Mamai collected a big army to conquer Moscow. Dmitry, supported by other Russian princes, also gathered a large army to meet the invasion. The Russians crossed the Don on September 7, 1380 and the next day fought a tremendous battle against the Mongols on the plains of Kulikovo. A strong wind favored the Russians and they won the battle but with great losses: only 40,000 were left out of 150,000. Mamai was gathering a new army when he was overthrown by a rival Khan, Tokhtamysh. Tokhtamysh then led an expeditionary army himself, captured Sespukhov and appeared before Moscow in 1382. Dmitry was away but the soldiers of Moscow fought very bravely.

Tokhtamysh besieged Moscow for several days but could not occupy it and finally had to withdraw.

Meanwhile another Mongol leader, Timur or Tamerlane the Great, had risen in the east and built a second vast empire in imitation of Chengiz Khan. He was descended in the female line from Chengiz Khan and rose in western Turkestan. By 1369 he had established an empire from North India to Asia Minor, spread his authority over Kipchak and Siberia, and assumed the title of Grand Khan. Tokhtamysh was appointed Khan by Timur but rebelled against him in 1395. After leading an army into Kipchak and crushing Tokhtamysh's forces, Timur entered Russian territory and occupied Elets. At that time Vasily I, son of Dmitry, was the Grand Prince and marched out to meet Timur. But for some reason Timur retreated and did not attack Moscow. In 1405 Edigei, the Vizier of the Golden Horde suddenly appeared before Moscow with an army, stayed there a month without attacking the city and finally withdrew after exacting a large sum of money. During his reign Vasily annexed Nizhny-Novgorod and made one visit to the Golden Horde in order to have this annexation confirmed by the Khan.

After Vasily I's death civil war broke out in the princely family of Moscow. Though Vasily II was confirmed as Grand Prince by the Khan his uncle Yury, brother of Vasily I, claimed the throne, and captured Vasily II and reigned in Moscow. But the boyars rallied round Vasily II and he was eventually restored to the throne. Two years later he was again seized by Shemyaka, son of Yury, blinded and dethroned. But the country rallied to Vasily II and restored him. Meanwhile the Golden Horde was having its own internal trouble. In 1437 Ulu Mehmet was expelled from the Horde and founded a separate principality of Kuzan. Later another separate horde was founded in Crimea. In 1451 the Mongols again appeared before Moscow but were defeated and fled at night, leaving all heavy baggage. Vasily II annexed Mozhaisk and Serpukhov and had a firm grip on Ryazan. The domain of Moscow had grown from 500 square miles during the reign of Daniel to 15,000 square miles at the death of Vasily II. (1462)

But it was Vasily II's son, Ivan III, who expanded his domain enormously and laid down the foundation of the later Russian empire. In 1463 what was left of the principality of Yaroslavl was voluntarily submitted to him. From 1465 to 1488 Ivan III absorbed, step by step, Novgorod the Great with its immense territory. In 1472 he subjected the vast region of Perm near the Urals and in 1485 he annexed the territory of Tver. Versa and Ryazan also became parts of his domain. Ivan III married Sophia, niece of the last emperor, Constantine Paleologus, whose influence hastened throwing off the Mongol yoke. In 1476 Ahmed Khan of the Golden Horde summoned Ivan III to Saray and received a refusal. A second envoy was sent and was insulted by Ivan III. When in 1480 Ahmed Khan led a large army to attack Moscow, Ivan III sent Sophia to Archangel and made preparations for his own flight. Moscow was furious and called Ivan III a coward. Even his son refused to leave the front. Ivan joined the army but only to leave it again. But on November 19 the Mongol army suddenly retreated and on his way back Ahmed was surprisingly attacked by the Nogays and was killed in his sleep. Thus Moscow finally got rid of the Mongol yoke and won its complete independence. Ivan III then took up the title of Sovereign of All Russia and even used the title Tsar in dealing with small foreign states. Ahmed's sons were finally overthrown by the Mongol Khanate of Crimea in 1502 and the Golden Horde was completely destroyed. Then in the middle of the 16th century, during the reign of Ivan the Terrible, Kazan and Astrakhan were captured by the Russians.

The Mongolian conquest of Russia was indeed cruel and barbarous: the Mongols looted, burned, and killed innocent people, and sometimes even massacred a whole town or city. Their long rule over the Russian was indeed harsh and not benevolent. But this long Mongol rule had great influence in shaping the Russian political and social structure. "The Mongolian state was built upon the principle of unquestioning submission of the individual to the group, first to the clan and through the clan to the whole state. This principle was in the course of time impressed thoroughly upon the Russian people... Under the influence of Mongolian ideas, the Russian state developed on the basis of universal service. All classes of society were made a definite part of the state organization".[11] The Mongols also introduced the principle of autocratic power of the Khan. When the rule of the Khan was weakened the view of the unlimited authority of the Khan was transferred to the Grand Prince of Moscow. Under Mongolian influence Moscow developed systems of taxation, census and post. The military organization of Moscow was also modelled after that of the Mongols and cavalry became the basic military force. Finally the Mongol rule did much to arouse the national sentiment of the Russian people and to help unite all Russia into one big empire under Moscow.

Mongol rule began in North China in 1213 and in South China in 1280; it ended in 1368. The Golden Horde ruled Russia from 1237 to 1480. So for almost 140 years China and Russia were parts of the same Mongol empire. During this time there must have been many contacts between the Chinese and the Russians. Many Russian princes paid visits to Karakorum in the 13th century and a Russian regiment was stationed at Peking during the reign of Tob-Timur Khan. There were also Russians among the imperial guards at Peking.[12] But unfortunately there were no writers like Italy's Marco Polo among the Russian princes, priests, soldiers and other travellers who went to Mongolia or China at that time and no accounts of their travels can now be found.

CHAPTER II

Russian Expansion Towards the Pacific

Three and a half centuries after the Mongol invasion and exactly a century after the collapse of the Mongol rule history reversed itself and the Russians began to push eastward. As early as the 11th century enterprising traders of Novgorod penetrated into western Siberia in search of valuable furs, but territorial annexation had not been contemplated until the middle of the 16th century. At that time Russia had expanded to the Urals and the Khanate of Sibir had disintergrated. Ediger, Khan of Sibir, was then challenged by Kuchun Khan, a new chieftain rising in the west. So in 1555 Ediger Khan sent envoys to Moscow to pay tribute and to beg Tsar Ivan the Terrible to protect the Khanate of Sibir against the attack of Kuchun. Ivan was interested but did not actually protect the khanate, which was taken by Kuchun Khan in 1563. In 1571 Kuchun Khan also sent envoys to offer his submission to the Tsar and so when Ivan the Terrible wrote to King Edward VI of England he already styled himself, besides other titles, "Lord of All Siber".[1]

But the actual penetration and occupation of Siberia at this early stage was mainly the result of private adventures. In 1558 a rich merchant family of Stroganov, whose mines and trade extended to the basin of the Kama near the Urals, petitioned the Tsar for permission to develop and exploit the region beyond the mountains. This request was granted and even the right to levy troops and administer justice was conferred upon the Stroganovs. Thereafter they frequently sent armed men to western Siberia and the Russian eastward expansion had begun. But the deep penetration did not take place until 1581. In that year the chieftain of Stroganov's private army, Yermak (his real name was Vasili Timofeiev) led 800 Cossacks into western Siberia. After engaging in several skirmishes Yermak reached the Irtysh in September 1582. Yermak then sent a deputation to Moscow to offer to the Tsar rich tribute in furs and the new acquired vast territory. Ivan the Terrible was highly pleased and pardoned him a sentence of death which had been imposed upon him for the misconduct of his followers. He was given a medal by the Tsar and was hailed as a great hero by the Russian people.

In 1583 Yermak extended his occupation by pushing forward along the Irtysh and the Ob. Mameitolik, a brave Tartar general, was captured by the Cossacks. In March, 1584 another Tartar general, Garaka, led a group of Tartars and Ostyaks and tried to besiege Sibir but was routed by Yermak. Then in June, when Yermak was searching Garaka along the Irtysh, he was surprised by the Tartars in a storm at night and defeated. Yermak tried to swim across the river but was drowned owing to heavy armor. Upon hearing the news of Yermak's death the Tartars, Voguls, Ostyaks, etc. all rose against the Russians. Consequently the remnant Cossacks, some 150, had to abandon Sibir and return to Russia. Thereupon the Kunchun Tartars re-entered Sibir.[2] In 1585 Tsar Feodor Ivanovich sent two generals with a Cossack army to Siberia who founded Tiumen as their base and cleared the nearby area of the Tartar forces. In 1587 Tobolsk was established. Next year the Russians lured Shejak Khan and Garaka from Sibir to Tobolsk and captured them there. Sibir was demolished. Thereupon the resistance of the native tribes in western Siberia ended and the Russians could push further east.

The Russian Government now turned its attention to actual colonization and administration. In 1590, 3000 peasant families were sent to western Siberia to cultivate the new land. Administration was directed from Tiumen and Tobolsk. Natives found little change in the Russian rule besides the fact that they paid tribute to the "Voyevodus", instead of the Tartar officers. "Ostensibly the duties of these 'voyevodus' were to maintain peace in the province and to prevent lawlessness, distilling, drunkenness, and gambling, which would diminish the revenue and unfit the men for service. In reality they were quite often corrupt and so busily engaged in feathering their nests. Neither the appointment of special customs officers, ('golova'), in charge of all money and tributes, nor other devices were successful in checking the corruption".[3] In 1604 Tomsk was founded on the Ob as the new seat of the Siberian Government. In 1619 the Cossacks reached the Yenissei and founded Yenisseisk. In 1628 they crossed the Yenissei and advanced to the Lena in eastern Siberia. In 1631 they sailed down the Yenissei and reached its mouth, flowing into the Arctic Ocean. In 1637 the fort of Yakutsk was established on the Lena as a base for pushing further east.

From Yakutsk a number of Cossack expeditions were sent forth to explore the unknown land to the east. The most successful expedition was that of Valilei Poyarkov in 1643. Poyarkov was sent by the Russian voivod of Yakutsk, Peter Patriovich Golovin, with 127 Cossacks and two interpreters to explore the Amur. His party left Yakutsk in June, 1643, sailed down the Lena and entered the Aldan on whose bank they spent the winter. Their food being exhausted, they practiced cannibalism and ate the flesh of the natives and even the corpses of their own comrades who died of starvation. In the next spring Poyarkov led the men southward across the Stannovoi or Outer Khingan mountains and finally reached the Amur. Then they built small boats and sailed down the river. In the spring of 1644 they entered the Sea of Okhotsk and sailed northward along its coast. After three months' sailing they reached the mouth of the Oud where they spent the winter. In 1646 they started from the bank of the Oud, crossed the Stannovoi again and returned to Yakutsk in the autumn. They spent more than three years and covered five thousand miles on their expedition. They suffered hunger, violent cold and disease and had to fight the wilderness and advance step by step. The record of their adventure is indeed a record of human bravery and endurance. Two years earlier Michaelo Stadukhin had sailed about a thousand miles from the mouth of the Lena eastward along the coast of the Arctic Ocean to the mouth of the Kolyma. In 1648 another expedition led by Simon Dejniev actually reached the Anadyr and later visited Kamchatka. At the same time some other Russians reached Cape Chukotsky and entered the strait which was later named Bering.

Thus, within the short period of sixty-seven years (1581-1648) Russia had pushed from the Urals to the Pacific and the vast territory of Siberia, (not including the Amur and Ussuri regions) totaling four and a half million square miles, was added to the Russian empire. This was indeed an unparalleled phenomenon in history, for it took the early American settlers about two centuries to push from the Atlantic to the Pacific.

There are two reasons which account for the rapid Russian occupation of Siberia. In the first place what the Russians penetrated into was practically a "no man's land". Siberia, while rich in mineral resources, is not productive agriculturally. Seventy-five per cent of its area is in the region of the "permanently frozen" earth where the soil never completely thaws.[4] Therefore food production in Siberia has not been able to feed a large population. The severe cold climate in the winter also checked the growth of the settlers. Consequently as late as the middle of the 19th century after three centuries of Russian colonization there were only 2,700,000 inhabitants in all Siberia.[5] At the time of Yermak's and Poyarkov's expeditions the number of native could not be more than 500,000. So except for a few towns and villages Siberia was simply a vast wilderness. Secondly Siberia was then not only a population vacuum but also a power vacuum. Besides the disintegrating Khanate of Sibir and the small Kuchun Khanate in Western Siberia there were no political organizations among the native tribes. Consequently after the collapse of the Khanate of Sibir and after conquering the Kuchun Tartars, the Russians fought not against men but against nature. Some weak opposition was offered by the Tungus in the Yenissei basin and by the Buryats near Lake Baikal but was easily suppressed. Most of the tribesmen simply submitted to the authority of the new conquerors without any resistance.

CHAPTER III

Early Sino-Russian Relations: Treaties of Nerchinsk and Kiakhta

In the middle of the seventeenth century when Russia was penetrating into eastern Siberia the Manchus rose in power in Manchuria. The Manchus started as a small tribe at the foot of the Changpei mountains. Under the leadership of Nurhachu (1583-1626) and his son Huang Taichi (1627-1643) they had subjugated all other tribes and ruled all Manchuria. The Ming dynasty, the last Chinese dynasty in China's long history, was then disintegrating and the Manchus were thus given a chance to conquer China. In 1644 Emperor Shunchih entered Peking and established the Ching or Manchu dynasty. It was this newly rising power which Russia had to deal with in her expansion towards the east.

In 1647 some Promyshleni in Siberia got the information that there existed a shorter and more commodious route to the Amur. Subsequently Cossacks were sent to make a preparatory exploration and came upon the Amur at a place half a day's journey below the mouth of Urka. Next year Yerofei Khabarov, a wealthy Promyshleni, offered to Dmitri Andrev Zin Transhekov, the newly appointed Voivod of Yakutsk, to bear the expenses of an expedition led by himself and to send the tribute collected to Yakutsk. Upon the consent of Transhekov, Khabarov left Ilimsk with about 70 men in the autumn, and reached the Amur on sledges in January 1650. The inhuman conduct of Poyarkov and his Cossacks had become known to the natives so they all fled at Khabarov's approach. He declared to Prince Lavkai of the Daurians that he had come merely for trade and a small tribute but the latter, unbelieving him, also fled from his forts. Khabarov then stayed in the strongest fort and discovered large pits filled with corn. He also found excellent fish in the river and valuable animals in the forests and regarded the surrounding country as suitable for settlement. He went back with a few men to Yakutsk to report while most of his party remained in Lavkai's forts and collected tribute from the neighboring tribes.

In the spring of 1651 Khabarov returned to the fort with 21 additional Cossacks and 117 Promyshleni as well as with cannons. In June Lavkai's forts were destroyed and the Russians sailed down the Amur in barges. All the villages on the banks of the Amur were deserted as the inhabitants heard the approach of the Russians. After a few days they reached a triple fortification recently built by three Daurian princes to check the Russian invasion. An encounter ensued and lasted two days. As the Daurians used only swords and arrows while the Russians had guns and cannons all the forts were taken. Six hundred and sixty-one Daurians were killed by the Russians and 243 women and 118 children were taken as prisoners. The Russians also got hundreds of horses and cattle and rich stores of grain. After staying there for some time Khabarov continued his journey. At the mouth of the Dzeya he again attacked a Daurian village and the forts of three other princes and took Princes Tolga and Tuanucha as hostages. The natives were compelled to swear their allegiance to the Tsar and to promise to pay tribute. But to supply 200 Russians with food was too much for them and in one night they all fled into the wood. The forts and village were burned down by the Russians who then proceeded on. Prince Tolga committed suicide by drowning himself in consequence of the tortures inflicted on him by Khabarov.[1]

Kharbarov sailed on until he had passed the mouth of the Sungari and came to the country of the Achans. At the end of September Khabarov built the fort of Achanskoi Gorod near an Achan village and spent the winter there. As the Russians seized food from the Achans without paying for it the enmity of the natives was aroused. So when about one half of the Russians left the fort on a foraging journey on October 5 the Achans and their ally, Duchers, attacked the fort from the land side. After two hours of fighting 117 natives were killed. The Russians lost only one man. After that the Achans had to pay a heavy tribute to the Russians. In anticipation of more attacks by the natives Khabarov strengthened his fort. This precaution proved to be wise; a few months later the first military engagement between the Manchus and Russians occurred on the spot.

All the native tribes in the Amur region were then under the protection of the Manchu empire. So when they realized that they were powerless to stem the Russian invasion they appealed to the Manchu authorities for help. General Haiseh, Defense Commissioner of Ninguta on the Sungari, hurried to the rescue of the Achans with 2000 horsemen, armed with bows and arrows, swords, spears and a few cannons and matchlocks. At daybreak on March 24, 1652, Haiseh attacked Achanskoi Gorod. The Russians were awakened from their sleep by the firing of the matchlocks and hastened for defense. The Manchus effected a breach of the fort with their guns and prepared to take it by assault but the Russians opened their cannon fire on the assailing column and repulsed the attackers. Then the Russians made a sortie and captured two of the Manchu guns. As a result the battle was won by the Russians. According to the Russian estimate almost 700 Manchus were killed and 17 matchlocks, a few prisoners and 830 horses were taken by the Russians, in addition to the two cannons. On the Russian side only ten were killed and 78 wounded.

Although the Russians proved victorious, Khabarov knew very well that his position was precarious and must withdraw before the arrival of the Manchus reinforcements. So he sailed upstream toward the end of April. At the mouth of the Sungari a large force of 6000 Manchus and natives was gathered to attack the Russians but a favorable wind enabled them to escape destruction. At the upper end of the defile of the Bureya mountains Khabarov unexpectedly met a party of 118 Cossacks and Promyshleni sent from Yakutsk to reinforce him. He then continued to ascend the river, collected tribute from the natives and was planning to build a fort opposite the Dzeya. But on August 1, 136 men deserted him and sailed down the Amur. Some of the men later returned to Khabarov but others either surrendered to the Manchus or were killed by the natives. After this incident Khabarov further ascended the Amur to the mouth of the Kamara where he built Kamarskoi Ostrog on an island opposite the mouth of the river.

Meanwhile, the Tsar was now interested in acquisition of the Amur region and had decided to send Prince Ivan Rostovskoi with an army of 2000 men to occupy the newly-explored territory. Dmitri Simoviov was sent in advance to prepare the way and left Moscow in March, 1652 with a small detachment. Simoviov met Khabarov and his men at the mouth of the Dzeya in August, 1653. Simoviov conveyed the instructions from Moscow as follows: Khabarov was to go to Moscow to report personally to the Tsar; Onufrei Stepanov was to take up the command after his departure; Tretiak Chechegin who had commanded the reinforcements which met Khabarov at the Bureya mountains was to proceed to Peking as an envoy; three forts were to be constructed, one at the mouth of the Dzeya, another on the site of the Albazas village,(one of the Lafkai's forts) and a third at the mouth of the Argun; soil was to be cultivated and one year's provisions for 6000 men were to be stored. Chechegin then departed for Peking with four men but they were slain on their way by the Duchers who served as guides. Khabarov proceeded with Simoviov to Moscow where he was warmly received by the Tsar and was created Synboyarskoi for his service.

After Khabarov's departure Stepanov did not cultivate the land nor build the forts as instructed by Moscow but began his adventures on the Amur. He descended the Amur to the mouth of the Sungari and obtained provisions from the natives. He wintered in the country of the Duchers and in the spring of 1654 he again explored the Sungari. After three day's journey from the mouth of the river he met a hostile flotilla with 3000 Manchus, Daurians and Duchers. Stepanov attacked the enemy boats and put them to flight but owing to lack of provisions and ammunition he had to retreat also. He then built a new fort at the mouth of the Kamara and wintered there. In March, 1655 several thousand Manchus with cannons, matchlocks and storming apparatus attacked the fort. But they failed to take the fort by assault; and after three weeks of siege they withdrew when their provisions were exhausted.

Then for three years Stepanov roved the Amur like a pirate chief and exacted heavy tribute or pillaged the natives. The proposed expedition under Rostovskoi had been abandoned by the Russian Government and a letter had been sent to Stepanov, encouraging him to make new enterprises but instructing him to treat the natives with leniency and to avoid collision with the Manchus. But the Manchus were bent upon revenge. They made necessary preparations and waited for an opportunity to annihilate Stepanov's force. In the spring of 1658 when Stepanov again descended the Amur a fleet of 45 Manchu boats with large and small guns under the command of Sha-er-hu-ta, Defense Commissioner of Ninguta, met him below the Sungari. One hundred and eighty of Stepanov's men deserted him when they saw the superiority of the enemy. In the ensuing battle Stepanov was killed and 270 men were killed or taken prisoners; only 47 escaped[2]. Thereafter for several years the natives in the Amur region were able to live in peace.

During the time when Khabarov and Stepanov were exploring the Amur in succession, Pashkov, Voivod of Yenisseisk, was penetrating into the Shelka region. In 1652 he sent Beketov with 100 Cossacks on an exploratory expedition. Beketov reached the Ingoda in 1654, sailed down the Ingoda and the Shelka and built an Ostrog opposite to the mouth of the Nercha rivulet. But as Beketov did not get along very well with the Tungus tribe he soon suffered from lack of provisions. He then proceeded to the Amur and joined Stepanov's force.

Not discouraged by the failure of Beketov's expedition Pashkov proposed to the Russian Government to found a town on the Shelka as a base for subjugating the surrounding territory. This proposal was approved by Moscow and Pashkov was appointed commander-in-chief of all Russian forces on the Amur to carry out the plan.

In July, 1656 Pashkov left Yenisseisk with 566 men and reached the Shelka in the spring of 1658 and founded Nerchinsk. While he was building the fort Pashkov sent Potapov down to the Amur to inform Stepanov of his appointment as commander-in-chief and to order Stepanov to send 100 men to Nerchinsk and to establish himself at the Albaza's village. Potapov met Pashkov's deserters on his way, was robbed of his provisions and had to return to Nerchinsk. The native tribes then appealed to the Manchu authorities for help and Bahai, son of Sha-er-hu-ta, led an expedition to fight the Russians. When Bahai defeated Pashkov's force at Kufatan village[3] in 1660 Pashkov removed his headquarters to Irgenskoi and left only a small garrison at Nerchinsk. In 1662 Larion Alexei Tolbuzin succeeded Pashkov who returned to Yenisseisk.

While on his way back from a fair at Kirensk in 1665 Lawrence Obukhov, Voivod of Ilimsk, was murdered by a lawless band whose leader was Nikitor Chernigovsky, a Polish exile. According to Witsen, one of Chernigovsky's sisters had been violated by Obukhov and so he killed Obukhov for revenge.[4] He then fled with 84 fugitives to the wilds of the Amur and after overcoming many difficulties they settled down at the site of Albaza's village in 1666 and rebuilt the fort of Albazin. Chernigovsky then made himself master of the region and exacted tribute from the natives. In 1669 Chernigovsky presented the re-conquered land to the Tsar and petitioned for a pardon which was granted. Tolbuzin was then appointed the voyevoda of Albazin.

The re-appearance of the Russians on the Amur attracted the attention of the Manchu Government and Emperor Kang-hsi ordered the Defense Commissioner of Ninguta to condemn the Russian authorities at Nerchinsk in a letter. Meanwhile Gantimur, a Tungus chief who had taken part in the battle of the Kamara against Stepanov had later deserted the Manchus and went over to the Russian side. The Manchus demanded his repartriation which was refused by the Russian authorities. Thereupon Emperor Kang-hsi decided to use force to settle the question with the Russians. But as at that time the Manchu Court was busily engaged in suppressing the rebellion of three Chinese princes, Kang-hsi had to be patient and wait for the proper moment.

In 1680 the rebellion was suppressed and the next year Generals

Lang Tan and Peng Chun were sent by Kang-hsi to the neighborhood of Albazin to study the situation. In 1681 and 1682 military preparations on a large scale were made and a large quantity of provisions was stored. A strong army of well trained and well equipped soldiers was gathered at Aigun on the Amur. In 1683 the Manchu forces had cleared the Amur of Russian Ostrogs and only Albazin remained to be taken. Emperor Kang-hsi then sent an edict, through two Russian prisoners, to Tolbuzin offering lenient terms for his surrender. Upon receiving no answer the Emperor, in February, 1684, ordered General Peng Chun to attack the fort. In his edict to Peng Chun, Kang-hsi declared: "We rule the empire with benevolence and do not like to kill persons... The Russians will not be able to resist our strong forces with superior equipment and will surely surrender with land. When that happens you should not kill one Russian but let them all go back to their own country".[5]

In June, General Peng Chun advanced from Aigun to Albazin with a Manchu army of 4000 to 5000 men carrying guns and matchlocks.[6] Tolbuzin had 430 Cossacks, 3 cannons and 300 muskets. General Peng Chun tried to pursuade Tolbuzin to surrender the fort but the latter refused. Thereupon the Manchu troops began their attack on June 15. After a few days of fighting more than a third of the Cossacks were either killed or wounded. Seeing the impossibility of further resistance Tolbuzin sued for mercy. For many years the Russians had maltreated the natives and killed all those who surrendered after resistance. But now Peng Chun, remembering the Emperor's instructions, treated Tolbuzin very magnanimously. The Cossacks were allowed to leave the fort not only with their goods but also with their arms. Forty of them who were willing to surrender were brought back to Peking where they were enlisted as the Emperor's bodyguards. Tolbuzin with the remnant force retreated to Nerchinsk. After destroying the fort the Manchu troops also returned to their base at Aigun.

Not long after the Manchu withdrawal the Russians broke their pledge and returned to Albazin. Tolbuzin was reinforced at Nerchinsk by the detachment from Moscow led by Afanei Beiton, a German, and marched back to Albazin with 460 men. By the next spring they had built an even stronger fort upon the ruins of the old. Learning this news General Sapusu of Aigun besieged Albazin again in July, 1686 with 8000 soldiers and 40 cannons. Tolbuzin was killed in action but the Cossacks held on under Beiton. Unable to take the fort after a few months' siege the Manchu troops retired for the winter.

In the spring of 1687 the Manchus came back to attack the fort again. By this time scurvy had broken out in the Russian camp and only 115 Cossacks were left. The fort was on the verge of falling into the hands of the Manchus when an edict from the Emperor arrived which instructed Sapusu to raise the siege immediately as China and Russia were ready to enter into negotiations.[7] So the Manchu troops withdrew 20 verst (about 13.3 miles) from Albazin to Djakan in the middle of May and retreated to Ninguta in August.

Since warfare between the two powers thus came to an end we may trace here their diplomatic relations. As early as 1567 during the reign of Emperor Lung-chin of the Ming Dynasty two Cossacks, Petroff and Yallysheff, arrived at Peking, claiming to be envoys of Ivan the Terrible. Because they did not bring any tribute the Emperor refused to receive them. In 1618 Ivashk Petlin and Ondrushka Mundiff, envoys of Tsar Michael, arrived at Peking. Without a tribute they were not received but they brought back a letter from Emperor Wan-li to the Tsar. Then in February, 1654 Tsar Alexei Mikhailovich formally appointed Theodore Isakavitch Baikoff as the first ambassador to China. He was given a letter to present in person to Emperor Shun-chih and was instructed "to learn secretly the Chinese military strength, and all the routes into the country; and to acquire information on the customs, population, financial condition and economic wealth of the country".[8] Baikoff first sent Setkoul Ablin to Peking to announce his coming and arrived at Peking in March, 1656. Officials of the Li-fan-yuan (Office for Vassal States) greeted him and requested his tribute. As Baikoff refused to present the Tsar's gifts until he had been received by the Emperor they were forcibly taken from him. Later when Baikoff refused to kowtow to the Emperor an audience was not granted, the gifts were returned to him and he was ordered to leave Peking. Even before Baikoff's return to Moscow the Tsar had sent another envoy, Ivan Perilieff, to Peking. Perilieff started for China with Ablin in February, 1658 and reached Peking in May 1660. When the Tsar's letter was delivered to the Manchu court it was found to show a lack of humility and Perilieff was dismissed without seeing the Emperor.[9]

In 1670 after Gantimur had deserted China and went over to the Russian side the Defense Commissioner of Ninguta wrote a letter to the Voivod of Nerchinsk demanding the surrender of Gantimur. Upon receiving this letter Daniel Archinsky, the Voivod, sent a Cossack, Ignashka Milovanoff to Peking with the proposal that Emperor

Kang-hsi accept Russian suzerainty.[10] Because of the internal trouble in China Milovanoff was well received by the Li-fan-yuan and brought back an edict from Kang-hsi stating "let my people not be attacked, nor harmed, and let the promise be given that the villagers live in peace and joy".[11]

When the news of this edict reached Moscow the Tsar decided to send another mission to China. Nikolai Garilovich Spathary was appointed ambassador in February, 1675, and reached Peking on May 15. Emperor Kang-hsi received Spathary on June 19; instead of kowtowing the latter was required to merely bow three times as he entered the palace and once before the Emperor. On August 13, Spathary was to receive, on behalf of the Tsar, gifts from the Emperor. But as Spathary refused to receive the gifts on his knees, they were withheld from him. The Li-fan-yuan then told Spathary that the Imperial Court would hereafter receive only letters, envoys, or merchants from Russia on the following conditions: that Gantimur be extradited to Peking, accompanied by a Russian envoy; that the envoy would do what the Imperial Court commanded, and that Russians along the borders should cease to disturb the peace. On the following day three more conditions were added: any communication to the Emperor from the envoy must be put in the form of a letter from an inferior to a superior power; gifts sent by a vassal state should be called tribute; and gifts sent in return to the vassal state, should be called gratitudes and not presents. He was compelled to leave Peking on September 18. While passing through Nerchinsk he warned the Russians at Albazin not to commit further outrages on the Amur.[12]

In November, 1685, Moscow received Emperor Kang-hsi's edict to the Russion garrison at Albazin dated 1683. Tsar Peter the Great then sent an envoy to settle the pending issues. Nicephore Venykoff and Ivan Favoroff were immediately dispatched; upon arriving at Peking in September, 1686, they announced the forthcoming arrival of a Russian High Ambassador and requested an immediate ceasefire at Albazin. The Emperor granted their request and ordered the siege to end. The High Ambassador, Theodore Alexeivitch Golovin left Moscow in June, 1686, with instructions to meet Chinese representatives at Selenginsk to discuss political and commercial questions. He was to propose that the boundary line between the two powers be fixed along the whole length of the Amur; in case of refusal by China, along the Amur and Bystra; in case of refusal again along the Amur and the Dzeya. He was also to persuade the Emperor to send ambassadors to Moscow. Commercially he was to collect information concerning river routes to China; the Ob, the Irtysh, the Selenga, etc; to ask for official regulations of trade, and to urge Chinese merchants to sell their goods in Russia. In September, 1687 while still on his way, he received secret instructions to cede Albazin in exchange for commercial privileges and to avoid bloodshed. On October 22, he arrived at Selenginsk.

Upon receiving notification of Golovin's arrival the Emperor appointed Prince So-eh-tu, Tung Kuo-kang, member of the grand secretariat, A-erh-ni, president of the Li-fan-yuan, General Sapusu, General Lang Tan and two Chinese officials, Chang Peng-ko and Chien Liang-tse, Chinese envoys to negotiate with the Russians. Two Jesuit priests, Jean Francois Gerbillion and Thomas Pereyra served as interpreters. So-eh-tu then submitted a memorial to the Emperor stating: "Nipchu (Chinese name for Nerchinsk) was originally the pasture lands of our Mao-ming-an tribe and Yaksa (Chinese name for Albazin) was the old home of Pei-li-erh, our Daurian chieftain. The territory, occupied by the Russians, is not theirs, nor is it a 'neutral' zone. The Amur has a strategic importance which must not be overlooked. If the Russians descend it, they can reach the Sungari. If they ascend the Sungari to the south they can reach the Naun and the Kamara, Kirin and Ninguta, and land of the Sibos, the Khorchins, the Solons and the Daurians. If they descend the Sungari to the north they can reach the sea. Into the Amur flow the Argun, the Bystra and the Dzeya. Along these rivers live our people, the Orochons, the Gilyaks, the Birars, as well as the Ho-chen and the Fei-ya-ko. If we do not recover the entire region our frontier people will never have peace. Nipchu, Yaksa and all the rivers and rivulets flowing into the Amur being ours, it is our opinion that none should be abandoned to the Russians. Gantimur and other deserters must be extradited. If the Russians will accede to these points we shall in return give up their deserters, expatriate the prisoners, draw the boundary line and enter into commercial relations; otherwise we shall return and make no peace with them at all".[13] This memorial was approved by the Emperor.

The mission left Peking with 800 guards in May, 1688, but before its arrival at Seleginsk it was recalled because of the Dzungharian invasion of Khalkha (Outer Mongolia) which blocked the way. Then the Manchus and Russians agreed to meet at Nerchinsk. So-eh-tu's mission left Peking again on June 3, 1689, with about 3000 Manchu soldiers and arrived at Nerchinsk on July 31. The Russian mission, headed by Golovin and Ivan Vlasoff, Voivod of Nerchinsk, arrived eight days later. The first conference was held on August 12 in a tent outside the fort. Golovin maintained that since the war was provoked by China the Amur region should belong to Russia on the basis of status quo ante bellum. So-eh-tu, on the other hand, blamed the Cossacks for starting the war and Tolbuzin for breaking his pledge and asserted that Albazin and the Daurian regions had always been Chinese territory. Golovin claimed that the Daurians had presented sable skins to the Tsar as a tribute but So-eh-tu said Russia had never actually occupied the Amur region and even the territory east of Lake Baikal had belonged to the Mongol Khan who had been a vassal to China. Then Golovin proposed to fix the Amur as the boundary line. Thereupon So-eh-tu declared that the Amur had belonged to China since the time of Alexander the Great and demanded the Russians to withdraw beyond Seleginsk and to surrender Nerchinsk, Albazin, and their environs to China otherwise Manchu troops would again attack Albazin. Golovin answered exitedly: "Threats of war should not be made during peace negotiations; but if China wants war, then declare it".[14] The conference thus ended in an unstatisfactory manner.

Due to the Dzungharian invasion Emperor Kang-hsi had instructed So-eh-tu before his departure from Peking: "At the opening of the conference you should still try to retain Nipchu. But if they beg for that city, you may draw the boundary along the Argun river".[15] So on the next day So-eh-tu made a concession by ceding Nerchinsk to Russia. But the Russians made further demands and the Manchus began to pack their tents, ready for departure. The two priests then went to see Golovin and pursuaded him to give up Albazin. On August 16, Golovin sent a Russian official to see So-eh-tu asking for minimum conditions China could accept. So-eh-tu then drew on a map a proposed boundary line running along the Kerbechi river and the Outer Khing-an mountains. Next day the two priests went to see Golovin again who drew another boundary line on a map running from the source of the Kerbechi to the mouth of the Amur. When the priests reported back the Manchu mission decided to break off the conference and to attack both Nerchinsk and Albazin.

As Golovin had only 1500 soldiers while there were more than 10,000 Manchu troops in the neighborhood of Nerchinsk, Golovin finally yielded. On August 18, he accepted the Argun and the Khing-an mountains as the boundary line and agreed to surrender Albazin but asked that the fort be destroyed. On August 19, Golovin asked for the right of the subjects of the two powers who had passports to trade with each other and So-eh-tu consented. The question of the repatriation of Gantimur was then brought up by So-eh-tu. It was learned that Gantimur, accompanied by his father, had gone to Moscow to join the Russian Orthodox Church and the matter was dropped. At this point of negotiation it was discovered that the Outer Khing-an mountains had two chains: the major chain or the Nosse turning northeastward while the minor chain curved southward. Between these two chains lay a vast country watered by the Oud. On August 22 So-eh-tu declared that he had intended the Nosse as the boundary; Golovin insisted the boundary should be along the minor chain. Finally they agreed that the area between the two chains should remain undecided until further negotiations.

The treaty of Nerchinsk, signed and exchanged on August 27, 1689, was the first treaty between China and a European power. It contained six articles and was in five languages: Chinese, Russian, Latin, Manchurian, and Mongolian. The Latin text, signed by the plenipotentiaries, was regarded as official. The boundary line was fixed along the Argun, continuing along the Amur to the mouth of the Kerbechi, thence along the Kerbechi up to its source, and thence along the mountain range (the Outer Khing-an) to the sea.[16] There was a serious discrepancy between the Latin text on the one hand and the Russian or Manchu text on the other. According to the Latin text the territory between the Oud and the northeastern branch of the Outer Khing-an mountains remained undecided; while according to the Russian or Manchu text what was left undecided (or neutral as in the Manchu text) was the territory between the southeastern branch of the mountains and the Oud.[17] This discrepancy remained, however, immaterial, as no negotiations had ever been conducted after 1689 on that point. Albazin was to be destroyed and the Russians living there were to return with their property to Russian territory. Hunters who transgressed the boundary line would be punished. Criminals and deserters after the conclusion of the treaty would be repatriated. Subjects of either power who now resided in the territory of the other could remain there. Subjects who held passports could cross the boundary line freely to do trade. This treaty, while not precise in language, marked the beginning of a period of 170 years of peace on the Siberian-Manchurian border.

Three years after the treaty, Peter the Great sent Everard Ysbrand Ides, a Dutch or German merchant, to head a trade mission to Peking. He was instructed to ascertain Chinese policy towards Russia, to obtain a site in Peking for the building of a Russian Orthodox church, to persuade the Chinese to send their merchants to Moscow with

Chinese products, and to make detailed inquiries as to the kinds of goods Russia could sell profitably in China. Ides left Moscow with a caravan of 400 men in March, 1692 and arrived at Peking in March of the next year. He stayed there almost a year and had four audiences with the Emperor. He was assured by the Li-fan-yuan that China had only friendly intentions towards Russia so long as the latter did not encroach upon Chinese territory. Permission for the building of a Russian church in Peking was not granted. Trade missions of not more than 200 men were allowed to visit Peking once every three years and could stay there for eighty days. What interested the Russians most was the privilege granted by the Manchu Court that all imported and exported goods were to be duty free.

The treaty of Nerchinsk settled the boundary disputes between Manchuria and Siberia but the boundary line between Mongolia and Siberia remained undecided. It was the irony of history that when the Russians pushed to eastern Asia at the beginning of the 17th century the first country they came into contact with was Khalkha (Outer Mongolia). After the collapse of the Yuan Dynasty in China, the Mongols had withdrawn to Mongolia. During the reign of Emperor Hsiao-chung of the Ming Dynasty Ta-yen Khan united Mongolia. He ruled Inner Mongolia and set up khanates in Khalkha to be ruled by his brothers and sons. In 1635, the Manchus conquered Inner Mongolia. At that time Khalkha was divided into four khanates. As early as 1616 Russia had sent its first mission to Altyn Khan, prince of the western part of Khalkha. The relations were soon broken off until 1632 when Altyn Khan sent an envoy to Tomsk to express his willingness to receive Russian protection. Thereafter several missions were exchanged. But after the Manchus had conquered China in 1644 Altyn Khan sent his son, Lobzdan, to Peking to pay tribute to the Manchu Emperor. After Altyn's death, Lobzdan was overthrown and the khanate disappeared. Tushetu Khan, prince of central Khalkha, was then quarreling with Dzhasaktu Khan, to his west. But soon they were both threatened by a rising power in Chinese Turkestan, Dzungharia.

The Dzunghars who were part of the Eleuth or Kalmuk tribes lived in the region between the Altai and the Tienshan mountains. After Galdan became the ruler of Dzungharia in 1671 it grew stronger and conquered all the neighboring tribes. Then in 1688 he invaded Khalkha and occupied Urianhai, Dzhasaktu, Tushetu, and Tsetsen khanates. At that time Galdan was on excellent terms with the Russians who without doubt secretly supported him to create troubles in China. The Khans of Khalkha and the Hutuktu (Living Buddha) fled to Chinese territory to ask for protection. In 1690 Emperor Kang-hsi led a large army himself and defeated Galdan at Chifeng and the Khans and Hutuktu returned to Khalkha. Next year the Emperor summoned all the Mongol Khans and nobles to a meeting at Dolun Nor where they swore their allegiance to him and thereupon Khalkha became a Chinese domain. In 1696 Kang-hsi again defeated Galdan at Chaomodo and the latter committed suicide.

In 1719 Tsar Peter the Great again sent to China an ambassador in the person of Leon Vasilievitch Ismailoff, a soldier with some diplomatic experience. Ismailoff was instructed to ask for complete free trade on reciprocal terms throughout the whole territory of both empires and the establishment of a Russian consulate-general in Peking and to explain to the Emperor that the Russian forts along the Irtysh and elsewhere in Siberia had been built for protection against unruly Cossacks and Dzunghars and were not intended for aggression towards China. He left Moscow with a large suite in July, 1719 and arrived at Peking in November, 1720. He agreed to kowtow to the Emperor on the condition that Chinese envoys should perform the same ceremony at the Tsarist Court, and was received a dozen times by Kang-hsi during his four months' sojourn at Peking. He was cordially treated by the Manchu Court which reminded him that the question of the Mongol frontier should be immediately settled. As many Dzunghars were then fleeing into Russian territory the Manchu Government demanded their repatriation according to the provisions in the Treaty of Nerchinsk. This was refused by the Russian Government and the Manchus became suspicious of a Russian intrigue. So Ismailoff's requests for the extention of trade and establishment of a consulate-general were not granted. But the Emperor approved the building of a Russian church in Peking and permitted his secretary, Lorenz Lange, to stay on after his departure.

Lange was arrogant and did not get along very well with the Li-fan-yuan officials. At that time in a battle with the Dzunghars several Russians were captured by the Manchus. Angered by Russian interference with China's internal affairs the Li-fan-yuan put guards at Lange's residence on the pretext of being there for his protection. Lange then threatened that when Russia had finished her war with Sweden the Tsar would turn his arms to China. When this threat became known he and the trade mission were compelled to leave Peking in 1722.[18] On his journey back to St. Petersburg he reported from Tsumhaitu: "At this moment the Chinese are in a critical position. Engaged in a terrible fight with the Dzunghars, they are afraid of Russia and at the same time look to us to supply their armies with provisions and horses. The moment is most opportune to intervene in Peking and demand that all restrictions imposed upon our caravans be removed; that the Russian mission be freed of the insufferable surveillance of the Mandarins, which hinders all trade; and that the dispute concerning frontiers be settled favorably. As long as the Dzunghars keep the Chinese in check on the battlefields the Chinese will not dare defy the Russian Court. We even believe that this is an excellent time to seek the extension of our frontier to the Amur river".[19] The Russian Government had sense enough not to follow his advice.

In 1723, Emperor Kang-hsi died and his son Yung-cheng succeeded him. In January, 1725 Tsar Peter the Great also died and Tsarina Catherine ruled Russia. In August Count Sava Vladislavich Ruguzinsky was appointed "Envoy Extraordinary and Minister Plenipotentiary" to the Court at Peking. He was instructed (1) to conclude a commercial treaty or to renew commercial relations that had been interrupted; (2) to fix the Mongolian-Siberian frontier; (3) to settle the question of deserters; and (4) to obtain a piece of land on which to build a Russian church. He was also asked to ascertain the military strength and resources of the Chinese empire. Vladislavich arrived at Peking in October, 1726 with a suite of 100 persons and a military escort of 1500 soldiers. Being well trained in commerce, diplomacy and spying he showed more tact, good taste and patience than any other European envoys who had visited the Manchu Court. By keeping good terms with Pere Parrenin, head of the Italian Jesuits in Peking, and by bribing a Chinese official named Machi and a Mongol official named Galdan, he obtained secret information concerning the Court. During his half a year's stay in Peking he succeeded in negotiating a new treaty concerning the frontier and trade. As the Manchu Court did not wish to have a treaty signed at the capital, Vladislavich left Peking in April, 1727 and reached Bura near Selenginsk in June. Many meetings were held at Bura between Vladislavich who was assisted by Lange and the Manchu envoys, Lon-go-tu, Posze-geh and Tu-li-sen. Lon-go-tu, who held a strong attitude towards Russia, was later recalled by the Emperor and replaced by Prince Thai-ling. Finally the treaty was signed on October 12, which became known as the Treaty of Kiakhta, where Vladislavich resided.

This treaty fixed the boundary line between Mongolia and Siberia from the Saian mountains and Sapintabakha in the west to the Argun river in the east (Article 3). The valley of the Uda (Oud in the Treaty of Nerchinsk) remained undecided (Article 7). Russian trade caravans to Peking were to be resumed once every three years with no more than 200 merchants at one time. Besides this other trade between Chinese and Russians was to be limited to Kiakhta and Nerchinsk (Article 4). This was a disadvantage to the Russians who had traded freely with the Mongols for a long time. Deserters and criminals who crossed the frontier after the conclusion of the treaty should be surrendered by both sides (Article 2).[20] This treaty was favorable to Russia in that by it China lost a large part of territory between the upper Irtysh and the Saian mountains and also the territory south and southwest of Lake Baikal. Declared Vladislavich: "... that the newly established frontier is highly advantageous to Russia and that actually the Russian possessions have been extended into Mongolia a distance of several days' march and in certain sections of even several weeks'".[21] Of course, some Russian high officials wanted even more than that but Vladislavich said the alternative he faced at Kiakhta was acceptance or war. When he returned to St. Petersburg in 1728 he presented a memorial to Tsar Peter II in which he described his plan of conquering China. He laid down four conditions for realizing his scheme: (1) the maintenance of peace in Europe so that time and money could be devoted to Siberia and the Amur region; (2) a decade of steady planting and reaping of crops in Transbaikalia so as to get sufficient provisions; (3) the training of 50 regiments of regulars and 20 regiments of irregulars to contend against the Manchu forces; and (4) encouraging the Eleuths, Mongols, and other non-Manchu tribes to strike for independence. The combination of these factions would open the way for a speedy conquest of China.[22]

After the ratification of the Treaty of Kiakhta in 1728 Russian trade caravans arrived at Peking again. In the same year the Russian Government sent four students to Peking who were assigned by Emperor Yung-chen to the Kuo-tze-chien, an office which took care of educational matters, to learn both Chinese and Manchurian. Trade at Kiakhta on the Russian side of the border and Maimaicheng on the Chinese side especially flourished. It was limited to barter system and no gold or silver was allowed as medium of exchange. Imports from Russia consisted mainly of furs, hides, leather goods and English textiles; while exports from China were tea, rhubarb, cotton and silk goods. In 1762 the Manchu Court closed the Peking market and thereafter Kiakhta became even more prosperous. Prince Tushetu and High Commissioner Chouta at Urga were entrusted with authority to regulate this trade.

In 1764 the market at Kiakhta was closed because the Russian authorities taxed Chinese goods and demanded reparation from China for Russian run-away horses. But Russian goods were smuggled into China with the tacit permission of the prince and the high commissioner who received bribes. When this became known the prince was dismissed from office and the high commissioner was executed. At the petition of High Commissioner Ching-Kwei the market was reopened in 1768 after the revision of Article 10 of the Treaty of Kiakhta. Eleven years later the market was closed for a year because the Russian authorities were giving asylum to Chinese criminals. In 1785 when Siberian tribesmen pillaged in Chinese territory the market was again closed. In 1792 upon the report of High Commissioner Sung-yun that the Russian authorities had repented their past wrongdoings and had requested the reopening of the market, Emperor Chien-lung instructed him to negotiate a new trade agreement with Russian representative Serabate. Although this new agreement was in the tone of a great power to its vassal state[23] the Russian Government under Tsarina Catherine II, was willing to accept it for the sake of the profit of the trade. After the conclusion of the agreement in February the market was reopened in May. Thereafter trade at Kiakhta was carried on without any interruption.

CHAPTER IV

Russian Acquisition of the Amur and Ussuri Regions

Russia was not satisfied with the Treaty of Nerchinsk because it checked her expansion to the east. While Russia gained much by the Treaty of Kiakhta she was also dissatisfied because it limited her trade with China to a few places. In the latter half of the eighteenth century merchants of western European countries and of the United States were already doing thriving business at Canton in South China. In 1806 when two Russian ships arrived at Canton and were making sales and purchases, the Chinese authorities received instructions from Peking that Russians were forbidden to trade by sea as they had already obtained the privilege of trading by land. Consequently the Russian ships were ordered to leave immediately. As long as the Chinese empire was strong and vigorous as under the reigns of Kang-hsi and Chien-lung or as it appeared to be so after the beginning of the nineteenth century Russia tolerated these treaties and kept friendly relations with China. But when the Opium War and the Treaty of Nanking (1842) completely exposed the weaknesses of this giant, Russia's ambitions in the Far East were revived and she wanted to get her share of the Chinese spoils.

It was Tsar Nicholas I who plunged himself into the Amur question again. In September, 1847 the Tsar appointed Nicholas Muraviev, a young and aggressive army officer, Governor-General of Eastern Siberia. In his conversation with Muraviev after the appointment Nicholas made remarks about the gold mining in eastern Siberia, the Russian trade at Kiakhta and the relations with China. Then he said: "As for the Russian river Amur, you will hear from us later" and concluded his talk by saying: "to one who knows how to listen even a few words are enough to understand".[1] Muraviev knew at once that the Tsar had ambitious plans about the Amur which the Tsar did not make public because of the opposition of his own government.

After assuming his office Muraviev sent emissaries to St. Petersburg to persuade the Russian Government to give him a free hand in far eastern affairs and to enlist the help of the navy in exploration of the mouth of the Amur and the Sea of Okhotsk. As a consequence Nicholas I appointed a young naval officer, Gennadi Nevelskoy, captain of the warship "Baikal" and sent him to the Far East to assist Muraviev. After spending a year at Irkutsk Muraviev proceeded east. He reached the fort of Okhotsk in May, 1849 and then crossed the sea to Kamchatka. On Sakhalin, while returning to Siberia, he met Nevelskoy, who had just discovered the Tartar Strait and proved Sakhalin to be an island instead of a peninsula, the importance of the mouth of the Amur being thus increased. Nevelskoy had also sailed up the Amur and discovered the site for a port some 25 verst from the mouth, and named it Nikolaievsk in honor of the Tsar. The Russian flag was hoisted on the spot. Muraviev was very much pleased with the discovery and went back to St. Petersburg to report in person to the Tsar.

The Russian Foreign Office was opposed to this adventure because it grossly violated the Treaty of Nerchinsk and advised immediate withdrawal. But Nicholas I was ambitious and supported Muraviev, saying: "When the Russian flag has once been hoisted, it must not be lowered."[2] Muraviev was instructed to go ahead with his scheme but received warning not to use arms against China. The Russian Government then notified Peking that the Russo-American Company had founded a trading post near the mouth of the Amur and for the sake of protection against the aggression from a third power a warship was stationed there. At that time the Taiping rebellion had already started and the Manchu Government had serious internal troubles. Therefore it overlooked Russia's violation of the Treaty of Nerchinsk and did not even make a protest to her.

Encouraged by this inaction of the Manchu Government, Muraviev requested St. Petersburg for the expansion of military forces under his command. When his request was granted he enlisted Tungus and Buryat tribesmen, gathering more than 10,000 men for his army. During the next few years Muraviev established a series of towns and forts along the left bank of the Amur, such as Blagoveshchensk, Khabarovsk, Mariinsk and Nikolaievsk and Cossacks, miners and farmers were transferred from Trans-Baikalia to settle in these places. Nevelskoy also made more explorations and illegally occupied Sakhalin, the Tartar strait, and the mouth of the Amur. In 1863 Muraviev returned to St. Petersburg to present to the Tsar the necessity of occupying the whole Amur region. When the Crimean War occurred Muraviev again pursuaded the Tsar to strengthen the defense of the Russian Far East against the invasion of an Anglo-French joint fleet.

Nicholas I entrusted the far eastern question to Muraviev and gave him full power to negotiate with the Manchu Government. Muraviev returned to Irkutsk early in 1854 and at once went ahead with an expedition down to the mouth of the Amur.

In April Muraviev sent a letter to the Manchu Government stating that as Russia was now at war with Britain and France it was necessary to transport troops and provisions via the Amur to protect Russian territory on the Pacific coast. He also requested the Manchu Government to send an envoy to settle the frontier question.[3] Without waiting for an answer he sailed down the Amur in May with a steamer, 85 boats and 2000 men including infantry, cavalry and artillery. Before reaching Aigun he sent emissaries to notify Hu Sun-pu, Deputy Military Governor of Heilungkiang, of his passage. Hu Sun-pu visited Muraviev on his steamer and tried to pursuade him not to proceed further. Since the Manchu authorities were not prepared they had to let the Russians pass through in order to avoid any possible conflict.[4] After visiting the mouth of the Amur and Kamchatka and having reinforced the various posts, Muraviev returned to Irkutsk in August. When the answer of the Manchu Government arrived, asking him to send a delegation to the Ussuri to discuss frontier matters, he postponed the negotiations to the following year.

Shortly after Muraviev's return to Irkutsk an Anglo-French small fleet bombarded Petropavlovsk on Kamchatka but was repulsed by the defense force. Realizing that Britain and France would attack again next summer, Muraviev recognized that it would be extremely difficult, if not impossible, for the fort at Petropavlovsk to prevail against a large fleet. In the spring of 1855 he withdrew the garrison from Petropavlovsk and personally conducted another expedition down the Amur with 104 boats, 8000 men, 300 horses, cannons, and guns. On reaching Aigun he again notified the Deputy Military Governor who, as before, had no power to stop him. Muraviev then set up his headquarters at Mariinsk and appointed Nevelskoy his chief of staff. The Anglo-French joint fleet entered the Sea of Okhotsk in the summer and searched for the Russian fleet but owing to its ignorance of the topography it dared not enter the mouth of the Amur.

In September envoys of the Manchu Government arrived at Mariinsk to discuss the frontier question. Muraviev at first avoided seeing them and Admiral Zavoiko read to them a document which asserted that all land on the left bank of the Amur should be granted to Russia for protecting the mouth of the Amur against foreign aggression. On September 23, Muraviev received the envoys and made the same demand. The Manchu envoys then produced a note from the Russian

Senate to the Li-fan-yuan, dated June 16, 1853, in which the Senate recognized the left bank of the Amur as Chinese territory. Thereupon Muraviev demanded the right of navigation on the Amur so that communications between Russian fortifications at its mouth and the inland could be maintained; the Manchu envoys agreed to submit this demand to Peking for its decision. The negotiations were then broken off without any result. After establishing more forts at Nikolaievsk Muraviev returned to Irkutsk.

Following the death of Nicholas I in 1855 Muraviev returned to St. Petersburg. Early in 1856 he reported to the new Tsar, Alexander II. A third expedition on the Amur which he had prepared was now entrusted to his aide, Colonel Gavsakoff. The latter sailed down the river in May, with about 100 boats and 1660 soldiers and established four more garrison posts on its left bank. Upon the petition of Muraviev the Russian Government set up the Maritime Province to administer Kamchatka, Sakhalin, and the mouth of the Amur. A plenipotentiary, Admiral Count Putiatin, was sent by the Russian Government to Peking to discuss the frontier question and to negotiate a new commercial treaty which would obtain for Russia the privilege of trade by sea at the treaty ports. Putiatin went to Peking via the overland route and had conversations with Muraviev at Irkutsk. When Putiatin reached Kiakhta he was refused permission to enter Chinese territory. He then proceeded by sea to the mouth of the Peiho near Tientsin but was again not pemitted to proceed to Peking from there. So he went by steamer to Hongkong where he joined the British, French and American envoys in demanding that the Manchu Government send a plenipotentiary to Shanghai to start negotiations with the powers. The answer they received was that negotiations with the British, French and American envoys would be conducted by the viceroy at Canton but that negotiations with Russia could only be conducted by the High Commissioner of Heilungkiang.[5]

Meanwhile hostilities between Chinese and British forces had occurred at Canton; the latter was occupied by the British at the end of 1857. The Taiping rebellion was also spreading far and wide. As a consequence the position of the Manchu Government was greatly weakened by both foreign aggression and internal troubles. Muraviev at once seized the opportunity and took the matter into his own hands. He first stationed over 10,000 troops along the Amur to its mouth and then notified Prince Yishan, High Commissioner of Heilungkiang, that he would conduct negotiations with the latter at Aigun before his departure for St. Petersburg. Upon learning this the Manchu Government appointed Yishan plenipotentiary to negotiate with Muraviev.

The meeting between Yishan and Muraviev began on May 11, 1858. On the pretext that the mouth of the Amur was acquired by Russia after repulsing the Anglo-French joint fleet Muraviev made the following demands: (1) the territory on the left bank of the Amur to the mouth of the Ussuri and that between the Ussuri and the sea should be ceded to Russia; (2) the right of navigation on the Amur and Ussuri should be limited to China and Russia; (3) rivers in the territory of one power should open to the other for trades; and (4) Chinese subjects who are now living on the left bank of the Amur should remove to its right bank within three years.[6] When Yishan insisted that the boundary line should be in accordance with the provisions in the Treaty of Nerchinsk, Muraviev threatened to use force and ominous cannon shots were heard at night. Yishan finally yielded and the Treaty of Aigun was signed on May 28, after Muraviev had made a few minor concessions. This treaty provided that the left bank of the Amur from the Argun to its mouth at the sea belonged to Russia while the right bank down to the Ussuri was part of China. The territory east of the Ussuri was to remain in the joint possession of Russia and China until the proper demarcation of the frontier in the future. The rivers Amur, Sungari, and Ussuri were to be open for navigation for Chinese and Russian vessels exclusively. The Manchus now living on the left bank of the Amur from the Dzeya to the village of Khormoldsin might forever remain there under the jurisdiction of the Manchu Government and the Russians should not render any injustice to them.[7]

While Yishan was conducting negotiations with Muraviev an Anglo-French joint fleet attacked and occupied the Taku forts at the mouth of the Peiho and the envoys of the four powers proceeded to Tientsin. Taking advantage of this situation, Putiatin negotiated with Kweiliang and Hwashana and then signed the Treaty of Tientsin on June 13, 1858. This treaty was mainly commercial. It extended Russian trade in China to the seven treaty ports—viz., Shanghai, Ningpo, Foochow, Amoy, Canton, Taiwan and Hainan—which had been opened to European powers and the United States (Article IV). Overland trade was to be subject to no restrictions in regard to the number of persons taking part in it, the quantity of imported goods, or the capital employed (Article IV). The Russian Government was to have the right to appoint consuls in these ports and to send warships there (Article V). Russia was to enjoy the right of consular jurisdiction in China (Article VII). Frontiers between the two powers not yet decided were to be surveyed and the agreement arrived at by the two governments would form an additional article to the present treaty (Article IX). What was most important for Russia was that she would receive "most-favored-nation" treatment. Hereafter all political and commercial rights and privileges enjoyed by other powers would be extended to Russia (Article XII).[8]

The article concerning the frontier was put into the treaty by Putiatin because he was unaware at that time that it had been settled by the Treaty of Aigun. When the terms of that treaty became known to the Manchu Government Yishan was dismissed for his stupidity and overstepping of authority. The Manchu Government had no intention to ratify the treaty and only consented to allow Russians "to reside in some places of the Amur basin and to cultivate the lands that were not occupied by anybody else".[9] In 1859 General Nicholas Ignatieff was appointed Minister to China to succeed Putiatin. Ignatieff proceeded to China via the overland route and had conversations with Muraviev at Irkutsk; both subsequently journeyed to Kiakhta together. At Peking Ignatieff exchanged ratifications of the Treaty of Tientsin on April 24, but he could not get the Treaty of Aigun ratified. The Manchu Government notified him that if Russia insisted on that China would discontinue any trade with her at Kiakhta, Chuguchak (Tarbagatai) and Kuldja (Ili).[10] Unable to obtain what he wished, Ignatieff left Peking in May.

Meanwhile warfare between China and the Anglo-French allies broke out again over the ratification of the 1858 treaties. The allied forces captured the Taku forts on August 21, occupied Tientsin on August 25 and marched on Peking in September. Yuenmingyuan, a summer palace near Peking, was occupied, plundered and burned down to the ground by the allied troops. Finally Peking was occupied on October 13 and Emperor Hsien-feng fled to Jehol. Ignatieff had already returned to Peking and offered his good offices for mediation between China and the allies. On the one hand he pursuaded Prince Kung and other high officials of the Manchu Court to recognize the danger of their position and to settle the differences with the allies immediately and on the other he urged the allied envoys not to push the Manchu Court too hard.[11]

After the Convention of Peking between China and Great Britain was signed on October 24 and that between China and France the next day the allied troops withdrew. Boasting that he had saved the Manchu Dynasty, Ignatieff then demanded as a reward not only the territory on the left bank of the Amur, as provided in the Treaty of Aigun, but also the area between the Ussuri and the sea. Since the Manchu Government was in no position to reject his demands, the Treaty of Peking was signed by Ignatieff and Prince Kung on November 14, 1860.

The Treaty of Peking made the Amur and the Ussuri the eastern boundary line between China and Russia. By a stroke of the pen the Amur and Ussuri regions with a total area of about 400,000 square miles were ceded to Russia (Article I). The western boundary line was also fixed as following the mountains, great rivers and the present line of Chinese permanent pickets. It ran from the lighthouse at Shabin-Dabag southwestward to Lake Zaisan, thence to the mountains situated to the south of Lake Issyk-kul and along these mountains as far as the Kokan's possessions (Article II). Delegates were to be appointed by the Chinese and Russian Governments to survey and map the frontier in the east from Lake Khanka to the Tumien river and in the west from Shabin-Dabag to the Kokan's possessions (Article III). Russian merchants were again permitted to travel from Kiakhta to Peking for commercial purposes and to trade at Urga and Kalgan en route. In Sinkiang, Kashgar was to be opened for trade besides Ili and Tarbagatai (Article VI). Russian consulates were permitted to be established at Ili, Tarbagatai, Kashgar, and Urga while the Chinese Government might appoint consuls in the Russian capital and other cities (Article VIII). Along the entire boundary line a duty-free barter trade was to be authorized (Article IV). Russians in China or Chinese in Russia were permitted to "freely carry on their business in the points open for trade without any annoyance on the part of local authorities; visit with the same freedom and at all times the bazaars, shops, houses of local merchants; buy and sell various goods at wholesale or retail, for cash or by barter; borrow or lend money, on mutual trust". The period of sojourn was not limited (Article VII).[12]

These three treaties (Aigun, Tientsin and Peking), unlike those of Nerchinsk and Kiakhta, were unequal treaties by which China not only lost vast territory but had to concede privileges to Russia unilaterally. For instance Russia was to enjoy consular jurisdiction and the most-favored-nation treatment in China while the latter did not enjoy the same in Russia. Consequently the relations between China and Russia thereafter could no longer be those between two equals but those between a superior power and an inferior one.

In a short period of thirteen years Muraviev had accomplished the task entrusted to him—the seizure of the Amur and Ussuri regions. What was more remarkable was that it was accomplished by bluff and deceit without the loss of a Russian life. At the same time Muraviev discovered the site of a good harbor at the south end of the Ussuri region and founded the port of Vladivostok (meaning "master of the east"). For his achievement the Tsar made Muraviev a count. One chapter of Russia's aggression in China was now closed but another was soon to begin.

CHAPTER V

Russian Expansion into Central Asia and Relations with Sinkiang

That part of Asia which is generally called Turkestan (including Sinkiang and Soviet Central Asia) had relations with China as early as two centuries before the birth of Christ. At that time there were more than fifty small countries in this vast region which the Chinese gave the general name "Hsi-yu" meaning "the western land". In 139 B.C. Emperor Wu of the Han Dynasty sent Chang Chien as envoy to Hsi-yu; he was detained by the Hunnus for many years but finally reached as far west as Bukhara. In 101 B.C. Emperor Wu sent General Li Kwang-li with an army to attack Ta-wan (Ferghana) and subjected it. Thereafter practically all the Hsi-yu countries paid tribute to the Chinese empire.[1] During the reign of Emperor Chang of the Later Han Dynasty (76-88 A.D.) General Pan Chiao was appointed Hsi-yu Tu-fu (Pacification Commissioner of the Western Land) and Kan Yin, a subordinate officer under General Pan, was sent on an expedition further to the west and reached the shore of the Persian Gulf. During the period of Three Kingdoms, the Tsing dynasty and the period of North and South dynasties, China was so disunited that communications between China and Hsi-yu were severed. Then when Emperor Tai-chung of the Tang Dynasty (627-649) again unified China communications with Hsi-yu were resumed and the office of Pacification Commissioner was restored. When the Tang Dynasty was weakened by civil strife Hsi-yu again broke away from China.

With the rise of Chengiz Khan in the east the whole region was conquered by the Mongols at the beginning of the thirteenth century and was later put under the rule of the Khanate of Zagatai. In the fourteenth century Timur the Great rose in this region and built a second Mongolian empire. After the disintegration of this empire local tribes formed small independent states. It was not until the reign of Emperor Chien-lung of the Ching Dynasty (1736-1795) that this vast territory was again brought under the rule of the Chinese empire after the suppression of the Dzunghar rebellion in 1757. That part of Hsi-yu which lies east of the Chung-ling mountains was renamed "Sinkiang", meaning "the new dominion". Manchu troops were stationed in different cities, with a Garrison-Commander at Ili and a High Commissioner at Kashgar. For the first time in history eastern Turkestan became a part of Chinese territory (hence the name "Chinese Turkestan"). Various native states west of the Chung-ling mountains, such as Kazaks, Burut (Kirgiz), Kokan, and Bokhara also offered their allegiance to the Manchu Emperor but owing to lack of communications they were not actually brought under direct control but were treated as vassal states.

It was about the same time that Russia began to penetrate into Central Asia from the north. At the beginning of the eighteenth century the Kazaks were divided into three hordes—the Little, the Middle and the Great—with separate Khans. In 1718 the three Kazak Khans, Tiavka, Kaip, and Abulkhair, all offered submission to the Russians in Siberia in the hope that the latter would aid them in their struggle against the Kalmuks. But the Russians did not give them much help and they were driven away from their homeland. After the complete rout of the Kalmuks by the Manchus the Kazaks appropriated the vacant pastures left by the Kalmuks and settled down under the rule of Sultans. In 1760 Sultan Abdul Faiz sent an envoy to St. Petersburg and submitted to the Russian sovereignty.

After the beginning of the nineteenth century Russia accelerated her speed in conquering Central Asia. In 1803 the Abdul tribe of Turkoman was put under Russian protection. In 1824 the first Russian caravan reached Bokhara. In 1831 the first Russian settlement was founded at Sergiopol. In 1839 a military expedition under General Perovsky was sent to conquer Khiva but completely failed owing to the severity of the winter. In 1844 the Great Horde of the Kazaks submitted to Russian rule. In 1847 Russians advanced to the Syl-daria. In the following year Russians began to colonize Semirechia in the east and the Russian line was pushed down to Khivan territory in the west. In battles fought between Russians and Kokandians in 1864 Hazret and Chimkent were taken by the Russian general Chernaieff. Shortly thereafter Tashkent was also captured. In 1868 Samarkand and Katte Kurgan fell into the Russian hands; in 1873 Khiva was conquered; three years later the Khanate of Kokan was annexed; in 1884 Merv was taken. Subsequently Bokhara was annexed and the conquest of Central Asia was completed.

Even before Russia's occupation of Central Asia Russian merchants had traded with the Taranchis at Kashgar under the rule of Galdan.

When the Dzunghars were defeated by the Manchus and fled to Russian territory in the middle of the eighteenth century the Manchu Government expelled all Russian merchants in Sinkiang and trade relations were severed. In 1811 Russian caravans proceeded to Ili and Tarbagatai for the first time. Although trade between Russia and Sinkiang was resumed thereafter it was done in an irregular and haphazard way. After having occupied Semirechia, the Russian Government requested the Manchu Court for the conclusion of a trade agreement with Sinkiang and the reopening of Kaṣhgar to Russian trade. The reopening of Kashgar was refused but negotiations for a trade agreement took place at Ili.

The Ili Trade Agreement was concluded in 1851 between Yishan, the Manchu Garrison-Commander, and Kovalousky, the Russian envoy. By this agreement Ili and Tarbagatai were opened for trade which was to be duty free.[2] Russian merchants were permitted to build homes warehouses, and churches. Nine years later the Treaty of Peking also opened Kashgar for trade. Although the Treaty of Tientsin had extended Russian trade to seven sea ports, most of the Russians who came to China for purposes of trade travelled by the overland route. At the request of the Russian Government the Sino-Russian Overland Trade Regulations were concluded at Peking in 1862. By these regulations duty-free trade was to be limited within a hundred li (about 33 miles) along the entire boundary line. Outside this limit custom duties were levied on Russian goods but the duties were to be one-third less than those imposed on the imports of other countries.[3]

Another question which rose after Russian occupation of Central Asia was that of boundary demarcation. In accordance with the provisions of the Treaty of Peking special commissioners were appointed to demarcate the boundary line. They met at Tarbagatai in October 1864 and were proceeding with their preliminary discussions when a new Islamic revolt broke out in Sinkiang. Chinese Commissioner Mingyi, being Garrison-Commissioner at Ili, had to hurry back to deal with the rebellion and thus the Boundary Treaty of Tarbagatai was concluded in great haste.

During the negotiations disputes arose concerning Chinese pickets. There were two kinds of pickets—permanent and movable. The permanent pickets were usually close to cities and towns, seldom extending beyond ten or fifteen miles. The movable pickets were established on the extreme frontier for the purpose of preventing native tribes in Central Asia from pasturing in Chinese territory. The Chinese Commissioner contended that the boundary line should be marked along the outermost pickets but the Russian Commisssioner insisted that it should follow the line of permanent pickets as provided in the Treaty of Peking. Thus a vast track of land to the south of Semipalatinsk, south east of Lake Zaisan, and north of Lake Issyk-Kul was lost. It was also provided in this treaty that where the boundary line was not yet clearly demarcated the two governments would appoint commissioners to finish the demarcation in the future. As a consequence three more boundary agreements were concluded between China and Russia in 1869 and 1870 by which the boundary lines along the Kobdo, Uliassutai and Tarbagatai regions were defined and boundary stakes were set up.

During the annexation of Sinkiang Manchu officials and troops gave the native Mohammedans (most were of Turkish descent) such harsh rule that the latter were quite dissatisfied. So in the autumn of 1864 Tuo-ming, a Tungan Mohammedan leader in Kan su, instigated the native populace of Urumchi to revolt. The uprising started at Kuchar and soon spread to other cities. An assistant Garrison Commander, So Fan-chang, himself a Mohammedan, supported the rebels and joined with Tuo-ming in leading an attack on Urumchi. The Manchu Commander was killed and Urumchi was taken. At the beginning of 1866 Ili fell into the hands of rebels and Garrison-Commander Mingyi met his death. Almost all the northern part of Sinkiang was now occupied by the forces under Tuo-ming.

Meanwhile another Mohammedan chieftan in southern Sinkiang, Chin Shan-ying, raised the standard of rebellion in 1865 and appealed to Yakub Beg, a Kokandian general in Andijan, for help. Being ambitious himself, Yakub Beg led an army into southern Sinkiang. He occupied Kashgar, Yengi Hissar, Yarkand and Khotan in 1866 and proclaimed himself Khan of Kashgar. He then marched his troops to northern Sinkiang in 1869, defeated Tuo-ming's forces and occupied Urumchi, Turfan and other cities. By that time Yakub Beg ruled the whole of southern Sinkiang and a greater part of northern Sinkiang and the only part still under the control of the Manchu Government was a narrow strip of territory from Hami through Baikul and Kucheng to Tarbagatai.

An ambitious scheme to form an independent Islamic state comprising Sinkiang and a part of Central Asia was then conceived by Yakub. He made Aksu his capital and devoted his time to the domestic affairs of his state. The Manchu Government of China was then exhausted after a long struggle against the Taiping Rebellion and could not send a military expedition to recover Sinkiang. Great

Britain was quite willing to see such a buffer state between Russian Central Asia and British India and gave Yakub Beg limited de facto recognition. British missions from India visited Aksu in 1873. Although opposed to such a state because it would be antagonistic to her own ambitions in Central Asia, Russia sent three missions to Aksu in 1872, 1875 and 1876. Trade agreements were concluded between Russia and Yakub in 1872 and between Britain and Yakub in 1873. Yakub also had relations with the Sultan of Turkey; the latter recognized Yakub as the emir of Sinkiang because he posed as a defender of the Mohammedan faith.[4]

Clearly determined to take advantage of the Mohammedan revolt to realize its own territorial aggrandizement ambitions, the Russian Government despatched troops to occupy the upper valley of the Tekes river, commanding the passes to the main route south of the Tienshan mountains. In June 1870, when the power of Yakub extended to Sinkiang, the Russian Government ordered the Governor of Turkestan to march on Ili with troops under the pretext of maintaining peace and order. The Mohammedan chieftain, Abdullah, surrendered and Ili was occupied by the Russians. In July the Russian minister in Peking, Vlangally, notified the Tsungli Yamen of this occupation. The Manchu Government was surprised by the unwarranted action on the part of Russia and demanded the reason for such occupation. In his reply the Russian minister asserted that the occupation was temporary and that the territory would be restored to China as soon as the Manchu Government was strong enough to extend its authority to that part of land. As pointed out by James Boulger, this pledge was probably made "in the happy belief that the Chinese would never be in a position to call for its redemption . . . ".[5]

Negotiations followed in the next year. The Russians insisted that Ili could be returned to China only after the latter had recovered the whole of Sinkiang and stipulated that Kobdo and other cities be opened to Russian trade to compensate Russian merchants for their losses. The Manchu Government now realized that unless it sent troops to suppress the revolt in Sinkiang Russia would permanently occupy Ili, but it was in no position to take any action. In 1873 and 1874 Japan was creating troubles in Taiwan (Formosa) and the two countries seemed to be drifting into war. Weary of the whole Sinkiang affair, the Manchu Government wanted to devote its full energy to its problems with Japan.

Sinkiang would have been abandoned if it were not for the unwavering attitude taken by Tso Tsung-tang, a Chinese statesman who became famous after suppressing the Taiping rebellion jointly with

Tseng Kuo-fan. In 1866 Tso was appointed the Viceroy of Shensi and Kansu with the mission of crushing Mohammedan rebels and other bandits in these two provinces. Within three years all the rebels and bandits in Shensi province were wiped out. During the next five years the Mohammedan revolt in Kansu was also suppressed by Tso. In 1875, when the Manchu Government asked his opinion concerning Sinkiang, Tso pointed out that if Sinkiang was abandoned the vast territory of China's northwest would be open to aggression and even the capital, Peking, would be threatened. He offered to recover Sinkiang with his troops, but the Manchu Government still hesitated because it felt that the cost of such a campaign would be too great a burden. However, Tso was so persistent that the Manchu Government finally gave its approval.

In preparing for action Tso moved his headquarters from Lanchow, capital of Kansu, to Suchow on the Sinkiang border in the spring of 1876. After making preparations for the transportation of necessary provisions, his troops, commanded by General Liu Ching-tang marched into Sinkiang. Liu's military campaign met with quicker success than expected. Urumchi was captured early in August and by the end of October northern Sinkiang was cleared of rebels. When the news of the recovery of Urumchi reached Peking Sir Thomas Wade, British minister, upon instructions from his government, proposed to the Tsungli Yamen that Yakub was now ready to surrender if only China would recognize him as head of a semi-independent vassal state and permit him to rule the eight cities in southern Sinkiang. In his note to the Tsungli Yamen Wade referred to Yakub as the Khan of Kashgar and asserted that if war continued it might give Russia a chance to invade Sinkiang to the deteriment of both China and India.[6] The Manchu Government notified Tso of this proposal to which Tso was strongly opposed.[7]

After a rest during the winter the campaign was resumed in the spring of 1877. Turfan was captured in April and the route to southern Sinkiang opened. Seeing that his cause was lost and that even the Mohammedans were rising against him, Yakub committed suicide at Kurla in May.[8] His second son, Hak Kuli Beg, then set out with Yakub's corpse to Kashgar, leaving the defense of Kurla in the hands of Hakim Tura; but before his arrival at Kashgar his elder brother, Beg Kuli Beg, saw in him a potential rival and sent men to murder him at Kuchar.

After the death of Yakub there was much disintegration among his subordinates. Hakim Tura proclaimed himself Khan at Kurla and Niaz Beg declared independence at Khotan. Thus the power of the

Andijanis was further weakened by internal strife. At this juncture Britain again tried to save the Andijanis from ultimate failure. The British Government proposed to Kuo Sung-tao, Chinese minister in London, that the Andijanis be permitted to keep Kashgar as the condition of their surrender. The Manchu Government again referred this proposal to Tso Tsung-tang who in his memorial to the Emperor stated: "Andijan is a tribe living outside the region of Kashgar while Britain and Russia are both friendly nations. If Britain wishes to protect Andijan against Russian aggression we can stand aside... If Britain wishes to establish an independent state for the Andijans in some other place she can give them some British territory or a part of India. Why should she seek the gratitude of the Andijanis by giving them our fertile land?... Kashgar has been a part of Chinese territory since the Han Dynasty. .. The request of the British Government, therefore, should not be granted."[9]

After another rest during the hot summer of Turfan, Liu Ching-tang's troops again advanced. At the beginning of October Karashar and Kurla were captured without any resistance. Ten days later Kuchar was taken after a battle and in another week Aksu was occupied. Niaz Beg now tried to surrender to the Chinese troops but was defeated by Beg Kuli Beg; the latter retook Khotan. Liu Ching-tang's forces then pushed forward rapidly. By the end of the year Kashgar, Yarkand, Yengi-Hissar and Khotan were all taken and the recovery of Sinkiang was thus completed. When Beg Kuli Beg and Hakim Tura fled into Russian territory the Russian Government refused China's request of extradition on the ground that they were political refugees.

The quick and complete success of the military campaign in Sinkiang was a great surprise to the Russians who were now unwilling to keep their pledge to return Ili to China. When in 1878 the Manchu Government made representations to Eugene Butzow, Russian minister in Peking, demanding the withdrawal of Russian troops from Ili, Butzow adopted delaying tactics. He maintained that the matter should be discussed not at Peking but at St. Petersburg. The Manchu Government than appointed Chung How minister plenipotentiary to negotiate with the Russian Government. After his arrival at St. Petersburg in December, 1878 negotiations began, the Russian representative being Butzow himself.

A Manchu nobleman who knew nothing about international politics, Chung How easily fell into the Russian trap. The Russian Government could not now go back on its words but intended to exact a high price for the return of Ili. On the other hand Chung How, ignorant as he was, cared only for the recovery of Ili without paying much attention to what price China had to pay. After seven months of negotiations Chung How signed, without the approval of the Manchu Court, the Treaty of Livadia. By this treaty Russia agreed to withdraw her troops from Ili on the following conditions: (1) the Tekes Valley—i.e., the larger and richer southwestern part of the Ili region—together with the passes through the Tienshan mountains[10] were to be ceded to Russia; (2) Russian merchants importing and exporting goods to and from Mongolia and Sinkiang were to be exempted from all duties; (3) Russian consulates were to be opened in seven cities, viz., Chiayukwan (Suchow), Kobdo, Uliassutai, Hami, Turfan, Urumchi and Kucheng; and (4) China was to pay 5,000,000 rubles (about 714,000 pounds) as compensation for Russian occupation costs.[11]

When the news of the treaty reached Peking the Manchu Government and the Chinese people were shocked. Many high officials denounced Chung How for his treacherous action. Both Tso Tsung-tang and Li Hung-chang advocated a firm policy to resist Russia's importunate demands; some officials urged preparation for war in case Russia refused to revise the treaty. Chang Chih-tung, who was to become a famous viceroy in later years, said in his petition to the Emperor: "Russia, though a powerful nation, is at present deficient in military strength and resources as a result of her recent war with Turkey. The Russian people are greatly dissatisfied with the government to the extent that an attempt on the life of the Tsar is rumored. If Russia should go to war with us it would be tantamount to her committing suicide. The new treaty gives China only the title of Ili; actually China loses 20,000 li of territory in addition to an annual expediture of 5,000,000 taels[12] for military defense. Under these curcumstances would it not be better for China to give up Sinkiang entirely? . . . I humbly beg the Throne to command Li Hung-chang to conscript and train necessary troops in readiness for war . . . We can make good use of the very payment to Russia provided in the new treaty to employ a large number of foreign mercenaries who will be ready to fight for us . . . ".[13]

Chung How was recalled and found to be guilty of disobeying instructions and overstepping his powers. He was discharged from his office and was sentenced by an imperial edict to be decapitated after imprisonment. Considering this punishment of Chung How an affront to itself, the Russian Government lodged a strong protest with the Tsungli Yamen. It demanded the release of Chung How on the ground that according to international practice, no government should punish an envoy for his failure in negotiations. Russia also threatened with the use of force by sending her fleet to the Far East and by increasing her troops in the vicinity of Ili to 90,000 men.

However, Tso Tsung-tang was bent upon retaking Ili by force of arms. He memorialized the Emperor: "Upon the occupation of Ili the Russians destroyed a large part of the city, using the material to build an extensive mart. It seems that Russia intends to make Ili a Russian colony... When a country is defeated in war it may be obliged to cede territory and to sue for peace. But up to the present moment not a single shot has been fired. Why should China sacrifice an important area to satisfy Russia's greed? It would be like throwing a bone to a dog to prevent it from biting. But when the bone has been eaten up, the dog would still want to bite. The loss at present is apparent and the trouble in the future will be endless!"[14] After sending more troops into Sinkiang in order to recover Ili, Tso proceeded to Hami in June. He was then 69 years old. To show his determination to do or die he ordered his coffin to be carried behind him. A Sino-Russian war seemed imminent and only a spark was needed to explode the powder keg.

The expected war did not materialize. While there was a strong war party among the officials and the literati, men like Li Hung-chang and Kuo Sung-tao (the latter was then back in China) asserted that China was no match for Russia's military might. Their view prevailed and the two Empresses Dowager[15]—they were the real rulers of China since Emperor Kwang-hsu was still a young boy—followed a course of compromise. In June, 1880 Queen Victoria of Britain sent a personal appeal to the Empresses Dowager in the form of a telegram begging for Chung How's life. This appeal proved successful; Chung How was pardoned. The face of Russia was saved and the door for negotiations was again open.

General Charles G. Gordon, whose service to the Manchu Government during the Taiping Rebellion had earned him great reputation and respect, was invited by Sir Robert Hart, Inspector-General of the Chinese Customs, to come to China to give his advice on the grave situation. Gordon offered the following alternatives to Li Hung-chang and other Chinese ministers: "If you will make war, burn the suburbs of Peking, remove the Emperor and archives from Peking, put them in the center of the country, and fight for five years, Russia will not be able to hurt you; issue letters of Mark (Privateer). If you want peace, then give up Ili in toto, and escape the payment of five million taels and all the articles in the Livadia Treaty concerning it. Ili, if the passes are held by Russia, will never be really Chinese;

it has always cost China more blood and money than it is worth."[16] Gordon's opinion also helped the Manchu Court to abandon the idea of war. Finally Tseng Chi-tse, son of Tseng Kuo-fan, China's great nineteenth century statesman, was transferred from the minister to Britain to minister to Russia and was charged with the mission of negotiating a revised treaty with the Russian Government. Meanwhile Tso Tsung-tang was recalled to Peking, nominally for consultations but actually to avoid any possible conflict with Russian troops at Ili.

Tseng Chi-tse knew very well that his task was extremely difficult, if not impossible. Before his departure from London for St. Petersburg he petitioned the Emperor to consider that there were three points of negotiations—boundary demarcation, a commercial agreement and an indemnity; and three ways of approach—war, defense and compromise. After lengthy presentation of the problem, he concluded that the best way out would be through compromise. In another petition he stated: "It seems to me that of all the three negotiable points the indemnity question is of the least importance. Then, comparing the demarcation issue with the commercial agreement, it is clear that the former is more important . . . In spite of the fact that the treaty entered into by Chung How is greatly detrimental to China's interests, I greatly fear that it could not be revoked in full. It is my humble opinion that we should stand firm as to the question of demarcation, as it is of a permanent nature, while the commercial agreement should be only amended in its most detrimental articles, approval being given to the rest... Negotiations will have to be carried step by step and in a compromising spirit, as one should not expect any concrete results in a short time."[17] Significantly, the Tsungli Yamen gave Tseng detailed instructions on what concessions to make if Ili could be wholly or partially restored.[18]

Tseng Chi-tse arrived at St. Petersburg in July, 1880 with two foreign advisers, Sir Halliday Macartney of Britain and Prosper Giquel of France.[19] Negotiations with Russian Foreign Minister de Giers soon began. Tseng presented China's point of view in six items: (1) China was not willing to cede any territory to any country and hoped that the whole region of Ili would be returned; (2) the boundary lines of Tarbagatai and Kashgar should remain unchanged; (3) China was willing to open Chiayukwan for trade and two trade routes through Nerchinsk and Kobdo if Ili was wholly restored; (4) a new Russian consulate might be opened at Chiaykwan while the establishment of other Russian consulates should be postponed; (5) Russia might choose a place among Hami, Kucheng and Barkul for storing goods along the lines allowed for in Kalgan; and (6) the question of custom duties on Russian trade should be open for further discussions.[20]

Initially the attitude of the Russian Foreign Minister was arrogant and uncompromising. At their first meeting de Giers told Tseng that he saw no ground for a renewal of discussions and asked for the ratification of the Treaty of Livadia. Later on he even threatened to break off the negotiations and to send Butzow back to Peking to negotiate with the Manchu Government. But Tseng Chi-tse's tact, patience and perseverance won the day and the situation took a more favorable turn for China. Finally an agreement on all main points was reached at the end of the year and Tseng sent the draft treaty to Peking for approval. Nearly two months later the Manchu Governments' approval was given and the Treaty of St. Petersburg was signed on February 24, 1881.[21]

While the Treaty of St. Petersburg did not entirely meet with the hopes of the Manchu Government and the Chinese people it did get back from Russia a large tract of land and many of the privileges which had been conceded by Chung How. The broad valley of the Tekes and all the passes between Ili and southern Sinkiang were saved for China and only a small area to the west of the Holkutz river was ceded to Russia for the purpose of accommodating those inhabitants who were forced to give up their lands in order to become Russian subjects (Article 7). Boundary lines east of Lake Zaisan and west of Kashgar as determined by the Treaty of Tarbagatai were to be redemarcated (Article 8). Russian consulates were to be established at Chiayukwan and Turfan but those at Kobdo, Uliassutai, Hami, Urumchi and Kucheng were to be postponed until trade there had prospered (Article 9). Free trade was to be continued in Mongolia, and temporarily permitted at Ili, Tarbagatai, Kashgar, Urumchi and other Sinkiang cities (Article 12). The trade stipulations of the treaty as well as the regulations serving as its complement were to be subject to revision after ten years (Article 15). The five million ruble indemnity provided in the Treaty of Livadia was increased to nine million rubles (1,431,664 pounds) to include the losses of Russian subjects in Ili (Article 6).

Viewed as a whole the Treaty of St. Petersburg was a diplomatic victory for China. Lord Dufferin, British ambassador in Russia, who had been a silent but interested observer of the Sino-Russian negotiations, commented on the treaty: China has compelled Russia to do what she has never done before, disgorge territory that she had once absorbed."[22] A famous author remarked: ". . . in her history of many centuries, China was accustomed to military victories, but a bloodless diplomatic triumph such as that of Marquis Tseng[23] was new in her experience."[24]

In accordance with the provisions in the Treaty of St. Petersburg, boundary agreements were subsequently concluded between China and Russia—one concerning the southern boundary of Ili in August, 1882, another concerning Kashgar in November, 1882, a third concerning Kobdo and Tarbagatai in July, 1883 and a fourth also concerning Kashgar in May, 1885. Due to the incompetence of the Manchu representatives China lost some territory in each of these agreements.

Then there arose the question of Pamir. Known as "the roof of the world," the Pamir plateau (where the boundaries of China, Russia, and India meet) averages 13,000 feet above sea-level. Encompassing an area of about 30,000 square miles, it was divided into eight Pamirs. On one of its peaks there was a stone tablet inscribed by Emperor Chien-lung, furnishing proof that the whole plateau was Chinese territory. In 1878, after Sinkiang had been recovered, General Liu Ching-tang established frontier posts along the border of Pamir. In 1891, Russia dispatched troops to protect scientific expeditions into Pamir and proclaimed it Russian territory. Britain then invaded Hunza, a vassal state of China, to counter-balance the expansion of Russia. Upon receiving reports from Tao Mu, Governor of Sinkiang, the Manchu Government protested to both Russia and Britain. In its reply the British Government stated that its action was a precaution against Russia; the Russian Government took the position that it occupied Pamir as a precaution against Britain. Afghanistan, at the instigation of Britain, occupied the central part of Pamir. In 1895 Britain and Russia compromised and concluded the Pamir Treaty to divide the plateau between them. Only one out of the eight Pamirs remained in Chinese hands. The Manchu Government again protested but to no avail.[25]

CHAPTER VI

Russian Penetration Into Manchuria

Since the Manchu Dynasty had risen from a tribe in Manchuria to become the master of whole China it naturally regarded Manchuria as its own sacred land and prohibited the Chinese people from migrating into Manchuria. It was not until 1776 that the prohibition of migration to Shenking province was relaxed and not until a century thereafter that the prohibition of migration to Kirin and Heilungkiang provinces was officially removed[1]. Consequently Manchuria was still very thinly populated in the 1850's; there were less than three million inhabitants in an area of about 364,000 square miles. Of these three million people two million lived in Shengking, an area adjacent to China proper, while Kirin and Heilungkiang had a combined population of less than a million.

The regions of Amur and Ussuri which lay to the north of Heilungkiang and east of Kirin were practically a land without people. When Russia acquired these two regions by the treaties of Aigun and Peking in 1858-1860 the entire population in this vast territory was less than 15,000. "It was a huge emptiness, with no agriculture, no trade, no roads, and, of course, no industry." Consequently the Russian Government encouraged the migration and settlement of Russians in this newly acquired Russian Far East. But this policy was not successful at the beginning. Owing to the enormous distance from Russia proper, difficult communications, and miserable living conditions few Russians cared to migrate to the new territory. In consequence the Russian Government sent criminals and so-called "Cossack armies" from Siberia to settle there. Prostitutes in the cities were seized in large numbers and sent there to become the wives of the settlers. Most settlers considered themselves deportees and were highly discontent with their lot. Przhevalsky, a Russian explorer who visited the Ussuri region at the end of the 1860's reported: "One hears bitter complaints about hardships, and sad reminiscences of former habitats. Most of them lack even bread, and every year the state must feed a great part of the population, to save it from famine. The bread looks like dried clay and burns the mouth. As a result of poverty, there is terrible demoralization. It is difficult to believe the extent of the corruption among the population of the Ussuri region."[2] The population in these regions did not increase as rapidly as the Russian Government had expected; at the end of the nineteenth century it did not exceed one third of a million.

For this reason, if for no others, Russia soon became dissatisfied with the acquisition of the Amur and Maritime provinces and her eyes turned to the more populous and fertile lands to the south—Manchuria and Korea. To the Russian mind control of these two countries were necessary if Russia was to be the dominant power in the Far East. Russia was also seeking an ice-free port and naval base in the Liaotung peninsula or in Korea. (Vladivostok, founded in 1860, is frozen in the winter even though it is a good port and base). But Russia had to wait for a proper moment to take action and had to first improve her system of communications in Siberia so that her military might could be brought to the Far East in a short time. Therefore Tsar Alexander III ordered, in 1891, the construction of the 3500 miles long Trans-Siberian Railway.

Even before the completion of this railway in 1901 the Sino-Japanese disputes concerning Korea gave Russia a chance to realize her ambitions. Korea, since the beginning of her history as a nation more than three thousand years ago, had had special relations with China. Sometimes, as during the reign of Emperor Wu of the Han Dynasty, the northern part of Korea was made a part of Chinese territory. Sometimes she was completely independent. But during the greater part of her history and up to the Sino-Japanese war Korea was a vassal state of China. As Japan grew stronger and stronger after the Meigi Reformation she began to think of annexing Korea as a stepping stone to her dominance in Manchuria. In 1876 Japan concluded a treaty with Korea by which the latter was recognized as an independent state. The Manchu Government was so incompetent at the time that it did not even take the trouble of lodging a protest with Japan. In 1882-1886 Korea concluded treaties with the United States, Britain, Germany, Italy, Russia and France but, due to the insistence of the Manchu Government, Korea announced in her notes to these countries that she was a vassal state of China.

There was a coup d'etat at Seoul in 1882 in which the anti-Japanese group burned the Japanese legation and killed several Japanese officers. The coup was soon suppressed by the Chinese army and navy sent from Tientsin but Japan also sent troops to Korea. After that Japan gradually assumed the role of a protector of Korea. In 1884 the pro-Japanese group made another coup and there were clashes between Chinese and Japanese troops in Korea. In April, 1885, after peace and order had been restored in Korea, Li Hung-chang concluded at Tientsin a treaty with Count Ito Hirobumi, Japanese envoy, by which China and Japan agreed: (1) to withdraw within four months troops stationed in Korea; (2) to refrain from sending officers to train the Korean army; (3) to previously notify each other in case of despatching troops to Korea in the future.[3]

In the meantime Britain and Russia were quarreling over Afghanistan. When Russia sent her fleet to Vladivostok, Britain landed her forces at Port Hamilton on Chuwen Island in March, 1885 to watch the Russian movement. The Manchu Government was ready to recognize British temporary occupation when the Russian minister notified the Tsungli Yamen that if China recognized the fait accompli Russia would occupy some other Korean territory. Consequently China continued to negotiate with Britain for the withdrawal of her troops from Port Hamilton. In 1886, when the tension in Afghanistan lessened, Britain notified China that if China could guarantee no other power would occupy the island British troops would withdraw. Li Hung-chang took the matter up directly with Russian Charge d'Affaires Ladygensky and got a pledge from the Russian Government that it would never violate Korean territory.[4] Thus assured, the British Government withdrew its troops early in 1887.

But before the Chinese-British settlement there had occurred an intrigue between Russia and Korea. In 1883 the Korean King had, at the recommendation of Li Hung-chang, appointed as his adviser P. G. von Moelendorff, a German who had been in the Chinese customs service. He came to enjoy the confidence of the King and later was used as a tool by the Russian. In 1896 von Moelendorff, in conspiracy with the anti-Chinese group in the Korean court, pursuaded the Korean Foreign Office to negotiate a secret convention with Russian Minister Waeber, by which Russia agreed to lend Russian officers to train the Korean army while Korea submitted to Russian protection and gave Russia the usufruct of Port Lazareff. When this news leaked out China, Japan, and Britain were alarmed. The Manchu Government threatened to use force if the scheme was carried out. In September the Korean King sent Hsu Hsiang-yu, Director of Foreign Affairs, to Tientsin to see Li Hung-chang with a personal letter from the King. The letter and Hsu's conversations with Li emphatically repudiated the secret convention and denounced as a forgery the document to the Russian minister asking for protection.[5] Von Moelendorff was summarily dismissed from his post. Thus Russia's plot was nipped in the bud and her ambitions in Korea were checked.

When the so-called Eastern Learning Society[6] started an uprising in Korea in May, 1895 the King appealed to the Manchu Court for a military expedition to suppress the revolt. The Manchu Government at once sent troops to Korea and stationed two warships at Inchon. When the Tsungli Yamen notified the Japanese Government of the despatch of Chinese forces the latter also sent troops to Korea. Upon learning of the approach of the Chinese troops the Eastern Learning Society dispersed and the revolt was over without any fighting. Then the Tsungli Yamen proposed to Japan that both countries withdraw their troops but Japan refused. Japan proposed in return joint action in reorganizing and reforming the Korean administration and met with a Chinese refusal. The Japanese then informed China of its intention to take such action alone. The Japanese envoy even demanded the Korean King to declare Korea an independent state and not a vassal of China.

Li Hung-chang tried to pursuade other foreign powers to bring pressure on Japan to withdraw her troops. The Department of State declined to take part "even in a friendly intervention".[7] The Russian Tsar did instruct his minister in Tokyo to advise the withdrawal of Japanese troops three times.[8] But as Japan refused to heed this advice Russian Minister Cassini told Li Hung-chang that his government was not willing to use force.[9] The British Government was quite willing to offer its good offices, but the Tsungli Yamen insisted that since Korea was a vassal state of China, Japan could not enjoy the same rights in Korea as China and that other questions could only be discussed after Japan had withdrawn her troops. British envoy O'Connor also withdrew from his mediation role.[10]

It becomes clear now that Japan intended at that time to win a war with China in order to elevate her place among the nations.[11] On July 25 Japanese warships sank in the Gulf of Chi-le the British steamer "Kowshing" which had been chartered by the Manchu Government to transport 1200 soldiers to Korea. Four day later Japanese troops attacked Chinese forces under General Yeh at Yashan with great loss to the Chinese. On August 1, both sides declared war. At that time the European powers and the United States over-estimated the strength of China and under-estimated that of Japan. To their mind China, although weak, was a huge and populous country while Japan, although having undergone 25 years' reformation, was a much smaller state. So in this war they expected neither side to win a decisive victory to affect the status quo in the Far East.

Japan, however, proved to be much stronger than the powers had thought and beat China both on land and at sea. Chinese troops were completely routed at Pingyang in the middle of September while the Chinese Pei-yang navy under the command of Admiral Ting Ju-chang was defeated in a battle off the mouth of the Yalu river, only two days latter. Towards the end of October the Japanese forces crossed the Yalu which formed the boundary between China and Korea and marched into Manchuria. As Japan now had control of the sea a second Japanese army landed on Liaotung Peninsula and soon occupied Dairen and Port Arthur. In December a battle lasting two days was fought near Haicheng and the Chinese were again defeated. In January, 1895 the Japanese landed 30 miles east of Weihaiwei to attack the remnant Chinese fleet which had taken shelter there. The forts on the shore were taken by the Japanese who then bombarded the Chinese warships with guns in those forts as well as guns of the Japanese fleet. Several Chinese warships were sunk, Admiral Ting committed suicide and what was left of the Pei-yang fleet surrendered. As the Chinese troops now lost the will to resist the Japanese occupied Liaoyang and Yingkow and could easily march through Shanhaikwan to China proper. There was nothing left for the Manchu Government to do but sue for peace.

In November, 1894 the Manchu Government had made through the American minister in Peking, peace overtures to Japan on the basis of an independent Korea and war indemnities,[12] but nothing came of this. Then at the end of the year an imperial edict appointed Chang Yin-hwan and Shao Yu-lien special envoys to Japan "to inquire what terms Japan will demand to bring the present war to an end". They arrived at Kobe in January 1895, but as their credentials were not of a plenipotentiary nature the Japanese refused to negotiate with them. In February Li Hung-chang was appointed ambassador extraordinary to negotiate peace with Japan. He arrived at Shimonoseki on March 19, and began negotiations the next day with the Japanese envoys, Prime Minister Ito Hirobumi and Foreign Minister Inutsu Munemitu.

At first the Japanese were very arrogant and would not even sign an armistice except on the condition that Japanese troops occupy Shanhaikwan, Taku Harbor and Tientsin. Then on March 24, a Japanese patriotic lunatic attempted to assassinate Li and seriously wounded him. This crime aroused the sympathy of the whole world towards Li and the Japanese Government was afraid that Russia might use it as a pretext for intervention. Six days later an armistice was signed. On April 1, the Japanese envoys presented a draft treaty to Li, the conditions of which were already mitigated but were still very harsh. After half a month's negotiations Japan made some slight concessions and the Treaty of Shimonoseki was signed on April 17. The main points of this treaty were: (1) China recognized the complete independence of Korea; (2) China was to cede to Japan Liaotung Peninsula, Taiwan (Formosa) and Penghu (Pescadores); (3) China was to pay to Japan an indemnity of 200,000,000 taels; (4) China was to open Shasi, Chungking, Soochow and Hangchow to foreign trade.[13] After this war the weakness of China was completely exposed while Japan was on her way to play the role of a major power.

The acquisition by Japan of Liaotung Peninsula would serve as a serious blow to Russian ambitions and was therefore intolerable to Russia. In an imperial conference presided over by Tsar Nicholas II, a conclusion was arrived at to give advice to Japan for her withdrawal from southern Manchuria and in case of Japan's refusal to take appropriate action.[14] Russian Foreign Minister Lobanov then notified the German and French envoys in Moscow of the decision and asked the support of their governments. In case of Japan's refusal pressure by armed forces would be applied and communications between Japan and the Asia mainland would be severed. The German Government under the ambitious Kaiser, Wilhelm II, at once gave its consent and ordered the German Far Eastern Fleet to cooperate with the Russian fleet. France did not wish to take joint action with Germany, but neither did she want to offend her new ally, Russia. Finally the French Government also agreed to give its support. Lobanov then invited Britain to join the three powers, but Foreign Secretary Chamberlain refused on the ground that Britain was not willing to take any military action against Japan.

On April 23, six days after the signing of the treaty the Russian, French and German ministers in Tokyo presented similar notes to the Japanese Foreign Office, asserting that the Japanese acquisition of Liaotung would threaten the capital of China, would make Korea's independence merely nominal and would disturb future peace in the Far East. Japan was advised to abandon Liaotung. Of course Japan strongly resented this interference but she was not in a position to wage a war against three major powers. So after two weeks of discussions and negotiations the Japanese Government replied to the three governments that she was willing to abandon Liaotung. But Japan was to exact a price from China for the retrocession of Liaotung.

In July Japan notified the three powers that China should pay an additional indemnity of 50,000,000 taels. After some negotiations between the ministers of the three powers and the Japanese Foreign Office the amount was cut down to 30,000,000 taels and Japan agreed to withdraw her troops from Liaotung within three months after the payment of this additional indemnity. A formal treaty between China and Japan embodying these points was signed at Peking on November

8. Eight days later the additional indemnity was paid and Japanese troops withdrew within the time limit.

By a masterly diplomatic move Russia gave Japan, a rising power, a serious blow at her ambitions on the one hand and won the gratitude of China on the other. Russia made a further pretense of friendship in the form of a loan of 400,000,000 francs (15,820,000 pounds) to enable China to pay her indemnity to Japan.[15] Of course Russia did not do all this for the sake of China. Her eyes were already on the proposed railway connecting Chita and Vladivostok via Manchuria. At that time the Trans-Siberian Railway had been built up to Transbaikalia and it was the opinion of Witte, who initiated the whole project, that if the railway could be extended to Vladivostok through Manchuria instead of following the course of the Amur it would be rendered 5000 verst shorter at great saving of time and expenses. This opinion was accepted by the Tsar and the only remaining question was how to make China give the concession for building this railway.

The retrocession of Liaotung and the loan made the Manchu Government and the Chinese people so grateful to Russia they completely forgot what Russia had done in the past. Many high officials now advocated an alliance with Russia against further Japanese aggression. Take Chang Chih-tung, viceroy of three Yangtze provinces, for instance. The same man who advocated a war against Russia during the Ili crisis 16 years previously petitioned the Emperor to conclude a secret alliance with her. His memorial read in part: "China and Russia have been friendly neighboring states for more than two hundred years without any military conflict. Her relations with us are different from those nations who have fought wars against us. Her policy is usually more generous and broad-minded than the western powers... Although Russia demanded the retrocession of Liaotung for the stabilization of the Far Eastern situation yet we are benefited by it. The dangerous expansion of Japan is also checked. How different from other nations who stood aside and simply wished to extend their trade. We should take this opportunity to strengthen our friendship with Russia by concluding a secret alliance."[16]

The Empress Dowager, Emperor Kwang-hsu and even Li Hung-chang now harbored all sorts of illusions about Russia. When the coronation of Tsar Nicholas II took place in May, 1896 the Manchu Court sent Li Hung-chang, who was then 73, as China's special envoy. Li Hung-chang left Shanghai by steamer in March and was met by Russian Prince Ukhtamsky at Port Said. Then he boarded a Russian warship to Odessa and arrived at St. Petersburg at the end of April, where he received a royal welcome. Tsar Nicholas II appointed Foreign Minister Prince Lobanov and Finance Minister Count Witte to negotiate with Li. When Witte first brought up the project of a railway through Manchuria Li objected and expressed the opinion that China should build it herself. But when later Tsar Nicholas II talked to Li personally and promised Russia's military help via the proposed railway in case China had troubles in the future, Li was willing to accept the proposal.[17]

After several more meetings both before and after the coronation the Sino-Russian Secret Treaty of Alliance was signed at Moscow on June 3, by Li on the one side and by Lobanov and Witte on the other. This treaty was kept a top secret at that time and its text was not published until after the First World War. It provided that in case Japan invaded Russian territory in eastern Asia, or Chinese territory or Korean territory the two powers should help each other via army and navy aid and by munitions and provisions; neither should negotiate a separate peace. During the time of war Russian warships should be permitted to enter any Chinese port and their needs be met with by the local authorities. China was to permit Russia to build a railway via Heilungkiang and Kirin to Vladivostok which was to be constructed by the Russo-Chinese Bank. The treaty was to be effective for fifteen years but could be extended.[18]

While the treaty was not published the news of the negotiations leaked out and there were many rumors concerning the secret alliance. *The North-China Herald*, an English newspaper in Shanghai, published on October 30, the so-called Cassini Treaty which was alleged to have been signed by Minister Wang and Cassini on September 29, and which provided, besides railway concessions, the lease of Kiaochow to Russia for fifteen years and the use of Port Arthur and Dairen by Russian forces in case of war. Judged by subsequent events this alleged treaty did not exist.[19]

After Li had left Russia the details of the railway concessions were worked out by Hsu Ching-tseng, Chinese minister at St. Petersburg and Romanov, Russian Assistant Minister of Finance. On September 8, an agreement concerning the construction of the Chinese Eastern Railway was signed by Hsu, representing the Manchu Government and Prince Ukhtomsky and Rothstern representing the newly formed Russo-Chinese Bank. For the construction of the railway the bank was to form a separate corporation, named the Chinese Eastern Railway Company, whose shares could only be bought by Chinese and Russians. The president of the company was to be appointed by the Manchu Government but its regulations were to be modelled after those of Russian railway companies. All public land needed would be donated to the company by the Manchu Government while private land would be purchased by the company. At the completion of the railway and the start of transportation the company would pay 5,000,000 taels to China. After thirty-six years China would have the right to redeem the railway. After eighty years Russia should return the whole line to China free of compensation.[20]

Another agreement with the Russo-Chinese Bank was signed by Hsu six days later by which China invested 5,000,000 taels in the capital of the Bank. The capital of the Chinese Eastern Railway Company was fixed at 5,000,000 rubles divided into 1,000 shares. Out of these 1,000 shares 700 were to be subscribed for by the Russian Government while the remaining 300 shares by individuals. If any of these 300 shares were not subscribed the Bank could request the Russian Government to take them up. The regulations of the Chinese Eastern Railway Company were approved by the Russian Government on December 4, 1896. The sale of shares was advertised in the Government Gazette on December 17, and the time for transactions was set to begin 9 a.m. of the same day. Naturally nobody was able to subscribe for any shares and a few minutes later the office was closed. Thus by a clever manipulation the Russian Treasury got all the shares of the company.

With the railway company thus established the survey work started in April, 1897 and construction began in August, 1898. In July, 1903 through trains began to run the whole line. Nominally it was jointly owned and operated but actually it was a Russian railway. The Chinese president of the company was a figure head and all the administrative power was in the hands of the Russian assistant president. The railway since its construction had served as the headquarters of Russian penetration into Manchuria. The railway company not only procured land but administered it. It maintained a strong police force in the so-called railway zone, issued regulations, imposed taxes on all merchants and claimed jurisdiction in the cities and towns which had developed within the zone.

After China's withdrawal from Korea Japan's influence in Korea became dominant. Korea was forced to get loans from Japan and as conditions for such loans Japan controlled Korean railways, post, telegraph and harbors. The Korean Government was now in the hands of the pro-Japanese group who even talked about the dethronement of the King. The King was thus alarmed and secretly negotiated with Russian Minister Waeber for his protection. Waeber was more than happy to give his consent and the King with the crown prince suddenly left the palace and went to the Russian legation in February, 1896. Thus under the Russian protection the King issued edicts to dismiss all the pro-Japanese ministers and form a new cabinet. Pro-Japanese Prime Minister Chin Feng-chi was excluded. Two Russian advisers were appointed to help consolidate Korean finance and military affairs and twenty Russian officers were engaged to train the army. A Russian language school was established.

Japan was yet no match for Russia and had to give in. After conversations between the Japanese and Russian ministers in Seoul an agreement was reached in the middle of May, by which Japanese troops stationed in Korea were to be limited to 800 soldiers and 200 military police while Russia had the right to station the same number of troops. A month later another agreement was signed by Field-marshal Yamagata, Japan's special envoy for the Tsar's coronation, and Russian Foreign Minister Lobanov, by which the relationships of Korea with Japan and with Russia were put on an equal basis. Then in April, 1898, Russian Minister Rosen, and Japanese Foreign Minister Nishi again signed an agreement in Tokyo, by which the two governments pledged themselves not to interfere with the internal affairs of Korea and to consult with each other when nominating military instructors or financial advisers to Korea. Russia recognized Japan's "peculiar interest" in Korea and would not obstruct the development of the commercial and industrial relations between Japan and Korea. These agreements temporarily settled the disputes over Korea between the two countries.[21]

Kaiser Wilhelm II was even more ambitious than his cousin, Tsar Nicholas II. When he heard that Russia had secured railway concessions in Manchuria he wanted to obtain some ports in China as a base for German expansion in the Far East. His eyes turned to Kiaochowwan in Shangtung, an ice-free bay suitable for a naval station. In the winter of 1895-1896 the Russian Far Eastern Fleet got the permission to winter there. So when the Kaiser visited the Tsar in Russia in August, 1897 he brought up the question of Kiaochowwan and asked the Tsar whether Russia wanted to take it. The Tsar denied to have such an intention, while Count Mikhail Muraviev, Russian Foreign Minister, declared to the German ambassador that Russia was willing to see Kiaochowwan in German hands so that it would not be seized by Britain.[22]

Thus assured of Russia's acquiescence the Kaiser waited for a proper moment to take action. He did not wait very long. In November two German missionaries were murdered at Chuyeh, Shangtung.

Using this as a pretext a German fleet sailed into Kiaochowwan; a small force landed at Tsingtao, seized the forts and occupied the port. A week later the German Government demanded of China the payment of an indemnity, dismissal of Governor Li Ping-heng of Shangtung, grant of a naval station at Kiaochowwan and sole right to construct a railway and open coal mines in Shangtung. China was helpless to resist German aggression and after four months' negotiations she conceded all these points. A convention was signed on March 6, 1898, leasing to Germany the land on both sides of the entrance to Kiaochowwan including Tsingtao and all the islands for ninety-nine years.[23]

When the German force dashed on Tsingtao Russian Foreign Minister Muraviev proposed to the Tsar that this was Russia's best opportunity to seize Port Arthur and Dairen. Witte was opposed to this proposal, asserting that such aggressive action would rouse strong opposition of the Chinese people which might affect construction of the Chinese Eastern Railway. But the ministers of war and the navy supported Muraviev and the Tsar decided to take immediate action. On November 22, 1898 Russian warships arrived at Port Arthur and landed marines there. H. Pablov, Russian Charge d'affairs at Peking, notified the Tsungli Yamen that Russia had no intention to occupy Chinese territory and that the Russian fleet was there to protect China against German aggression and would withdraw as soon as the German fleet withdrew from Kiaochowwan. When the Tsar received Chinese Minister Yang Yu in February, 1898 he still promised to withdraw the fleet in the spring but it might return in the winter.[24]

In March the Manchu Government sent Hsu Ching-tseng as special envoy to negotiate with the Russian Foreign Office on this problem. Muraviev demanded the lease of Port Arthur and Dairen and the extension of the Chinese Eastern Railway to these ports in the interests of both countries. The Tsar also told Hsu that the Russian fleet could not withdraw from Port Arthur as the situation in the Far East had changed. Both Britain and Japan advised China to stand firm but the Manchu Government was afraid to offend Russia. So on March 27 a convention was signed at Peking, by Pablov for Russia and Li Hung-chang and Chang Yin-hwan for China, by which Port Arthur and Dairen and its adjacent territory were leased to Russia for twenty-five years. By an additional convention concluded in May at St. Petersburg the leased territory was extended to include Chinchow.[25] The Convention of Peking also gave the Chinese Eastern Railway Company the right to build a branch line. By a supplementary agreement with the railway company in July the branch was to be built from Harbin to Port Arthur and Dairen and was to be named the South Manchurian branch.[26]

France, as one of the three powers which had forced Japan to return Liaotung to China, now wanted her share of compensation. Although French Foreign Minister Hanotaux declared in February, 1898 that France had "not the slightest intention of imitating Germany in seizing a naval base in China";[27] French warships sailed into Kwangchowwan in Kwangtung province and raised the French flag there on April 22. A convention for the lease of Kwangchowwan with its dependencies to France as a naval base for ninety-nine years was submitted to the Tsungli Yamen on May 27, but it was not ratified by China until February 19, 1900.[28]

Then in June, 1898 Britain, taking advantage of this situation, obtained a convention to extend Hongkong territory across the bay to Kowloon under lease of ninety-nine years "for the proper defense and protection of the colony" and in July another convention for the lease of Weihaiwei together with adjacent islands across Chih-li Strait from Port Arthur "for so long a period as Port Arthur shall remain in the occupation of Russia".[29]

There was also, at that time, a scramble for spheres of influence in China by the powers. The sphere of influence was implied in the so-called "declaration of non-alienation". The first such declaration was made by the Manchu Government to France. In March, 1897 France asked China to declare that she would not "alienate or cede the island of Hainan to any other foreign power either as final or temporary cession, or as a naval station or coaling depot", and the Tsungli Yamen replied, disclaiming any intention of ceding Hainan to any power.[30] In February, 1898 China gave Britain "a definite assurance that China will never alienate any territory in the provinces adjoining the Yangtze to any other power whether under lease, mortgage or any other designation".[31] Two months later France got a similar assurance concerning provinces bordering on French Indo-China.[32] In the same month Japan got an assurance that China would not alienate any part of Fukien, the province across the strait from Taiwan, to any power whatsoever.[33] Germany regarded Shangtung as her sphere of influence while Russia regarded Manchuria as hers. In April, 1899 Britain and Russia exchanged notes, by which Britain agreed not to interfere outside the Great Wall while Russia agreed not to interfere in the Yangtze basin.[34]

Thus at the end of the nineteenth century China was on the verge of being dismembered by the powers. The only major power which was not seeking concessions or a sphere of influence in China was the United States which had no territorial ambitions and was only interested in doing trade with China. Fearing that China might be broken up into colonies of the powers the American Secretary of State, John Hay, on September 6, 1899, instructed the American ambassadors to Britain, Germany and Russia to present a circular note to these governments respectively asking for a formal assurance that each government would in no way interfere with any treaty port or any vested interest within any so-called "sphere of interest" or leased territory it might have in China; that only the Chinese Government should collect customs duties which should be according to the Chinese treaty tariff; and that no preferential harbor dues or railway charges in the "sphere of interest" should benefit its own subjects. In September similar notes were presented to the French, Italian[35] and Japanese governments.

The British Govenment was the first to reply that Britain adhered to the principle of equal opportunity concerning trade in China and would make such a declaration if the other powers concerned did the same. France, Japan, Italy, Russia and Germany then all replied one after another that they would accept the principle if it was acceptable to other powers. Only Russia made the reservation that "the settlement of the question of the customs duties belongs to China herself".[36] When all replies were in, Secretary Hay again notified each of the six governments in March, 1900 that "the condition originally attached to its acceptance—that all other powers concerned should likewise accept the proposals of the United States—having been complied with, this Government will therefore consider the assent given to it... as final and definitive".[37] Thus the famous open-door policy in China was inaugurated.

The declaration of this policy was very timely for within a short time the Boxer rebellion broke out in China. The Boxers were ignorant fanatics who resented foreign encroachment and acted with patriotic motives. But they did not know what was the right thing to do to make China strong and independent and followed a blind anti-foreign course. Encouraged by the stupid Empress Dowager[38] and Manchu noblemen they created troubles in North China especially in Peking and Tientsin in the spring of 1900. Foreign missionaries and Chinese Christians alike were massacred by them and their houses burned down.

There was then a rumor that the powers were demanding the return of political power to the Emperor and the Empress Dowager was enraged. So an imperial edict declaring war against foreign powers was issued on June 21. German Minister Ketteler on his way to the Tsengli Yamen had been murdered by an unruly soldier a day before and the legations in Peking were now attacked by Boxers and troops. Fortunately for China, the viceroys and governors of various provinces ignored the edict and were trying to keep peace and order in the regions under their control. Viceroy Liu Kun-yi of Kiangsi and Anhwei and Viceroy Chang Chih-tung of Hupei and Hunan even negotiated a modus vivendi with the foreign consuls in Shanghai, by which the viceroys agreed to protect the lives and properties of foreigners in accordance with the treaties within their respective jurisdictions while the foreign powers agreed not to despatch forces to the Yangtze valley. This principle was also accepted by Li Hung-chang who was then the viceroy of Kwangtung and Kwangsi. Yuan Shih-kai, Governor of Shangtung, adhered to the same policy. Thus despite the imperial edict troubles were confined to Chihli, Shansi and Manchuria.

Eight powers—viz., Austria, Britain, France, Germany, Italy, Japan, Russia and the United States—now organized an allied force to suppress the uprising and to save their diplomatic representatives in Peking. Foreign warships attacked the Taku forts on June 24 and took them the next day. Reinforced with a Japanese division the Allied army occupied Tientsin on July 14. Early in August the Allied army marched on Peking and entered the capital on August 14. The Empress Dowager and Emperor Kwang-hsu fled to Sian and Li Hung-chang was appointed plenipotentiary to negotiate a settlement with the powers. The Manchu Court had grossly violated international law and the Chinese empire was now humiliated as it had never been before.

Had the tendency of the powers to grasp concessions and spheres of influence in China continued in 1900 China would have been completely dismembered. So at the beginning of the military expedition in China Secretary Hay sent another circular note to all the powers concerned which asserted the attitude of the United States in settling the Boxer problem and concluded: "the policy of the government of the United States is to seek a solution which may bring about permanent safety and peace to China, preserve Chinese territorial and administrative entity, protect all rights guaranteed to friendly powers by treaty and international law, and safeguard for the world the principle of equal and impartial trade with all parts of the Chinese Empire." As the powers, orally or in writing, gave consent to Hay's statement, he declared on October 29 that the United States had had "the gratification of learning that all the powers had similar views".[89]

Britain was also anxious to see the status quo in China maintained. So British Prime Minister Lord Salisbury concluded with German Ambassador Herzfeldt an agreement on October 16 to the effect that all Chinese ports should open to trade without discrimination; that they would not take advantage of the existing tumultuous situtaion to acquire any territory in China; and that if other powers wanted to obtain territorial advantage they would consult with each other about measures to protect their interest in China.[40] The two powers then invited Austria, France, Italy, Japan, Russia and the United States to accept these principles and they all answered favorably.

Consequently when the International Protocal was signed at Peking on September 7, 1901, between Li Hung-chang and the envoys of eleven powers[41] it contained no cession of territory. The main points were: (1) the appointment of Prince Tsaili and Vice-Minister Natung as special envoys to express regrets to Germany and Japan[42] respectively; (2) the punishment of those officials who were responsible for the crime; (3) payment of 450,000,000 taels as indemnity; (4) demolition of all forts between Peking and the sea; (5) the Legation Quarter in Peking to be policed and defensed by the legations; and (6) station of foreign troops to keep the route between Peking and the sea open.[43]

While China escaped from dismemberment Russia was bent upon seizing Manchuria on this occasion. As the people in Manchuria hated Russia for her penetration, the anti-foreign movement had spread there. The Chinese Eastern and South Manchurian railways, being under construction, were seriously damaged by Chinese rioters. After the declaration of war by the imperial edict the Manchu generals attacked the railways and burned down Russian churches. All the Russians in Manchuria now withdrew either to Siberia or to the leased territory in Liaotung. Manchu troops in Heilungkiang attacked Russian steamers on the Amur and even bombarded Blagoveshchensk. The Russians retaliated by driving Chinese merchants and their families, 3000 men, women and children, into the Amur.[44]

When the news of the trouble reached Moscow, Minister of War Kuropatkin told Witte that it made him happy because he now had a chance to occupy Manchuria. When Witte asked him what to do with Manchuria, Kuropatkin said that it would be made a second Bokhara.[45] Then the Russian Government sent a strong force into Manchuria. As the Manchu troops were no match for the Russians both Kirin and Heilungkiang were occupied in August and September. Another Russian force attacked Shengking in September from its base in the leased territory and a month later occupied the whole province. Thus within three months all Manchuria was under Russian occupation.

When the Russians occupied Mukden, capital of Shengking, Garrison-Commander Tseng-chi, a Manchu nobleman, fled and hid himself in a nearby village. He was found out by General Alexeieff, Commander of the Russian forces, and was compelled to send Chow Mien to negotiate and sign a temporary agreement concerning Shengking, with Russian envoy Korostovetz at Port Arthur on November 11, 1900. By this agreement Russian guards were to be stationed in Manchuria to protect the construction of the railway; Chinese troops in Shengking were to be disbanded and their arms surrendered; all forts and arsenals in Shengking were to be demolished; cities occupied by the Russians were to be administered by them until the complete pacification of the province; and the Garrison-commander was to give the Russian resident at Mukden full information respecting any important measure he might take.

When this agreement was known in Peking the Manchu Government dismissed Tseng-chi from his post and instructed Yang Yu, Chinese minister at Moscow, to negotiate with Russia for the return of Manchuria. In February 1901, after several conversations, Count Lamsdorff, Russian Foreign Minister, handed Yang Yu a draft consisting of twelve articles which were even more harsh than those in the temporary agreement. Russia promised to return Manchuria to China on the conditions that Russian troops would be stationed to protect the railway; that Chinese troops would not be stationed in Manchuria until the completion of the railway and thereafter the number of Chinese troops in Manchuria would be determined by consultation with Russia; that arms would not be imported into Manchuria; that China wouuld dismiss any garrison-commander or high official in Manchuria on the request of Russia; that China would give no railway, mining or other concessions in Manchuria, Mongolia and Sinkiang to any other power and would not build railways in these regions without Russia's permission; and that China would pay occupation expenses and compensate the railway for its losses.[47]

When these demands leaked out other powers became alarmed and all advised the Manchu Government not to conclude a separate treaty with Russia but to settle the question in the general protocol. Japan was especially opposed to Russian domination in Manchuria and pressed the Manchu Government not to conclude such a treaty. Viceroys like Liu Kun-yi, Chang Chih-tung also petitioned the Manchu Court not to be intimidated by Russia. Negotiations dragged on and then Lamsdorff presented a revised draft to Yang, on March 17, in which the station of Chinese troops in Manchuria were to be permitted by consultations with Russia; the area in which China would give no railway, mining and other concessions to any other power was limited to Manchuria; and the demand that China would not build railways without Russia's permission was omitted.[48] Lamsdorff also set a deadline for the signing of the draft treaty—March 22. Li Hung-chang was inclined to sign it but viceroys, governors and envoys abroad were almost all opposed to it. The Manchu Government finally decided to reject it and Lu Tseng-hsiang, who was then an interpreter in the Chinese legation but later to become the Prime Minister of the Chinese Republic, was sent to notify Lamsdorff.[49] Two days later the Russian Government issued a declaration blaming the interference of other powers in the Sino-Russian negotiations and asserting that Russia would wait until the appearance of a stable government in China to further negotiate the withdrawal of Russian troops and the return of Manchuria.[50]

Realizing the grave situation in the Far East created by the ruthless action of Russia, Britain and Japan began to negotiate an alliance in April, 1901. After several months of discussion the Anglo-Japanese Agreement was signed in London on January 30, 1902. This agreement was, in fact, a treaty of alliance which provided that either power might take such action as was necessary to protect its interests in China and Korea; that if either power were attacked the other power would "maintain a strict neutrality and use its efforts to pevent other powers from joining in hostilities against its ally"; and that if any other power should join in the hostilities then the other power would come to the assistance of the ally and conduct the war and make peace in common.[51]

Russia knew very well that the Anglo-Japanese Alliance was aimed at her and adopted a milder policy towards China . The newly established Waiwupu (formerly Tsungli Yamen) then negotiated with Russian Minister Paul Lessar for an agreement which was signed at Peking on April 8 by Lessar and Yi Chuang and Wang Wen-shao representing China. By this agreement Russia agreed to withdraw her troops from Manchuria in three periods: from the territory west of the Liao river in six months, from the west of Shengking and Kirin in twelve months, and from Heilungkiang in eighteen months. Chinese troops were to reoccupy Manchuria only after previous agreement with Russian authorities with regard to their number and the places to be stationed. Arrangements were to be made for the restoration of Chinese railways and for the compensation of Russian expenses.[52] This agreement was certainly far more reasonable than the drafts presented by Lobanov.

The territory west of the Liao and the railways between Shanghaikwan and Sinmingting were restored to China within the first six months after the conclusion of the agreement, but when the second period expired in April, 1903, Russian troops failed to withdraw from the west of Shengking and Kirin. Instead, Lessar presented to the Waiwupu, as conditions for further withdrawal, a convention of seven points which were: (1) no new treaty ports or foreign consuls in Manchuria to be allowed; (2) no foreigners other than Russians to be employed in the public service in North China; (3) the status of the administration in Mongolia to remain unchanged; (4) the receipts of the Niuchwang customs to continue to be deposited in the Russo-Chinese Bank; (5) the sanitary commission at Niuchwang to be dominated by Russians; (6) Russia to retain control of the Port Arthur-Yingkow-Mukden telegraph line; and (7) no territory in Manchuria to be alienated to any power.[53]

Lessar urged the Waiwupu to keep these demands a top secret, but the latter purposely leaked the news out. The United States, Japan and Britain protested to Russia for such demands and warned China not to accept them. The Russian Government categorically denied them, but secretly pressed China for their acceptance. Encouraged by the firm attitude of other powers the Manchu Government rejected the Russian demands. Then in September Russia proposed a new agreement of a milder character but still contained the provision that China would never cede to any power any part of the three Manchurian provinces.[54] While China and Russia were still negotiating about the evacuation of Russian troops the Russo-Japanese War broke out in February, 1904.

Ever since July, 1903, Japan had tried to reach a settlement with Russia concerning Manchuria and Korea. On August 12, the Japanese minister in St. Petersburg presented an outline of general principles for the settlement of the Manchurian and Korean questions, which provided that the two powers were to agree to respect the independence and territorial integrity of China and Korea; that Russia was to recognize Japan's paramount interest in Korea and Japan, Russia's special interest concerning Manchurian railways; that for protecting their interest or for suppressing revolt, Japan could send troops to Korea and Russia could send troops to Manchuria, but they must be withdrawn when the mission was completed; and that Russia was to recognize Japan's rights to help Korea in her political and military reforms.[55]

At that time the opinion of the high officials in the Russian Government concerning relations with Japan was divided. Lamsdorff, Witte and even Kuropatkin advocated a policy of peace towards Japan. But General Bezobrazov, a confidential adviser to the Tsar, and Admiral Alexeieff, commander of the Russian troops in Liaotung wanted war. The Tsar being ambitious himself, was easily influenced by Bezobrazov and Alexeieff. So on the same day, when the Japanese envoy presented his memorandum, the Tsar appointed Alexeieff Imperial Lieutenancy of the Far East who was to have supreme power in the regions under his jurisdiction, independent of the ministries in Russia. This was indeed a sign pointing to the pendng war.

After almost two months of delay, Russian Minister Rosen handed to Japanese Foreign Minister Komura a counter-proposal of eight articles concerning Korea, in which it was provided that Japan and Russia agreed not to use any part of Korean territory for strategic purposes and not to send troops north of the 39th parallel.

At the end of October, Komura gave Minister Rosen a revised draft agreement which included both China and Korea, but in which refraining from using Korean territory for strategic purposes was omitted. Then in the middle of December, Rosen presented another revised draft to Komura, which again only referred to Korea and in which the article of the prohibition of strategic use of Korean territory was again inserted. Japan was then prepared to sacrifice Manchuria in exchange for a free hand in Korea, but even this Russia refused.

After dragging on for nearly another two months without definite result, the Japanese minister in St. Petersburg presented on February 6, 1904, an ultimatum to the Russian Foreign Office and broke off diplomatic relations. Two days later the Japanese navy attacked and defeated the Russian fleet off Port Arthur. On February 10, Japan and Russia declared war simultaneously. China declared her neutrality at the beginning of the war but she was too weak to prevent them from fighting on Chinese territory. So the Manchu Government regarded the territory east of the Liao as war area, where the war was actually fought. Other powers also declared their neutrality and later requested the belligerents not to send troops into China proper and the latter agreed.

To the suprise of the world Japan, a small Asian country, beat colossal Russia both on land and at sea. After the declaration of war Japanese troops landed at Chemulpo in Korea, met little Russian opposition and crossed the Yalu at the beginning of May. Then two

Japanese armies landed at Pitzewo and Takushan in Liaotung Peninsula. The Russian forces were pushed back in a series of engagements and finally the Russians defending Port Arthur were separated from their army to the north. Dairen was occupied by the Japanese on May 30 and Port Arthur was beseiged. In June, Kuropatkin took over the command in person but could not turn the tide. The Russian forces were defeated at Telisze, Tashihchiao, Fenghwangcheng and Liaovang in succession. The battles of Liaoyang, fought in September and October, resulted in heavy losses to the Russians.

On January 1, 1905 Port Arthur surrendered to the Japanese, who took 24,000 prisoners of war. From February 23 to March 10 the greatest battle of the war was fought near Mukden in which 400,000 Russians and 350,000 Japanese took part. It again resulted in Japanese victory and Mukden was occupied by them. Tiehling and Changtu soon fell into Japanese hands. Kuropatkin then resigned and General Linievitch succeeded him. The Russian Far Eastern Fleet had been locked up at Port Arthur since the beginning of the war. Later it tried to escape but only a few ships got away seriously damaged. The Baltic Fleet under Admiral Rodjestvensky, arrived in the Sea of Japan on May 27. On that very day the Japanese fleet, commanded by Admiral Togo attacked it off Tsusima and practically annihilated it.

Russia suffered defeat time and again but Japan was also near the point of exhaustion. Early in May the Japanese Government indicated to President Theodore Roosevelt its wish that he act as the peacemaker. At the end of the month Japan made a formal request to the president. On June 6 the Tsar also expressed his willingness to negotiate peace. Two days later American Ambassador Meyer at Moscow and American Minister Griscom at Tokyo presented identical notes to the Russian and Japanese Foreign Offices respectively, urging them in the name of President Roosevelt to appoint plenipotentiaries to consider terms of peace, but disclaiming any intention of intervening in the discussion on the part of the United States. The two governments promptly accepted and appointed plenipotentiaries: Komura and Takahira for Japan and Witte and Rosen for Russia.

They met at Portsmouth, New Hampshire, on August 9. At first the Japanese envoys demanded the transfer to Japan of Liaotung Peninsula (including Port Arthur and Dairen) and of the railway from Harbin to Port Arthur; cession of Sakhalin Island (which was under Japanese occupation); fishing concessions; and payment of indemnity. But the Tsar declared that he would not cede an inch of territory or pay a ruble of indemnity. Witte remarked in the conference that Russia was not a defeated nation. Japan then made concessions by giving up the demand of indemnity and by returning the northern half of Sakhalin to Russia at a price. But Russia still refused to accept these terms. The discussions came to a deadlock in two weeks and negotiations almost broke off. Then President Roosevelt mediated and asked the Kaiser to urge the Tsar to make peace on the basis of no indemnity and cession of the southern half of Sakhalin. The Tsar accepted this proposal and the Peace Treaty of Portsmouth was signed on September 5. By this treaty Russia recognized Japan's "paramount political, military and economic interests" in Korea; the two powers agreed to withdraw their troops from Manchuria; Russia, with the consent of China, transferred to Japan the lease of Port Arthur, Dairen and adjacent territorial water and land and the railway from Changchun to Port Arthur and coal mines pertaining to it without any compensation; Russia ceded to Japan the southern half of Sakhalin; and Japanese subjects were given fishing rights near the Russian coast of the Sea of Japan, the Sea of Okhotsk and the Bering Sea.[56]

Before the opening of the Portsmouth Conference the Waiwupu on July 6, sent identical notes to the two powers expressing its joy over the news of peace but asserting that all items in the future peace treaty affecting China would not be recognized by China unless given her previous consent. Many items in the Treaty of Portsmouth certainly concerned Chinese territory and interests but the two parties did not take any trouble to consult with China. It was more than two months after the conclusion of the treaty that the Japanese Government sent Foreign Minister Komura as a special envoy to negotiate a new treaty with China. Negotiations took place at Peking, in November and December 1905. China was very weak and could not but recognize the fait accompli. So the Manchurian Convention was finally signed on December 22, by which China agreed to all the transfers made to Japan as provided in the Treaty of Portsmouth. By a supplementary agreement, China agreed to open sixteen cities in Manchuria to foreign trade and residence; Japan agreed to withdraw her railway guards on the conditions that order had been established in Manchuria and that Russia would also withdraw her railway guards; and China agreed to establishment of a Sino-Japanese lumber company to cut lumber in the forests on the right bank of the Yalu.[57]

During the Russo-Japanese War the American people had shown their sympathy for Japan as little David in a conflict with giant Goliath. But after the opening of the peace conference, Witte by his clever diplomacy and dominant personality won the American public over to his side. When the peace treaty was signed there was a big celebration in Portsmouth and the local populace congratulated Witte for his achievement.[58] On the other hand the terms of peace were bitterly disappointing to the Japanese who had expected a huge indemnity and the acquisition of much Russian territory. For the failure of their diplomacy they blamed partly their own government and partly the United States. On September 6, one day after the signing of the treaty, almost one hundred thousand Japanese held a mass meeting in Tokyo and after the meeting the angry mob burned down the official residence of the Minister of the Interior, police stations, a pro-government newspaper and many Christian churches, most of which were American. The riots spread to other cities, lasting three days until martial law was proclaimed on September 8.

The decision of the San Francisco school board in October, 1906 to bar Japanese children from schools for white children intensified the anti-American feeling among the Japanese people. Consequently, Japanese foreign policy after the war changed from seeking American friendship to regarding the United States as a potential enemy and the Japanese Government under Prime Minister Saionji began to seek a rapprochement with Russia. Russia, feeling now the pressure of the aggressive policy of Germany from the west, also wished to have a settlement with Japan. Encouraged by Britain and France the two powers held negotiations at Moscow in the summer of 1907.

On July 30, Russian Foreign Minister Iswolsky and Japanese Ambassador Motono signed an agreement in which each of the two powers agreed "to respect the actual territorial integrity of the other, and all the rights accruing to one and the other Party from the treaties, conventions and contracts in force between them and China . . ." and both "recognized the independence and the territorial integrity of the Empire of China and the principle of equal opportunity in whatever concerns the commerce and industry of all nations in that Empire . . ." Besides this open agreement there was signed on the same day a secret convention, by which Japan recognized Russia's special interests in northern Manchuria and Outer Mongolia, while Russia recognized Japan's special interests in southern Manchuria and Korea. A supplementary article provided the line of demarcation between northern and southern Manchuria.[59] Thus in less than two years after the end of the war the former enemies agreed in a friendly manner to recognize each other's sphere of influence at the expense of China.

The American railroad king, E. H. Harriman, had long dreamed of extending his railroad empire to Asia; during the peace conference he talked with Komura about the rehabilitation of the South Manchurian Railway with American capital as a joint American-Japanese enterprise. If this could be done, Harriman reasoned, Russia might also be willing to sell the Chinese Eastern Railway. In 1906 Harriman visited Japan and signed on October 12, a "Memorandum of Preliminary Understanding" with the Japanese Premier, Count Katsura, concerning the formation of a syndicate to provide the necessary funds.[60] Later the Japanese Government changed its mind and the matter was dropped.

Willard Straight, American consul-general at Mukden, became very much interested in this scheme, believing that only the neutralization of the railways could save Manchuria from being taken over by Japan and Russia. Straight later served as acting chief of the newly formed Division of the Far Eastern Affairs of the Department of State and persuaded Secretary Philander C. Knox to accept his idea. So in November, 1909, Secretary Knox formally proposed the Knox plan to the powers, i.e., the formation of an international banking consortium to purchase the Chinese Eastern and South Manchurian railways and to put them under international management. Knox, at that time, was unaware of the secret Russo-Japanese Agreement of 1907 and wished to see the carrying out of the Open Door policy in Manchuria. The British Government which had helped bring about the Russo-Japanese rapproachement was very cool towards this plan. France, as Russia's ally, could not support it. Russia and Japan were strongly opposed to the plan and threatened China not to accept it. Only Germany, whose interest in international affairs was opposed to that of Britain and Russia, supported the plan whole-heartedly. Thus Knox completely failed in his efforts to save Manchuria.[61]

Knox's attempt made Russia and Japan seek closer cooperation than what was provided in the agreements of 1907. On July 4, 1910 Iswolsky and Motono signed two more conventions, one open and one secret, at St. Petersburg. By the open convention the two powers agreed "to lend each other their friendly cooperation with a view to the improvement of their respective railway lines in Manchuria... and to refrain from all competition prejudicial to the attainment of this proposal"; and to respect the status quo in Manchuria resulting from all existing treaties and agreements between themselves or between them and China. In case any event endangering the status quo should be brought about they would consult with each other concerning the measures to be taken. By the secret convention, Russia and Japan undertook to refrain from all political activity and not to seek concessions and privileges within each other's sphere of special interest in Manchuria. They would "enter frankly and honestly into communication in all matters of common concern to their special interests" and in case these interests were threatened they would "agree on the measures to be taken in regard to common action or the support to be accorded for the protection and defense of these interests."[62]

This secret convention amounted almost to an alliance and its aim was either the United States or Germany. In December, 1910, Sukhomlinov, Russian Minister of War, actually demanded at a cabinet meeting the annexation of northern Manchuria as a counter move against American interference in Manchuria. But Foreign Minister Sazonov warned that the moment was unfavorable as the situation in Europe called for attention and military reserves. The government decided to postpone annexation to a later date.[63] When the Waiwupu was notified of the open convention it issued a circular note to the powers that since Russia and Japan pledged to respect existing treaties, Chinese sovereignty in Manchuria and the principle of equal opportunity as provided in the Treaty of Portsmouth were reassured and China would do her part in the development of the commerce and industry in Manchuria to the benefit of all concerned. Evidently it was completely ignorant of the two secret agreements concluded in 1907 and 1910.[64]

After the Russo-Japanese War there had been some negotiations of minor importance between China and Russia in northern Manchuria. Since the construction of the Chinese Eastern Railway the railway company had usurped the administrative power in Harbin. In 1906, Harbin was opened to international trade and some powers soon established consulates there. They objected that the administrative power of a city should be in the hands of a corporation and Russia announced that she would not infringe China's sovereignty but would only keep police power in the railway zone. But in 1908, the railway administration suddenly proclaimed regulations to tax both Chinese and foreigners residing in Harbin. This aroused the opposition of Chinese and foreign merchants and after long negotiations an agreement was concluded in May, 1909, between the Waiwupu and the Russian minister in Peking, by which municipal councils were to be established in all cities and towns in the railway zone whose members were to be elected by Chinese and foreign residents.[65] Thus these cities and towns were to enjoy a certain degree of home rule under the supervision of the Chinese president of the railway company. In 1908, China and Russia also concluded regulations concerning the customs in northern Manchuria, by which free trade within 100 li (about 33 miles) which had, since 1881, applied to trade in Mongolia and Sinkiang was now extended to northern Manchuria. Goods transported beyond 100 li from the border were to be exempted one-third of the duties.[66]

CHAPTER VII

Russia and Outer Mongolia

Since the conclusion of the Treaty of Kiakhta in 1727 the relations between Russia and Outer Mongolia had been mainly commercial. Although Muraviev had sent Zenovitch to Mongolia to induce a Mongol revolt against China nothing came of the plot.[1] But as Russian ambitions in southern Manchuria were checked by the Russo-Japanese War her eyes now turned elsewhere. Outer Mongolia, with an area of 622,000 square miles, was of great strategic value to Russia, as the semi-official *Torogovo-Promyshlennaya Gazetta* declared in 1940: "Our frontier with China is incorrect, winding, difficult to defend, and does not correspond at all to physical-geographic conditions. The natural frontier between Russia and China must be the Gobi desert."[2]

There was a native tribe in Siberia called Buryats who were of the Mongolian race and believed in Lamaism. The Russian Government sent a number of these Buryats to Mongolia to instigate the native populance against the Manchu rule. Tsar Nicholas II also sent personal representatives to see the Hutukhtu, Living Buddha of Outer Mongolia, with expensive gifts for him and other princes. Thus a pro-Russian atmosphere was gradually created at Urga. Seeing the danger of Russian penetration, the Manchu Government raised the ban on Chinese immigration and many Chinese peasants flocked into Mongolia. Chinese garrison forces in Mongolia were also increased and some stringent administrative changes were put into effect. Many new offices were created, greatly increasing the burden of the Mongols. These measures caused dissatisfaction among the princes and lamas. Moreover, the high commissioner at Urga, a Manchu official named Santo, also alienated Mongols in general by his greedy behavior.

The terms concerning free trade in Mongolia which were provided in the Treaty of St. Petersburg of 1881 and had been extended in 1891 and 1901 were due to expire in August, 1911. Six months before the latter date the Manchu Government notified St. Petersburg of its intention to revise these terms. The Russian Government not only refused to consider this request but presented to China new demands which included the right of residence in Mongolia and Sinkiang for the Russian consulates in Kobdo, Uliassutai, Urumchi, Kucheng and Hami.

The Manchu Government at first stood firm, but when Russia concentrated troops at Dzharkent and on the border of Heilungkiang, China yielded and conceded to Moscow's demands in April.

It was under these circumstances that a conspiracy developed in Outer Mongolia. In July, 1911, at the instigation of the Russians, the Hutkuhtu and princes held a meeting at Urga and decided to appeal to the Tsar for help against the Manchu Government. A delegation headed by Prince Hanta Dorchi, who claimed to be the foreign minister appointed by the Hutukhtu, went to St. Petersburg with a letter to the Tsar signed by the Hutkuhtu and four high princes. The letter stated: "The omnipotent white Tsar of the great Russian people, being powerful, strong and charitable, protect the yellow peoples and is himself the incarnation of virtue; if we assist one another, we will not lose our former position. The yellow peoples will flourish and eternal peace will reign. According to the experience of many nations, any small people can become strong if it is supported by a great and powerful people. There is a saying that a great and strong state aids the small state. Mighty Tsar, consider our condition with pity and magnanimity. Humbly imploring aid and protection as do those who long for rain in times of great drought, speaking but the truth, we present you this worthless gift."[3]

Russia would surely have annexed Outer Mongolia at that time had the international situation been ripe. The Russian Government decided to concentrate its effort on the separation of Mongolia from China. In August the Russian minister lodged a protest with the Waiwupu against the administrative reforms in Outer Mongolia on the pretext that the Mongols were opposed to them and demanded their immediate abolition; otherwise Russia would take appropriate measure.[4] Meanwhile Russian troops were sent to Urga to reinforce the small consular guard. Santo then negotiated with the Hutkuhtu for the recall of Prince Hanta and discontinuation of Russian troop arrivals. The Hutkuhtu agreed on the condition that all reforms be terminated. The Manchu Government finally accepted this request and abolished the newly formed offices, but Hanta did not return to Urga while Russian troops continued to arrive from Kiakhta.

On October 10, the Chinese revolution against the Manchu Dynasty broke out at Wuchang and soon spread to all parts of the country. As the power of the Manchu Government was thus greatly diminished the Mongols saw their chance of independence. At the end of November the Hutkuhtu and princes decided at a meeting in his palace to declare independence from China, to drive away all Manchu officials in Outer Mongolia, and to strictly prohibit Chinese immigration.[5] On the same day Santo received an order from the Hutkuhtu to leave Urga with his assistants and guards. At that time there were 4,000 Mongolian soldiers and more than a thousand Russian troops while the Chinese guards numbered 130 men. Santo had no choice other than to withdraw. The next day the Chinese guards were disarmed. On December 2, the Russian consul-general invited Santo to stay in the consulate and three days later Santo proceeded to Kiakhta under the protection of Russian soldiers to return to Peking via Siberia. All Chinese merchants in Outer Mongolia also had to leave, suffering untold losses at the hands of Mongolian and Russian soldiers.

On December 16, the so-called "Mongolian Empire" was proclaimed and the Hutukhtu was chosen by the princes to become emperor with the title Bogdo Cheptsun Damba Hutukhtu Khan.[6] Sometime later an edict was issued which clearly showed who was behind the scene. It read: "Henceforth in Mongolia, religion will be systematically welded with state government. Chinamen shall be compelled to embrace Lamaism, provincial officials shall be nominated from among the adherents of Lamaism. The highest state officials shall in future wear uniforms of Russian cut and design; subordinate public servants shall dress in Mongolian fashion, not like the Chinese. The taxes and imposts which are at present in vigor are repealed, and fresh taxation will be levied in accordance with laws which will be framed in concert with Russia."[7] On December 28, the coronation of the "Emperor" took place at a thoroughly Russian ceremony. On this occasion the Russian Government presented to Outer Mongolia a number of Russian guns.

Five ministries were established—viz: the Ministries of the Interior, of Foreign Affairs, of Finance, of War and of Justice—but the ministers, being ignorant Mongolian noblemen, were merely figureheads. The Russian Government also loaned 2,000,000 rubles to Outer Mongolia with Mongolian gold mines as security and on the condition that a Russian adviser was to be appointed to the Ministry of Finance whose consent was necessary for any payments. The Mongolian Government also appointed two Russian advisers to manage a state bank and 45 Russian military instructors to train a new army. The four tribes[8] of Outer Mongolia were each required to recruit 10,000 men and 2,000 Manchurian Hunghutse bandits were enlisted and stationed along the Chinese-Mongolian border. Large quantities of ammunition were purchased from Russia.

At the end of the year the Russian minister presented a note to the Waiwupu demanding: (1) that China grant Russia the right to build a railway from the Russian border to Urga; (2) that China conclude a treaty disclaiming any intention to send troops and immigrants into Outer Mongolia and to interfere with Mongolian internal affairs; (3) that China receive Russia's consent first in case she wished to make any administrative reforms in Outer Mongolia. On the other hand Russia would recognize China's sovereignty over Outer Mongolia and would guarantee that the Mongols would fulfill their obligations to China.[9] On the verge of complete collapse, the Manchu regime did not even try to negotiate with the Russians.

On January 1, 1912, the Republic of China was proclaimed at Nanking with Dr. Sun Yat-sen as provisional president. In March, the Manchu Emperor abdicated. Yuan Shih-kai succeeded Dr. Sun as provisional president and China was united. Sometime later Yuan sent a lengthy telegram to the Hutukhtu saying in part: "For a nation to exist independently, she must have a large population, abundance of wealth, a strong army and a sound system of government. Although your Mongolia has a large territory, yet your people are too small in numbers . . . the economic existence of your people is miserable and they certainly cannot bear the taxes necessary for the maintenance of an army. To resort to foreign loans is to invite interference which would endanger the very existence of your country... The salvation of Mongolia, therefore, depends on China. With the immense wealth at her disposal and the great man-power at her command China can easily transform Mongolian weakness into strength, Mongolian poverty into wealth. The Chinese Government has resolved to sweep aside the corrupt government of the old days in Mongolia and to install a new reign of righteousness and justice. Therefore, any suggestions or proposals that you think fit to present will be carefully considered by me. It is earnestly desired that the Mongolian independence will be immediately cancelled. Thoughtful and intelligent as you are, I am sure you will make the right choice between good and bad, happiness and misery, and not be deceived by the intrigue of false friends."[10]

In his reply the Hutukhtu said that since Outer Mongolia was "hemmed in between powerful neighbors" independence was its only hope and then added: "Personally it is as easy for me to cancel our independence as to discard a pair of old shoes. But this declaration was proclaimed before the abdication of the Manchu Dynasty and has already been promulgated to the outside world. Consequently, my hand is being tied from taking an independent course of action. However, if Your Excellency should insist on this step being taken, it is desirable that our neighbor (Russia) be consulted and an understanding reached between China and Russia. Therefore, the very existence of Mongolia is in Your Excellency's hands. I beg Your Excellency not to take too severe a measure lest it drives the Mongols to desperation, and I also hope that Your Excellency's generous heart will hear the supplications of the Mongolian people and open for them a way through which they may save themselves from destruction." [11] This telegram from the Hutukhtu showed two things: (1) the so-called independence had been brought about by Russia and (2) the Mongols were now afraid of a Chinese punitive expedition. As the internal problems of China were not yet solved and as the recovery of Mongolia by force would have international complications Yuan was not ready to take such a step.

Upon receiving this answer, Yuan sent another telegram to the Hutukhtu asserting that inviting foreign intervention in the adjustment of internal affairs would be tantamount to throwing away the inalienable right of sovereignty. He concluded: "In this connection I beg to make assurance that in the event of Mongolia's cancelling its independence, all the Mongol princes and Mongol people will be most favorably treated and accorded every opportunity for self-government and development. As there are so many things that cannot be said in a telegram, I am therefore despatching a special envoy to Urga to discuss matters with you in detail and I hope when he arrives you will give him courtesy and consideration." This proposal was promptly rejected by the Hutukhtu, who said in his answer: "I am also fully aware that foreign intervention infringes on our sovereign rights, but such a recourse is necessitated by considerations beyond my control, and after careful deliberation with my ministers, we have come to the final conclusion that the best thing for us to do at the present time is to solicit the good offices of our neighbor for the settlement of our differences."[12]

Then in June, 1912, the Russian minister in Peking presented to the Waichiaopu[13] as basis for negotiations on the Mongolian question between China and Russia three principles, viz., (1) China would not station troops in Outer Mongolia; (2) China would not send immigrants into Outer Mongolia; and (3) in case Mongolian independence was cancelled the Mongol people should enjoy self-government. The Chinese Government considered the Mongolian question as its internal affair and refused to negotiate with Russia.[14]

The Russian Government at that time knew very well that an outright recognition to Outer Mongolia's independence would be a violation of China's territorial integrity and might bring about opposition from other powers, especially Britain and Japan. In his memorandum to the Russian cabinet Foreign Minister Sazonov frankly admitted: "The definite settlement of this difficult question which especially affects Russian interests, must be postponed to a future date, for we have to take into account our political interests which, in principle, are directly opposed to the maintenance of China's territorial integrity. In this way the Chinese will be prevented from estabishing their authority over these districts." He then recommended cooperation with Japan by saying: "If we proceed with Japan, we shall be able to reckon all the sooner upon the fulfillment of our wishes as we succeed in assuring ourselves on the support of our French ally just as England might also give her support to Japan."[15]

So Russia, on the one hand, helped Outer Mongolia to occupy Kobdo in August, 1912 and threatened that if China sent troops into Outer Mongolia Russia could not stand aside;[16] and on the other, approached Britain and Japan for an agreement. An understanding was reached between Russia and Britain, whereby Russia granted Britain a free hand in Tibet in exchange for Britain's recognition of Outer Mongolia, northern Manchuria, and western China as Russian exclusive spheres or influence.[17] With Japan a secret convention was concluded at St. Petersburg on July 8, by which the line of demarcation of their spheres of special interests in Manchuria as provided by the secret treaties of 1907 and 1910 was extended to Mongolia. Outer Mongolia remained Russia's sphere while Inner Mongolia was divided into two parts, east and west of the Peking meridian. The eastern part was to be a Japanese sphere while the western part, Russia's.[18]

With diplomatic arrangements completed Russia sent Jean Korostovetz, former minister to China, to Urga to negotiate with the Hutukhtu. The Hutukhtu requested Russia to immediately recognize Mongolia's independence and employ military force to help bring about the incorporation of Inner Mongolia into the new state. Since Russia was not in a position to do these things Korostovetz had a difficult time explaining matters to the Mongols. On November 3, an agreement was signed by Korostovetz and by Sain-noyen Khan, Mongolian Prime Minister and all other five ministers. In its preamble the agreement stated: "In accordance with the desire unanimously expressed by the Mongolians to maintain the national and historic constitution of their country the Chinese troops and authorities were obliged to evacuate Mongolian territory, and Djebzoun-Khutukhtu (Cheptsun Hutukhtu) was proclaimed ruler of the Mongolian people. The old relations between Mongolia and China thus came to an end."

By this agreement Russia promised to "assist Mongolia to maintain the autonomous regime which she had established, as also the right to have her national army, and to admit neither the presence of Chinese troops on her territory nor the colonization of her land by the Chinese" (Article I). Mongolia, on the other hand, agreed to grant to Russian subjects and trade the rights and privileges enumerated in the annexed protocol (Article 2). In case Mongolia should conclude a separate treaty with China or another foreign power, the new treaty should neither infringe nor modify the present agreement and the annexed protocol without the consent of Russia (Article 3).

The protocol, annexed to the agreement and signed on the same day, enumerated the rights and privileges Russian subjects were to enjoy in Mongolia, including the right to reside and move freely; to engage in commerce, industry and other business; to import and export without paying dues; to hold allotments on lease or to acquire them as their own property; and to enter into agreements with the Mongolian Government respecting the working of minerals and timber, fisheries, etc. Russian consulates were to be established wherever this was deemed necessary and a Russian postal service in Mongolia was to be instituted.[19]

When the Chinese Government learned the news of Russian-Mongolian negotiations it lodged a protest with the Russian minister at Peking and also instructed Liu Chin-jen, Chinese minister at Moscow, to declare to the Russian Government that Outer Mongolia, being a part of Chinese territory, had no power to conclude treaties with foreign states. After the signing of the agreement the Russian minister handed its text to the Waichiaopu and the latter refused to accept it. Strong feeling against Outer Mongolia was aroused among the Chinese people and a storm of protest broke out throughout China. Mass meetings were held in big cities and provincial capitals and telegrams by the thousands poured into Peking from every part of China, demanding the despatch of a military expedition to Outer Mongolia even at the risk of provoking an armed conflict with Russia. Military governors of several provinces declared that they were ready to send troops to Outer Mongolia. Foreign Minister Liang Yu-hao, under strong attack from every quarter, left his post and fled to Tientsin.

But the newly-born republic was no match for Russia in military strength and no other power was ready to act in China's behalf. Britain and Japan had understandings with Russia while France was Russia's ally. The United States and Germany were opposed to Russia's move but were not willing to actively interfere. Russian

Foreign Minister Sazonov threatened the Chinese minister at Moscow that "If China assumed a reasonable attitude her sovereign rights can still be safeguarded. If not, the situation might grow worse". So Yuan Shih-kai decided to settle the question through diplomatic channels. Lu Tseng-hsiang was appointed Foreign Minister to succeed Liang Yu-hao and negotiations with Russia began at the end of November, 1912.

Lu Tseng-hsiang presented to Russian Minister Krupensky as basis for discussions a memorandum containing seven points: (1) China's sovereignty over Outer Mongolia must be recognized; (2) no foreign power would maintain troops in Outer Mongolia or transfer its subjects there for reasons of colonization; (3) the Chinese Government would not increase its agents in Outer Mongolia; (4) China would maintain a police force for the protection of Chinese residents; (5) pasture lands belonging to the Chinese Government could be freely used by Mongol princes and chiefs; (6) agricultural, mining and railway projects in Outer Mongolia must obtain the consent of the Chinese Government; and (7) no treaties might be concluded by the Mongols without the authorization of the Chinese Government and those already concluded must be cancelled[21] These points were far from what Russia was prepared to accept and Krupensky made a counter proposal of four points, viz., (1) the Russo-Mongolian Agreement would remain in force; (2) Russia would furnish loans to Mongolia for administrative reforms; (3) Russia would build railways in Mongolia; and (4) Russia was to have a free hand in Mongolia without Chinese interference.[22]

Long and laborious negotiations followed until a draft agreement was reached on May 20, 1913. This draft provided: (1) that Russia recognized Outer Mongolia as an integral part of Chinese territory; (2) that China agreed not to modify the historical autonomy of Outer Mongolia and to give the Mongols in Outer Mongolia the right to keep military forces and police, as well as the right to prohibit the immigration of non-Mongols; (3) that Russia promised not to send troops, except consular guards, into Outer Mongolia, not to undertake the colonization of Outer Mongolia, and not to institute officials in Outer Mongolia other than consuls; (4) that China, being desirous of using peaceful means in the exercise of her authority over Outer Mongolia, declared herself to be prepared to accept the good offices of Russia to establish her relations with Outer Mongolia; (5) that China agreed to grant Russian subjects in Mongolia commercial rights enumerated in the protocol of 1912; and (6) that hereafter all international acts concerning the governmental systems of Outer Mongolia which might be concluded between the Russian Government and

Mongolian authorities would become effective only after direct negotiations between China and Russia and with the approval of the Chinese Government.[23]

The Chinese Government approved this draft at a cabinet meeting on May 26. It was then sent to the newly elected National Assembly for deliberations. It passed the Tsung-yi-yuan (Chamber of Deputies) on July 8, but was rejected by the Tsan-yi-yuan (Senate) three days later. Meanwhile a military uprising by members of the Kuomintang against Yaun Shih-kai, known as the second revolution, broke out in South China and Sino-Russian negotiations were interrupted. Within two months the Kuomintang forces were crushed by the superior military strength of Yuan Shih-kai and negotiations were resumed on September 18, between Foreign Minister Sun Pao-chi and Krupensky. Sun Pao-chi wanted to use the six points contained in the draft agreement as basis for discussion but Krupensky insisted that they no longer fitted the changed circumstance and presented new principles. After ten meetings an agreement was reached on October 31. As by now the National Assembly had ceased to function owing to the illegal dismissal of Kuomintang legislators, the agreement in the form of a joint declaration was approved by the Chinese Government and signed on November 5.

In this declaration Russia recognized China's suzerainty over Outer Mongolia while China recognized the autonomy of Outer Mongolia. Both China and Russia pledged not to intervene in the internal affairs of Outer Mongolia, nor to send troops, and to refrain from colonizing. China also pledged not to institute officials, either civilian or military, in Outer Mongolia except her representatives at Urga and some other places. China agreed to accept the good offices of the Russian Government in the settlement of her relations with Outer Mongolia in accordance with the present agreement and the protocol of 1912. With regard to other questions concerning Chinese and Russian interests in Outer Mongolia, China and Russia agreed to settle them in future conferences.

An exchange of notes took place on the same day, by which Russia recognized Outer Mongolia as part of Chinese territory. Outer Mongolia was to participate in the conferences as provided in the declaration. Autonomous Outer Mongolia was to comprise the regions under the jurisdiction of the former High Commissioner at Urga, the Garrison Commander at Uliassutai and the High Counselor at Kobdo. The most important point was that: "As regards questions of a political and territorial nature, the Chinese Government shall come to an agreement with the Russian Government through negotiations in which the authorities of Outer Mongolia shall take part"[24]

Although China kept nominal suzerainty over Outer Mongolia, it had come to be under the joint protection of China and Russia. The area of Outer Mongolia was considerably extended by adding to it the region of Kobdo, which was situated between Mongolia and Sinkiang and was not a part of former Khalkha. The initial zeal of the Chinese public over Outer Mongolia had died down, while Yuan Shih-kai was now a virtual dictator who would tolerate no voice of opposition in China. Consequently, although the Chinese people were dissatisfied with the settlement they tolerated it in silence. But it was a mistake to say that it "was generally considered in China as a victory for national diplomacy".[25]

The Mongol princes and lamas were also discontent with the agreement, because it was distinctly short of their desire. Sain-noyen Khan, Mongolian Prime Minister, was then in St. Petersburg seeking Russian assistance for Mongolia's complete independence and absorption of Inner Mongolia. Sazonov had to point out to Sain-noyen Khan "the great importance of this agreement for Mongolia, since by this act the Chinese Government officially recognized the existence of a Mongol state which, although in a relationship of vassalage to China, in fact remained independent in every respect except for territorial questions and foreign politics, and even in regard to these questions, Mongolia retained a voice in the decisions to be taken." He also explained to Sain-noyen Khan that: "Most of the powers do not wish to see China disintegrate. It was only through the efforts made by Russia that an autonomous Mongolia was created at all. Urga's declaration of independence in 1911 had indeed produced a very unfortunate impression on the great powers, especially England and Japan; we succeeded in preventing foreign intervention in the Sino-Mongol conflict only by giving positive assurances that under no circumstances would we support the Mongol hope of separating from China those regions where either Japanese interests (Inner Mongolia) or English interests (the regions of Kukunor and Tsaidam, bordering Tibet) already existed."[26]

The Sino-Russian-Mongolian tripartite conference, as provided in the agreement and notes, took place at Kiakhta, on September 9, 1914. China was represented by General Pi Kuei-fang and Chen Lu, Minister to Mexico; Russia by Alexandre Miller, Consul-General in Mongolia; and Outer Mongolia by E-er-te-ni Chonang, Vice chief of Justice and Tushetu Khan, Chief of Finance. At the beginning of negotiations the Chinese envoys demanded that Outer Mongolia should renounce its independence and the Hutukhtu should give up the title of emperor. The Mongolian delegates refused to comply and the conference almost broke up on several occasions. As the First World War had already started in Europe and soon took an unfavorable turn for Russia the Russian Government wanted to reach a settlement with China and urged the Mongols to accept these demands. Then in January, 1915, Japan presented her well-known twenty-one demands to China and the Chinese Government was hard pressed in its dealings with Japan. So the attitude of the Russian and Mongolian delegates again stiffened and negotiations dragged on for several months. Finally the Chinese Government instructed its envoys to make concessions and the tripartite agreement concerning Mongolia was signed on June 7.

Besides embodying all the points in the Sino-Russian declaration and exchange of notes this agreement provided that Outer Mongolia recognized the validity of the Sino-Russian Declaration of 1913 and the notes exchanged and also recognized China's suzerainty (Articles 1 and 2); that the title "Bogdo Cheptsun Damba Hutukhtu Khan" was to be conferred by the president of China (Article 4); that Outer Mongolia was "to attend to all the affairs of its internal administration and to conclude with foreign powers international treaties and agreements respecting all questions of a commercial and industrial nature" but not respecting political and territorial questions (Articles 3 and 5); that the military escort of the Chinese dignitary at Urga was not to exceed 200 men and those of his assistants at Uliassutai, Kobdo and Kiakhta in Mongolia were not to exceed 50 each, while the Russian consular guard at Urga was limited at 150 and at other consulates at 50 each (Articles 7 and 8); and that goods imported into Outer Mongolia by Chinese merchants were to be exempted from customs duties (Article 12).[27] By an exchange of notes between the Chinese and Russian delegates China granted a full amnesty to all the Mongols who had submitted to the Autonomous Government of Outer Mongolia, gave the Mongols the freedom, as before, of residence and travel in Inner and Outer Mongolia and would not place restraint upon Mongols going in pilgrimage to Urga.[28] Soon after the conclusion of the agreement Chen Lu was appointed Tuhuhsih (Defense Commissioner) at Urga and the Mongolian question was settled for the time being.

In connection with this agreement the Sino-Russian agreement concerning Hulunbuir may be mentioned. Hulunbuir was an administrative area in Heilungkiang situated on the border of Outer Mongolia. Owing to its adjoining Mongolia there was a large Mongolian population in that region. So when Outer Mongolia declared its independence in 1911 the Mongols in Hulunbuir followed suit. As now the Mongolian question was settled the Russian Government urged China to settle the question of Hulunbuir also. So after some negotiations an agreement was signed by Lu Tseng-hsiang and Krupensky at Peking on November 6. By this agreement Hulunbuir was made "a special district directly subject to the Central Government of the Chinese Republic." The deputy military governor of Hulunbuir was to be appointed by the president and must be a Mongolian. In normal times the military forces of Hulunbuir would consist of local militia. In case of serious troubles the Central Government might send troops there, after giving in advance notice to the Russian Government, and the troops must be withdrawn after order was restored. In case foreign capital was required for the construction of a railway in Hulunbuir the Chinese Government should address itself in the first instance to Russia to obtain such capital. The contracts which had been concluded between Russian investors and Hulunbuir authorities and examined by a Sino-Russian Commission were confirmed by the Chinese Government.[29]

The Mongols soon began to become disillusioned with Russia. Not only their so-called independence was a farce, even their autonomy which they had enjoyed more than two centuries began to disappear. The policy of Russia regarding Outer Mongolia was nothing less than making it a Russian protectorate. The first eye-opener was Tannu Urianhai, a region situated at the northwestern corner of Mongolia and almost as large as Great Britain. The native people were a tribe of the Mongols and numbered about 60,000 at the time of the Chinese revolution. The region had been under the jurisdiction of the High Counselor at Kobdo. Russian merchants had been doing trade there since the 1860's while Chinese merchants began to come through Mongolia in the 1890's. Later Russian peasants migrated into Urianhai and settled down there. This movement was encouraged by the Russian Government and there were soon thousands of Russians there. As the natives were mainly ignorant nomads and hunters they were powerless to resist Russian aggression.

When the Chinese revolution broke out in October, 1911 the Russian envoy in China advised St. Petersburg to take advantage of the situation and to annex the region immediately on the ground that it was a disputed territory between China and Russia. But at a cabinet meeting on November 21, Foreign Minister Sazonov reported that the Treaty of Chuguchak of 1864 clearly defined Urianhai as a part of Chinese territory and the cabinet adopted a cautious policy. When Outer Mongolia proclaimed its "independence" it claimed jurisdiction over Urianhai and the Urianhai Mongols wished also to be incorporated into Outer Mongolia. To the great disappointment of both Mongolia and Urianhai, Russia prevented this unification, the reason, as pointed out by Mr. Dallin, being "that Outer Mongolia, large in territory and better known to the world, had to be recognized as an autonomous organism, which small and obscure Tuva (Urianhai) could easily be annexed by Russia."[30]

The region was renamed Tannu Tuva and a special "border commissioner" was appointed in 1913 by the Russian Government, who actually served as its governor. In the same year the authorities of two of the five Khoshuns[31] in Urianhai were forced to appeal to the Tsar to annex their land into the Russian empire. But Sazonov was again opposed to the annexation and advocated the establishment of a protectorate. What Sazonov wanted was "the quiet occupation of the region by Russians and the acquisition of de facto possession."[32] In July, 1914, Amban Gombodorchzhi, Chief Tannu of the Urianhais of the other three Khoshuns, addressed a petition to the Tsar, expressed his "joy over the Tsar's acceptance of Urianhai into the protection of Russia and pledged to have no independent, direct contact with Mongolia and other foreign powers. But he also begged "to leave to our Urianhai population their customs, the Buddhist religion which they practice, their way of life, self-government, ranks, and nomad camps, permitting no special alterations which would tend toward a loss of power."[33] In 1915, the application of Russian civil and criminal codes was extended to Urianhai and the Russian consul-general at Urga warned the Mongolian Government not to send its agents or troops into Urianhai. In 1916 a large number of natives were arrested because of their anti-Russian sentiment.

After declaring its "independence", Outer Mongolia had the naivete to think of having relations with other powers. It was permitted by Russia to conclude a treaty with Tibet in January 1913, by which Outer Mongolia and Tibet recognized each other's "independence" and pledged to assist each other. But in dealing with Japan the story was different. In September, 1913, when Kodama, representative of the South Manchurian Railway, passed through Urga, the Mongolian Government offered to him a railway concession in Inner Mongolia in exchange for Japan's assistance in preventing Chinese troops from entering Inner Mongolia. Naturally, the Japanese were interested. But when the Russian Government heard this news it at once instructed its ambassador at Tokyo to make inquiries at the Japanese Foreign Office, and Foreign Minister Makino denied such a project.

When Sain-noyen Khan arrived at St. Petersburg a few months later, he handed the Russian Foreign Minister a letter from the Hutukhtu to the Japanese Emperor and asked that it be delivered through the Russian embassy in Tokyo. In the letter the Hutukhtu recounted the story of Mongolia's independence and his negotiations with Kodama and begged the Emperor "to make strong representations to the Chinese Government that it refrain hereafter from sending its troops into Inner Mongolia so that we may carry into effect what we aspire to—the union of Inner Mongolia with our Outer Mongolia."[84] After studying the letter Sazonov instructed Malevsky-Malevich, charge d'affaires in Tokyo, to deliver it to Baron Makino, Japanese Foreign Minister and to inquire "to what extent the visits and the activity of Mr. Kodama take on the character of a low political intrigue, impeding the actual delimitation of the Russian and Japanese spheres of influence, on which the Tokyo cabinet itself had insisted." Baron Makino, after talking with Prime Minister Yamagata, returned the Hutukhtu's letter to the Russian charge d'affaires because the Emperor could not accept the letter of the chief of a state with which Japan had no diplomatic relations and gave categorical assurance that Kodama had no mission to undertake negotiations in Urga. Returning the letter to Sain-noyen Khan, Sazonov told the latter that the Japanese Government considered the Hutukhtu's attempt childish and that this incident should be a good lesson to the young Mongolian state.

Having politically separated Outer Mongolia from China in 1912, Russia proceeded with economic exploitation of Mongolia. In December, 1912 an agreement was concluded by which the Mongolian Government granted Russian subjects the right of mining in Outer Mongolia. A mining company was to be established with mainly Russian capital but Mongols might subscribe for up to 20% of the shares. No nationals of other states were allowed to own shares.[85] In September, 1914, by an an agreement concerning railways in Outer Mongolia the two governments pledged to jointly deliberate and decide upon the most advantageous direction in which the railways were to serve Mongolia and Russia, as well as upon the manner in which the construction of such railways was to be proceeded with. In case Outer Mongolia was to give railway concessions to any one other than Russians it should consult with Russia first.[86] By two agreements, one signed in May, 1913 and the other in September, 1914, Outer Mongolia gave Russia the right to construct telegraph lines from Kosh-Agatch in Siberia to Kobdo and from Monda also in Siberia to Uliassutai.[87] But owing to the occurrence of the First World War, few of the economic projects were actually carried out.

CHAPTER VIII

China and the Russian Revolution

Ever since the outbreak of the First World War the Russian army had made a poor show in fighting against the Germans. In the summer of 1915 it was crushingly defeated by the Germans in Poland and suffered heavy losses. Thereafter Russia's attention was centered on Europe and her relations with the Far East were generally inactive. In proportion to her reverse in the war her prestige and influence abroad were diminished.

Her only important diplomatic move in the Far East at that time was the conclusion of two conventions with Japan at Moscow on July 3, 1916. The open convention provided that Russia and Japan "having resolved to unite their efforts for the maintenance of permanent peace in the Far East, agreed not to enter any arrangement or political combination hostile to each other" and that should the territorial rights or the special interests, in the Far East, of either power be menaced they would "confer in regard to the measures to be taken with a view to the support or cooperation to be given each other in order to safeguard and defend those rights and interests."[1] But by the secret convention which was later revealed by the Soviet Government, the two powers actually concluded a military alliance by which they agreed that China should not fall under the political domination of any third power who might be hostile to Russia or Japan, and would communicate with each other whenever circumstances demanded and agree on the measures to be taken. In the event of war between either of them and a third power the other should come to its aid at its demand and they would not make peace without a previous agreement between themselves. But neither party was bound to lend its ally armed aid "without being assured by its Allies of cooperation corresponding to the gravity of the approaching conflict." The convention was to remain strictly confidential and would continue in force for five years or until twelve months after either party should have disclaimed it.[2]

This alliance could not be directed against Germany since Germany was already at war with both Russia and Japan and there was no need of keeping an anti-German treaty secret. Its aim could very well be the United States as the United States was still a neutral and the Open Door policy was in conflict with Russian and Japanese interest. It is interesting to note that when the Bolshevik Government published the treaty in 1918 it was given the title: "Secret Agreement between Russia and Japan, with reference to a possibility of their armed conflict together against America and Great Britain in the Far East before the summer of 1921."[3]

Repeated defeat at the front and corruption and misgovernment in the rear brought about the long-expected revolution. In March 1917, dissatisfied soldiers joined the mass of people to overthrow the Tsarist regime. Soviets of workers' and soldiers' deputies were formed and the Petrograd (St. Petersburg) soviet was dominated by the Socialists parties, the Mensheviks and the Social Revolutionaries. A Provincial Government was set up with Prince G. Lvov as Prime Minister and Alexander Kerensky as Minister of Justice and later Minister of War. As the Russian army was now in process of disintegration and national economy was on the verge of collapse the Russian people wanted to quickly end the war. On May 18, the Provisional Government declared that it aimed at "the speediest conclusion of peace without annexations and indemnities, based on the self-determination of nations".[4] On June 16, Foreign Minister Tereshchenko notified the Allied governments that Russia was renouncing all claims to foreign territories and proposed an Allied conference to reconsider war aims. The Socialist leaders, however, did not wish to desert the Allied cause and to capitulate to the Germans. So when Kerensky succeeded Prince Lvov as Prime Minister in July, he attempted desperately an offensive on the German-Austrian front which ended in a serious defeat.

When the revolution broke out in March, the Bolshevik leaders were in exile. Consequently, when the Petrograd Soviet was first created the Bolsheviks constituted a small minority. Then Nikolai Lenin, Grigori Zinoviev, and others who had lived in Switzerland went back to Petrograd in April through Germany in a sealed car with the permission of the German General Staff, which was thinking of ruining Russia through the hands of these revolutionaries. Leon Trotsky arrived from Canada. Lenin and his followers at once preached two things: a separate peace with Germany and the immediate seizure of land by peasants. They organized extensive fraternization between Russian soldiers and the enemy along the front line and were regarded by the Russian people as agents of Germany. In July, they even attempted to seize the capital, but failed. The Provisional Government then arrested Trotsky and others and Lenin had to hide. But in September Kerensky had quarrels with the commanders at the front and his position was weakened. In October, the Bolsheviks were set free and at once proceeded to overthrow the Kerensky Government. On November 7, they staged a coup. Kerensky fled the country after an unsuccessful attempt to suppress the revolution and most of the ministers were taken prisioner. Thus the Bolsheviks (later to be named Communists) came into power in Russia.

Soon after the seizure of the government Lenin started negotiations with the Germans. An armistice was signed on December 14, which enabled Germany to transfer her troops from the eastern to the western front. Then on March 3, 1918 the Soviet Government signed the Peace Treaty of Brest-Litovsk with Germany. The peace conditions were humiliating and disastrous to Russia. Poland, Finland, Lithuania, Estonia, Latvia and Ukraine were granted independence and a part of Transcaucasia was ceded to Turkey. "Russia lost 26% of her total population, 27% of her arable land; 32% of her average crops; 26% of her railway system; 33% of her manufacturing industries; 73% of her iron industries; 75% of her coal fields."[5] She also had to pay a large war indemnity; an accompanying economic treaty provided for economic exploitation of Russia by Germany. Lenin accepted these terms in order to drag Russia out of the war and thus to enable the newly formed Soviet Government to consolidate its position at home.

Because of capitulation of the Soviet Government to Germany to the detriment of the Allies and because of its repudiation of the Tsarist and war debts the Allied powers not only withheld their recognition of the Soviet Government but actually adopted a policy of intervention. At that time military officers under the Tsarist regime and Cossack leaders were rising in every part of Russia against the Bolshevik rule: Denikin and Wrangel in the Kuban region, Krasnov in the Don region, Chernov in Samara, Yudenich near Petrograd, and Kolchak and Semenov in Siberia. In the spring of 1918, British marines were landed at Murmansk and in August they were again landed at Archangel. A provisional government of the northern area was then established at Archangel under the protection of the Allies. Later in May, 1919, when Admiral Kolchak was at the zenith of his power the Allied Supreme Council informed him that they were disposed to assist his government with munitions, supplies and food so as to establish it as the government of all Russia.

During 1918 and the early part of 1919 the position of the Soviet Government was indeed precarious, but the table was soon turned in its favor. Due to the fact that the Allied intervention in Russia was half-hearted and insufficient military assistance was given to the anti-

Bolshevik leaders, and that these leaders were bad administrators and could not hold popular support they were crushed one by one by the Bolshevik forces. By the end of 1920 the civil war was practically over and the rule of the Soviet Government became secure.

In the Far East Japan had seen, from the beginning of the Bolshevik revolution, a chance not only to supplant Russia in northern Manchuria and Outer Mongolia but even to bring a large part of Siberia under her influence if not under her control. A month after the Brest-Litovsk peace Japanese troops landed in Siberia. They were few in number as the Japanese Government wanted to see what the international repercussions would be. Then in June the Czechoslovak Legion, which was composed of prisoners of war in Russia and had fought against the Germans, was on its way across Siberia to reach the western front via the United States, and was attacked at Irkutsk by Siberian Bolshevik forces. The Czechoslovaks then seized the Siberian Railway from Omsk to Vladivostok. Meanwhile about two hundred thousand German and Austrian prisoners of war were set free in Siberia. France and Britain were now anxious that intervention should take place. The Allied Supreme War Council decided on July 2, that there should be a joint operation in Siberia participated by Japan, the United States, China, Great Britain, France, Italy and newly-independent Czechoslovakia to safeguard the free transportation of the Czechoslovak Legion through Siberia and to prevent any possible action of the German and Austrian prisoners of war.

It was agreed that each power was to send no more than 7000 troops for these purposes and Vladivostok was soon taken over by the Allies. But from August on 72,000 Japanese troops were sent to Siberia and occupied not only the Russian Far East but also the Transbaikalian region. Seven thousand American troops also arrived to allow Japan no single-handed control of Siberia and to watch and check Japanese aggressive policies. Britain, France and Italy also sent troops but in much smaller number (Britain 1600, French 700, Italy 2000). The Peking Government of China which was then in the hands of a group of pro-Japanese politicians, called the Anfu Clique, had concluded with Japan military and naval pacts in May, in which the two powers agreed, as participants in the war, to take concerted action against the common enemy. By a supplement to the military agreement signed on September 6, they again agreed to conduct joint operations in the Siberian provinces of Transbaikalia and Amur and the Chinese forces in these two provinces were put under Japanese command.[6] Chinese troops did appear in Kiakhta, Vladivostok and other places in Amur province but owing to internal trouble the number was very small.

The intervention was in fact a Japanese rather than an Allied intervention. Japanese industrial and commercial firms extended their business to eastern Siberia. Russian ships were taken over by Japanese shipping companies while economic concessions were acquired by Japanese subjects. Japanese goods were brought into Siberia duty-free over the Chinese Eastern and Siberian railways in sealed cars while Russians found it practically impossible to transport their goods. The Allied powers supported the government of Admiral Kolchak at Omsk but Japan gave aid to Cossack leader Semenov who controlled the railway at Chita and cut off the communications between Omsk and Vladivostok.

At the instigation of the Japanese an intense anti-American propaganda developed in eastern Siberia. In November the American Government protested to Japan both at Washington and at Tokyo. For a time there was war talk in Japan but finally reason prevailed as the armistice was signed in Europe. Then the Japanese forces in Siberia were cut almost by half. After the conclusion of the Versailles Peace Treaty in June, 1919, the reason for the allied intervention in Russia no longer existed. So after the collapse of the Kolchak Government in January, 1920, the United States announced its intention to withdraw its forces from Siberia. The withdrawal began in the middle of January and was completed at the beginning of April. During the same period the British, French, Italian and Chinese forces also departed. On March 31, Japan issued a statement denying any political designs against Russia and promising that when matters would be settled satisfactorily she would also withdraw her troops from Siberia. This continued occupation of the Russian Far East by Japan presented a serious threat to Russia.

Lenin then carried out a very shrewd diplomatic move. He instructed the Communists in eastern Siberia to create an "independent" non-Soviet state, called the Far Eastern Republic. It embraced the Transbaikalia, Amur and Maritime provinces with its captial at Verkine-Udinsk (now Ulan Ude). The new republic was proclaimed on April 6, 1920, with Alexander Krasnoshchekov, a Russian-American, as its head and was recognized by the Soviet Government on May 14. The Russian Socialist Federated Soviet Republic and the Far Eastern Republic even changed envoys but in reality the policy of the latter was directed by the Central Committee of the Communist Party at Moscow.

While the Soviet Government denounced all Western powers as imperialistic, the Far Eastern Republic pretended to be a genuine democracy, which could get along very well with the West. It got de facto recognition from Japan and began to negotiate with her concerning the withdrawal of Japanese troops. In August, Japanese forces began to withdraw from Transbaikalia. In October, Semenov fled from Chita and the capital of the Republic was removed there. During the Washington Conference of 1921-1922, it sent three delegates to Washington. While they were not admitted to the conference, they did much to influence American public opinion in their favor. Pressed by the United States, the Japanese troops at last completely withdrew from Siberia at the end of October, 1922. Its object having been achieved, the Far Eastern Republic was dissolved and its territory was incorporated into the Russian Socialist Federated Soviet Republic in November.

After the Bolshevik revolution in Russia, China, like other Allied powers, withheld her recognition of the Soviet Government. Prince Kudachev, who was the Tsarist minister at Peking, and other diplomatic and consular officials were still regarded as legitimate representatives of Russia. After China's participation in the war against Germany the Allied ministers in Peking agreed in November, 1917, to suspend the payments of the Boxer indemnity for five years. Russia was made an exception in that the greater part of the Russian portion of the indemnity was still to be paid and "kept in safe custody by the Russo-Asiatic Bank so as to be transferred to the future Russian Government formally recognized by China".[7] So China continued to pay two-thirds of these funds which were used by the Russian legation and consulates to support their existence and activities.

It was not until the position of the Soviet Government had been stabilized and the mission of Yurin had arrived at Peking that the indemnity payments were suspended in August, 1920 and the recognition of the Russian minister and consuls was withdrawn in September. In the same presidential mandate of September 23, which deprived the Russian minister and consuls of their status, it was stated that China would adopt an attitude of neutrality towards the Russian civil war, that Russian subjects in China would be given due protection with regard to person and property and that Russian concessions and the railway zone of the Chinese Eastern Railway would be dealt with by the ministeries and provinces concerned.[8] The Russian legation was then turned over to the control of the Diplomatic Corps in Peking in accordance with the protocol of 1901 and all Russian consulates were taken over by local authorities. The Russian concessions in Hankow and Tientsin were also taken over and made special administrative districts of the two cities. Russian post offices in China were closed. Russian subjects in China, of whom there were between 200,000 to 300,000, were now placed in the position of non-treaty foreigners without extra-territorial rights of any kind. They were to be tried and sentenced by Chinese courts if any crimes were committed.

The question of the Chinese Eastern Railway had come up even earlier. According to the contract of 1896, between the Manchu Government and the Russo-Chinese Bank, for the Chinese Eastern Railway the president of the railway company was to be appointed by the Manchu Government. The first president of the railway was Hsu Ching-Cheng, former minister to Russia. After Hsu's execution in 1900 during the Boxer rebellion, no president had been appointed by the Manchu Government. All the administrative power of the railway was in the hands of the Russian assistant president. At the time of the March revolution the assistant president was General Horvath who was related to the Romanov dynasty and was strongly opposed to the revolution. So he declared his independence from the Provisional Government and tried to rule the railway zone as a dictator.

After the Bolshevik revolution Lenin instructed the Russian Communists in Harbin to chase Horvath away and to seize power in the railway zone. The Russian workers and railway guards, divided into Red and White factions, fell to quarrelling among themselves. Then Communist leader Rutin organized the Red workers and guards and created some trouble. The consulate corps at Harbin notified Horvath that the consuls were all opposed to the Communists and would support the latter in his efforts to keep order in the railway zone. Chinese authorities at Harbin then reinforced Chinese garrison forces outside the railway zone and notified the consular corps that China would interfere with armed force in case of emergency. On December 12, the so-called soldiers' and workers' council issued a declaration that from then on the council would officially represent the Soviet Government and all the Russian offices in Harbin must obey its orders. Six days later the council issued an order dismissing Horvath and Russian consul-general Pappov. Pappov sought protection in the office of the Chinese Commissioner for Foreign Affairs and the commissioner warned the council of armed intervention by Chinese troops. Thus the plot of the council was not carried out.

But the activities of Rutin and his followers continued and both

Chinese and foreign residents in Harbin petitioned local authorities for a final settlement. American, British, French and Japanese consul-generals also sent notes to local authorities asking for immediate action. General Tao Hsiang-kwei, newly appointed garrison commander of the railway in Kirin, then sent Chinese troops into the railway zone on December 26 and disarmed and interned Rutin and about 4,000 Red Russian railway guards. By an agreement between General Tao and Horvath, Rutin and the disarmed guards were repatriated to Russia and the peace and order in the railway zone at Harbin would be jointly maintained by Chinese forces and railway authorities. The provisional authorities of Heilungkiang now adopted similar measures. In February, 1918, General Chang Hwan-hsiang was appointed garrison commander of the railway in Heilungkiang and made necessary defense preparations along the border line. Meanwhile the Peking Government appointed Kuo Tsung-hsi, Governor of Kirin, president of the Chinese Eastern Railway. A meeting of the shareholders of the railway was called at Peking on April 29, by the Russo-Asiatic Bank, which had been reorganized from the former Russo-Chinese Bank and which now had French backing. A new Board of seven directors was elected and Horvath kept his position as the assistant president.[9]

After sending their troops into Siberia the Allied governments, in view of the disorganization of the transport system, approved the American plan of the formation of an Inter-allied Committee composed of all the Allied powers having military forces in Siberia. A Technical Board and a Military Transportation Board were set up under the committee. The Technical Board with an American engineer as its president was to deal with the technical operations of both the Siberian and the Chinese Eastern railways but the general management of the latter railway was left in the hands of Horvath.

At first the Peking Government objected to the inclusion of the Chinese Eastern Railway in the plan but in March, 1919, a compromise was reached, by which the Chinese Eastern Railway was to be under the protection of the Chinese forces and the only foreign troops permitted to stay in Manchuria were 1,000 Americans at Harbin and the Japanese troops at Manchuli. Despite this agreement Japan, taking advantage of the stipulation in the military pact of 1918, deployed many troops in northern Manchuria. The Peking Government then appointed General Pao Kwei-ching, Military Governor of Kirin, commander-in-chief of the garrison forces of the Chinese Eastern Railway. Under General Pao three commanders were also appointed, one for each of the three sections of the railway; Harbin-Manchuli, Harbin-

Changchun, and Harbin-Suifengho. Chinese troops were stationed along the whole line.

Meanwhile, Horvath continued to create troubles for the Chinese Eastern Railway. After attending the Board of Directors' meeting at Peking in May, 1918, he led more than a thousand railway guards to Chita to join forces with Semenov to fight against the Communists. When the Omsk Government was formed in June, Horvath participated in it. After returning to Harbin, he used the railway funds for his political activities. The Chinese president of the railway warned him time and again that he should confine himself to railway matters but he paid no heed to these advices. So the railway finance became tight and the pay of the employees was two months in arrears. A general strike by the Russian employees against Horvath occurred in March, 1920. The Chinese president then notified Horvath demanding his immediate resignation. Horvath complied and was later appointed by the Board of Directors high adviser to the railway. All the Russian railway guards and police in the railway zone were disarmed by Chinese troops. A bureau of railway police was created by the Chinese Ministry of the Interior to be under the direction of the president and China was now in complete control of the railway for the first time since its construction.

The Chinese president of the railway announced that in the future no Russian parties or individuals would be allowed to make use of the railway for political puposes. Then the Chinese Ministry of Communications negotiated with the Russo-Asiatic Bank for the revision of the contract of 1896. After long negotiations a supplement to the original agreement was signed on October 2. By this supplement it was provided that the rights and obligations of the railway company were to be of a commercial nature and any political activities were to be forbidden and suppressed by the Chinese Government; that the Chinese Government was to appoint four Chinese members to the Board of Directors, which consisted of nine members including the Chinese president of the railway; that the Chinese Government was to appoint two auditors out of a total of five; that the railway company was to pay the Chinese Government a sum of 5,000,000 taels in accordance with the original contract at 6% compound interest from the date of the opening of traffic up to 1920; and that Chinese and Russian employees of the railway were to be impartially distributed and to receive equal treatment.[10]

Since 1895 Russian steamers had plied on the Amur, Sungarai and Ussuri rivers as the Treaty of Aigun of 1858 stipulated that only China and Russia had the right of navigation.[11] The Chinese Eastern Railway had a navigation department and its vessels also plied on these rivers. After the Bolshevik revolution most of the Russian steamship companies wound up their business for fear that their ships might be confiscated by the Soviet authorities. Chinese merchants in Manchuria, taking advantage of this situation, organized the Wutung Steamship Company, bought 29 Russian vessels and started operations in July, 1919. At first these ships, whenever touching the Russian bank of the Amur, were detained by the Russian authorities. After strong protests the right of navigation on the Amur by Chinese steamers was recognized. In the spring of 1920, the navigating lines extended from Khabarovsk to Nikolaievsk at the mouth of the Amur on the Tartar Strait and to Fulin on the Ussuri.

In January, 1924, the Peking Government issued orders forbidding vessels belonging to the Chinese Eastern Railway and those flying the Tsarist flag to ply on the Sungari, a Chinese river. Subsequently, in 1925, the Wutung Company was taken over by the Manchurian authorities and reorganized into the Northern Navigation Bureau. In the next year, acting on the precedent established by the Soviet Government in taking over the Golden Horn Wharf in Vladivostok together with 11 tug boats belonging to the Chinese Eastern Railway, the Manchurian authorities also took over 11 steamers, 30 tug boats, and other properties of the Steam Navigation Department of the Chinese Eastern Railway. From then on no more foreign vessels appeared on the Sungari.

Besides Manchuria, the regions in China which were affected most by the Russian revolution were Sinkiang and Outer Mongolia. At the time of the Chinese revolution the Russian Minister of War again wanted to occupy Ili, but the Foreign Minister was opposed to such action and the plan was dropped. In 1914, the Turkistan-Siberian Railway from Novosirbi to Semipalatinsk[12] was completed and Russia's ambition in Sinkiang was revived. Five divisions were stationed in Central Asia to wait for a proper moment to strike. But the First World War soon broke out and the troops had to be transferred to the European front. During the tumultous time immediately after the revolution Russian trade with Sinkiang greatly decreased and Russian influence in Sinkiang almost disappeared.

When civil war broke out in Central Asia, remnants of the defeated White armies, numbering about 10,000, under General Bakich and Atamans Dutov and Anenkov, retreated into Sinkiang. These White troops not only sought shelter in Sinkiang but wanted to use it as a base of operations to carry on the war against the Reds. Sinkiang was then under the rule of an able military governor, Yang Tseng-hsin. Governor Yang adopted a policy of strict neutrality toward the Russian civil war and with shrewdness and courage he disarmed and interned these remnant troops. Thus no Red-White Russian conflict took place in Sinkiang as did later in Outer Mongolia. Thousands of natives of Central Asia also entered Sinkiang as refugees. These natives, unlike the White troops, were Mohammedans and belonged to the same ethnic stock as the natives of Sinkiang. So they came over the border with their horses and cattle to settle in Sinkiang.

When the Soviet situation became stabilized the Russian Turkestan Government at Tashkent wanted to resume trade with Sinkiang. Governor Yang seized this opportunity to revise the trade stipulations in the Treaty of St. Petersburg, by which Russian goods entered Sinkiang duty-free. With the approval of the Peking Government, Governor Yang sent a delegation to Tashkent in the early part of 1920. The Russian representatives proposed that the Russian soldiers and refugees in Sinkiang should be repatriated; that the arms seized from the Russian troops should be returned; that no White Russian organizations should be permitted in Sinkiang; and that a Soviet trade representative should be permitted to reside in Ili. The Chinese delegates replied that the Russian soldiers and refugees would be persuaded to return to Russia if they were offered an amnesty; that the seized arms would be returned when a legally constituted government had been recognized by China; and that a trade agreement based on the principles of equality and reciprocity should be concluded before the exchange of trade representatives. The Chinese delegates also proposed that due protection should be given to Chinese citizens residing in Soviet territory and that restrictions on immigration should be modified.

A second conference took place at I-ning City, Ili and the Trade Agreement in the form of a series of resolutions was signed on May 27, 1920. This agreement contained three parts. Part I provided for the mutual establishment of a commercial and foreign affairs organization at Wei-nei-sai in Russian Turkestan and I-ning, the designation of trade routes through Ni-kan, customs duties levied on goods passing through the border, and passports for Chinese and Russian nationals who crossed the border on business. Part II concerned with the repatriation of White Russian soldiers and refugees. The Tashkent authorities asserted the existence of an amnesty and the Chinese authorities agreed to the visit of a Soviet commission to Ili to cooperate with the Ili Foreign Affairs Bureau to carry out the repatriation. Part III dealt with the compensation of the lossses sustained by

Chinese nationals during the Russian revolution. The Soviet representatives declared that an Investigation and Compensation Bureau had been established and the Chinese authorities could take up the matter with that bureau. They also agreed to transmit Chinese demands to the Soviet authorities at Tashkent for an amicable settlement.[13] The agreement was approved by the Peking Government in September. Technically this was an agreement between local authorities and not an international treaty. But it governed the trade regulations between Sinkiang and Central Asia for eleven years and Russian goods entering Sinkiang was thereafter taxed for the first time.

In 1921, the trade stipulations of the Treaty of St. Petersburg and the Overland Trade Regulations of 1881 expired for the fourth time after a ten-year period. China was bent upon revising these stipulations and regulations but as the Soviet Government had not yet been recognized there was no way to start negotiations. So on January 8, 1922, President Hsu Hsi-chang issued a mandate stating that pending the conclusion of a new treaty "all provisions for the reduction of duties by one-third, duty-exempted areas, duty-exempted commodities, etc., as specified by the Sino-Russian treaties and the Overland Trade Regulations, be abrogated and the procedure relative to the above be discontinued as from April 1 of the present year. All merchandise seeking entry into China and all Chinese and foreign goods sent to Russia should be subject to the imposition of import and export duties, according to the scale of rates of the maritime customs".[14]

The story of Outer Mongolia during and immediately after the Russian revolution was quite different. During the Manchu Dynasty the Mongolian princes had taken care of political affairs while the lamas had attained only to religious matters. After the so-called independence of 1911, the lamas began to serve as high officials in the government and to take over the power from the hands of the princes. The princes gradually became dissatisfied with the 'independent" and later the autonomous, government of Outer Mongolia. As Russia's prestige decreased in Mongolia owing to her reverse in the war the inclination of the princes towards China increased. So in 1916, merely a year after the conclusion of the tripartite agreement which granted autonomy, some princes secretly approached Chen Lu, Chinese Resident Commissioner at Urga, for the abolition of autonomy on the condition that a dignified position be given to the Hutukhtu and that a large sum of funds be given to the Hutukhtu and princes as rewards. As the Chinese Government was then very tight in finance this proposal was dropped.[15] In January, 1917, the Hutukhtu sent Minister of

Justice Tsetsen Khan and Vice-Minister of War E'erh-te-ni as special envoys to visit Peking and they were cordially received by the Peking Government.

Since 1911, Russian rubles had become the medium of exchange in the Mongolian market. After the outbreak of the revolution the value of the ruble sharply dropped and Mongolian merchants suffered great losses. Soon White and Red Russians were fighting near Kiakhta, threatening to invade Outer Mongolia. The Mongols now began to regret that they had demanded separation from China. Seizing this opportunity Chen Yi, who succeeded Chen Lu as the Resident Commissioner, negotiated with the Mongolian Government for the despatch of Chinese troops into Mongolia. Upon its consent the Peking Government sent two battalions of cavalry to Urga in March, 1919. This troop movement was very timely, for soon Semenov was to create trouble on the border.

Atamen Grigori Semenov, a Cossack leader, occupied Chita in 1918 with the assistance of Japan. There he formed an "Asiatic Corps" with Buryats to fight against Communist forces because he thought the Russians were not reliable as they had already been contaminated with Communism. Later he enlisted Mongols and Tibetans into this corps and conceived of an ambitious plan to create a "Pan-Mongolian State" which would include the Buryat region in Transbaikalia, Outer and Inner Mongolia, Hulunbuir, and Tibet. This plot was secretly encouraged by Japan as she also had the ambition to see such a state under her protection. He called two Mongolian conferences in quick succession. The first conference met at Chita early in 1919, of which we know very little. The second conference took place at Verkhne-Udinsk in March and adopted a program as follows: (1) a central government for all the Mongols was to be established at Hailar. capital of Hulunbuir; (2) an army of 20,000 Mongolian-Buryat soldiers was to be created; (3) 4,000 troops were to be sent to Urga immediately to overcome the hesitations on the part of the Hutukhtu; (4) a delegation was sent to the Paris Peace Conference to seek formal recognition; and (5) Semenov was to be conferred the title of Mongol Prince.[16]

Japan and Semenov had pressed the Hutukhtu to sever his relations with China and to join the "Pan-Mongolian State." As the Hutukhtu had not accepted their proposal, Semenov now threatened him with the use of force. After the second conference Semenov again instigated the Hutukhtu to take action. The Hutukhtu then called a meeting of the princes and lamas to discuss this important matter. It was decided to abrogate autonomy but the lamas were opposed to that.

After the meeting Prince Chei-lin, representing all the princes, secretly asked Chen Yi, in August, to request the Chinese Government to restore formal status of Outer Mongolia and to protect Mongolia against Russian invasion. Chen Yi told Chei-lin that the princes must send a petition to the Chinese Government requesting the abrogation of autonomy so that China could tell Russia and other powers that the initiative came from the Mongols themselves. Chei-lin agreed to this principle but suggested many measures to be adopted after the abrogation, such as the establishment of local self-government, the reorganization of the Mongolian ministries, the appointment of Mongols to high positions, etc. Later even the Hutukhtu accepted the idea and Chen Yi agreed with the representatives of the princes on 63 points as conditions of the abrogation of autonomy which were forwarded to the Peking Government for its final approval.

The threat of Semenov to invade Outer Mongolia never materialized as the Red force had defeated him and driven him away from Kiakhta. A peaceful restoration of Outer Mongolia to China seemed now not only possible but even imminent if not for the ruthless action of General Hsu Shu-tseng, an adventurous militarist. After China's entry into the First World War, Tuan Chi-jui, one-time Prime Minister of the Peking Government, was appointed Director of the War Participation Board. When the peace treaty was concluded the War Participation Board was reorganized into the Frontier Defense Board also with Tuan as the director. Hsu served under Tuan as Defense-Commander and Commissioner of the Northwest Frontier. As Outer Mongolia now lay in his area of defense, Hsu sent more troops to Urga in the summer of 1919. When Hsu heard that a movement to abrogate autonomy was under way he proceeded to Urga himself in October. Difference of opinion soon developed between Hsu and Chen Yi.

When Hsu saw the Mongolian Prime Minister he told him that the Hutukhtu should petition the Peking Government for the abrogation of autonomy and the latter would so declare by a mandate, and that all the conditions should be discussed after the abrogation. This proposal was rejected by the Hutukhtu. When the Hutukhtu received Hsu in an audience Hsu had his troops lined up in front of the palace to display his superior force. But the Hutukhtu was not to be intimidated and stubbornly refused to accept Hsu's proposal. Hsu then struck out those clauses in the 63 points agreed to by Chen Yi which promised good treatment to the Mongols and substituted for them eight conditions which were harsher. On the next morning an ultimatum was addressed to the Hutukhtu that if the new terms were not accepted in 36 hours the Hutukhtu and the Prime Minister would be arrested and transported to Kalgan. The Hutukhtu then referred these terms to the Assembly of the Princes and Lamas for consideration. Great indignation was aroused and hot debate ensued. But the princes and lamas knew that it was impossible for the Mongol soldiers to fight against Hsu's army and submitted to the terms.

A petition renouncing autonomy, the Russian-Mongolian treaties, and the Sino-Russian-Mongolian Tripartite Agreement, and asking for the reintegration of Outer Mongolia into the Chinese Republic, was sent to both Hsu and Chen Yi with the signatures of ministers, princes and lamas but without that of the Hutukhtu. Upon receiving this petition a presidential mandate on November 22, 1919 declared that the request of the ministers, princes and lamas was granted with satisfaction and that hereinafter Outer Mongolia was back in "the family of five nations".[17] To the protest of the Tsarist minister in Peking against the abolition of the tripartite agreement of 1915, the Waichiaopu answered: "In 1911, the Mongols, of their own accord, broke away from China and the situation thus created, demanded Sino-Russian-Mongolian Agreements. Today, again of their own accord, they renounce their autonomy, thus making the agreements concluded purposeless." The Russian minister knew he had no power to interfere and the matter was dropped. Tannu Urianhui and Kobdo had been recovered by Chinese troops in the summer of 1919. Then Hulunbuir also petitioned in January, 1920, for the abolition of its status as a special district and it again became an administrative unit of China.

Although Outer Mongolia renounced its autonomy the highhanded policy of Hsu Shu-tseng alienated the Hutukhtu and princes. In December, 1919, the office of the Resident Commissioner was abolished and Hsu was appointed by the Peking Government to assume charge of the rehabilitation of Outer Mongolia. Hsu then enlarged the office of the Northwest Defense Commissioner to include eight administrative bureaus and absorbed all Mongolian ministries into them. This action increased the dissatisfaction of the Mongols. Then in July, 1920 a civil war broke out between Tuan Chi-jui on the one side and warlords Tsao Kun and Wu Pei-fu on the other. Hsu's troops in Urga were sent back to take part in the fighting near Peking. The war quickly ended in Tuan's defeat and Hsu sought asylum in the Legation Quarter.

The Peking Government appointed Chen Yi Pacification Commissioner of Outer Mongolia, Uliassutai, Kobdo and Tannu Urianhai in September with his headquarters at Urga. By now the Mongolian princes and lamas were secretly conspiring to drive Chinese forces out and to restore autonomy. The invasion of Outer Mongolia by Baron Ungern von Sternberg gave them a chance. When Semenov's "Asiatic Corps" was defeated by the Reds in Transbaikalia in the autumn of 1920 Ungern, one of Semenov's White generals, led a remnant force of three thousand men into Mongolia. At first he intended to reach Troitskosavsk, a Russian town near Kiakhta and to join the anti-Communist partisans there. Finding it impossible to cross the mountainous region of Kentai he turned towards Urga. Arriving at the Barum Tereledge river about 18 miles from Urga in November he requested permission to enter the capital and stay for a short time and offered to buy provisions for his troops with gold. Before receiving an answer Ungern suddenly decided to attack Urga and was repulsed by the Chinese garrison with heary losses. Living in the open air under light tents in the severe Mongolian winter and unable to obtain provisions his officers and men began to desert the camp. What remained of the detachment had to pillage Mongolian and Chinese caravans for food.

Then fortune turned in favor of Ungern. A group of princes and lamas in Tsetsen Khan's clan got in touch with him and obtained his promise to help them fight against the Chinese. Later he even established connections with the Hutukhtu's entourage. Thereafter food and horses arrived in abundance and Mongols and even Tibetans came from all sides to enlist under his flag. On the night of February 1, 1921, a group of Tibetans under the command of a Buryat officer, rescued the Hutukhtu from the palace where he was interned by Chinese soldiers. On the next day Ungern again attacked Urga with 5000 Buryats, Mongols and Tibetans and took it by assault. The Chinese garrison suffered heavy casualties and retreated northward to Maimaicheng on the border. The Hutukhtu returned to the palace and proclaimed an "independent" Mongolian Government. Ungern was appointed Supreme Military Adviser and was admired as a great hero by the Mongols.

But his dramatic adventure soon came to a tragic end. Intoxicated by his sudden success Ungern began to conceive of confused and even contradictory plans. In one plan he would put himself at the head of a "Pan-Mongolian State" coming to grips with China; in another he would seek for an alliance of the Mongols with the Chinese for the restoration of the Manchu dynasty. He regarded Communism as the "universal enemy" and announced at the Hutukhtu's coronation festival that he would lead a punitive expedition against it. Sometimes he even attacked all western nations as the "foul Occident" and intended to purify it with sabres and guns. Once he declared to his officers:

"with my Mongols I shall go to Lisbon".[18] His incoherent plans made him suspicious to the Mongol princes and lamas; while his cruel purge of Chinese, Mongols and Russians,—wholesale execution of suspects—and the looting and extortion indulged in by his troops finally changed Mongols' admiration for him to hate. After suffering a setback in his encounter with the Red forces a revolt broke out in his ranks. He fled Urga in June, reentered Transbaikalia and occupied Selenginsk. But soon he was forced by the Reds to retreat into Mongolia again. His troops then deserted him en masse and he was captured by a Mongol detachment. The Mongol soldiers bound him hand and foot and abandoned him on the steppe of Elzin-gol. He was discovered by Red soldiers, brought back to Siberia, tried and publicly executed.[19]

Ungern's adventure gave the Soviet Government an excuse to interfere with Mongolian affairs. At the time of Ungern's first attack on Urga the Soviet Foreign Commissar sent a telegram to the Peking Government stating that at the request of the Chinese authorities at Urga Soviet forces had been ordered to enter Outer Mongolia to assist the Chinese garrison in suppressing the "Semenov-Ungern bands". But before the Soviet troops could arrive Ungern had been repulsed. The Soviet Government declared on November 27, that the previous order of an expedition had been cancelled but the Soviet Government would send troops in the future when again requested by the Chinese authorities. But on December 31, the Chinese minister in London handed to Soviet representative Krassin, for dispatch to his government, a formal denial that the Chinese authorities in Urga had ever requested Soviet aid in the expulsion of White invaders and asserted that China had no intention to ask for Soviet aid in the future.[20]

Now the Soviet Government had to fabricate a pretext for intervention. So early in 1921 a Mongolian People's Revolutionary Party was created with a membership of 160 and was soon admitted as a unit of the Communist International. In March a party conference was held at Kiakhta and a so-called Provisional Mongolian People's Revolutionary Government was proclaimed. This government appealed in April to Russia and the Far Eastern Republic for assistance to annihilate the Ungern forces and it was promptly given. In June, combined Russian and Far Eastern forces defeated Ungern and in July they marched into Urga. The Mongolian Government under the Hutukhtu then transferred its power to the Provisional Revolutionary Government on July 12. The Hutukhtu was kept as a nominal head but the actual power was now in the hands of the Prime Minister,

Comrade Bodo, who had served as typist in the Russian consulate-general at Urga.[21]

Immediately after seizing power in Outer Mongolia, the Provisional Revolutionary Government addressed a request to the Soviet Government "not to withdraw the Soviet troops from the territory of Mongolia until the complete removal of the menace from the common enemy who is now seeking reinforcements in the Eastern Steppes".[22] The Soviet Foreign Commissar, Chicherin, said in his reply to the Provisional Revolutionary Geovernment: "Having firmly decided to withdraw its troops from the territory of autonomous Mongolia, which is bound to Soviet Russia only by the ties of mutual friendship and common interests, just as soon as the menace to the free development of the Mongolian people and to the security of the Russian Republic and the Far Eastern Republic shall have been removed, the Russian Government, in complete harmony with the People's Revolutionary Government of Mongolia, notes that this moment has not yet arrived. In response to the request addressed to it by the People's Revolutionary Government, the Russian Government announces its decision to give this request complete satisfaction".[23]

Then on November 5, an agreement was signed between Soviet Russia and Outer Mongolia at Moscow. This agreement provided that the Government of the Russian Socialist Federated Soviet Republic and the People's Government of Mongolia recognized each other as the only government in its territory respectively; that they agreed to respect each other and not to allow on their territory the formation of groups for the recruiting of troops, nor to allow through their territory the transportation of arms and the transit of troops, hostile to one of the contracting parties; that they would send plenipotentiary representatives to each other's capital and consuls to each other's cities; that the frontier between Russia and Mongolia would be decided by a special commission; and that the citizens of each power residing on the territory of the other would enjoy the rights and perform the duties in an equality with citizens of the most favored nation.[24] Thus Outer Mongolia was in the grip of Soviet Russia—a firmer grip than the Tsarist one. Uliassutai and Kobdo were again occupied by Mongolian troops with the help of Russians. Tannu Urianhai, still unable to join Outer Mongolia, was created into an "independent" Tuvinian People's Republic in 1921.

CHAPTER IX

Soviet Declarations of 1919 and 1920 and the Sino-Soviet Agreement of 1924

For reasons to be discussed in the following chapter, the eyes of Soviet Russia early turned to China. As early as July, 1918, George Chicherin, Foreign Affairs Commissar, told the Fifth Congress of the Soviets that the Soviet Government would renounce the Tsarist conquests in Manchuria, all indemnities, and particular rights on the Chinese Eastern Railway.[1] In the summer of 1919 when the Allied troops were still marching along the Siberian Railway and the White Russians were very active in eastern Siberia, the Soviet Government made its first overture to the Chinese people. Leo Karakhan, Soviet Deputy Commissar for Foreign Affairs, made the famous Soviet declaration to China. In view of its importance it is quoted here at length:

"All people, whether they are great or small, whether they have lived until now a free life, or whether they form against their own will a part of another country, shall be free in their inner life, and no power shall interfere with them within their limit. The Government of Workers and Peasants (The Soviet Government) has then declared null and void all the secret treaties concluded with Japan, China and the ex-Allies, the treaties which were to enable the Russian Government of the Tsar and his Allies to enslave the people of the East and principally the people of China by intimidating or buying them for the sole interests of the capitalists, financiers and the Russian generals.

"The Soviet Government invites, henceforth, the Chinese Government to enter into negotiations with the object of cancelling the treaty of 1896, the protocol of Peking of 1901, and all the agreements concluded with Japan from 1907 to 1916. That is to say, to give back to the Chinese people all the power and authority which were obtained by the Government of the Tsar by tricks or by enticing into understandings with Japan and the Allies.

"We herewith address the Chinese people with the object of making them thoroughly understand, that the Soviet Government has given up all the conquests made by the Government of the Tsar, which took away from China, Manchuria and other territories...

"The Soviet Government returns to the Chinese people, without demanding any kind of compensation, the Chinese Eastern Railway, as well as all the mining concessions, forestry, gold mines, and all other things which were seized from them by the Government of the Tsar, that of Kerensky and the brigands, Horvath, Semenov, Kolchak, the Russian ex-generals, merchants and capitalists...

"The Soviet Government gives up the indemnities, payable by China for the insurrection of the Boxers in 1900 . . .

"The Soviet Government has abolished all the special priviledges and all the factories owned by Russian merchants in Chinese territory; no Russian official, priest or missionary should be allowed to interfere with Chinese affairs; and if they should commit any crime, they must be judged according to the local laws in local courts. No authority or law court should be allowed to exist in China except the authority of the Chinese people.

"Besides these principal points, the Soviet Government, represented by plenipotentiaries, is ready to negotiate with the Chinese people all the other questions and to settle once for all cases of acts of violence and injustice of Russia, acting together with Japan and the Allies."[2]

To the Chinese people who were then suffering from the injustice done to them by the Versailles Peace Treaty which gave Japan the former German rights in Shangtung this declaration sounded like "a diplomatic Magna Charta." They rejoiced over this idealistic and anti-imperialistic policy of a new Russia and warm praise for Soviet Russia came especially from university professors and students. But owing to the disruption of communications the official text of this declaration was not forwarded to Peking until March 26, 1920. Before that date the Peking Government was very much in doubt as to its authenticity and even after receiving the text some officials suspected it to be a forgery.[3]

The Peking Government under the presidency of Hsu Shi-chang was very weak and dared not accept the declaration lest it might offend other powers, particularly Japan. It was not until September of the same year that a Chinese mission with General Chang Shih-lin at its head visited Moscow. On September 27, Karakhan handed General Chang the second Soviet declaration to China for transmission to the Peking Government. This declaration expressed the Soviet Government's regret that a rapproachement between China and the Soviet Union had been long delayed and that the Chinese mission was not given full power to start negotiations with the Soviets. It then proposed to the Chinese Foreign Office eight points of a new Sino-Soviet treaty of friendship which were based upon the principles in the declaration of 1919. These points were as follows:

"(1) The Government of the Russian Socialist Federated Soviet Republic declares null and void all the treaties concluded with China by the former governments of Russia, renounces all seizures of Chinese territory and all Russian concessions in China, and restores to China, without any compensation and forever, all that had been predatorily seized from her by the Tsar's Government and the Russian bourgeousie.

"(II) The Governments of both Republics shall take necessary measures for immediately establishing regular trade and economic relations. A special treaty to this affect shall be subsequently concluded on the principle of the clause of the most favored nation, applying to both contracting parties.

(III) The Chinese Government pledges itself: (1) not to proffer any aid to Russian counter-revolutionary individuals, groups or organizations, and not to allow their activities in Chinese territory; (2) to disarm, intern and hand over to the Government of the R.S.F.S.R. all the detachments and organizations to be found in the Chinese territory at the signing of this treaty which are fighing agtainst the R.S.F.S.R., or states allied with her, and to give over to the Government of R.S.F.S.R. all their arms, munitions and property; (3) the Government of R.S.F.S.R. shall bear the same responsibility towards Chinese counter-revolutionary individuals or organizations.

"(IV) All Russian citizens residing in China shall be subject to all the laws and regulations acting in the territory of the Chinese Republic and shall not enjoy any rights of extra-territoriality. Chinese citizens residing in Russia shall be subject to all the laws and regulations acting in the territory of the R.S.F.S.R.

"(V) The Government of the Chinese Republic pledges itself: (1) immediately after the signing of the present treaty to sever connections with persons styling themselves as diplomatic and consular representatives of the R.S.F.S.R., and to deport such persons from China; (2) to hand over to the Russian state, in the person of the R.S.F.S.R., the buildings of the embassy and the consulates and other property and archives of the same situated in Chinese territory and belonging to Russia.

"(VI) The Government of the R.S.F.S.R. renounces any compensation paid out by China as indemnity for the Boxer rising, provided that under no circumstances shall the Government of the Chinese Republic pay any money to the former Russian concerns or to any other persons or Russian organizations putting up illegal claims thereto.

"(VII) Following immediately upon the signing of the present treaty, there shall be mutually established diplomatic and consular representatives of the Republic of China and the R.S.F.S.R.

"(VIII) The Russian and the Chinese Governments agree to sign a special treaty on the way of working of the Chinese Eastern Railway with due regard to the need of the R.S.F.S.R., and in the conclusion of the treaty there shall take part, besides China and Russia, also the Far Eastern Republic."[4]

When we compare the two declarations we readily find one big difference in their language about the Chinese Eastern Railway. In the first declaration it was clearly stated that "the Soviet Government returns to the Chinese people, without demanding any kind of compensation, the Chinese Eastern Railway . . .", while in the second this generous offer was nowhere to be found and only "a special treaty on the way of working" of the railway was proposed. This alteration clearly indicated that the Soviet Union intended to keep the Chinese Eastern Railway under Sino-Soviet joint control. The change of policy was probably due to the fact that the Soviet Government was far more stable in September, 1920 than fourteen months ago. It also furnished the first evidence that the Soviet Government would not keep its own pledges in international dealings.

It was the nominally independent Far Eastern Republic which sent Ignatius Yurin with a large staff of experts to China towards the end of 1920, the first mission after the revolution. He was technically a delegate of the Far Eastern Republic to negotiate a trade agreement, but was considered by China as a representative of the Soviet Government. The Peking Government proposed four points of discussion: (1) the mission must refrain from engaging in propaganda work; (2) an indemnity should be paid to Chinese merchants in Siberia to cover their losses and damages; (3) the protection of the Chinese in Siberia should be guaranteed; and (4) measures should be taken to prevent recurrences of incidents. Although Yurin was willing to negotiate along these lines, negotiations did not go further owing to the lack of written confirmation on these points from the Soviet Government. Yurin had to content himself with his work of getting in touch with members of the Chinese National Assembly and prominent educators. Through the introduction of university professors he also cultivated the friendship of Chinese students. Since his mission could not be fulfilled he returned to Siberia in the summer of 1921.

In December, 1921, a Soviet representative, Alexander Paikes, arrived at Peking. At that time Red forces had occupied Urga and the Soivet-Mongolian Agreement had been concluded. When the Waichiaopu first inquired about the news of the agreement, Paikes denied the existence of such a treaty and dismissed the news as a mere rumor. A few months later the text was made public and Paikes had to admit it. On May 1, 1922, the Waichiaopu lodged a strong protest with Paikes which stated in part: "The Soviet Government has repeatedly declared to the Chinese Government that all previous treaties made between the Russian Government and China shall be null and void, that the Soviet Government renounces all encroachments of Chinese territory and all concessions within China, and that the Soviet Government will unconditionally and forever return what has been forcibly seized from China by the former Imperial Russian Government and the bourgeoisie... It must be observed that Mongolia is a part of Chinese territory and as such has long been recognized by all countries. In secretly concluding a treaty with Mongolia, the Soviet Government has not only broken faith with its previous declarations but also violates all principles of justice". In conclusion the Waichiaopu emphasized that such a treaty would not be recognized by China.[5] Thus the Paikes mission failed to open negotiations with China and he soon returned to Moscow.

After Great Britain had concluded a treaty with the Soviet Union in 1922, Krassine, the Soviet representative in London, approached Dr. Wellington Koo, Chinese Minister to Britain, requesting resumption of diplomatic relations between China and the Soviet Union. Upon instructions from the Waichiaopu Dr. Koo informed Krassine that China was ready to enter into negotiation on the condition that the Soviet declarations of 1919 and 1920 be used as basis for discussions. The Soviet Government agreed to this point and sent Adolf Joffe to China in the summer of 1922. Joffe was a man of much greater calibre than Yurin or Paikes, having served as a professor of international law in Russia and having successfully negotiated a trade agreement with Germany after the revolution. After arriving at Peking in August he made a series of speeches denouncing Western imperialism and advocating the liberation of colonial and semi-colonial peoples and soon gained the sympathy and admiration of the Chinese intellectuals.

Early in September he proposed to Dr. Koo who was now Foreign Minister to open a Sino-Soviet conference immediately. But Dr. Koo demanded withdrawal of Soviet forces from Outer Mongolia as a guarantee of Soviet good faith before opening negotiations. In his reply Joffe declared that "the stationing of Soviet troops in Mongolia concerns Chinese interests no less than the Soviet interests"[6] and energetically rejected the demand. He also blamed the Peking Government for shielding White Russians who used Chinese territory as a base to attack the Soviet Union. The Peking Government immediately ordered local authorities to disarm all White troops who might seek shelter in Chinese territory but insisted that the Soviets must evacuate Urga before the conference could begin.

Besides this, there was another point in dispute. The Peking Government asked Joffe to declare that the Soviet Government would return to China the Chinese Eastern Railway without compensation as promised in the declaration of 1919. Joffe flatly denied that and stated: "even if Russia vests in the Chinese people her title to the Chinese Eastern Railway, this will not annul Russia's interest in this line, which is a portion of the Great Siberian Railway and unites one part of Russian territory with another." Because these disputes could not be settled the proposed Sino-Soviet conference never took place. The Chinese people began to suspect that Soviet policy towards China was following the lines of Tsarist Russia. In January, 1923, Joffe went to Shanghai to get in touch with Dr. Sun Yat-sen and soon proceeded to Japan at the request of Baron Shimpei Goto who was strongly in favor of a Soviet-Japanese rapproachement. But nothing came out of their meetings and Joffe soon returned to Moscow because of his poor health.

Then in the summer of 1923, the Soviet Government sent Karakhan himself as special envoy to China to negotiate a Sino-Soviet treaty. Karakhan arreived at Peking on September 2 and received a rousing welcome because he was the author of the two Soviet declarations. In his public speeches in Peking Karakhan called the Chinese people "the best ally of the Russians in Asia". Prior to his arrival the Peking Government had already appointed Dr. C. T. Wang as head of the Sino-Soviet Negotiations Commission. Karakhan at first demanded China's recognition of the Soviet Union, which was formally proclaimed in July of that year, before negotiations, but Dr. Wang insisted that an agreement be reached on general principles which would cover recognition and other important pending issues. These preliminary discussions lasted almost three months with several exchanges of notes in which Karakhan accused the Peking Government of retaining vesssels of the Russian Volunteer Fleet, interfering with a mail train on the Chinese Eastern Railway, permitting outrages against the Soviets on the Chinese border, and using the Boxer Indemnity Fund for payment to former Tsarist officials, while the Waichiaopu gave explanations to these allegations. Then Karakhan agreed to talk on pending issues and negotiations began.

Outer Mongolia and the Chinese Eastern Railway soon became the stumbling block of an agreement. With regard to Outer Mongolia Wang demanded that all treaties between Russia and Outer Mongolia be clearly declared null and void in the new Sino-Soviet agreement and Soviet forces in Outer Mongolia be immediately withdrawn; while Karakhan only conceded that the Soviet Union would recognize Outer Mongolia as a part of China and would declare all treaties and agreements between Tsarist Russia and any third party or parties detrimental to China null and void. Soviet forces would be withdrawn from Outer Mongolia after the necessary conditions for withdrawal, such as checking White Guard's activities, were agreed upon in a future conference. Concerning the Chinese Eastern Railway Wang demanded its return to China without compensation but Karakhan stated: "Never and nowhere could I have said that all the rights on the Chinese Eastern Railway belong to China . . . But even now I can confirm what was said four years ago, namely, that the sovereignty of China in the territory of the railway is fully recognized by us and that we shall not insist on any one of these privileges which the Tsarist Government had, and which the other Foreign Powers still have today, in the railway zone."[8] The Soviet mission even published what they called the authorized version of the declarations, in which the clause providing for the restoration of the Chinese Eastern Railway to China without any compensation in the 1919 declaration was omitted.

In February, 1924 Great Britain accorded the Soviet Union de jure recognition and this fact strengthened the Soviet position in international affairs. In the meantime the Peking Government was weakened by incessant civil wars among the war-lords. Wang, therefore, made concessions to Karakhan in their negotiations and a draft agreement on general principles and another draft agreement on the provisional management of the Chinese Eastern Railway were signed on March 14.

In the draft agreement on general principles it was provided that diplomatic and consular relations between the two powers be immediately re-established and that a conference should be held within one month after the signing of the agreement (1) to annul "all conventions, treaties, agreements, protocols, contracts, etc., between the Government of China and the Soviet Government and to replace them with new treaties, agreements, etc., on the basis of equality, reciprocity and justice as well as the spirit of the Declarations of the Soviet Government of 1919 and 1920"; (2) to agree upon the time limit of the withdrawal of Soviet troops from Outer Mongolia and the measures to be adopted in the interests of the safety of the frontiers; (3) to re-demarcate the national boundaries; and (4) to conclude a commercial treaty and a customs tariff agreements in accordance with the principles of equality and reciprocity. The governments of the two powers pledged themselves not to permit within their territories the existence and activities of any organizations or groups whose aim was to struggle by acts of violence against either power; and not to engage in propaganda directed against the political and social systems of either power. The Soviet Government agreed to give up the Russian portion of the Boxer Indemnity, to relinquish the rights of extra-territoriality and consular jurisdiction, and to renounce the special rights and privileges related with all concessions in all parts of China acquired by the Tsarist Government. The Soviet Government recognized that Outer Mongolia was an integral part of China, respected China's sovereignty therein and declared all treaties, agreements, etc., concluded by the former Tsarist Government and any third party or parties affecting the sovereign rights or interests of China null and void.

With regard to the Chinese Eastern Railway the question was to be settled at the forthcoming convention; and pending the final settlement the rights of the two powers as provided in the contract of August 1896 for the construction and operation of the Chinese Eastern Railway which did not conflict with the present agreements should be retained. The draft agreement for its provisional management provided that China and the Soviet Union each appoint five directors of the railway. A Chinese director was to be the President of the Board and also the Director-General while a Russian director was to be the Vice-President and the Assistant Director-General. Russians were to be the Manager and one Assistant Manager while a Chinese was to be the other Assistant Manager. Thus we see that contrary to its public declarations the Soviet Union was to keep all its rights on the Chinese Eastern Railway.

The final copies of those agreements were to be formally signed on March 16; but the Peking Government did not approve those drafts, blamed Wang for overstepping his authority and instructed him to continue negotiations in order to make some alterations. Upon learning of this turn of events Karakhan sent an ultimatum to Wang on March 16, stating that agreements must be signed within three days beyond which he would not be bound by the conditions specified therein. He also sent a note to the Waichiaopu, warning the Peking Government "against making irreparable mistakes, which might affect the future relations between China and the Soviet Union".[9] The Peking Government then instructed Wellington Koo, Chinese Foreign

Minister, to negotiate directly with Karakhan but the latter refused to discuss any alteration of the drafts. The deadlock lasted over two months.

In the meantime negotiations between Japan and the Soviet Union were going on and it was rumored that the Soviet Union was ready to sell to Japan the southern section of the Chinese Eastern Railway from Harbin to Changchun. Rumors were also in the air that both the Canton Government and Marshal Chang Tso-lin in Manchuria were negotiating with the Soviets. This news made the Peking Government uneasy and it finally gave in to Karakhan. After a few secret talks Wellington Koo and Karakhan signed the two agreements on May 31, 1924.[10] The final official text of these agreements was practically the same as that of the drafts. The only alterations were in the declarations by the two governments accompanying the agreements with regards to questions of the reciprocal transfer of real estate and immovable property and of the Boxer Indemnity Funds which were of minor importance. Within a month of the signing of these agreements the Soviet Union appointed Karakhan its first ambassador to China while China appointed Cheng Yen-hsi charge d'affaires at Moscow. Diplomatic relations were thus resumed.

At that time Manchuria under Marshal Chang Tso-lin was practically independent of the Peking Government and its orders were certainly not to be obeyed in Manchuria. Karakhan knew this very well and before his arrival at Peking he broke his journey at Mukden to have an interview with Chang. After the signing of the agreements he was aware that unless they were approved by Chang Tso-lin the stipulations concerning the Chinese Eastern Railway could not be carried out. So in June, 1924 he sent Nikolai Konznetsoff as his representative to Mukden to secretly negotiate with Chang Tso-lin. After three months' negotiations an agreement between the Soviet Government and the so-called Government of the Autonomous Three Eastern Provinces of China was secretly concluded. It embodied all the important points in the agreements concluded with the Peking Government. The only new provision was that the Chinese Government should enter gratis into possession of the Chinese Eastern Railway after sixty years instead of eighty as originally provided. This agreement was approved in March, 1925 by the Peking Government as a supplementary document to the Sino-Soviet Agreement of 1924.[11]

According to the Sino-Soviet Agreement on General Principles a conference should be held within a month of its signing to settle all pending issues. But it was not until March, 1925 that the Peking

Government appointed C. T. Wang and Cheng Chien Chinese delegates to the conference and not until August 26 that the opening ceremony of the conference took place. The next day Karakhan went back to Moscow and the conference was interrupted. When Karakhan returned to Peking at the beginning of December the negotiations were continued. Owing to an incident in the Chinese Eastern Railway in which the Russian Manager Ivanoff was arrested by the Railway Guard Commander, General Chang Hwan-hsiang, because he instigated railway employees to strike; Sino-Soviet relations became tense and the negotiations were again suspended. Then a settlement was reached between Chang Tso-lin and the Soviet consul-general at Mukden. Both Ivanoff and Chang Hwan-hsiang were dismissed from their posts and the traffic was resumed. Thereafter the conference was unofficially shifted to Mukden. Several meetings were held between General Yang Yu-ting and Shelebrokoff, the Soviet representative, to discuss affairs of the Chinese Eastern Railway, but no agreement was reached. Because of his attitude in the railway incident Chang Tso-lin had strong feelings against Karakhan. Consequently, the Peking Government demanded his recall and the Soviet Government finally complied with this request. Karakhan left China in September, 1926 and the Soviet Government sent Chernik to serve as Charge d'Affaires. Since the northern expedition of the Canton Government had started and the Peking Government was now on the verge of collapse, the Sino-Soviet conference was never resumed.

CHAPTER X

Soviet Role in the Chinese Revolution

After the November revolution the Russian Bolsheviks expected workers in London, Paris and Berlin to follow suit and thus start a proletarian world revolution. But the workers in the Western countries turned a deaf ear to the call of the triumphant Bolsheviks and they were disappointed. Lenin sought for an explanation and came to the conclusion that "the surplus profits from the explotation of colonies and semi-colonial countries such as China had enabled the European capitalists to maintain their wage-slaves above the starvation level which would make revolution inevitable. To free such countries from capitalist exploitation would therefore be a long step towards the proletarian world revolution".[1] So his attention was led to Asia and especially to China as the largest semi-colonial country in Asia.

At that time the revolutionary tide in China was also rising. Domestically, although China became a republic in 1912 it had since then been ruled by militarists or war-lords such as Yuan Shih-kai, Tuan Chi-jui, Feng Kuo-chang, etc., who knew nothing about democracy. Dr. Sun Yat-sen had led a revolutionary movement against the war-lords but unsuccessfully. Internationally, imperialist powers had long exploited China and the Chinese people had strong resentment against them. When at the end of the First World War the three big empires in Europe, Russia, Austria-Hungary and Germany, collapsed one after another the Chinese people had high hopes that international justice and righteousness would now prevail. But the Paris Peace Conference of 1919 which, ignoring all moral principle, gave former German rights in Shangtung to Japan, completely disillusioned them. College students in Peking staged a big demonstration on May 4, 1919 in protest of this unjust decision of the Peace Conference, and burned the house of one high official, Tsao Ju-lin, and beat up another high official, Chang Tsung-hsiang, for their treacherous collaboration with the Japanese Government. This patriotic movement soon spread over the whole country and the people were awakened to the danger of bad government within and aggression from without. The Chinese Revolutionary Party led by Dr. Sun Yat-sen was then reorganized into the Chung-Kuo-Kuo-Min-Tang (we usually use its abbreviated name,

Kuomintang). Many intellectuals and patriotic elements flocked to its banner.

It was at this juncture that Lenin began to spread Communism to China. Early in 1920 Lenin sent Grigori Voitinsky, head of the Eastern Department of the Communist International (hereinafter Comintern), to China to start a Communist movement. Upon his arrival in China Voitinsky found that a Society for the Study of Marxism had been founded in Peking by Li Ta-chao, professor of history at National Peking University, Chen Tu-hsiu, head of the Department of Literature in the same institution, Chang Kuo-tao, a student, Mao Tse-tung, a clerk in the university library, and some others. These intellectuals had been impressed by the success of the Russian revolution and began to be baptized by Communism. Chen Tu-hsiu had also established a branch of the society in Shanghai where he was then residing. Voitinsky at once got in touch with them and set up his headquarters in Shanghai. With the help of Soviet funds Communist classics, such as Marx's *Communist Manifesto* and Kautsky's *Class Struggle* were translated into Chinese and widely circulated. Many youths, however, read these publications at that time simply for the sake of curiosity.

Voitinsky then directed those he considered as good Communist timber to organize Communist cells: Chen Tu-hsiu formed one in Shanghai; Li Ta-chao, one in Peking; Mao Tse-tung, one in Changsha; Tung Pi-wu, one in Hankow; Chen Kung-po, one in Canton; Teng Enming, one in Tsinan; Chou Fo-hai, one in Japan; etc. A group of Chinese students in France, Tsai Ho-sheng, Chou En-lai, Li Lih-san, Wang Jo-fei, Li Fu-chun, etc., were also attracted by Communist propaganda and established a Chinese Communist Youth Corps at Paris. Accompanied by Chen Tu-hsiu, Voitinsky called on Dr. Sun Yat-sen at his home in Shanghai. This was the first time that the leader of the Chinese revolution and a representative of the Comintern came into contact but their conversations were confined to Dr. Sun's inquiry about the Russian revolution and his desire to have better communications with the Soviets.[2]

In the same year the Second Congress of the Comintern adopted a resolution to maintain the closest contact with the revolutionary forces in the politically and economically oppressed nations which were working for the overthrow of imperialism. A Committee on Nationality and Colonial Problems was created under the personal direction of Lenin. As the result of the work of this committee a Congress of the Peoples of the East was held at Baku in September, 1920. At that Congress Grigori Zinoviev, head of the Comintern, declared: "The real revolution will blaze up only when the 800,000,000 people who live in Asia unite with us, when the African continent unites, when we see hundreds of millions of people in revolt."[3] After this congress the work of agitating a revolution in China was accelerated. Voitinsky was transferred to Japan and G. Maring, (Sneevliet, a Dutchman) secretary of the Committee on Nationality and Colonial Problems, was despatched to China early in 1921. Chen Tu-shiu had by then gone to Moscow and come back with the assignment from the Comintern to form a Chinese Communist Party.

In the presence of Maring the First National Congress of the Chinese Communist Party was held at Shanghai in July with thirteen delegates representing some fifty Communists. Sources disagree as to the delegates present at the meetings. According to Robert Payne, Mao Tse-tung recalled eleven delegates besides Mao, viz., Chen Tu-hsiu, Li Ta-chao, Chang Kuo-tao, Chou Fu-hai, Chen Kung-po, Shih Tseng-tung, Pao Hui-sheng, Tai Chi-tao, Li Han-chuen, Li Ta, and Shao Li-tsu.[4] But according to Chen Tan-chiu, who wrote an article about the congress fifteen years later, thirteen delegates representing Communists in seven places were present, viz., Chang Kuo-tao (Peking), Chen Kung-po (Canton), Li Han-chuen (Shanghai), Li Ta (Shanghai), Liu Jen-ching (Peking), Mao Tse-tung (Changsha), Pao Hui-sheng (Canton), Teng En-ming (Tsinan), Tung Pi-wu (Wuhan) and Wang Tsing-mei (Tsinan).[5] Both Mao and Chen were present at the meetings but Chen's account seemed to be accurate. In this case either Mao's memory failed him or Payne misquoted him because Chen Tan-chiu did not appear on Mao's list while Chen Tu-hsiu was in Canton and Ta Chi-tao and Shao Li-tse, being Kuomintang members, could not attend the Congress.

Owing to the interference of the police in the French concession of Shanghai where the meetings were held the delegates went to Niehbu Lake in Chiahsing, Chekiang province, about a hundred miles from Shanghai and carried on the work of the Congress on a hired boat. The delegates found themselves in serious disagreement concerning the party program and organization. In a written program proposed by Chen Tu-hsiu, who was then serving as commissioner of education in Canton, he emphasized the necessity of giving education to the members of the party, the guidance of the party in a "democratic" spirit, the development of discipline and the advisability of approaching the masses cautiously so as to bring them into the Communist camp. Li Han-chuen asserted that the revolutions in Russia and Germany should be studied on the spot before adopting a program

platform which advocated the overthrow of the war-lords; unification of China proper and Manchuria into a genuine democratic republic; establishment of a federated republic by uniting China proper, Manchuria, Mongolia, Tibet and Sinkiang; establishment of universal sufferage; promulgation of freedoms of speech, press, assembly and strike; initiation of compulsory education; introduction of progressive income tax; abolition of contract labor; initiation of eight-hour working day; regulation of child and woman labor, etc. A constitution was adopted in which it was expressly provided that the Chinese Communist Party was to be a part of the world Communist movement and join the Comintern to establish its relationship with the international revolution.

Prior to the Second Congress the Chinese Communist Party had on June 10 issued a statement on the existing political situation in China in which it proposed a joint conference with the Kuomintang for the purpose of forming a united front in order to liberate the Chinese people from the "dual yoke" of war-lords and foreign exploiters. But this proposal was not accepted by Dr. Sun Yat-sen. Then in August Maring, who had gone to Moscow and returned, called a special plenary session of the Central Committee of the Chinese Communist Party at Hangchow to discuss this problem. According to the account of Chen Tu-hsiu, Maring urged the Chinese Communists to join the Kuomintang because the Kuomintang was "not a bourgeois party but a coalition party of all classes" and could therefore be transformed, under proletarian leadership, into the driving force of the Chinese revolution. Chen Tu-hsiu and four other members of the Central Committee, Li Ta-chao, Chang Kuo-tao, Tsai Ho-shen and Kao Yu-han were strongly opposed to this proposal on the ground that the conglomeration of forces within the Kuomintang would check the independent policy of the Chinese Communist Party. Answering this strong opposition Maring simply said it was a Comintern decision and asked the members of the Central Committee whether they wanted to disobey the Comintern.[12] Thus the question was settled and the Central Committee adopted a resolution instructing party members to join the Kuomintang.

At the same time as the Second Congress was being held Dr. Sun Yat-sen was fighting against Chen Chiung-ming at Canton. Chen Chiung-ming had been a longtime Kuomintang member and close ollower of Dr. Sun. It was his troops who had defeated war-lords Lu Yung-ting and Mo Yung-shing and welcomed Dr. Sun back to Canton towards the end of 1920. After Dr. Sun was elected Provisional President by the National Assembly in April, 1921 Chen had served under him as Minister of War and concurrently Commander-in-Chief of the Kwantung Army. But a breach was soon developed as Chen was strongly opposed to Dr. Sun's plan of a northern expedition. In the spring of 1922 Dr. Sun dismissed Chen as Commander-in-Chief of the Kwangtung Army and thereupon Chen retired to his native city. But Canton was still garrisoned by Chen's troops who at the instigation of Chen, rebelled against Dr. Sun during the night of June 16-17. Dr. Sun was awakened from his sleep by loyal advisers and escaped from his official residence barely half an hour before the rebels attacked it. Dr. Sun then boarded the warship "Yung-feng" and personally conducted fighting against the insurgents for almost two months. When he saw that it was useless to continue the fighting he left Canton for Hongkong and returned to Shanghai on August 14.

This unexpected turn of events had much to do with the future relations between the Kuomintang on the one hand and the Soviet Union and the Chinese Communist Party on the other. For being defeated by his own close follower made Dr. Sun realize that the Kuomintang was not closely knit as it should be. He was then determined to learn a lesson from the success of the Bolshevik revolution and to reorganize the Kuomintang completely.

In January, 1923 the Comintern adopted a resolution on the Chinese revolution that "in view of the weakness of the Chinese labor movement and of the inability of the Chinese working class to become a completely independent social force, it was necessary for the young Chinese Communist Party to seek the cooperation of the Kuomintang; that if the Kuomintang was able to pursue an objectively correct policy the Chinese Communist Party should lend a helping hand in all movements relating to the national revolutionary war; but that the Chinese Communist Party should never be amalgamated with the Kuomintang and to lose identity." [13]

Joffe who was then at Peking was instructed by Lenin to approach Dr. Sun at Shanghai. Joffe again proposed cooperation between the Kuomintang and the Chinese Communist Party and Dr. Sun who was then thinking of securing Soviet aid for his revolutionary cause was easily impressed by Joffe's argument. So after several conversations Dr. Sun and Joffe issued a joint declaration on January 26, 1923 stating: "Dr. Sun Yat-sen holds that the Communist order, or even the Soviet system cannot actually be introduced into China, because there do not exist here the conditions for the successsful establishment of either Communism or Sovietism. This view is entirely shared by M. Joffe, who is further of the opinion that China's paramount and pressing problem is to achieve national unification and attain full national independence, and regarding this task he had assured Dr. Sun Yat-sen that

China has the warmest sympathy of the Russian people and can count on the support of Russia." In this statement Joffe also declared to Dr. Sun "that the Russian Government is ready and willing to enter into negotiations with China on the basis of the renunciation by Russia of all the treaties and exactions which the Tsardom imposed on China, including the treaty or treaties and agreements relating to the Chinese Eastern Railway," and that the Russian Government had no intention to pursue an imperialistic policy in Outer Mongolia or to cause it to secede from China.[14] Satisfied with such explicit pledges Dr. Sun, in turn granted Joffe's request that members of the Chinese Communist Party be admitted as members of the Kuomintang.

At that time Chen Chiung-ming was ousted from Canton and Dr. Sun returned there in February, 1923. He assumed the title of Commander-in-Chief of the Armed Forces and established his headquarters. Then the so-called "cooperation with the Soviet Union" policy of the Kuomintang began to be put into effect. In August Dr. Sun sent General Chiang Kai-shek, a young soldier of 36 and his chief-of-staff, to Moscow "to discuss ways and means whereby our friends there can assist me in my work in this country."[15] Letters of introduction to Lenin, Trotsky and Chicherin by Dr. Sun were given to General Chiang who received favorable treatment in the Soviet capital. When Karakhan arrived at Peking in September letters of greetings were exchanged between him and Dr. Sun who informed Karakhan of General Chiang's mission.

On September 23 Karakhan wrote Dr. Sun that: "The absence in Canton of a permanent and responsible representative of our government has long been keenly felt at Moscow. With the appointment of M. M. Borodin an important step has been taken in this direction... Please regard Comrade Borodin not only as a representative of the Government but likewise my personal representative with whom you may talk as frankly as you would with me."[16] This act clearly showed the two-pronged policy of the Soviet Government towards China. On the one hand it sought for recognition by the Peking Government, and on the other it officially helped Dr. Sun and the Canton Government whose avowed policy was to overthrow the Peking regime.

Mikhail Marcovich Borodin (or Gruzenburg) was born in Russia, was brought up and educated in Latvia, and emigrated to the United States after spending some time in a Russian jail for his revolutionary activities. After the Russian revolution he returned to Moscow where his knowledge of English and Spanish became very useful in the Bolshevik camp. He had been first sent to Mexico and later to England to do party work and was now assigned the job of outwardly assisting the Kuomintang but actually grasping the power of the Kuomintang from within. He arrived at Canton on October 6, 1923, and was appointed by Dr. Sun high adviser to the Kuomintang. He brought with him a staff of Russian Communists and had vast financial resources placed at his disposal by the Soviet Government.

Meanwhile the Third National Congress of the Chinese Communist Party had been held at Canton in June of the same year and attended by twenty delegates representing some 300 members. It adopted a resolution that the Chinese Communist Party should lead the Chinese revolutionary movement but in view of the long history and experience of the Kuomintang the Chinese Communist Party had to acknowledge the latter as the central agency of the Chinese revolution. It decided to lay emphasis on the activities in Canton because the city was under the Kuomintang control and, taking advantage of the Kuomintang's acquiescence to propagate the labor and peasant movements. The fact that after two years' existence the Chinese Communist Party still had only 300 members almost all of whom were intellectuals clearly proved that the Communist movement was extremely unpopular among the masses of the Chinese people and that it did not originate as a workers' party.

At that time some Communists, such as Li Tai-chao, had already become Kuomintang members. So the Central Committee, in its plenary session in December adopted a resolution defining the work of those Communists who were also Kuomintang members as "the absorption of the best young members of the Kuomintang into the Communist fold, the splitting of it into left and right wings, and the initiation of a program to win over the former and isolate the latter".[17] This resolution which was kept a secret at that time clearly showed that the Communists never intended to sincerely cooperate with the Kuomintang but adopted from the very beginning the tactics of "divide and rule" towards it.

In December, 1923 Dr. Sun appointed nine influential Kuomintang members of whom one was a Communist, Tang Ping-shan, to form a Provisional Central Executive Committee whose duty was to register party membership, to organize party units from the bottom up, to select party cadre and to convene a National Congress. On December 12 a declaration was issued by Dr. Sun stating that past failures of the party were due to lack of strict organization and training and therefore it should be immediately reorganized. The First National Congress of the Kuomintang was held from January 20 to January 30, 1924 at Canton, and was attended by 165 delegates from all the provincial and overseas party branches. It was indeed an epoch-making event in the history of the Kuomintang.

In the first place it proclaimed a manifesto reiterating and defining the Three People's Principles and embodying a party platform on both domestic and foreign policies. Internationally it advocated the abolition of all unequal treaties; conclusion of new treaties based on equality and a mutual respect of sovereign rights; cancellation of foreign loans which "were put through by bribery or by any other illegal process, also such loans as were obtained solely for the purpose of financing the militarists in their purely personal campaigns, or to enable them to fill their own pockets,..." and the repayment of all legitimate foreign loans for which a conference should be called to discuss plans and measures. Domestically, it called for the distribution of power between the Central and provincial governments; local self-government; universal suffrage; freedoms of belief, residence, publication and speech; a system of civil examination; a system of conscription; labor laws; equality between the sexes; universal education; land reform; and state ownership of monopolistic enterprises.[18]

Secondly it adopted a new constitution which emphasized organization and discipline. The party structure was now organized into five echelons: the basic units were chu-fen-pu or sub-divisions; next higher were chu-tang-pu, or divisional branches; next higher were hsien-tang-pu and shih-tang-pu, or district and municipal branches; next higher were sheng-tang-pu or provincial branches, and finally there was the Chung-yang-tang-pu, or Central Party Headquarters. (This five-echelon organization has stayed ever since 1924.) Any member who disobeyed party resolutions or who said or did something in violation of the party's policies or principles was to be reprimanded or expelled.

Thirdly it passed a resolution to admit Chinese Communists to the Kuomintang as the latter's own members. Fourthly, a Central Executive Committee and a Central Supervisory Committee were set up in the Central Party Headquarters whose members were to be elected by the delegates of the National Congress. The Central Executive Committee was the highest authority in the party when the National Congress was not in session while the Central Supervisory Committee was in charge of disciplinary matters and saw to it that the party's policies were faithfully carried out. Thus instead of the former one-man rule in the party it had now a group of elected persons to direct party affairs. Dr. Sun, being the founder of the party, was proclaimed in the party constitution to be the Tsungli or Director-

General of the party for life and kept the power of veto over the Central Executive Committee.

Even before the National Congress many Kuomintang members had already become suspicious of the Communist motives in joining the party. Towards the end of November, 1923 a group of Kuomintang members led by Teng Tse-ju submitted a petition to Dr. Sun in which they exposed the intrigue of the Communists and severely condemned Chen Tu-hsiu. So when Dr. Sun introduced the resolution to admit Communists at the National Congress many delegates were opposed to it. It was only under the pressure of Dr. Sun and after Li Ta-chao, on behalf of the Communists, had announced their complete acceptance of the principles, policies, and discipline of the Kuomintang that the resolution was adopted. In the election of the members of the Central Executive Committee, upon the recommendation of Dr. Sun, Communists Tan Ping-shan, Li Ta-chao, and Yu Shu-teh were elected members, and Lin Tsu-han, Han Ling-fu, Mao Tse-tung, Chang Kuo-tao, Yu Fang Chow, Chang Wei-chuen and Chü Chiu-pai reserve members.

In the establishment of the Central Party Headquarters key positions were assigned to Communists. Tan Ping-shan became Director or Organization and Lin Tsu-han, Director of Peasant Affairs. Such an arrangement showed clearly how much Dr. Sun trusted the good faith of the Chinese Communists. But the Communists who believed the end justifies the means betrayed this trust from the very beginning. As soon as they infiltrated into the Central Party Headquarters they started their subversive work. They created the names of leftists and rightists among Kuomintang members and played one against the other. Taking advantage of his position, Tan Ping-shan sent Communists to various provinces and cities to organize local branches. These Communists controlled mass movements and induced students, workers and peasants to drift away from the Kuomintang and towards the Chinese Communist Party. Under the protective cover of the Kuomintang Communist organizations were extended and the membership of the Chinese Communist Party grew to 1500 within a year of their admission to the Kuomintang. Such subversive actions naturally aroused the enmity of many loyal Kuomintang members and they pleaded with Dr. Sun to expel the Communists from the party. But Dr. Sun, thinking of strengthening the revolutionary force, refused to do so.

Although Dr. Sun permitted Chinese Communists to join the Kuomintang and trusted them to work harmoniously with Kuomintang members for the success of the revolution he strongly objected to

Communism as unfit for China. In order to make Kuomintang members and the Chinese people in general better understand his ideals and the difference between them and Communism he gave eighteen public lectures on the Three People's Principles at Kwantung Normal College between January and August, 1924.

In his first lecture on the Ming-sheng-chu-i or Principle of People's Livelihood he said: "The Principle of People's Livelihood is socialism, it is Communism . . ."[19] Now this sentence was intended to remove the doubt in the minds of loyal Kuomintang members concerning the admission of Communists. But he went on to criticize the Marxist theories such as the material interpretation of history, class struggle, and surplus value. Dr. Sun maintained that "the problem of livelihood is the central force in social progress; and the social progress is the central force in history". He pointed out four economic achievements in recent years in Europe and the United States, viz: (1) improvement of the social conditions of the working class; (2) socialization of transportation and communications facilities; (3) creation of direct taxation; and (4) socialization of distribution. These achievements were caused not by class struggle but by the harmony of the economic interests of society, or by mutual understanding between capital and labor. "Class struggle, therefore, is not the cause of social progress, but a kind of social disease, which develops when a social group lacks the means of livelihood and resolves as the last resort to use abnormal means of obtaining its livelihood. Marx's trouble was that he mistook a social pathological condition for the cause of social progress; so rightly he should be called a 'social pathologist', not a 'social physiologist'." Marx's surplus value theory "overstressed the contribution of labor in the process of production, and neglected the contribution of society in general." Taking the huge net profit, or surplus value, of the cotton mills in China as an illustration, Dr. Sun asserted that the surplus value was contributed not only by the laborers in these mills, but also by farmers, agriculturists, manufacturers, inventors of machines, railway men, steamship crews, miners and consumers.[20] Borodin was present at this lecture and furiously argued with Dr. Sun afterwards for the latter's criticism of Marx.[21]

After spending three months in the Soviet Union General Chiang returned to China and submitted a memorandum to Dr. Sun in which he proposed among other things the establishment of a military academy to train cadre for the revolutionary army. The Whampoa Military Academy, after four months' preparatory work, was opened early in May, 1924, with approximately 500 cadets who came from every part of China and were anxious to serve the revolutionary cause. General Chiang was appointed its superintendent and devoted himself to cadre training. Meanwhile the Soviet Government had sent two generals to Canton to assist Dr. Sun in reorganizing the armed forces under him. General Kisanko, was appointed military adviser to the Canton Government and General Vasili Bluecher, under the assumed name of Galen, was assigned to the Whampoa Academy as its advisor. Under Kisanko Soviet officers of lesser rank were appointed advisers to every army and division. Political officers, most of whom were Communists, were also installed in the armed forces. These officers were supposed to teach the rank and file Dr. Sun's principles but secretely indoctrinated Communist theories. Chou En-lai, a Communist, later became the head of the Political Department of the Whampoa Academy.

Dr. Sun was bent upon a northern expedition to wipe out the war-lords and to unify China. On September 18, 1924 he issued a statement declaring the aim of the northern expedition to be the overthrow of war-lords Tsao-kün and Wu Pei-fu and the imperialism which supported them. Five weeks later, before the military campaign had begun, a coup d'etat took place at Peking by which Tsao-Kün was compelled to resign from the presidency of the Peking Government and Wu Pei-fu was later defeated by the joint forces of Feng Yu-hsiang and Chang Tso-lin. Tuan Chi-jui then became the Provincial Chief Executive of the Peking Government and invited Dr. Sun to Peking to solve political problems. Dr. Sun arrived at Peking on December 31. As he was already seriously ill with liver trouble he was confined to bed at his residence and never saw Tuan Chi-jui. Taking advantage of Dr. Sun's absence from Canton, Chen Chiung-ming attacked the city from the East river region. In February, 1925 Chen's troops were badly defeated by the newly formed revolutionary army under General Chiang Kai-shek and with Whampoa cadets as officers. This news made Dr. Sun happy in his sickbed but could not cure his illness. He died on March 12, at the age of 59, without seeing the unification of China under the revolutionary movement which he cherished so much.

Less than three months later an incident occurred at Shanghai which greatly strengthened the Communist position in China. On May 30, a demonstration of students and workers was staged in the international settlement of Shanghai as a gesture of sympathy for a worker who was killed and a dozen others who were wounded in a strike dispute in a Japanese textile mill. When the demonstrators paraded on Nanking Road the Municipal Police intervened and opened fire. As a result ten persons were killed, fifteen seriously wounded, and fifty-three arrested. The Communists at once took advantage of this incident to inaugurate an anti-imperialist, especially anti-British, (because the Shanghai Municipal Police was controlled by the British) movement. A Shanghai Labor Union was formed with Li Lih-san as its chairman and its 200,000 members immediately went on strike. Students, merchants, and even Chinese constables all joined the strike as a protest. It soon spread to other cities of the country and even overseas Chinese raised money to support the strikes. British and Japanese goods were boycotted. Then on June 23 another incident occurred at Canton in which dozens of paraders were killed and wounded by the British troops stationed at Shameen. Thereafter Chinese workers in Hongkong joined the strike and went back to Canton en masse. Under such circumstances it was easy for the Communists to appeal to the patriotism of the people and the membership of the Chinese Communist Party rose from 1500 in January, 1925 when the Fourth National Congress was held at Shanghai to over 10,000 at the end of the year. In December, 1925 the Soviet Government, seeing the rapid growth of the Chinese Communist Party, founded the Sun Yat-sen University at Moscow ostensibly as a memorial of Dr. Sun but actually to train cadres for the Chinese Communist Party.

When Dr. Sun left Canton in December, 1924 Hu Han-min served as Acting Commander-in-Chief. After his death a struggle for power developed between Hu and Wang Ching-wei, who had been friends of long standing. Wang, being a very ambitious man without a principle, sought the support of Borodin and the Communists by allying with them. So when the National Government was first formed on July 1, 1925 in accordance with the Program of National Reconstruction proclaimed by Dr. Sun in April, 1924, Wang was chosen as Chairman while Hu was appointed Minister for Foreign Affairs. About a month later, Minister of Finance Liao Chung-kai, another veteran Kuomintang member who was friendly towards the Communists (his son Liao Cheng-chi actually joined the Chinese Communist Party), was mysteriously assassinated. In taking advantage of this incident Wang and Borodin attacked Hu Han-min for complicity in the assassination and banished him from Canton. Thereafter, Borodin and Wang Ching-wei had the Kuomintang firmly in their grip, but General Chiang Kai-shek was rising rapidly both in power and prestige. The revolutionary army under his command, due to its strict discipline and intensive training, was growing into a formidable force. He annihilated war-lords Yang Si-ming and Liu Tseng-kuan's troops at the outskirts of Canton in June, wiped out the remnant forces of Chen Chiung-ming in the East river region in October, and suppressed the rebellion of Teng Peng-yin in southern Kwangtung in December. Thus the province of Kwangtung was unified under the National Government and could serve as a base for the revolutionary movement. Many people, especially youths, both inside and outside the Kuomintang, began to look to General Chiang for a new leadership.

As the Chinese Communists grew in number and in influence they quickened their pace in destroying the Kuomintang from within. The publications of the Chinese Communist Party even openly attacked the Kuomintang and criticized the Three People's Principles. A group of loyal members of the Central Executive Committee, mostly Dr. Sun's longtime followers such as Chang Chi, Chu Cheng, Hsieh Chih, Tsou Lu, etc., could no longer tolerate such a situation and decided to take action. They held a special session of the Central Executive Committee in December, 1925 at the Pi-yun Temple in the Western Hills near Peking where Dr. Sun's coffin was placed. (Hence the name Western Hills group.) They adopted a resolution to expel all Communists from the Kuomintang and to dismiss Borodin and other Soviet advisers for their treacherous actions. But they formed only a minority of the Central Executive Committee and the Central Party Headquarters condemned them for violating the party constitution which provided that plenary sessions of the Central Executive Committee must be held at the site of the National Government. The Western Hills group then established a Central Party Headquarters of their own at Shanghai. They convened their Second National Congress in 1926 and elected their Central Executive and Supervisory Committees. Thus the Kuomintang was split wide open to the delight and satisfaction of the Communists.

The Second National Congress of the Kuomintang was held at Canton on January 4, 1926 and lasted sixteen days. Of the 250 delegates over 100 were Communists. These Communists and the so-called leftists under the leadership of Wang Ching-wei dominated the Congress. It adopted strong disciplinary measures against the Western Hills group in order to teach the anti-Communist elements in the party a lesson. Fourteen Communists were elected members and reserve members of the Central Executive Committee (approximately one-fourth of the total number) and three of them were elected members of the Standing Committee of the Central Executive Committee (one-third of the total number). In the reconstructed Central Party Headquarters Tan Ping-shan and Lin Tsu-han remained Directors of Organization and Peasant Affairs respectively, Mao Tse-tung was made Deputy-Director of Publicity, and four more Communists were appointed secretaries in the Departments of Women, Labor, and Overseas Affairs and in the secretariat, Mao was concurrently Director of the Peasant Movement Training Center and there he had the chance to train cadres for future peasant uprisings.

Realizing that General Chiang was the only man who could succeed Dr. Sun as the leader of the Kuomintang and thus the only obstacle to his completely taking over the Kuomintang, Borodin now concentrated his efforts on ousting Chiang from power. Young Communists who had infiltrated into the Whampoa Academy formed a Young Soldiers' Union to create troubles in the academy. General Chiang had a hard time fighting against Communist intrigue and yet not breaking openly with them. Borodin even tried to force Chiang to leave Canton like he had done to Hu Han-min. At one time the pressure was so great and the future of the struggle was so uncertain that General Chiang became pessimistic. So one day in February 1926 he drove down with Chen Li-fu, his secretary and confidant, from his residence at Canton, to the wharf to board a steamer for Hongkong whence he would go to Shanghai. But before the limousine had reached the wharf he suddenly said to Chen with clenched fists: "Li-fu, we will fight on for our cause and must not give up." Thereupon he ordered the chauffeur to turn back to his residence.[22]

Borodin then conceived a daring plot to exile Chiang according to which Chiang would be lured to board the warship "Chung-shan" (former S.S. "Yung-feng") and kept as a prisoner there while the vessel steamed at full speed to Vladivostok where Chiang would be handed to Soviet authorities and sent to Moscow. The Communist controlled labor unions would declare a general strike and create chaos and disturbances. Borodin then left Canton for North China to confer with Feng Yu-hsiang and entrusted Kisanko to carry out the plot.

Fortunately for China, an influential Chinese Communist named Wu, who remained an admirer of Chiang, learned of the plot and informed Chiang at midnight of March 19.[23] General Chiang took prompt action the next day. Li Chih-lung, acting chief of the Naval Bureau, a Whampoa graduate and a Communist, who had sent the "Chung-shan" to Whampoa without orders from higher authorities, was arrested and Soviet military advisers were detained in their houses. The labor unions were closed and the Canton Headquarters of the Canton-Hongkong Strike Committee was disarmed. Wang Ching-wei immediately left Canton under the pretext of poor health and went abroad.

At that time many loyal Kuomintang members expected that General Chiang would break with the Soviet Union and the Communists completely. But General Chiang was thinking of Soviet military supplies which were on their way to Canton and which were badly needed to carry out the northern expedition as wished by Dr. Sun. So he compromised and did not go to the extreme. Kisanko and some Soviet military advisers who were directly involved in the conspiracy were sent back to Moscow but others remained. The Young Soldiers' Union was dissolved. On the Soviet side Stalin also did not want to end his cooperation with the Kuomintang. Voitinsky, writing in *International Press Correspondence,* simply dismissed reports of Chiang's action in foreign newspapers as imperialist propaganda.[24] When Borodin returned to Canton in May he recognized the fait accompli and kept cordial relations with Chiang for the sake of appearence. General Bluecher was then on leave of absence at Moscow and probably knew nothing about the plot. He was welcomed back to China by General Chiang to succeed Kisanko as the head of the Soviet military advisers.

On May 15, a plenary session of the Central Executive Committee adopted a resolution, introduced by General Chiang, to the effect that Communists should not form more than one-third of the Committee members in the Central Party Headquarters and provincial branches; that they could not be directors of departments in the Central Party Headquarters; that the Chinese Communist Party should hand over to the Central Party Headquarters a complete list of the names of those Communists who had joined the Kuomintang; and that all instructions given by the Chinese Communist Party to Communists inside the Kuomintang should be first submitted to a Kuomintang-Chinese Communist Party joint session for approval.[25] Thereupon Tan Ping-shan, Lin Tsu-han and Mao Tse-tung were relieved of their positions as directors and deputy-director. Although the Communists did not faithfully carry out the provisions in this resolution their subversive work within the Kuomintang was checked for the time being.

CHAPTER XI

From the Northern Expedition to the Communist Insurrections

With the temporary settlement of the Kuomintang-Chinese Communist Party disputes and the arrival of Soviet military supplies consisting of howitzers, machine guns, rifles and ammunition, preparations for a northern expedition began earnestly in the spring of 1926. The same plenary session of the Central Executive Committee which adopted the resolution to regulate the relations between the Kuomintang and the Chinese Communist Party on May 15 also adopted a resolution to launch the northern expedition. The military forces under the National Government were reorganized into seven armies of the National Revolutionary Army and General Chiang Kai-shek was appointed its Commander-in-Chief (hence the title Generalissimo).

On July 9, the Generalissimo assumed his command at a solemn ceremony and the expedition immediately started. The main force under the personal command of the Generalissimo and with General Bluecher as the chief military adviser pushed northward from Kwangtung into Hunan, while the Eastern Route Army commanded by General Ho Yin-ching advanced from the East river region into Fukien. Due to the strict discipline and high morale of the National Revolutionary Army the northern expedition met with quicker success than expected. From the beginning the revolutionary troops not only fought bravely but kept close relations with the people. On the other hand the soldiers of the war-lords were usually unruly and were hated by the people. Consequently, when the troops of the war-lords passed through towns and villages the townsmen and peasants fled to the hill and woods; while when the revolutionary troops appeared they lined the streets and roads to cheer them, offered food and drinks, and volunteered their services as guides.

Within two and a half months the troops under war-lord Wu Pei-fu in Hunan and Hupei were crushed despite their numerical superiority to the revolutionary forces and the two provinces were occupied. The walled city of Wuchang, capital of Hupei, held out longer and was not taken until October 10. At the end of September the Generalissimo led his troops eastward into Kiangsi. There he again crushed the troops of war-lord Sun Chuan-fang and the province was taken early in November. Thereupon it was generally believed that the war-lords would all be wiped out and the National Revolutionary Army would eventually unify China. So many generals in Szechuan, Kweichow, Anhwei, etc., simply swore their allegiance to the National Government and changed their flag.

As the Generalissimo rose rapidly in popularity and prestige the Communists became more and more jealous and hated him intensly. They did everything possible to stop his advance but failed. After the capture of the Wuhan cities (Wuchang, Hankow and Hanyang) the Kuomintang and the National Government decided in November to move their headqquarters there as those cities were more centrally located than Canton. As Generalissimo Chiang had now to conduct the campaign at Nanchang, capital of Kiangsi, Hunan and Hupei, including the Wuhan cities, were controlled by the troops under General Tang Sheng-chi, a longtime Kuomintang member but a very ambitious man. Taking advantage of this situation Borodin and some Chinese Communists approached Tang for a secret alliance against the Generalissimo to which Tang readily agreed for his personal aim to replace Chiang himself. Anti-Chiang posters, speeches and newspaper articles began to appear in the Wuhan cities. When the members of the Kuomintang Central Committees as well as high officials of the National Government passed through Nanchang on their way to Hankow in December, 1926 the Generalissimo pursuaded them to stay in Nanchang. But the Communists and Kuomintang leftists who regarded Wang Ching-wei as their leader, refused to comply and moved on to Hankow in February, 1927.

Meanwhile the Seventh Plenum of the Comintern took place towards the end of November. In his opening speech Nicolai Bukharin declared: "We address ourselves to the great Chinese people who stand in a gigantic revolutionary liberation struggle. We promise in the name of the entire Communist International, in the name of the whole working class of the world, that we will support this world historical struggle with all means, with all forces, at any price."[1] Tan Ping-shan, one of the speakers at the Plenum, analyzed the membership of the Kuomintang into five groups: (1) the extreme Right representing the interests of compradors and big landowners; (2) the Right Wing, composed of big bourgeoisie, wealthy emigrated merchants and well-to-do peasants; (3) the Middle Wing, represented by Tai Chi-tao, the ideologist, and Chiang Kai-shek, the military man;

(4) the Left Wing of the middle and petty bourgeoisie; and (5) the Communist Wing, including all Communists working within the Kuomintang, all urban proletarians and landless peasants. The real power of the Kuomintang, according to Tan, lay in the Left Wing which controlled nine-tenths of its organizations. The task of the Communists should be to support the Left Wing in opposition to the Right and to isolate the Middle Wing.[2]

The Plenum adopted a thesis on the Chinese question, prepared by Bukharin, Andrei S. Bubrov, and M. N. Roy, an Indian Communist, which emphasized agranian revolution through the channels of the Kuomintang. "If the proletariat does not put forward a radical agrarian program," according to the thesis, "it will fail to attract the peasantry into the revolutionary struggle and will lose hegemony in the national revolutionary movement." After reaching the peasantry the Communists could develop the Kuomintang "into a real people's party—a solid revolutionary bloc of the proletariat, peasantry, the urban bourgeoisie and other oppressed and exploited strata".[3] After the Plenum Stalin sent Roy to China to carry out the program in the thesis.

In all the newly occupied provinces Communists now propagated the mass movements. They organized labor, peasants', shop employees' and students' unions, ostensibly under the direction of the Kuomintang but actually with pro-Communist and anti-Kuomintang leanings. The work was especially carried out in Hunan and Hupei due to the pro-Communist attitude of Tang Sheng-chi. Communists there agitated workers to seize factories, and shop employees to seize shops. Capitalists, merchants and landowners were arrested, jailed, tortured or even executed. The good reputation and popular support earned by the Revolutionary Army at the beginning of the expedition were now counter-balanced by the atrocities committed by the Communists. The Generalissimo and other loyal Kuomintang members disapproved such actions and tended to check the activities of these Communist-controlled unions in the areas under their control. Thus the rift between the Generalissimo and the Communists grew wider and wider.

The military campaign, however, continued unabated. The Eastern Route Army had occupied Fukien in December, 1926 and Chekiang in February, 1927. The Generalissimo moved his headquarters to Anking, capital of Anhwei, early in March for the operations in the lower Yangtze. On March 23, Nanking fell into the hands of the Sixth Army. In order to put the Generalissimo in trouble and discredit him before the eyes of the world, the political officers of that army who were almost all Communists, instigated soldiers to loot and burn the residences of foreigners in that city. Some foreign missionaries and consular officials were murdered by the unruly soldiers. The United States and British gunboats stationed in the Yangtze to the north of the city opened fire and killed a number of Chinese. But the mutinous elements were soon arrested by loyal troops and were punished and order was restored.

The situation at Shanghai was even more serious. Taking advantage of the complete demoralization of the garrison forces the Communist-controlled Labor Union was ready to disarm these troops and take the affairs of Shanghai into their own hands. Had the Communist plot materialized a reign of terror would have taken place. Fortunately, the Generalissimo ordered the Eastern Route Army to rush to the scene. It occupied Shanghai on March 22 and some days later dissolved the unruly Labor Union. Thus no incidents occurred and the situation was secured.

At this juncture, Wang Ching-wei returned from Europe. In Shanghai he conferred with the Generalissimo concerning the political situation, but secretly conspired with Chen Tu-hsiu, the Communist leader. At the beginning of April he suddenly left for Hankow without notifying either Chiang or other Kuomintang leaders. Immediately after his departure a joint statement by Wang and Chen Tu-hsiu was issued on April 5, in which they emphasized the necessity of the alliance between the Kuomintang and the Communist Party and dismissed all news concerning disruption between them as rumors.[4]

Meanwhile, at Nanchang, the first open struggle between the Kuomintang and the Communists occurred. During the rule of the warlords, the provincial party branch, like those in many other provinces, was controlled by Communists. After the occupation of Nanchang a provincial party convention was held in December, 1926 and provincial government appointed by the National Government when it the efforts of loyal Kuomintang delegates out of the nine members of the executive committee only two were Communists. The provincial government appointed by the National Government when it passed through Nanchang in January, 1927, consisted of only loyal Kuomintang members. General Li Lieh-chün, a veteran Kuomintang member and a native of Kiangsi, was appointed chairman of the provincial government. General Chu Pei-teh, commander of the Third Army which had taken part in the conquest of Kiangsi and which now garrisoned Nanchang, was appointed a member and was dissatisfied. The municipal party branch was in the hands of Communists and defied the decision of the provincial executive committee to reorganize it. The Communists also controlled the Labor Union, Peasants' Union and Students' Union and made troubles in the name of these civic organizations. General Chu Pei-teh took a neutral attitude towards the Kuomintang-Chinese Communist Party struggle while Chu Ko-ching, head of the Political Department of the Third Army and Chu Teh, commander of the Training Regiment and concurrently chief of police of Nanchang, both Communists themselves, gave support to the Communists. The provincial government was reorganized by the Wuhan Government on April 1 and General Chu Pei-teh was appointed chairman. The next day the Communists struck. Several hundred students and labor pickets attacked provincial party office with revolvers, rods and spears. Nine loyal Kuomintang members were wounded and arrested,[5] and the provincial party committees were dissolved.

With the arrival of Wang Ching-wei at Hankow on April 10 the position of the Communists and Kuomintang leftists was strengthened. The Wuhan Government then abolished the position of the Commander-in-Chief of the National Revolutionary Army, created five army corps and appointed Generalissimo Chiang one of the five commanders. Subsequently the Wuhan Government ordered Chiang's arrest for his "anti-revolutionary" activities. Loyal members of the Kuomintang were branded as Chiang's henchmen and were jailed or put to death. Under such circumstances the Kuomintang had to take some drastic action. A Central Party Headquarters was set up in Nanking and on April 12 the Central Executive Committee held a special meeting, unanimously approved the impeachment of Communists by Wu Chih-hui, a veteran member of the Central Supervisory Committee and adopted a resolution to purge Communists. That night important Communists hidden in Nanking, Shanghai, Canton and other cities under the Kuomintang rule were rounded up and put on trial. Those who had committed crimes were punished. Soviet military advisers had either fled to Hankow or were sent back to Moscow. On April 18 the National Government was established at Nanking with Hu Han-min as its chairman and the military campaign of the northern expedition continued.

In the meantime the Peking Government under Marshal Chang Tso-lin also had a showdown with the Soviet Union. Ever since its establishment the Soviet embassy at Peking had become the headquarters of Communist activities and intrigues in North China. Chang Tso-lin, after the defeat of Wu Pei-fu by the Revolutionary Army, went to Peking in November, 1926 and took over the Peking Governmen. Thereafter he adopted strong measures against both Kuomintang members and Communists. Students of both parties were arrested and prominent Communists sought safety in the Soviet embassy.

In March, 1927 there were rumors that Communists would soon stage an uprising in Tientsin and foreigners were evacuating the city. A messenger boy who delivered notices for the Communist meetings at the Soviet embassy was caught by the Peking police and concrete evidence of the conspiracy was obtained. Chang Tso-lin then decided to search the Soviet embassy and his headquarters negotiated with the Dutch minister, William Oudendyk, who, being the "Senior Minister", acted as the dean of the Diplomatic Corps in the absence of the Soviet ambassador, for the permission to enter the Legation Quarter.[6] This permission was obtained and Wu Chin, Foreign Commissioner of Chang Tso-in's headquarters, led a large body of police and searched the offices of the military attaché, the Chinese Eastern Railway and the Boxer Indemnity Fund on the morning of April 6. More than six Chinese Communist suspects and 19 Russians were arrested by the police.

The Communists, as soon as they knew a raid was on, set the office of the military attaché on fire. Minister Oudendyk who was an eyewitness, described the scene thus: "Suddenly a great column of smoke was seen rising from the western part of the barrack. Before long a Chinese fire engine was brought to the scene, and a hose was laid over the building and water pumped down the chimney. This quenched the fire, but an enormus quantity of documents, and no doubt the most incriminating ones, must have meanwhile perished in the flames . . ."[7] Enough secret documents were seized to prove the plot of the Soviet Union to communize China, and its close relations with the Chinese Communist Party. These documents were later published by the Waichiaopu of the Peking Government.[8] The Soviet Government naturally dismissed them as forgeries but no person with an open mind who cares to read them will doubt their authenticity. The arrested Chinese Communists were tried by a special tribunal headed by a general. Twenty of them including Li Ta-chao and Lu Yu-yü were sentenced to death and the rest to imprisonment of from 2 to 12 years. The Russians were not sentenced and were set free in June, 1928 when the Revolutionary Army conquered Peking.

The Peking Government immediately protested to Soviet Charge d'Affairs Chernik for fostering Communist activities against China in violation of the Sino-Soviet Agreement of 1924. On the other hand the Soviet Government was indignant over this incident. At its instigation mass demonstrations took place in many cities. Chicherin, acting Commissar for Foreign Affairs, handed Cheng Yen-hsi, Chinese charge d' affairs, a strong protest demanding: (1) the withdrawal of Chinese troops and police from the office of the embassy; (2) the immediate release of the arrested Russians; (3) the return of all documents taken from the office of the military attaché; and (4) the return of all articles taken by the troops and police to the proper owners. Upon the rejection of these demands by the Peking Government Chernik and other officials of the Soviet embassy were all recalled. They left Peking on April 19 and the Soviet embassy was closed. But Soviet consulates in Manchuia and in South China remained. Cheng Yen-hsi and Chinese consular officials also stayed on in the Soviet Union.

At that time the struggle for power between Stalin and Trotsky in the Soviet Union was at its height. Stalin controlled the Communist Party but Trotsky was still leading a strong opposition. Stalin had been in favor of cooperation of the Chinese Communists with the Kuomintang while Trotsky had always opposed this idea and advocated independent actions for the Chinese Communist Party. So after the purge of Communists in Nanking the Trotskyites attacked Stalin for this setback in China and demanded immediate Communist withdrawal from the Kuomintang at Wuhan and the formation of Soviets. Stalin argued that such an action would mean "to weaken the Communist Party, to undermine the revolutionary Kuomintang (Left Wing) ... and to deliver the flag of the Kuomintang, the most popular flag in China, into the hands of the Right Wing members of the Kuomintang ... It follows, therefore, that the Opposition . . is playing into the hands of the enemies ..."[9] The Comintern then directed the Chinese Communist Party to support the Kuomintang Left, to develop the agrarian revolution in the areas under the control of the Wuhan Government and to conduct an intensive campaign of agitation and disruption within the forces of Nanking.

At the end of April the Chinese Communist Party convened its Fifth National Congress at Hankow. It was attended by about a hundred delegates representing 58,000 members, almost forty times as many as at the time of the Fourth National Congress. The congress accepted the Comintern's resolution on the Chinese question and adopted a resolution to carry out the agrarian revolution. Chu Chiu-pai and Jen Pei-hsi attacked Chen Tu-hsiu for his opportunism and a resolution condemning opportunism was passed. But despite it Chen was again chosen as the secretary-general of the Chinese Communist Party.

Although Wang Ching-wei had declared that Kuomintang members and Communists should live and die together the cooperation between the so-called Kuomintang Left and the Chinese Communist Party did not last long. Borodin had become the power behind the throne and resorted to torture and murder to cow the people into submission. A ruthless G.P.U. inspector, Petroff, was sent by Moscow to Wuhan to spread the reign of terror. Roy had also agitated the confiscation of farmland belonging to landowners. In the Kuomintang Central Party Headquarters at Wuhan, Communist members of the Central Executive Committee proposed formally to adopt such a policy and put it into practice in Hunan as an experiment. Owing to the opposition of Wang Ching-wei this proposal was not adopted. But Communists in Hunan, under the directions of Roy, put it into practice anyway.

The Communist-controlled peasants' unions seized farm land which exceeded 3 or 4 acres and jailed or executed landowners. Many military officers who came from landowning families and who were fighting at the front heard the news that their land was confiscated and their parents or brothers were liquidated. A group of these officers who were stationed at Changsha, capital of Hunan, could tolerate the situation no longer; under the leadership of General Hsu Ko-hsiang, a division commander, they took matters into their own hands. On May 21 they dissolved the Communist-controlled provincial party branch, and labor, peasants', and students' unions and arrested prominent Communists. When the news reached Hankow Borodin and other Communists proposed that the Central Executive Committee should order an attack on the revolting units and severely punish the guilty officers. Wang Ching-wei, knowing that other commanding generals sympathized with Hsu Ko-hsiang, only agreed to send General Tang Sheng-chi, chairman of the Hunan Provincial Government, to investigate the affair and to restore order. Thereupon the Communists began to attack Wang and the Kuomintang Left Wing.

Meanwhile the Eighth Plenum of the Comintern had taken place in Moscow. It again endorsed Stalin's policy toward China and condemned the opposition. Dissatisfied with the work of the Chinese Communist Party, Stalin gave a new directive to Borodin and Roy. It read in part: "Without an agrarian revolution victory is impossible. Without it the Central Committee of the Kuomintang will be converted into a wretched plaything by unreliable generals . . . We are decidedly in favor of the land actually being seized by the masses from below . . . A large number of new peasant and working class leaders from the ranks must be drawn into the Central Committee of the Kuomintang . . . (It is necessary to liquidate the unreliable generals immediately.)[10] This dependence upon unreliable generals must be put to an end. Mobilize about 20,000 Communists and about 50,000 revolutionary workers and peasants from Hunan and Hupei, form several new army corps, utilize the students of the school for commanders, and organize your own reliable army before it is too late . . . Organize a revolutionary tribunal headed by prominent non-Communist Kuomintangists. Punish officers who maintain contact with Chiang Kai-shek or who set soldiers on the people, the workers and the peasants. Persuasion is not enough. It is time to act. The scoundrels must be punished."[11]

This directive in the form of a telegram reached Hankow sometime towards the end of May. Borodin decided to keep it a secret, fearing that it would certainly alienate the Kuomintang leaders. But Roy invited Wang Ching-wei to meet him on June 1 and showed Wang the original Russian text and its Chinese translation. Wang Ching-wei was astonished on learning Stalin's attitude and told Roy that on no account could the Kuomintang accept the conditions in the telegram. Upon Wang's request Roy sent a copy of the telegram to Wang the next day with the remark: "I am glad I have shown you the telegram which you can take as an ultimatum. If you accept the tenor of the telegram and grant facilities for its execution, the Comintern will continue to cooperate with you. If not, it will have nothing to do with the Kuomintang." Wang replied: "The conditions for cooperation between the Kuomintang and the Third International laid down by Joffe and Borodin in 1923 were entirely different from these presented in your ultimatum. It is not for us to refuse your conditions, for it is you who have violated the agreement."[12] When Borodin learned that Roy had handed over the telegram to Wang he was very much annoyed and at once requested Stalin to recall Roy. Roy defended his position by arguing that as the Kuomintang Left Wing could only survive when in alliance with the Communists they should be informed of the directive. A majority of the Chinese Communists agreed with Borodin and blamed Roy for his reckless action. Soon after the episode Roy left Hankow for the Soviet Union.

Subsequent events proved the correctness of Borodin's view. Upon learning the plot of the Comintern Wang Ching-wei immediately conferred with other Kuomintang leaders then in Hankow. Most of them felt indignant over the telegram and wanted the expulsion of the Communists from the Kuomintang but a few like Madame Sun Yat-sen and Eugene Chen advised caution because military operations were still in progress and Soviet help was needed. After ten days' secret discussions at Wang's residence the Presidium of the Government Council made a decision to take immediate measures for the expulsion of the Communists. This decision was kept a top secret for the Communists had already infiltrated into the National Revolutionary Army under the Wuhan Government and the news of their repulsion might easily bring about a revolt. So loyal troops were ordered to return to the vicinity of Wuhan to prepare for any emergency.

Finally on July 15, Wang proposed in the Political Council of the Central Executive Committee the expulsion of the Communists. The Communist members, sensing what was in store, did not attend the meeting, neither did Madame Sun and Eugene Chen, and the council unanimously adopted Wang's proposal. The Kuomintang now recognized the Chinese Communist Party as a political as distinct from a governing party with its individual members fully enjoying the rights of citizenship. Borodin's resignation which had been tendered some time ago was accepted at the meeting. He left Hankow on July 27 and went back to the Soviet Union via Mongolia. Communist members in the Wuhan Government had also resigned their posts but the Chinese Communist Party instructed its members not to withdraw from the Kuomintang but to utilize evey opportunity to incite disorder and destroy the party from within.

Even before July 15 reports of the impending break between the Kuomintang Left Wing and the Chinese Communist Party had reached Moscow. The Executive Committee of the Comintern then adopted a resolution on the Chinese revolution on July 14. This resolution denounced the Kuomintang Left Wing that dispite the advice of the Comintern they had not only deprived the agrarian revolution of their support but had "sanctioned the disarmament of the workmen, the sending of punitive expeditions against the peasants, and the repressions by Tan Shen-tsi (Tang Sheng-chi) and others". It also blamed the Chinese Communist Party for the Wuhan failures. "The present leadership of the Chinese Communist Party has committed recently several grave blunders. The Chinese Communist Party should, according to the directions of the Comintern, welcome and advance the agrarian revolution, openly criticize and unmask the indefinite and cowardly position taken by the 'radical' leaders of the Wuhan Government and of the Central Committee of the Kuomintang, warn the masses about the possibility of betrayals on the part of the generals, arm more and more of the workingmen and push with all possible energy the Kuomintang and the National Government towards the true revolutionary road. Neither the Central Committee nor the Polit-bureau of the Chinese Communist Party has fulfilled those directions." The Comintern then instructed the Chinese Communists to withdraw from the Wuhan Government but not to leave the Kuomintang, to intensify their work among the workers and peasants, to build up militant extra-legal apparatus of the party, to strengthen the ties of the rank and file on the basis of Comintern resolutions and to get rid of the opportunism of the present leadership of the party.[13]

Meanwhile Stalin sent two other Communist agents to China: Besso Lominadse, a Georgian of 29, and Heinz Neumann, a German of 26. Lominadse carried instructions for a military uprising against the Wuhan Government. Upon his arrival at Hankow the Communists who had infiltrated into the Revolutionary Army immediately took action. Ho Lung, commander of the 20th Army and Yeh Ting, commander of the 24th Division, both Communists, suddenly marched their troops to Nanchang without orders from their superiors. At Nanchang Chu Teh, Chang Kuo-tao, and Chou En-lai joined them and staged a military coup on July 31 with about 20,000 troops. A Revolutionary Committee was established to carry on the agrarian revolution and a reign of terror soon prevailed. But loyal troops under General Chu Pei-teh and General Chang Fa-kwei soon attacked the city and the revolt was suppressed within five days. The Communists fled southward to Kwangtung and captured Swatow on September 24. This news was reported with jubilance in the Comintern publication *International Press Correspondence,* which even predicted an advance on Canton.[14] But the joy was short-lived; the insurgents were soon dispersed by government troops.

After the failure of the Nanchang revolt, on August 7 Chu Chiu-pai, under the direction of Lominadse and Neumann called a special conference of the Chinese Communist Party in great haste to which twelve regular members and three alternate members of the Central Committee attended. In this conference Chen Tu-hsiu and Tan Ping-shan who were absent, were severely condemned and dropped from positions of leadership. An emergency "Politburo," including Chu Chiu-pai, Hsiang Chung-fa, Li Lih-san, Mao Tse-tung, Chou En-lai, Li Wei-han and Liu Shao-chi, was set up to direct party affairs and Chü Chiu-pai replaced Chen Tu-hsiu as secretary-general. In a circular letter to all party members the conference declared: "The CI (Comintern) has severely criticized the opportunist line of the

CC, (Central Committee) which has in reality betrayed the Chinese revolution. We agree that this criticism is entirely just and the policy of the Comintern regarding the Chinese problem is entirely correct. We welcome recent instructions of the Comintern which have made possible the unmasking of the past mistakes of the (party) leadership and have saved our party (from destruction). We positively agree that in the past the leadership of the CC carried out an opportunist, unrevolutionary policy and that it is necessary to carry out a thorough revision of our policy on the basis of lessons of the past"[15] The conference also resolved to break away from the Kuomintang and to devote the Chinese Communist Party to the agrarian revolution, armed uprisings against the Kuomintang and the creation of Chinese Soviets.

After the conference Mao Tse-tung went back to Changsha to organize an Autumn Crop Uprising. The purpose of the insurrections, according to Mao, was to achieve a final severing of the Communist-Kuomintang alliance on local levels; to organize a peasant-workers' army; to confiscate the property of small, middle and large landlords; to set up Communist power in Hunan independent of the Kuomintang; and to organize Soviets."[16] Some 5,000 peasants were organized by Mao into the 1st Division of the Chinese Workers' and Peasants' Army and the uprising broke out on September 8. The area affected included Pinkiang, Liuyang, Liling and Chuchow in Hunan, and Pinchi, Hsienning, Chiayu, Tungshan, and Chingyang in Hupei. The original object of Mao was to occupy Changsha but these peasants who had no training in fighting were soon crushed by government troops. Mao fled with a remnant force of 400 men to Chingkangshan in Ningkang district of Kiangsi. As this uprising had not been sanctioned by the Central Committee of the Chinese Communst Party Mao was repudiated by the committee after its failure. He was dropped from the Politburo and from the Party Front Committee.[17]

There were more Communist insurrections in the latter part of 1927. In Kwangtung, Peng Pai, head of the Communist peasant movement, used the remnant troops of the Nanchang revolt as a nucleus, gathered several thousand local peasants and started a peasant uprising on October 30. The insurgents occupied Haifeng and Lufeng, two districts in the East river region, and immediately set up a Soviet Government. Land was redistributed, title deeds were burned and landowners and gentry were liquidated. They held out over a month and were finally suppressed. Another uprising, led by Liu Tsu-tan, broke out at Weinan and Huaying, Shensi and after its collapse the insurgents fled to the northern part of the province where they laid the foundation for a later Communist base at Yenan. Sporadic and minor uprisings also occurred in several districts in Kiangsu and Chekiang but they were all short-lived.

When the Communists were in Swatow, Chü Chiu-pai from Communist headquarters in Shanghai wired Chang Tai-lei, a Communist leader in Canton, that the enemy was ready to retreat and that an insurrection should be staged in Canton. Chang wired back that "The objective situation in Canton is not really favorable to insurrection." Even after the defeat at Swatow, Chü Chiu-pai again asked Chang Tai-lei to start an insurrection no matter how difficult the circumstances were, because that was the order from the Comintern. When the 15th Congress of the Communist Party of the Soviet Union took place in November, 1927 Lominadse reported the defeats suffered by the Chinese Communist Party during recent months and declared that the fundamental reason for these defeats was that the rise of labor and peasant movements had not coincided. "The question now confronting the party in Kwangtung and several other provinces", according to Lominadse, "is that of taking up a struggle for power and the organization of armed insurrection".[18] Stalin was then using the 15th Congress to force a purge of Trotskyites from the party and wanted a victory in China to cover up "the physical extermination of the Russian opposition".[19] Consequently the Comintern sent one or two cables every day urging insurrections in other cities. "They badly needed insurrections and a Soviet Government", as recorded by Li Ang, "even if it lasted three minutes . . ."[20]

Under such circumstances the Chinese Communists had to comply, otherwise they would be expelled by the Comintern. The situation in Canton also gave them a chance. General Li Chi-shen and General Chang Fa-kwei, then stationed at Canton, were engaged in a struggle for complete control of Kwantung. On November 17, Chang Fa-kwei, supported by Wang Ching-wei, had staged a coup and Li Chi-shen was ousted from Canton. After that Chang's troops were fighting against those under Li outside of Canton. Two regiments under the command of Yeh Chien-ying, a Communist, remained in Canton for garrison duties. Chang Tai-lei, Yun Tai-ying, Yeh Ting and Peng Pai now all came to Canton and a military uprising known as the Canton Commune, was staged early in the morning of December 11. A Soviet Government was immediately set up with Su Chao-cheng as its chairman. Thousands of coolies and vagabonds were recruited into the insurgents and Yeh Ting was appointed Commander-in-Chief. Slogans such as "Bread for the workers!, Land for the peasants!, Down with the power of the Kuomintang!, All power to the workers, peasants, and soldiers!, All powers to the Soviets!," etc., were posted.

A policy of arson and massacre was adopted. In three days more than 1500 houses were burned down and 2300 people were slaughtered.

On hearing of the revolt, Chang Fa-kwei hurried back with loyal troops and attacked the city on December 13. Members of the Labor Union and the Merchants' Union also organized "Dare-to-die Corps" to attack the so-called Soviet Government. Thus the insurrection was crushed in three days. Chang Tai-lei was killed and other Communist leaders fled. During the insurrection the Soviet consulate was used as a revolutionary headquarters and consular officials took active part in it. When loyal troops entered the city Soviet Vice-Consul Abram Isaakovich Hassis was caught with an assistant in front of the Communist headquarters. The inmates of consulate were arrested and five consular officials who participated in the insurrection were shot. The National Government at Nanking then withdrew its recognition of the Soviet consulates at Canton, Shanghai, and Hankow and closed all Soviet state enterprises there. Consular officials and employees of the state enterprises were sent back to Moscow.

When this news reached Moscow the 15th Congress was still in session and it resolved that despite the failure of the Canton Soviet the Chinese revolution was gathering its force for a new beginning and a broader offensive along all fronts. In February, 1928 the 9th Plenum of the Executive Committee of the Comintern adopted a resolution on the Canton Uprising presented by Stalin. This resolution listed a whole series of blunders such as: insufficient preliminary work among workers and peasants; insufficient subversion of enemy forces, a faulty appraisal of the loyalty of non-Communist workers, insufficient organization of strikes, improper organization of the Chinese Communist Party and Young Communist League, etc. It held Neumann and some others as partially accountable for the defeat and declared: "To play with insurrections instead of organizing a mass uprising of the workers and peasants is a sure way of losing the revolution." Stalin maintained that although the first revolutionary war was over worker and peasant movements in China would move towards another mighty upsurge. The work of the Chinese Communist Party hereafter was to win over the masses and to unite many small guerrilla units into one common National Red Army so as to carry out the agrarian revolution.[21]

CHAPTER XII

Sino-Soviet Hostility Over the Chinese Eastern Railway

In June, 1928, the National Revolutionary Army occupied Peking. All the powers except the Soviet Union now recognized the National Government at Nanking as the de jure government of China. But the Chinese charge d'affaires at Moscow and consular officials in the Soviet Union appointed by the Peking Government were not recalled and continued to hold their posts. The Soviet consular officials in Manchuria also stayed in their offices after Chang Hsueh-liang, son of Chang Tso-lin, declared his allegiance to the National Government at the end of 1928. Thus although the National Government of China and the Soviet Government of Russia did not recognize each other, some informal relations remained. The reason for this rather abnormal relationship between the two countries was the existence of the Chinese Eastern Railway, which had to be jointly managed, and the settlement of tens of thousands of Chinese merchants and workers in the Soviet Union, especially in Siberia. These facts made a complete severance of relations undesirable if not impossible. Yet under such circumstances the relations could hardly be satisfactory.

Despite its repeated declaration that it wouuld renounce all the concessions in China the Soviet Government had no intention to give up its privileges on the Chinese Eastern Railway. In March, 1926 the Politburo of the Communist Party of the Soviet Union appointed a commission with Trotsky as its chairman and Voroshilov, Chicherin and Dzerzhinsky as its members to formulate a Soviet policy with regard to the Chinese Eastern Railway. It adopted a resolution which advocated "the strict maintenance of the factual control of the line in the hands of the Soviet authorities".[1] Consequently, after 1924, the Chinese Eastern Railway remained a Soviet "sphere of influence" in China. Although the Chinese Eastern Railway was declared a purely commercial enterprise it had become a state within a state. It owned a large tract of land in excess of its needs as a railway, established its own schools and museums, engaged in construction activities and even maintained its own river flotilla. It also controlled the telephone and telegraph system of northern Manchuria. Besides, the Chinese

Eastern Railway harbored Communist activities: the Russian employees formed Communist cells and clubs while Chinese Communist, persecuted by the Manchurian authorities, sought shelter in the railway zone.

During his rule Marshal Chang Tso-lin had tried to curtail the influence of the Chinese Eastern Railway. From 1924 to the summer of 1928 he had confiscated excessive land of the railway; disbanded the Russian Municipal Council in Harbin; taken over the schools. museums and libraries operated by the railway; seized the river flotilla; and succeeded in having the dividends of the railway divided in accordance with Chinese wishes. After Chang Hsueh-liang's succession to power he continued his father's policy towards the Chinese Eastern Railway.

Disputes soon developed over its management. According to the Sino-Soviet Agreement for the Provisional Management of the Chinese Eastern Railway the employment of persons in the various departments should be in accordance with the principle of equal representation between Chinese and Russians, and the statutes of the Chinese Eastern Railway Co., approved by the Tsarist Government in December, 1896 should be revised within six months of the formation of the new board of directors.[2] But after the establishment of the new board the Russian directors had persistently refused to carry out these provisions. The Russian manager of the railway exercised just as much power as under the Tsarist Government. In 1928 three quarters of the railway personnel were Russians; out of 18 departments there were 13 Russian departmental chiefs. So on March 1, 1929 the Chinese president of the board, Lü Yung-kwan, proposed to the board several measures which would limit the authority of the manager and carry the principle of equal distribution of positions. The Russian vice-president and other directors rejected these demands and presented counter-proposals to the board. Negotiations dragged on for three months without any result. Then an event occurred which soon led to a crisis.

Upon receiving confidential information that a conference under the auspices of the Comintern was to be held in the Soviet consulate at Harbin on May 17, the Chinese police raided the consulate while the conference was in progress. All doors of the consulate were closed and when the police broke in most of the documents had been burned in the stove. But enough documents were confiscated to prove the ties between the Comintern and both consular and railway authorities; the existence of a Communist network in central China; the smuggling of arms and explosives into China for terroristic purposes;

and the plot to turn the so-called Christian General Feng Yu-hsiang against the Generalissimo.[3] Thirty-nine Russians were arrested on the spot of whom most were railway employees.

The Manchurian authorities, with the permission of the National Government, then instructed the Bureau of Tele-communications to forcibly take over the Telegraph Office of the railway so that the railway could no longer secretly communicate with Moscow. In July Lu Yung-kwan, ordered that five more Chinese should be appointed chiefs of departments and that hereafter all orders and documents issued by the Russian manager must be countersigned by the Chinese assistant manager. Upon the refusal of Manager Yemshanov to carry out this order Lu Yung-kwan dismissed the Russian manager, assistant manager and 59 high-ranking railway officials who participated in Communist activities and deported them to the Soviet Union. The Chinese assistant manager Wan Chi-kwang, was appointed acting manager and the railway administration was thus forcibly taken over.

On the day following the search of the consulate at Harbin, the Soviet authorities at Vladivostok protested to the Chinese consul-general there. Three days later a formal note of protest was received, demanding the immediate release of the Russians detained and restoration of documents and properties. On June 3 Karakhan, who was then again Deputy Foreign Commissar, in a strong protest to Hsia Wei-sung, Chinese charge d'affaires at Moscow, made the same demand, attacked the National Government violently and warned that the Chinese legation and consulates in the Soviet Union would no longer be accorded diplomatic status.

Then the Soviet Government sent Cheleplanhoff, Commissar of Communications, as envoy extraordinary to China to start negotiations. But before his arrival the taking over of the Chinese Eastern Railway had taken place and Karakhan sent an ultimatum to the Chinese charge d'affaires on July 13, demanding that: (1) a conference should be called without delay to settle all pending questions of the Chinese Eastern Railway; (2) all illegal actions concerning the Chinese Eastern Railway on the part of the Chinese authorities should be nullified; and (3) all Soviet citizens in detention should be immediately released and all oppressive actions against Soviet citizens and offices should be stopped. "The Government of the Soviet Union", threatened the note at its conclusion, "hopes the Mukden Government and the National Government of the Republic of China will carefully consider the serious consequences of opposing these proposals made by the Soviet Government. The Soviet Government expects a reply from the Chinese Government to the above mentioned items within three days, and wishes to state in advance that failing to receive a satisfactory reply the Soviet Government will be forced to adopt other measures to safeguard the rigths and privileges of the Soviet Union."[4]

In its reply to Karakhan on July 17, the National Government asserted that "Soviet Russia has been conducting organized propaganda and other activities to instigate the Chinese people to take destructive measures against the Chinese Government and society, thus compelling the government to take such steps as are necessary for the maintenance of peace and order in the country"; that "the authorities of the Three Eastern Provinces in ordering the search of the Soviet consulate at Harbin, and in taking such steps as already have been taken with reference to the Chinese Eastern Railway have but in view the prevention of the sudden occurrence of incidents"; and that "the Soviet manager and other important Russian officials of the Chinese Eastern Railway from the very beginning have never observed the terms of the 1924 Sino-Russian Agreement for the Provisional Management of the Chinese Eastern Railway". The National Government also complained that the Soviet Government had arrested more than 1,000 Chinese merchants without any provocation whatsoever and most Chinese mechants in the Soviet Union had been reduced to wretched circumstances owing to Soviet oppression. Consequently, the National Government proposed that if the Soviet Government would release all Chinese merchants arrested and detained and give them adequate protection and facilities the National Government would be ready at the appropriate time to take similar measures towards the arrested Soviet agents and the closed office buildings.[5]

Upon receiving this reply Karakhan immediately sent another note to Hsia declaring that the Soviet Government would now take the following measures: (1) recall of Soviet consular representatives in China; (2) recall of all Russian officials on the Chinese Eastern Railway; (3) severance of railway communications between China and the Soviet Union; and (4) immediate departure of Chinese diplomatic and consular officials in the Soviet Union.[6] Thus the relations between China and the Soviet Union were completely broken off. The Waichiaopu made a declaration to the world and published the documents seized in the Soviet consulate at Harbin.

Prior to his departure from Harbin, Soviet Consul-General Melnikov had an interview with Governor Chang Tso-hsiang of Kirin on July 24 concerning the Chinese Eastern Railway incident. Four days later

Melnikov telegraphed Tsai Yun-sheng, Chinese Commissioner for Foreign Affairs at Harbin, asking Tsai to proceed to Siberia for discussions. In the meantime the commander of the Chinese Eastern Railway guards at Manchuli also received a telegram from the Soviet Military Command in Siberia stating that the Soviet Government had appointed Melnikov as representative to discuss questions with Tsai. With the approval of the National Government, Tsai went to Siberia on July 30 and met with Melnikov at a small station, twenty miles from Manchuli. The conversations were satisfactory, and a second meeting took place at Manchuli on August 2. But the next day Melnikov sent his secretary to inform Tsai that he had received instructions from the Soviet Government to present the following proposals to the Chinese authorities: (1) the dismissed officials of the Chinese Eastern Railway should be reinstated and the system of management restored; (2) Soviet troops should have the right to protect the railway; and (3) supervision over the Far Eastern Bank should be removed. On the condition that the Chinese authorities agreed to these proposals the Soviet Government would send representatives for a formal Sino-Soviet conference and railway communications over the border could be resumed. The National Government instructed Tsai to reject these proposals as detrimental to the sovereignty of China and the Tsai-Melnikov conversations were ended.

Then on August 6, Chu Shao-yang arrived at Harbin as Chinese plenipotentiary to negotiate with the Soviets, but Melnikov avoided meeting him. Chu appealed directly to Karakhan at Moscow who in a long-distance telephone conversation with Chu informed the latter that the demands in the ultimatum of July 13 must be accepted as a basis for discussion in the proposed Sino-Soviet conference. As this could not be accepted Chu left Harbin for Nanking.

At that time an idealistic view of the world situation prevailed, especially in the United States. The Kellogg-Briand Pact of 1928 outlawing war as an instrument of national policy had been signed by all the major powers including the Soviet Union and President Herbert Hoover had set July 24, 1929 as the day for a solemn celebration of that covenant. Hopes ran high that thereafter international disputes would be settled by peaceful means and war might be done away with forever. So when the struggle for the Chinese Eastern Railway developed into a crisis the world was alarmed lest a war might be precipitated.

Although the United States had not yet recognized the Soviet Government, Secretary of State Henry L. Stimson took the initiative to seek for a peaceful settlement. On July 25, Stimson invited the ambassadors of Great Britain, France, Italy, Germany and Japan to the State Department and read to them a draft which proposed the appointment of a prominent neutral citizen acceptable to both China and the Soviet Union as the provisional president and manager of the Chinese Eastern Railway pending the settlement through negotiations. Britain, France and Italy favored Stimson's plan. Germany being then on good terms with China and the Soviets, was willing to mediate but declined to take part in any collective action of the major powers because this would offend the Soviet Union.

The attitude of Japan was quite a surprise to the American Government. Since the interests of Japan in Manchuria were basically in conflict with the Soviet interests the world expected Japan to side with China against Soviet domination over the Chinese Eastern Railway. The Japanese Kwantung Army was far superior to Soviet forces in Siberia and without Japan's tacit consent the Soviet Government would not dare to resort to military action. Yet Japan was opposed to Stimson's proposal and decided not to intervene. The best explanation for this policy is that while Japan was by no means friendly towards the Soviets she disliked far more to see the extension of Nanking influence over Manchuria and also feared that the taking over of the Chinese Eastern Railway by China might set a precedent concerning the Japanese-owned South Manchurian Railway.

Japan's neutral role greatly satisfied the Soviet Government. Commenting on the failure of Stimson's efforts, the *Communist International* said: "American imperialism . . . has run into sharp opposition from Japan, which has justly found a threat to its influence in Manchuria in the effort of the United States of America to put its hands, in some form or other, on the Chinese Eastern Railway."[7] Reassured that Japan would not intervene the Soviet Government now mobilized its forces along the Manchurian border for military actions. A Special Far Eastern Red Army consisting of 100,000 men with tanks and planes was created and General Bluecher was appointed its commander. On August 12, a week after the breaking off of the Tsai-Melnikov conversations, Soviet troops attacked and occupied three strategic towns in Chinese territory. But General Chang Hsueh-liang did not mobilize his troops until August 15, and General Chang Tso-hsiang did not proceed to Harbin to direct defensive operations until August 22. In equipment and training Chinese troops were no match for those of the Soviets. So Russia attacked and occupied Mishan on August 23 and Wangching on August 28.

On August 27 the German Government offered its good offices

for mediation and proposed that both sides issue a joint manifesto containing the following main points: (1) both sides should immediately appoint representatives to start negotiations and all questions should be settled in accordance with the Sino-Soviet Agreement, especially in regard to the redemption of the railway in Article 9, Section 2; (2) conditions in the Chinese Eastern Railway after the incident should be accordingly readjusted to the Sino-Soviet Agreement and Soviet-Mudken Pact but with previous agreement of representatives of both sides; (3) the Soviet Government might nominate a candidate each for the manager and assistant manager to be appointed by the board of directors and all Russian employees of the railway should be instructed by the Soviet Government to strictly observe Article 6 [8] of the Sino-Soviet Agreement; (4) both sides were to set free immediately all persons arrested in connection with the incident.

The Soviet Government agreed to the proposal, but made the following alterations: (1) all outstanding disputes in connection with the Chinese Eastern Railway should be settled at the conference; (2) the appointment of the Soviet manager and assistant manager should be made simultaneously with the issue of the joint manifesto; (3) both governments were to order their respective employees of the Chinese Eastern Railway to strictly observe Article 6 of the Agreement; and (4) both sides were to free persons arrested since May 1, 1929. The National Government did not agree to these alterations and the German Government persuaded the Soviet Government to modify them to some extent. But the National Government insisted that the appointment of the manager could not be made before the conclusion of the negotiations. To this point the Soviet Government simply did not reply and the German good offices brought no result.[9]

Upon the failure of the German mediation, the Soviet Government sped up its military activities. But at that time Stalin's power was not quite absolute and there were Communist idealists like Karl Radek who advocated that the Chinese Eastern Railway should be returned to the Chinese. So some justification had to be found for the use of force for the control of the Chinese Eastern Railway and an official explanation was given in the *Communist International.* "The Soviet proletariat carries out the administration of the Chinese Eastern Railway jointly with the Chinese (bourgeois-landowners) Government in the interest of preventing the transfer of the railroad into the hands of the imperialists subjugating China; in the interest of an easier transfer of the railroad into the hands of the Chinese people after the (genuine and not social-democratic) victory of the national revolution—to the Chinese people which will have done away with the imperialists, their bourgeois-landlord pillars within China proper; and finally in the interests of the defense of the Soviet Union itself—that country which is building socialism—from the threats of invasions on the part of hostile capitalist countries."[10] This means that the Soviet Union would only return the Chinese Eastern Railway to the Chinese people when a Communist regime emerged in China.

On October 12, Soviet forces attacked Tungkiang, a strategic city on the Amur, with nine gunboats, eighteen planes, and more than 3000 infantry and calvarymen. Chinese defense forces were inferior in number and equipment and suffered heavy casualties. Upon the fall of Tungkiang the National Government strongly protested to the Soviet Union through the German Government which then represented China's interests in the Soviet Union. On November 1, Soviet troops occupied Fuchin across the Sungari from Suiping. Soon the Soviet Government extended warfare to another sector. On November 17, Soviet forces attacked Chalainoerh on the Chinese Eastern Railway about 25 miles southeast of Manchuli, with cannons, planes, tanks and three divisions of infantry. The Chinese defense forces fought bravely. Out of the 7000 men only about 1000 escaped with their lives. General Han Kwang-ti, a brigade commander, and two regiment commanders were killed in action. Afterwards the occupation of Chalainoerh Manchuli became completely encircled and soon fell into Soviet hands. General Liang Chung-chia, the defense commander, was also killed in action.[11]

After the Soviet occupation of Tungkiang, the National Government notified all the signatories of the Kellogg-Briand Pact of the Soviet responsibility for the failure of German mediation and of the Soviet offensive actions at Tungkiang. After the loss of Chalainoerh and Manchuli it again notified the powers of the atrocious actions of the Soviet troops and requested them to do something to stop Soviet aggression. On November 26, upon receiving these notes, Secretary Stimson again proposed to the five powers that they should jointly ask both sides to refrain from warlike acts in accordance with the Kellogg-Briand Pact, but Germany and Japan once more refused to participate.

Then at the beginning of December, the United States, Great Britain, France and some other States which had signed the Pact sent notes to both China and the Soviet Union requesting them to stop hostilities at once and to seek solutions of the disputes through peaceful means. The National Government immediately expressed its willingness to comply, but the Soviet reply to the State Department through the French ambassador at Moscow stated: "It cannot admit the intervention of anybody in these pourparlens or in the conflict."[12] The Soviet press attacked the powers violently for their diplomatic intervention and blamed the United States for starting the conflict in order to get the Chinese Eastern Railway into the hands of the American capitalists. When the conflict was over Maxim Litvinov, the Foreign Commissar, made a report to the Central Committee of the Communist Party of the Soviet Union in which he bitterly attacked the United States and the Nanking Government but warmly praised Japan.[13]

In the later part of 1929 the National Government was busily engaged in suppressing the revolt of several generals in Central China and could not send any reinforcements to Manchuria to help fight against Soviet aggression. As a consequence, in November it hinted to General Chang Hsueh-liang to seek for peace with the Soviet Union. Commissioner Tsai, under the instruction of General Chang, then sent a Soviet employee of the Chinese Eastern Railway to Khabarovsk to see Soviet Consul-General Simanovsky and to express China's desire for peace. In the meantime Tsai also telegraphed this desire to Karakhan and the latter instructed Simanovsky to negotiate with Tsai. They met at Nikolsk Ussuriisk and after several conversations agreed to the terms of armistice on December 3. These terms restored the status quo ante on the Chinese Eastern Railway, but the Soviet Union agreed to recall Yemshanov, the manager and Sismont, the assistant-manager who had been dismissed by China.

Then on December 22 a protocol was signed at Khabarovsk by Tsai and Simanovsky to restore peace on the border and to settle the disputes over the Chinese Eastern Railway. This protocol provided that the status quo ante on the Chinese Eastern Raiway be re-established, Soviet consulates and trading missions in Manchuria and Chinese consulates and commercial organizations in the Soviet Far East be reopened; all persons arrested on both sides in connection with the conflicts be set free; armed forces in the occupied area be withdrawn; and the "White Russian" units in Manchuria be disarmed and their leaders expelled. It was also provided that the resumption of diplomatic relations, trade and other outstanding questions were to be discussed and settled at a Sino-Soviet conference to be held at Moscow on January 25, 1930.[14]

When the terms of the protocol became known there was an outcry against it in Chinese public opinion. The National Government was also dissatisfied and condemned Tsai Yun-sheng for exceeding his authority in signing an agreement which contained articles not concerned with the Chinese Eastern Railway. So the National Government issued a statement repudiating those articles which were not related to the Chinese Eastern Railway but expressed its willingness to negotiate with Moscow concerning the permanent settlement of the Chinese Eastern Railway question, trade relations and other problems. But so far as Manchuria was concerned all the provisions in the protocol were carried out. The new Soviet manager and assistant-manager assumed office on January 4, 1930 and exercised just as much power as their predecessors.

In February, 1930, the National Government appointed Mo Teh-hui Chinese plenipotentiary to the Sino-Soviet Conference at Moscow. But as a major civil war now was brewing in China the Soviet Union was not anxious to open the scheduled conference. The date was postponed first to April 15 and again to June 1. Mo Teh-hui arrived at Moscow on May 9, and the Soviet Government appointed Karakhan its plenipotentiary. In their informal talks Mo and Karakhan had different opinions on the agenda of the conference. Mo wanted to put the redemption of the railway on the agenda while Karakhan was opposed to it. Karakhan insisted that the conference should discuss such topics as trade relations, navigation on the Amur and Sungari, Outer Mongolia and Sinkiang, but Mo wished to limit the discussions to the Chinese Eastern Railway.

It was not until October 11, when the civil war in China had been ended that the conference was formally opened. The first question discussed was the Chinese Eastern Railway. Mo asserted that the Chinese Eastern Railway question should be settled according to the Sino-Soviet and Soviet-Mukden Agreements but Karakhan declared that the Khabarovsk Protocol should serve as the basis for settlement. Many conversations and several exchanges of notes took place concerning China's recognition of the Khabarovsk Protocol without any definite result. In their second meeting on December 4 the two plenipotentiaries agreed to set up three committees to study (1) the Chinese Eastern Railway, (2) trade and (3) resumption of diplomatic relations. Then Mo went back to China to report to the National Government. At the end of March, 1931, Mo returned to Moscow. Owing to the illness of Karakhan the third meeting of the plenipotentiaries did not take place until April 11. Karakhan agreed to the principle of redemption but adopted delaying tactics. From the middle of April to the beginning of October twenty-two more meetings were held to discuss the redemption, temorary management and organization of the Chinese Eastern Railway without arriving at any conclusion. By that time the Mukden incident had occurred and the Soviet Government declared that the Sino-Soviet conference could not be continued until the Manchurian problem had been settled. Thus the conference was abruptly ended and Mo left Moscow.

CHAPTER XIII

The Soviet Union and Outer Mongolia

Outer Mongolia can claim the distinction of being the first non-Russian nation which was put behind the iron curtain after the Bolshevik revolution. Despite its professed friendship towards China and despite the repeated protests lodged by the Peking Government the Russian Socialist Federated Soviet Republic and later the Soviet Union had not for a moment loosened its grip over Outer Mongolia since July, 1921. Zinoviev, president of the Comintern, once remarked: " . . . . a definite solution of the Mongolian question will not become possible until the Chinese themselves shall liberate themselves from the yoke of their oppressers, until they chase from their borders the soldiers of foreign imperialist nations, until the revolution shall be victorious in their country."[1] This means that Outer Mongolia would not be returned to China until and unless China herself became a Soviet satellite. This policy naturally aroused opposition in China, even among the intellectuals whose pro-Soviet feeling was otherwise quite strong. For instance in 1923 a certain Professor Liu sent an open letter to Joffe saying: "During my stay in southern China I read with tremendous interest your energetic protests against the continued occupation of the northern part of Sakhalin Island (by Japan). I must recognize the propriety of your claims. At the same time I have the honor of reminding you that Russia is committing an exactly similar act in keeping Urga under its control to this day. The city is an absolutely Chinese one, and nonetheless you are occupying it. . . .How can Russia hold under its control a part of Chinese territory while it is protesting the Japanese occupation of Sakhalin?"[2] Even after the conclusion of the Sino-Soviet Agreement of 1924 by which the Soviet government recognized Outer Mongolia as an integral part of China and respected China's sovereignty therein, Outer Mongolia continued to be ruled by Moscow.

The Soviet rule was, of course, carried out by its fifth columnists in Outer Mongolia – the Mongolian People's Revolutionary Party which formed so-called Mongolian People's Government. It was paraded before the world as an independent government but was actually a stooge of the Soviets. After the signing of the Soviet-Monogolian Agreement in November 1921 two Russian Communists, Okhtin and Berezin, arrived at Urga and became "the power behind the throne." Butin, another Russian Communist, was appointed financial adviser by the People's Government. Soviet economic agencies such as the Oil Syndicate, the Siberian State Trade, and Wood Purchasing Agency immediately opened offices in Urga. Soviet military instructors were sent to Outer Mongolia to train the newly formed Mongolian Army. A sovietized educational system was also adopted, the professor and teachers being mainly Russians and Buryats. A Mongolian Youth Revolutionary Corps along the lines of the Komsomoe in the Soviet Union was organized and consisted mostly of Mongolian fugitives who during their exile in Soviet territory had been baptized with Communism. This corps took orders directly from Moscow and spied on the activities of the Mongolian People's Revolutionary Party. A secret police, modelled after the G.P.U., was formed in 1922. It soon unearthed the reactionary activities on the part of Prime Minister Bodo and other high officials and they were ousted from power in April.[3] Other "counter-revolutionary" plots were again discovered at the end of the year and also in 1923.

After the mysterious death of the Hutukhtu in May, 1924 the monarchical form of government was abolished and the so-called Mongolian People's Republic was proclaimed on July 8. In the next month the Third Congress of the Mongolian People's Revolutionary Party was convened. At that time some Mongols expressed the desire to incorporate Tannu Tuva into the newly formed republic and Vassiliev, the Soviet representative, told the congress that the Soviet Union would not permit it. He also emphasized the role of the Comintern in the development of Outer Mongolia. Delegates to the congress, being dissatisfied with their lot, criticized economic and political conditions and the state of the army. Some even mentioned the possibility of establishing trade relations with other foreign countries. This independent attitude towards the Soviet Union alarmed Russia; clearly something had to be done. When Danzan, Vice-Premier and Minister of War, made a violent speech on August 30 saying that too close relations with the Soviet Union would put Mongolia under the Soviet yoke Ricino, a Buryat and leader of the Left Wing of the party, staged a coup d'etat and arrested and shot Danzan.[4] Vassiliev at once praised this move as a contribution to Soviet-Mongolian unity and thereupon all free talks ceased.

A new constitution was promulgated on November 21 which was faihfully patterned after the Soviet model. It provided that in the People's Republic "the whole government belongs to the laboring people" who exercised their power through the Great Hural which was a copy of the Congress of the Soviets. The Great Hural chose a Little Hural to operate when it was not in session. The Little Hural, in turn, elected a "Presidium" and the cabinet. All exploiters of others' labor such as merchants, usurers, former princes, Hutukhtus, and religious persons residing in monasteries were disfranchised. The primary object of the People's Republic consisted "in the destruction of the principles of the new republic order on the basis of complete democratization of the state administration." The land and natural resources were to be nationalized and a state monopoly of foreign trade was to be introduced gradually. With regard to the foreign policy it stated: "In view of the fact that the toilers of the world are aspiring after the radical abolition of capitalism and the attainment of socialism (Communism) the People's Republic of the toilers must conduct its foreign policy in conformity with the interests and fundamental tasks of small oppressed nations and of the revolutionary toilers of the entire world."[5]

Since Outer Mongolia was now in its firm grip the Soviet Government was bent upon the economic exploitation and sovietization of Outer Mongolia. There was no longer need of stationing troops and consequently the Soviet Union withdrew its forces from Mongolian territory on March 6, 1925. On the same day Foreign Commissar Chicherin reported to the Congress of the Soviets at Tiflis: "The Soviet Government recognizes Mongolia as a part of the whole Republic of China, enjoying, however, autonomy so far reaching as to preclude Chinese interference with the internal affairs and establish independent relations with Mongolia. It ought to be noted that after several crises the internal situation in Mongolia has settled down and been consolidated on a basis somewhat similar to the Soviet system."[6] According to some sources a secret agreement had been concluded between the Soviet Union and Outer Mongolia in February 1923 by which Outer Mongolia agreed to nationalize all lands, forests and mineral resources within its territory, to distribute its unclaimed lands to Soviet citizens and the Mongolian proletariat for cultivation, to grant gold mining concessions to Soviet labor union, etc.[7]

A railway connecting Kiakhta and Ulan Bator (the new name for Urga, meaning the red warrior) was built with Soviet capital and roads and water transport were also improved. In 1924 a Mongolian

Industrial and Commercial Bank was established under Soviet control and a period of rapid growth in Soviet-Mongolian trade followed. There was a steady rise in Soviet exports to Outer Mongolia, particularly of grain and oil, and the trade balance turned in favor of the Soviet Union, in striking contrast with the situation under the Tsarist regime. "From 1926, Soviet commercial transactions became more and more interwoven with the Mongol State economic machinery."[8] By 1928 the wool trade was completely in the Russian hands. By 1934 91% of Mongolian foreign trade was done with the Soviet Union, the only important non-Soviet item in Mongolian imports being tea from China but also through Soviet hands.

Meanwhile the Soviet Government wanted to isolate Outer Mongolia and to reduce its contact with other foreign countries to the minimum. Some Mongolian Communists had the naivete to seek the unification of all Mongols in Buryat, Manchuria, Tannu Tuva and Inner and Outer Mongolia into a big Mongol State and were promptly rebuked by Moscow. No foreign states besides the Soviet Union, were allowed to send official representatives to Outer Mongolia. Even the Swedish missionaries were expelled in 1924 and since then no foreign missionaries had been allowed to enter. A Mongolian trade delegation was sent to Berlin in 1925. It bought German cars, tractors and machines and hired German geologists for research work in Mongolia. Forty-five Mongolian boys were sent to study in Germany. But it was withdrawn in 1928 when the German Foreign Office proposed de jure recognition of the Mongolian Republic and establishment of normal diplomatic relations. Between 1925 and 1930 some German, Swedish, Swiss and Hungarian technicians were employed by the Mongolian Government to build power stations, brick factory and other installations. But they were got rid of as soon as their contracts expired. Foreign firms which had done business in Outer Mongolia found themselves increasingly handicapped and by 1928 they had all closed down. From 1924 on, visas for Outer Mongolia could only be obtained either at Ulan Bator or Moscow.

In 1929 when the Soviet drive towards collective farming and industrialization was on its way the Seventh Congress of the Mongolian People's Revolutionary Party also adopted a resolution setting "the creation of a socialist economy" as the immediate goal. Soon the Mongolian Government began to expropriate the properties of the princes, lamas and monasteries which consisted mainly of cattle. Before 1929 the princes and lamas had owned over 29% of the herds, by 1930 they owned only 1%. During the same period a vigorous anti-religious campaign took place and the number of lamas dropped from 95,000 in 1928 to 82,000 in 1932.

The Soviet Kolkhoz was also experimented in Outer Mongolia. The entire wealth of 600 "feudals" (princes and monasteries) were taken over by the government and given to the newly formed collectives. By the summer of 1931, 740 collectives with 175,000 members and dependents had been created, this number representing almost one-fifth of the total population. But this experiment was bound to be a failure. At that time 97% of the population were illiterate. The members of the collectives, being unable to read, write or keep an accounting system, simply could not run a highly organized economy. Thousands of shepherds who resented collectivization killed their livestocks or attempted to cross over into Inner Mongolia, Manchuria or Sinkiang. Many of them were shot by frontier guards while making the attempt but about 20,000 succeeded in their escape. In 1932 a revolt broke out in the western part of the country and was only suppressed after serious fighting.

The People's Revolutionary Party had now to admit, with Moscow's consent, that Outer Mongolia was not yet ripe for socialism. In a Plenum of its Central Committee in June 1932 it condemned its own policy as a "left-wing deviation." Premier Gendun, in his speech to the Seventh Great Hural, declared: "Our Republic is a bourgeois democratic Republic of the new type, anti-feudalistic and anti-imperialistic, gradually advancing on the road of non-capitalistic development. But our national-democratic and anti-feudalistic revolution did not reach the socialistic stage. In order to build a strong foundation for the Mongolian national economy we should develop private (though not unrestricted) economics. . . Of course we should aim for the gradual limitation of exploiting elements while doing everything in order to improve the private economy and the material well-being of the poor and middle Arats."[9] The Kolkhoz experiment was abandoned and the right of the herdsmen and peasants to hold private property was again recognized. But trade, especially cattle trade, remained to be concentrated in the hands of a "cooperative" enterprise which was practically an agency of the state.

Together with the change of the economic policy there was also a new policy towards the lamas. Instead of attacking the lamas as a whole an effort was now made to drive a wedge between the upper hierarchy and the poorer lamas. Said Gendun in the same report to the Great Hural: "We must make a distinction on the one hand between the high lamas who used to exploit both the low-ranking lamas and arats and, on the other hand, the low lamas. The low-ranking monks and lamas should be treated differently from the high dignitaries of the church. They should receive education (and in this case be exempted from special taxes) and if they take part in work they should be allowed to vote. The Government should try to separate them from the hierarchy who exploit them. The Government should apply compulsory education to all illiterate officials and by all means try to advance the culture and national economy of Outer Mongolia, emulating the example of the Soviet Union."[10]

After the establishment of the puppet state, Manchukuo, in 1932 Japan tried to win the Mongols over to her side. A Mongolian province, Hsingan, was created with the right of self-government as a lure to the Mongols both in China and in Outer Mongolia. Meanwhile as there had never been a clear-cut boundary line between Manchuria and Outer Mongolia when they were parts of the same empire border disputes naturally arose when they became puppets of two rival powers. From 1933 on border incidents along the Mongolian-Manchurian frontier occured frequently. In 1934 the Manchukuo regime proposed to Outer Mongolia to recognize each other and to send a mission to Ulan Bator. This offer naturally displeased the Soviet Union and was emphatically turned down by Outer Mongolia. When the Japanese attitude became threatening the Soviet Union made a "gentlemen's agrement" with Outer Mongolia on November 27, providing for mutual assistence in case of an invasion. Thereafter Soviet troops were again stationed in Outer Mongolia.

Then a serious border fight took place at Lake Buir in January 1935 and both sides sufferd heavy casualties. In June a Mongolian-Manchuko Conference was held at Manchuli to settle border disputes. The Manchukuo delegation, backed by the Japanese Kwantung Army, demanded the "opening" of Outer Mongolia and the establishment of three commissions, with one operating in Ulan Bator. The Mongolian delegation, with Soviet support, rejected these demands. The conference was in session for five months without reaching any agreement. Thereupon the Manchukuo press threatened: "Manchukuo does not consider Mongolia an ordinary normal state, and therefore Manchukuo now claims that, viewing Outer Mongolia as an incomprehensible and dangerous country, it intends to regulate all issues and settle all disputes by force of arms as it sees fit."[11] In the same year the so-called Mongolian Inter-tribal

Autonomous Government was created by the Japanese at Peiling-miao in Suiyuan, a part of former Inner Mongolia.

From December 1935 on more border clashes occurred. Early in 1936 there was wide-spread speculation of a Japanese invasion of Outer Mongolia and Stalin made a warning to Japan that in case such invasion took place the Soviet Union would go to war. In a press interview he declared on March 6 "If Japan should venture to attack the Mongolian People's Republic and encroach upon its independence, we will have to help the Mongolian People's Republic. Stomonyakov, Litvinov's assistant, recently informed the Japanese ambassador in Moscow of this and pointed to the immutable friendly relations which the U.S.S.R. has been maintaining with the Mongolian People's Republic since 1921. We will help the Mongolian People's Republic just as we helped it in 1921."[12]

A few days after this declaration the gentlemen's agreement was put down in writing in the form of a Soviet-Mongolian Protocol of Mutual Assistance signed at Ulan Bator by Tairov of the Soviet Union and by Amor (chairman of the ittle Hural) and Gendun (Premier) of Outer Mongolia. It provided that the two powers would consult with each other in case of military menace to either; that they would render each other assistance, including military assistance, in case of a military attack upon either, and that troops of either which were on the territory of the other party in order to carry out the obligation of this protocol would be immediately withdrawn when the need was over.[13] When the protocol was made public in April the Chinese Government lodged a strong protest with Moscow contending that "Outer Mongolia being an integral part of the Republic of China, no foreign state has the right to conclude with it any treaties or agreements." The Soviet Government had, by concluding a military alliance with Outer Mongolia, broken its pledge to China, infringed upon China's sovereignty and violated the Sino-Soviet Agreement of 1924.

In its reply the Soviet Government argued that as the protocol did not contain any territorial claim by the Soviet Union and neither did it change the relations hitherto existing between the Soviet Union and China or between the Soviet Union and Outer Mongolia therefore it did not violate in the slightest degree China's sovereignty over Outer Mongolia. The Soviet Government further cited as precedent the Soviet-Mukden Agreement of 1924. The Chinese Government found this reply unsatisfactory and lodged another protest a few days later which reiterated China's stand and pointed out that in 1924 the then Peking Government did repeatedly protest against the Soviet-Mukden Agreement and that the agreement was later submitted by the Mukden authorities to the Peking Government for its approval.[14] These protests, of course, did not affect the determinated policy of the Soviet Union at all.

Ever since 1935 there had been border incidents between the two puppets, Manchukuo and Outer Mongolia. The most serious one occurred in the summer of 1949. These will be treated more fully in another chapter.

The Mongolian People's Revolutionary Party, being a protégé of the Communist Party of the Soviet Union, suffered the same periodic purges as the latter. Its membership which was only 160 at the time of its formation in 1921 rose to 6,300 in 1924. Then there was a purge and it dropped to 3,000 a year later. After a while the growth of the party was resumed and the membership grew to 12,000 in 1929 and 42,000 in 1932. Then came another purge and by the end of the year only 12,000 members remained in the party. The tendency to diminish continued and by 1934 only 7,500 members were left. During 1936-39 when the bloodiest purge took place in the Soviet Union the same thing happened in Outer Mongolia. Many high officials including two former premiers, Amor and Gendun, and a minister of war, Gemid, were either executed or committed suicide Only Choibalsan, who became premier during the great purge, had stayed in power until his death in 1952. The Mongolian Youth Revolutionary Corps also suffered from the purges. Its membership had steadily grown until the number reached 22,000 in 1931. After a large-scale purge only 5,000 were left in 1934.

In 1940 a new constitution of the Mongolian People's Republic, the so-called Choibalsan Constitution, was promulgated. It declared the the future of Outer Mongolia lay "along non-capitalist lines and a subsequent development into Socialism." "Industry, mines, railways, banks, (and) means of transportation by car, water, and air" were all made the exclusive property of state. With regard to religion it provided for both freedom of worship and freedom of anti-religious propaganda. The organization of the hurals remained the same but all voting in the hurals must be public, i.e. not secret. Four years later the franchise was extended to former members of the "exploiting classes."[15]

CHAPTER XIV

The Soviet Union and Sinkiang

While the Soviet Union had just as much aggressive intention towards Sinkiang as towards Outer Mongolia its penetration into Sinkiang took quite a different course. As told in Chapter VIII, Russian influence in Sinkiang disappeared after the revolution. Then in 1924 after the conclusion of the Sino-Soviet Agreement the Soviet authorities sent an envoy to Urumchi to negotiate the re-establishment of five consulates in Sinkiang. Governor Yang Tseng-hsin agreed to this on the condition that five Chinese consulates be opened in Central Asia. By an exchange of notes in October 1924 Soviet consulates were opened at Urumchi, Tarbagatai, Ili, Altai and Kashgar; while Chinese consulates were opened at Tashkent, Andijan, Alma Ata, Zaisan and Semipalatinsk. As the Peking Government had very little real power these Chinese consular officials were appointed by the Sinkiang provincial government. So even after the disruption of diplomatic relations in 1927 or during the Sino-Soviet hostility in 1929 these consulates continued to exercise their functions.

At that time the two autonomous People's Republics of Khiva and Bokhara were incorporated into the Soviet Union and Central Asia was again firmly in the Russian hands. In 1927 the Soviet Government began the construction of that part of the Turksib Railway which runs from Semipalatinsk through Sergiopol and Alma Ata to Chemkent. The whole length of this line was about 900 miles and was completed in April, 1930. For more than 400 miles this railway runs almost parallel to the border lines of Sinkiang. It was intended for the economic penetration into Sinkiang as shown by an official commentary at the time of its construction which said: "The construction of the line from Turkestan to Siberia simultaneously solves the problem of transportation from this lost country (Sinkiang), which will be increasingly attracted to the Soviet Union economically, particularly if, in addition to this great line, other lines are opened and if (other) roads are improved..."[1] Several good roads were later built which connected the Turksib Railway with Ili in Northern Sinkiang and Kashgar in the south. After that the quickest way to go to Sinkiang from China was via the Trans-Siberian and Turksib railways. This of course gave the Soviet Government a measure of control through the issue of visas.

The internal political situation in Sinkiang after 1930 also gave the Soviet Union a good chance to invade Sinkiang. On July 7, 1928 Governor Yang was assassinated by one of his subordinates[2] and Chin Shu-jen, Commissioner of Civil Affairs under Yang, succeeded him as governor. Chin was weak in character and incompetent and the delicate balance between Chinese officialdom and the non-Chinese population of Sinkiang, which was well kept by Yang, was soon upset. The growing Soviet control of foreign trade in Sinkiang was detrimental to the interests of local merchants and cotton growers. Heavy taxation and currency difficulties increased the volume of discontent.

Since Sinkiang had been Chinese territory for only two hundred years several tiny Moslem principalities managed to remain in existence. During Governor Yank's seventeen years' rule their autonomous status had been gradually abolished. The last remaining autonomous principality was the one in Hami. When the Moslem prince died in 1930 Governor Chin saw his chance to abolish this principality. So the new prince, Nei-tse-erh, was ordered to Urumchi and his domain was divided into three administrative districts with a magistrate for each appointed by the governor. The prince's estate was surveyed and licenses were issued to his tenants giving them the right to continue ownership by paying taxes to the local government. At that time there was famine in Kansu and many Chinese fled to Hami for settlement. One of the magistrates allocated tilled land to these refugees which was taken from Moslems who were given untilled land as compensation. This unjust act aroused the opposition of Moslems. Due to Chin's poor administration what had started as a local struggle between natives and Chinese settlers soon developed into an all-out Moslem uprising, second in importance only to the Yakub Beg rebellion in 1868.

The rebels now appealed to General Ma Chung-ying, a Tungan Moslem leader in Kansu, for help and Ma led his troops into Sinkiang in 1931 and assumed the leadership of the revolt. Ma was then only 23 but had been a general for six years. He was brave and a good strategist and won battle after battle against Chin's forces. His cruelty was extraordinary and left behind him thousands of corpses wherever he went. Sometimes the inhabitants of entire villages were slaughtered by his troops and he instilled terror among the people of the whole province. As the National Government was then busily engaged in suppressing the Communists in China proper and could send no reinforcement to Sinkiang, Chin turned to the Soviet Union for help.

In order to extend its influence in Sinkiang Moscow could have helped either Chin or Ma. But as Ma, like the Moslems of Central Asia, was strongly opposed to the Soviet Union for national and religious reasons Moscow decided to take Chin's side. So a secret trade agreement with four annexes was signed by Chen Chi-san, representing the Sinkiang provincial government, and Slavusky, Soviet representative. The text of these documents was kept a close secret until the downfall of Chin in April 1933. In exchange for Soviet machines and technical experts for the reconstruction of Sinkiang Chin gave the Soviet agencies far-reaching trade concessions and privileges. Annex II granted the Soviet Union the right to establish financial bureaus in Sinkiang.[8] Military support was not mentioned in these documents but was understood.

Yet even with Soviet arms Govenor Chin could not stem the onrush of Ma's troops for lack of a trained army. So he turned to the White Russian refugees who had military training and fighting experience. A contingent of 1,500 White Russian soldiers was created under the command of Pappengut, a White Russian general. The Soviet representative at Urumchi protested strongly against such action but Chin ignored him. The White Russian army proved effective but owing to its small size it could only hold Urumchi against Ma's troops but could not defeat them. Then in March, 1933 about 10,000 Manchurian troops under General Sheng Shih-tsai arrived in Sinkiang. These troops were the remnant forces of General Ma Chan-san who as commander-in-chief of Heilungkiang had founght against the Japanese after the Mukden incident in 1931. Being defeated by the Japanese they retreated into Siberia and were interned there. Now the Soviet Government saw fit to transport them to Sinkiang and to put them at Chin's disposal. After their arrival 3,000 were stationed in the Ili district and 7,000 proceeded to Urumchi.

On April 12, while the Manchurian troops were fighting against the Tungan rebels at the front, the White Russians staged a coup d'etat in Urumchi with the sole purpose of overthrowing Chin. The corruption and inefficiency of Chin had so alienated not only the White Russians but even his Chinese colleagues and subordinates that the Chinese officials sided with the Russians and formed a Political Maintenance Council which elected Liu Wen-lung, acting Governor and Sheng Shih-tsai, provisional Border Defense Commissioner pending the confirmation of Nanking. Chin fled to the outskirt of Urumchi during the tumult and led some troops who were loyal to him to attack the city. He was defeated by the Russians, and retreated to Turbagatai.[4] Sheng returned to Urumchi on April 14 and order was restored. In May Nanking announced its acceptance of Chin's resignation and Chin went back to China proper via Siberia and Vladivostok. Upon his arrival at Tientsin he was arrested for secretly concluding an agreement with a foreign power, put on trial and sentenced to three and a half years' imprisonment. In August the National Government appointed Liu Governor and Sheng Shih-tsai Border Defense Commissioner. This coup d'etat put Sheng Shih-tsai in power who had since then ruled Sinkiang with an iron hand while Governor Liu and his successors became mere figure heads.

Upon hearing the news of the coup d'etat in Urumchi Ma Chung-ying again advanced towards the capital. At first Sheng tried to come to terms with Ma by sending a peace mission to Kucheng where Ma had set up his headquarters. Ma was offered the title of Commander-in-chief in southern Sinkiang where his troops would be stationed. They were to be counted and enrolled with the regular army of the province and the provisional government would be responsible for their pay.[5] At first Ma was ready to accept these terms but his staff members advised him that he could easily take Urumchi by force and he changed his mind. The National Government sent General Huang Mu-sung, assistant chief-of-staff, in June and Dr. Lo Wen-kan, Foreign Minister, in August to Sinkiang to pacify the Moslems and to end the civil war but both missions failed. Rebellion now spread to southern Sinkiang and a "Republic of Eastern Turkestan" was proclaimed in August.

As Nanking could give Sheng no effective help he turned to the Soviet Union. When Sheng first seized power he issued an eight-point declaration of which the first point was the carrying out of the equality of nationalities. Sheng stressed that all weak and suppressed nations, in order to obtain an equal position with the strong nations, must fight a relentless war against imperialism. This had some Communist flavor but did not satisfy Soviet authorities. So when Sheng coveted Soviet assistance he announced his six basic policies: (1) anti-imperialism, (2) pro-Sovietism, (3) equality of nationalities, (4) integrity, (5) peace, and (6) reconstruction.[6] But mere words were not sufficient so Sheng had to sign a secret agreement with the Soviet representative, Pogodin. By this agreement Sheng granted the Soviet Union economic concessions and the right to build a railway from Sergiopol through Tarbagatai to Urumchi in exchange for Soviet military support. The White Russian general, Pappengut, and several of his officers were shot and the White contingent was now placed under the command of Soviet officers. Many Chinese officials in Sinkiang who had an anti-Soviet trend were removed from office.

After a few months' rest at Turfan and having recruited more Moslem soldiers Ma Chung-ying again marched on the capital in the spring of 1934. His troops soon occupied all strategic points near Urumchi. General Chang Pei-yuan, garrison commander at Ili, who had ill-feeling against Sheng Shih-Tsai, cooperated with Ma and sent 3,000 troops to attack Urumchi. The fall of Urumchi seemed to be imminent and even the Manchurian and White Russian troops could not have saved it. Then the Soviet Government intervened by sending two brigades of G.P.U. troops with tanks and artillery "to clear the roads and liquidate the rebellion". Even the Soviet air force was mobilized. As reported by Alexander Barmine who was in charge of Soviet supplies to Sinkiang: "Meanwhile, on the order of the politburo, we shipped a number of planes and bombs to the borders of Sinkiang. There they were stuck for some time, as the road to Urumchi, capital of Sinkiang, was blocked by the rebels. Finally the command of the Red Army Air Force operating there took charge of this shipment. They delivered our cargoes, consigned to the governor, by dropping the bombs on the rebel forces gathered round the capital, and by landing the planes right on the air-field of the beseiged fortress. I was instructed to send the bill for the bombs, as well as the other goods, to the governor.'[7] Of course Ma and Chang's forces were no match for this superior strength. Chang's army was practically annihilated and he committed suicide. Ma's troops suffered heavy losses and Ma had to flee to Kashgar for his life. Later Ma entered Soviet territory with a small group of body-guards but accompanied by the secretary of the Soviet consulate at Kashgar. Ma was well treated in the Soviet Union and appointed an officer in the Red Army. Apparently the Soviet Government regarded Ma as a potential asset in Soviet activities in the Moslem world and wished to keep him for future use.

By June, 1934 all fighting in Sinkiang had ended. Even the so-called Republic of Eastern Turkestan in Southern Sinkiang disintegrated. Almost all of Sinkiang was now under the control of Sheng Shih-tsai except Khotan and its adjacent areas which were occupied by remnant Tungan forces under Ma Ho-san, a relative of Ma Chung-ying, until his suppression in 1937, again with Soviet help. In April 1939, when Dr. Sun Fo, President of the Legislative Yuan, was in Moscow on a mission Stalin explained that the Soviet Government had helped Sheng Shih-tsai against Ma Chung-ying in 1934 because Sheng was legally appointed by the Chinese Goverment while Ma had advanced to Sinkiang on his own accord. "Furthermore, it was reported that the Japanese were backing Ma Chung-ying, supplying him with ammunition and money. Should Ma Chung-ying capture Sinkiang with the Japanese behind the scene, then Soviet Central Asia would be threatened. Therefore a prompt response was given to Sheng Shih-tsai, who asked for immediate military assistance, by sending two brigades of Soviet troops disguised in Chinese military uniform to demolish the formidable force of Ma Chung-ying. Such troops were instantly called back as soon as the task had been carried out. The Soviet Government, therefore directly helping Sheng Shih-tsai who had no connections with the Soviet whatsoever, was indirectly helping the Chinese Government to quell the rebels. The financial aid for the reconstruction of industry could be looked upon in the same way."[8]

As Sheng owed his survival and his position in Sinkiang to Moscow he became practically a Soviet puppet. The executive posts of the provincial government remained in the Chinese hands but actual power rested with Soviet representatives. Soviet advisors were appointed to every important civil or military office. There was a Financial Committee which controlled budget and appropriations but all the decisions and payments made by it must be approved by its Soviet adviser. A special agency, the Sovsintorg (Soviet-Sinkiang Trade) was created by the Soviet Government to monopolize the foreign trade of Sinkiang. Its headquarters was in Moscow with offices in Urumchi, Ili and other Sinkiang cities. It controlled transportation facilities between Sinkiang and Central Asia.

When the rumor reached Nanking in June 1934 that Sinkiang was negotiating a loan with Soviet authorities the Waichiaopu had sent a note to Russian Ambassador Bogomolov, declaring that any foreign loans not approved by the National Government would not be regarded as valid. Then in July Sheng Shih-tsai petitioned the Chinese Government for its approval of a loan of 4,000,000 gold rubles from the Sovsintorg to be paid back in five years with native products. In its reply the Government instructed Sheng to send the draft agreement for consideration. Meanwhile the Chinese embassy in Moscow notified the Foreign Commissariat that before the Chinese Government expressed its approval to the Soviet Government the Sovsintorg should not sign such an agreement. Then in August Vice-Minister Hsu Mo of the Waichiaopu had a talk with Bogomolov, concerning this loan. Bogomolov asserted that it was not a loan but a commercial deal but Hsu insisted that any economic agreement or contract concerning local authorities and a foreign agency must be approved by the Central Government before its conclusion. There were more conversations and notes but neither the Soviet Government, nor Sheng Shih-tsai, was willing to disclose the conditions of the proposed agreement. Then on May 24, 1935 Sheng Shih-tsai telegraphed the National Government that the contract between the Sovsintorg and Sinkiang had been signed on May 16 by which the Sovsintorg was to furnish a loan of 5,000,000 rubles for productive purposes and to be paid back with native products in five years with a 4% annual interest. The contract itself had never been submitted to the Government for its approval. It was not until March 1950 when the Chinese Government had moved to Taipei that Sheng Shih-tsai told the Waichiaopu that the contract had been signed by the Sinkiang Commissioner of Finance; that the Soviet Government had not given Sinkiang gold rubles as Sheng expected but with silver bullion which could not be freely circulated and had been used as security for issuing bank notes; and that the loan had been paid back with sheep and wool.[9]

On January 22, 1935, Japanese Foreign Minister Hirota informed the Diet of "reports of the Sovietization of Sinkiang". Six days later Molotov answered Hirota by declaring in the Seventh All-Union Congress of Soviets: "One is struck by the fact that special efforts to spread this slander against the U.S.S.R. are being made in Japan whose policy in relation to China is known to everybody and cannot possibly be covered up by the spreading of inventions. I consider it necessary to emphasize the real Soviet policy towards China: the Soviet Union considers as incompatible with its policy the seizure of foreign territories, and is absolutely adherent to the independence, integrity and sovereignty of China over all of her parts including Sinkiang."[10]

But despite this emphatic denial the Soviet grip over Sinkiang became even firmer after the conclusion of this loan. Sinkiang was to be developed under Soviet direction. Soviet engineers, physicians, military instructors and other experts arrived by the hundreds. A number of factories, mills, hospitals and highways were built under the supervision of the Russians. A military academy and an aviation school was established. In public schools Russian took the place of English as the required foreign language. Hundreds of boys were sent to Tashkent to study military science while a number of girls went to the Soviet Union to learn other subjects. Even a vigorous anti-religious campaign was conducted which met with great opposition from the Moslems. When the great Swedish explorer, Sven Hedin, passed through Urumchi in 1935 he was invited to give a speech at a Soviet club to 250 Soviet officials and officers. Later Hedin wrote in his book: "There was . . . only one man in Urumchi who was more powerful than Sheng Tupan—M. Apresoff."[11]

Barmine also reported "Sinkiang was to become a sphere of exclusive Russian influence and to serve as a bulwark of our power in the East. We had to equip 10,000 Sinkiang troops completely from boots to Kuomintang insignia. Soviet advisers who actually exercised the authority of ministers, were placed at the governor's elbow. A commission headed by Stalin's brother-in-law, Svanidze, was sent to Sinkiang to draw up a plan of reconstruction for the province. My trust was instructed to send engineers to build roads, airdromes and hangars all over Sinkiang. Sinkiang was soon a Soviet colony in all but name. The Soviet Government had guaranteed her currency with a huge loan of silver, dominated her trade, and was directing her policies."[12]

The *Moslem World* later reported a third secret agreement which had greater political significance than the previous two. It was alleged that the Soviet Union and Sinkiang agreed to take care that no foreign influence should penetrate into Sinkiang; that in case of external attack upon Sinkiang the Soviet Union would assist it politically, economically and by armed force; and that in case Sinkiang decided upon the declaration of independence or the formation of a separate state the Soviet Union was bound to assist it.[13] There has been no evidence to support the authenticity of this agreement.

For many years Britain had had trade relations with Sinkiang, especially its southern part, via the route of India, but now the Soviet Union was determined to get the British out of Sinkiang. An anti-British movement had broken out in southern Sinkiang in 1934 and Sir Erich Teichman, a staff member of the British embassy in Nanking, was sent to Urumchi and Kashgar in the fall of 1935 to investigate and negotiate. He was cordially received by Sinkiang authorities but his mission completely failed. In March 1939 all foreign, i.e. British and Indian, merchants in southern Sinkiang were ordered to sell their goods and leave the country within a week. The British consul-general at Kashgar protested. The consulate was then boycotted and its couriers were molested along the trade route from India.[14] Later a despatch from Delhi reported that: "Thirty three British-Indian refugees, including nine women and twelve children who had been deported from Sinkiang have arrived at Gilgit frostbitten and destitute . . ."[15] The British consul-general then went to Urumchi to take up the matter with the provincial government but to no avail. Thereafter trade between Sinkiang and India no longer existed.

Unlike Outer Mongolia, no revolutionary party was created in Sinkiang. The reason is simple: a political party would need some popular propaganda on behalf of the natives of whom 75% were Moslems. The Moslems were against Communism as well as against Chinese rule. So it was easier for the Soviet Government to control one man who was willing to serve as a Soviet stooge than to control a political party. Consequently instead of a revolutionary party an Anti-Imperialist League was formed in Sinkiang whose propaganda was directed against Britain and Japan in line with the Soviet policy in Asia during that period. This league had its headquarters at Urumchi and branches all over Sinkiang. On New Year's Eve of 1937 tremendous anti-imperialist demonstrations were staged in all large cities. In October 1938 an All-Sinkiang Congress of the Anti-Imperialist League was held in Urumchi. As the Sino-Japanese War was then in full swing it adopted a resolution to contribute ten planes to the Chinese Air Force and to keep the overland route to China proper open. After the conclusion of the Soviet-German pact in August 1939, the *Sinkiang Daily News* described the non-Soviet world as divided between two imperialist camps, Britain and the United States in one and Germany, Italy and Japan in the other. For Sinkiang the clash of the two imperialist camps meant peace.[16]

As a result of his capitulation to the Soviet Union Sheng also co-operated with the Chinese Communists. The brother of Mao Tse-tung was made Commissioner of Finance in the provincial government. In 1937 when the Sino-Japanese War had broken out and when Chen Shao-yu, Kang Sheng and Teng Fa, representatives of the Chinese Communist Party, passed through Sinkiang on their way from Moscow to Yenan, Sheng applied for admission to the Chinese Communist Party. It was granted by Mao Tse-tung but the Comintern objected on the pretext that it might offend the Kuomintang and British imperialism to the detriment of Sinkiang. Early in 1938 a regiment of Soviet troops was sent to Hami and stationed there on the pretext of preventing Japanese invasion of Sinkiang. In September Sheng went to Moscow to see Stalin and again applied for membership in the Communist Party. Stalin told Sheng to become a member of the Soviet Communist Party first and promised to transfer his membership to the Chinese Communist Party later. But that transfer never took place, evidently because Stalin did not wish to see too much relationship between Sinkiang and Yenan.[17]

Then in November 1940 Stalin sent Bakulin to Urumchi to see Sheng with a draft agreement on tin mines in Sinkiang. According to this draft Sinkiang granted to the Soviet Union "exclusive rights for the prospection, investigation and exploitation of tin mines and its ancillary minerals". In this connection the Soviet Government was also given the right to build offices, warehouses, dormitories, hospitals, schools, power stations, railways, roads, etc. The materials and equipment used for these purposes would be admitted to Sinkiang duty-free for the first ten years and products of the tin mines and its ancillary minerals would also be exported duty-free. Soviet engineers, technicians and workers could be employed to do these jobs and would have the freedom of residence in various places in Sinkiang. The agreement was to be effective for 50 years. A trust with the short title of "Sin-tin' was to be established by the Soviet Government to carry out the project.[18] In short Sinkiang was to be put under economic control of the Soviet Government through its agency, Sin-tin. Sheng wanted to modify some of the terms and to shorten the duration of the lease but was told by the Soviet emissary "that not a single word was alterable and that, being a member of the U.S.S.R. Communist Party, I should obey the orders of the party and struggle the more vigorously for the interests of the Soviet Union". Sheng was also reminded that during the rebellion of Ma Chung-ying much of Soviet blood was shed in Sinkiang for which the Soviet Union had not yet been compensated. Sheng was thus compelled to sign his name on the agreement but refused to have the seals of the provincial government and the Border Defense Commissioner's office attached to it.[19]

The National Government was quite aware of Sheng's relations with the Soviet Union but it tolerated him for fear that if Sheng was dismissed from his office he would openly revolt and it would have no power to suppress him, its hands being tied in dealing with both Japan and the Communists. Later, after the outbreak of the Sino-Japanese War, it was through Sinkiang that Soviet military supplies reached Chungking and the National Government had the least desire to offend either the Soviet Union or Sheng. It waited for a proper moment to exercise its authority over Sinkiang; it finally came in 1943.

Ever since 1934 a Pao-an-chu, Security Preservation Bureau, a counter-part of the NKVD in the Soviet Union, had been established at Urumchi. A Chinese was its nominal head but its Pao-an-twei, Security Police, was under the control of Pogodin, NKVD leader in Sinkiang. The Russians were always suspicious of Chinese, Mongols, and Moslems alike and Sheng himself was cruel. So executions became routine and large scale purges took place several times. According to the estimates of some natives 120,000 persons, including officials, officers, scholars, merchants, peasants, etc. were liquidated during Sheng's twelve years of rule. After German invasion of the Soviet Union in June 1941 most of the Soviet troops in Central Asia had to be transferred to the front. The serious defeat of the Soviet army by the Germans diminished Soviet prestige in Sinkiang. So the Russians became suspicious of Sheng and tried to liquidate him. In the spring of 1942 a conspiracy was under way to assassinate Sheng and other high officials at a mass meeting to be held on April 12, anniversary of the coup d'etat of 1933. Soviet consular representatives, advisers, miltary officers and Chinese Communists, all participated in the plot. But before that date Sheng's brother, Shih-chi, was murdered by some Soviet officers who were probably Trotskyites and the whole plot was unearthed. Sheng then executed all the Chinese Communists in Urumchi, including the brother of Mao Tse-tung and, according to some sources, even his own wife. The Anti-Imperialist League was dissolved.

Thus breaking away from the Soviet Union Sheng turned towards the National Government for support. He sent his brother, Shih-ji, to Chungking to see Generalissimo Chiang and to pledge his allegiance. In July Generalissimo Chiang sent General Chu Shao-liang, Commander-in-Chief of the Eighth War Zone (Northwest), to Urumchi to assure Sheng the support of Chungking; it was at this juncture that Sheng revealed his past relations with the Soviet Union in a long and confidential letter to Chiang. In August Madame Chiang personally flew to Urumchi to celebrate the re-unification of Sinkiang with China. Government troops were sent into Sinkiang early in 1943 and the authority of the National Government was established for the first time since 1927. The provincial government was reorganized and new officials were appointed to replace the old. A provincial office of the Kuomintang was established at Urumchi with Sheng at its head. The Central Planning Board worked out a ten-year plan for the development of the Northwest and a "Go Northwest" movement was inaugurated at Chungking to induce young officials, engineers, scholars and party workers to proceed to the Northwest, especially to Sinkiang. The British and American consulates in Urumchi were also reopened in 1943.

This sudden shift of Sheng's allegiance must have extremely antagonized Moscow but as the Soviet Union was engaged in a life or death struggle against Germany it had no strength to settle the account with Sheng at the moment. Besides, an open break with China, one of the principal allies, would certainly create unfavorable impressions in the United States. So Stalin decided to acquiesce in this episode and to withdraw temporarily from Sinkiang. The Russian consul-general at Urumchi told Sheng on April 10, 1943 that the work of the Sin-tin would be immediately suspended and all geologists who had been investigating in Sinkiang and all equipment which had been sent to Sinkiang since 1940 would be withdrawn. By June the geologists and their families had all left Sinkiang and the equipment of the Sin-tin had been removed. Soviet troops in Sinkiang had also been withdrawn in April 1943. Soviet advisers were gradually recalled and the offices of the Sovsintorg were closed.

With regard to the Tu-shan-tze oil mine which had been illegally exploited by Soviet agencies in Sinkiang since 1939 the National Government had tried to make it a Sino-Soviet joint enterprise. Negotiations had been going on between Fu Ping-chang, later Victor Hu, Vice Minister for Foreign Affairs, and Wong Wen-hao, Minister for Economic Affairs, on the one hand and Soviet Ambassador Paniushkin on the other from September 1932 to May 1933. The National Government was quite willing to make some concessions to the Soviet Union but Paniushkin demanded terms which could not be accepted. Then on May 17, 1943, Paniushkin notified the Waichiaopu that the Soviet Government had decided to abandon the mine and to remove the equipment. Later it was agreed that China was to pay 1,700,000 U. S. dollars for the buildings and equipment of the mine.[20]

Sheng, who had been a Soviet favorite, was now regarded as Public Enemy No. 1 in Sinkiang. The Soviet Government sent to Chungking a copy of its correspondence with Sheng before the rupture to show that Sheng was not so loyal to China as he claimed. When Vice-President Henry Wallace visited Chungking in June, 1944 he pointed out to Generalissimo Chiang Kai-shek that Sheng was an obstacle in the way of Sino-Soviet cooperation.[21] Thereupon Sheng was removed from his posts as Border Defense Commissioner of Sinkiang and chairman of the provincial government and appointed Minister of Agriculture in the National Government. General Wu Chung-hsin, a veteran Kuomintang member, succeeded Sheng as the head of the provincial government. In July 1945 during the negotiations of the Sino-Soviet Treaty of Friendship and Alliance Sheng was again dismissed from his post as Minister of Agriculture.[22]

CHAPTER XV

Sino-Soviet Relations After the Mukden Incident

As told in a previous chapter Japan had as much ambition in China as Russia. But after the First World War her ambition was checked by the Washington Conference and the Nine Power Treaty of 1921-1922. As long as China was disunited Japan was contented with the status quo in Manchuria where her influence was dominant. But when China showed signs of unity the Japanese militarists became uneasy and wanted to grasp Manchuria from China. So in June 1928 when the National Revolutionary Army under Generalissimo Chiang Kai-shek was marching on Peking and Marshal Chang Tso-lin, war lord of Manchuria, fled from Peking back to Mukden he was killed by the explosion of a mine placed under the railway track near Mukden by the Japanese Kwantung Army. It was the calculation of the Kwantung Army that the sudden death of Chang Tso-lin would create chaotic conditions in Manchuria which would furnish a good pretext for the Japanese to occupy it. But Chang Hsueh-liang, eldest son of Chang Tso-lin, quietly returned to Mukden and assumed his father's position, and peace and order were thus maintained. The plot of the Kwantung Army was nipped in the bud.

Owing to the assassination of his father Chang Hsueh-liang hated the Japanese. So at the end of 1928 when his authority in Manchuria was consolidated he swore his allegiance to Nanking and Manchuria was peacefully brought back under the rule of the Central Government for the first time since 1917. Thereafter the Kwantung Army was even more anxious to get rid of Chang Hsueh-liang and to seize Manchuria. The civil wars in China during 1929 and 1930, the failure of the American efforts to check Soviet aggression on the Manchurian border in 1929 and the subsequent business depression in the United States greatly encouraged Japanese militarists to take bold action. After taking part in the suppression of the revolt of Yen Hsi-san and Feng Yu-hsiang in October 1930 Chang Hsueh-liang stayed most of the time in Peiping[1] seeking pleasures and neglected his duties in Mukden. The Japanese militarists saw their chance and struck. In the evening of September 18, 1931 a Japanese soldier, patroling in the South Manchurian Railway zone, heard an explosion on the track and discovered that a section of the rail had been blown apart. The damage was very slight and an express train passed over the spot within a few minutes without any disturbance. But the Kwantung Army command at once charged the Chinese forces near Mukden with a plot to blow up the South Manchurian Railway, a Japanese enterprise. Japanese troops then besiged the Chinese barracks, captured military stores and disarmed Chinese garrison forces. Within a few hours Mukden and nearby strategic points were all occupied by the Japanese.

The Mukden incident was staged by the Kwantung Army without the previous consent of Japanese Premier Wakatsuki and Foreign Minister Shidehara. After its occurrence they were alarmed and Shidehara told his friends that swallowing Manchuria would be tantamount to swallowing a bomb. But the Ministry of War was backing this adventure and the Japanese cabinet was powerless to check the militarists. So the aggressive action beginning at Mukden spread and within four months all Manchuria was under the occupation of the Kwantung Army. Most of the Chinese troops in Manchuria were either disarmed without resistance or retreated inside the Great Wall. Only the forces under General Ma Chan-san in Heilungkiang resisted fiercely but was defeated and had to cross the border into Siberia.

The National Government knew that China was too inferior in military strength to fight a full-scale war against Japan and appealed to both the League of Nations and the United States for checking Japanese aggression as it grossly violated the League Covenant, the Nine Power Treaty and the Kellogg-Briand Anti-War Pact. The Council of the League passed resolutions first at the end of September and again in October calling upon Japan to withdraw her troops into the railway zone and Secretary of State Stimson sent notes to the Japanese Foreign Office to the same effect.[2] To both the League and Washington Shidehara replied in a conciliatory tone, promising to call back unruly soldiers but the Japanese militarists simply paid no heed to what the foreign minister said. When it became known that Japan intended to remain in Manchuria Secretary of State Stimson suggested that the United States would have to resort to economic sanctions against Japan in order to safeguard world peace but met the refusal of President Hoover. Mr. Hoover was afraid that economic sanctions would lead to war and was only willing to apply moral pressure. So on January 7, 1932, four days after the Kwantung Army had completed its occupation of Manchuria, Secretary Stimson sent identical notes to the Chinese and Japanese governments declaring that the United States "cannot admit the legality of any situation de facto nor does it intend to recognize any treaty or agreement entered into between those governments, or agents thereof, which may impair the treaty rights of the United States or its citizens in China, including those which relate to the sovereignty, the independence, or the territorial and administrative integrity of the Republic of China, or to the international policy relative to China, commonly known as the open-door policy; and that it does not intend to recognize any situation, treaty or agreement which may be brought about by means contrary to the covenants and obligations of the Pact of Paris of August 27, 1928, to which treaty both China and Japan, as well as the United States, are parties".[3] This policy has been known as the doctrine of non-recognition.

There were also talks of economic sanctions in the League Council among the small-nation members but the great powers like Britain and France did not approve such an idea. In fact the British representative in the League was actually helping Japan in justifying her action in Manchuria. The council finally decided to send a commission of inquiry to examine the issue on the spot and to recommend what could be done to safeguard the interest of both parties. The five-man commission, headed by Lord Lytton of Britain, arrived at Shanghai in March, 1932, but before that Japan had started a military offensive at Shanghai and had set up a puppet state, Manchukuo, in Manchuria. The League then promoted direct negotiations concerning a cease-fire between China and Japan and hostilities around Shanghai stopped in March. The Lytton Commission, after spending six months in the Far East, submitted its report to the League in September. In this report the commission asserted that Japan's military action could not be justified, as Japan had claimed, as legitimate self-defense and that the establishment of the Manchukuo did not represent the wishes of the Manchurian people but was engineered by Japan. It proposed a special administration for Manchuria under Chinese sovereignty but with a large degree of autonomy in local affairs. Both Chinese and Japanese forces would be withdrawn and special gendarmerie would be entrusted with the maintenance of peace and order. Japan's interests in Manchuria would be safeguarded by a treaty between China and Japan.[4] The League Assembly adopted the report in February 1933 and advised all members not to recognize Manchukuo "either de jure or de facto". Japan responded by notifying the League of her intention of withdrawing from it.

The inability of the League of Nations to check aggression greatly disappointed China. The National Government then turned to the Soviet Union for possible help in China's struggle against Japan. The

Central Executive Committee of the Kuomintang adopted a resolution in June 1932 to resume diplomatic relations with the Soviet Union. When the Disarmament Conference was in session at Geneva in the fall of 1932 Dr. W. W. Yen, Chinese delgate, was instructed to approach Maxim Litvinov, Soviet representative, on the question of resumption of diplomatic relations. The Soviet Union, as its own security was being threatened by the aggressive policy of Japan, was quite willing to resume normal relations with China. Consequently the conversations between Yen and Litvinov proceeded very smoothly and an agreement was soon reached. The National Government had also proposed the conclusion of a non-aggression pact by which it hoped that Soviet representatives in China would refrain from taking part in Chinese Communist activities, but the Soviet Government insisted on the resumption of relations before the discussion of other subjects. As China was more anxious to have official relations restored the National Government finally accepted the Soviet view.

On December 12 the following identical notes were exchanged between the two envoys: "In pursuance of our recent conversations during our pleasant meetings at Geneva, I am duly authorized to inform you that, being desirous of promoting the interests of peace and friendly relations between our two countries, the Government of China (or the U.S.S.R. in the Soviet note) has decided to regard normal diplomatic and consular relations as having been re-established as from to-day."[5] Dr. W. W. Yen was appointed the first Chinese ambassador to the Soviet Union while Dimitri Bogomolov was appointed Soviet ambassador to China. They both presented their credentials in May 1933, and diplomatic relations were resumed after six years' rupture. But somehow the proposed non-aggression pact did not materialize until four years later.[6]

While the Soviet Government at that time was willing to cultivate China's friendship its policy toward Japan had been since the Mukden incident that of appeasement. After the conclusion of the Soviet-Japanese Treaty of 1925 the relations between the two powers were marked by the absence of political conflicts. Molotov told the Central Committee of the Soviet Union Communist Party in December 1933 that "From the time of the Peking agreement to the end of 1931, the best good-neighborly relations existed between us and Japan".[7] The Mukden incident naturally caused anxiety in the Foreign Commissariat but Japanese Ambassador Koki Hirota soon assured Foreign Commissar Litvinov that Japan would limit her military activities to the southern part of Manchuria and that she would not penetrate into the sphere of the Chinese Eastern Railway. Thereupon the Soviet Government decided to pursue a policy of "strict neutrality" in the Sino-Japanese struggle. The Soviet press did not attack Japan for her aggression while the official publication of the Comintern blamed the antagonism between Britain and America for the Far Eastern crisis.

But Japan did not keep her promise and her troops marched into Kirin and Heilungkiang (northern Manchuria) after Liaoning (southern Manchuria) had been occupied. In Heilungkiang Japanese forces met the resistance of General Ma Chan-san. The Japanese Government at the end of October protested to the Soviet Union against its giving assistance to General Ma. Moscow replied that it not only was not helping General Ma but had no intention of interfering in the Manchurian conflict. Japan then demanded the Chinese Eastern Railway must no longer transport Chinese troops on the ground that the South Manchurian Railway had not transported Chinese troops in the Sino-Soviet conflict of 1929. In his reply Litvinov denied any similarity between Soviet action in 1929 and the Japanese invasion in 1931 but promised that in no case would the Soviet Government agree to the transport of troops of either side to the front.[8]

Towards the end of 1931 Litvinov proposed to Japanese Foreign Minister Yoshizawa who was passing through Moscow on his way home the conclusion of a non-aggression pact. The Japanese Government ignored the Soviet offer for a year and then made a counter-proposal that all causes of possible disputes should be eliminated before the conclusion of such a pact. As this was unacceptable to the Soviet Government the matter was dropped.[9] In February 1932 the Japanese Government demanded the use of the Chinese Eastern Railway for the transport of Japanese troops and Moscow readily yielded. When Sir Eric Drummond, Secretary-General of the League of Nations, invited the Soviet Government to participate in the Lytton Commission, Litvinov refused the invitation and reiterated in his reply that the Soviet Government had adopted "a course of strict neutrality". In August a fisheries agreement between Japan and the Soviet Union was concluded by which new concessions were granted to Japan and in September another agreement provided for the delivery of Soviet gasoline to Japan over a period of five years. On December 12, the same day when resumption of Sino-Soviet relations was announced, Litvinov made a declaration in which he said: "The Soviet Union has its hands unfettered by any secret political combinations and agreements, consequently the improvement of relations with one country is not a means of rendering worse relations with another. Only such a policy can genuinely assist in strengthening general peace".[10] Of course this was meant for the ears of Japan. Yet such an explanation failed to remove the apprehension of the Japanese Government which officially asserted that "the elements most disturbing to the peace of the world have now joined hands and Japan stands squarely against these forces".[11]

Despite the Soviet policy of appeasement towards Japan the Japanese Government which was now under the domination of the militarists was bent upon eliminating the Soviet influence in Manchuria completely. Its attention was centered on the Chinese Eastern Railway. After the establishment of the puppet state of Manchukuo in March 1932 the Chinese Eastern Railway hoisted the Manchukuo flag and accepted Li Shao-keng, appointee of the puppet regime, as its director-general. Li, backed by the Japanese soon had troubles with the Soviet officials of the Chinese Eastern Railway. The Soviet Government, being aware of the possible seizure of the railway by Japan, secretly ordered the Chinese Eastern Railway to gradually remove a large part of the rolling stock into Siberia. When this action was later discovered by the puppet regime Li Shao-keng, at the beginning of April 1933, delivered a strong note of protest to the Soviet assistant director-general, Stephen Kuznetzov, demanding the immediate return of the rolling stock detained in Siberia. As this protect brought no result, Japanese-Manchukuo troops blocked Manchuli and delivered to Kuznetzov on April 12 an ultimatum demanding the return within thirty days of the detained rolling stock consisting of 83 locomotives, 190 passenger cars and 3,000 freight cars. The next day another blockade was effected at Suifengho (Pogranitchnaya) at the east end of the railway. Three days later Karakhan, acting Foreign Commisar, lodged a protest with Japanese Ambassador Ota and asserted that the detained rolling stock was the property of the Soviet Union and not of the railway. The Japanese Government was not satisfied with this explanation and at the end of May the connection between the Chinese Eastern and the Ussuri railways was cut off at Suifengho.

Now the Soviet Government had to decide either to defend its interest in the Chinese Eastern Railway with armed force as it had done in 1929 or to withdraw from Manchuria completely. Of course it was not willing to give up its sphere of influence in northern Manchuria which had existed for more than thirty years, yet it knew very well that its military strength in the Far East had not yet been built up and a conflict with Japan would end in Soviet crushing defeat. So the Soviet propaganda followed two seemingly contradictory lines: peace and resistance. The Comintern advocated "resistance to Japanese aggression", blamed the Chinese Government for concluding truce with Japan and attacked the Western powers for their appeasement of Japan. But on the other hand the Soviet press asserted that the Soviet policy was the maintenance of peace in the Far East so as to save the world from another catastrophe. As pointed out by Mr. Dallin, "Actually, the two were part of the same policy: resistance by the other nations in order to weaken Japan wherever possible and to prevent her from attacking Russia, and Soviet concessions to Japan in order to safeguard peace. Both means served the same end: to prevent a defeat of the Soviet Union at the hands of Japan".[2] As a consequence on May 2 Litvinov directly proposed to Ota to sell the Soviet interests in the Chinese Eastern Railway.

The news of the sale of the Chinese Eastern Railway reached Nanking on the heels of the arrival of the new Soviet ambassador and the Chinese people were very much puzzled. The National Government instructed Dr. Yen to inquire at the Foreign Commissariat and Karakhan assured Yen on May 11 that no such sale had been contemplated. A day later Livinov declared, through the Tass Agency, that: "During the negotiations between Ota, the Japanese Ambassador, and myself, I did mention that the actions of the Manchukuo authorities caused serious difficulties to the Chineses Eastern Railway and aggravated controversies between Japan, Manchukuo, and the Soviet Union. In order to arrive at a possible solution, I therefore suggest that there may be a chance for Manchukuo to redeem the Chinese Eastern Railway; that is to say, the Soviet Government would sell the interests of the Chinese Eastern Railway to Manchukuo which is considered as one of the radical methods of solving the present difficulties".[13]

Nanking then lodged a strong protest with the Soviet Government against the proposed sale of the railway and charged the latter with violation of the Sino-Soviet Agreement of 1924 which expressly provided that "the governments of the two Contracting Parties mutually agree that the future of the Chinese Eastern Railway shall be determined by the Republic of China and the U.S.S.R."[14] In reply Litvinov told Ambassador Yen that the National Government and its subordinate authorities (meaning authorities in Manchuria) had ceased to be actual partners of the U.S.S.R. on the Chinese Eastern Railway of more than eighteen months and that the sale of Soviet interests was rather favorable to China in that the railway could not be removed to Japan and as China had expected to recover Manchuria, they would ultimately get the railway back without paying the Soviet Union for it.[15] In a press interview Litvinov justified the sale of the railway with a high-sounding motive by saying: "In the building of the road in Manchuria, in foreign territory, the Tsarist Government unquestionably was pursuing imperialist aims. After the October revolution the road lost the significance it had for the people of the Russian empire as an instrument of penetration".[16]

After three weeks' consideration the Japanese Government advised the Manchukuo regime to accept the Soviet offer. The puppet government then notified Moscow of its willingness to negotiate the purchase of the Chinese Eastern Railway, expressed its hope that Japan would mediate in this matter and suggested Tokyo as the place for negotiations. On May 29 Ota formally replied to Litvinov to the same effect and asserted that the matter should be settled politically but not technically, meaning that the railway had depreciated in value since the Mukden incident and therefore its price could not be based on its initial cost. The Soviet Government promptly accepted these suggestions and negotiations started in Tokyo on June 26. The Soviet Union was represented by Ambassador Yurenev; Japan, by Foreign Minister Uchida; and Manchukuo, by its minister to Japan Ting Shih-yuan and its Vice-Minister for Foreign Affairs Chuichi Ohashi, a Japanese. The Chinese Eastern Railway also sent Sheng Jui-ling as its representative. By holding meetings with Manchukuo representatives the Soviet Government practically accorded the puppet state de facto recognition.

At the third meeting both sides submitted their concrete items. The greatest difference between them was the price: the Soviet representative proposed to sell all properties belonging to the railway except the detained rolling stocks for 250,000,000 gold rubles, while the Manchukuo bid for the railway was 50,000,000 yen, equivalent to 20,000,000 gold rubles. Yurenev at first also claimed sole Soviet ownership of the railway on the ground that it was built by the toiling masses of Russia with their hard earned money. The Manchukuo representatives rejected such a claim and asserted that the entire work except the steel structures were carried out by Chinese laborers paid with Tsarist bank-notes which were later repudiated by the Soviet Government.[17] They actually demanded compensation for the losses of the Manchurian people who had worked for the railway and owned such bank-notes. After much contention over the question of ownership both sides agreed to drop it and the sale price became the stumbling block of the negotiations.

After a long standstill the Soviet representative brought down the price to 200,000,000 gold rubles but the Japanese-Manchukuo side stuck to 50,000,000 yen. Meanwhile all kinds of trouble was happening on the Chinese Eastern Railway. Manchurian armed bands were frequently damaging the railway traffic. According to official Soviet sources in 1933 there had occurred 11 intentional train wrecks, 39 attempts at wrecking, 38 raids on trains, 19 cases of arson, 60 murders of employees, 197 cases of robbery and assault, and kidnapping of 400 persons.[18] No attempt was made by the Manchukuo authorities to maintain order along the line. Besides, the Japanese were planning to construct other lines parallel to the Chinese Eastern Railway which, when completed, would render the railway valueless. Under such pressures the Soviet Government had to give in and in February 1934 lowered the price to 200,000,000 yen. In April the Manchukuo delegation raised its offer to 100,000,000 yen including 30,000,000 yen for allowances given to the discharged employees of the railway. Negotiations then dragged on with the Soviet side gradually lowering its demand while the Japanese-Manchukuo side gradually raising its offer.

Finally in September 1934 an agreement was reached to fix the purchase price at 140,000,000 yen, with Manchukuo bearing the discharging allowances of 30,000,000 yen. One-third of the price was to be paid in cash and of this amount one half was to be paid simultaneously with the signing of the agreement while the other half was to be paid with Manchukuo treasury bonds at 3% annual interest redeemable within three years. The other two-thirds of the price were to be paid with goods in installments over three years. With this question settled other details were agreed upon smoothly. The Japanese Government gave its guarantee to the payments by Manchukuo and the agreement was signed at Tokyo on March 23, 1935.[19] After its taking over by the puppet state the Chinese Eastern Railway was re-named the North Manchurian Railway and incorporated into the South Manchurian Railway Company.

Upon learning the conclusion of the agreement the National Government again protested strongly with the Soviet Union and sent a circular memorandum to the signatories of the Nine Power Treaty. In this memorandum China refused to recognize any party as a successor to the rights and interests in the railway; and asserted that "Russia's present action constitutes without the shadow of a doubt a direct violation of China's contractual as well as sovereign rights" and that "the painful fact that the Chinese Government has been prevented by circumstances—for which it is not responsible—from exercising its rights in connection with the administration of the Chinese Eastern Railway, does not in the least affect the validity of the provisions of the agreement of 1924, nor the status of the railway".[20] The Soviet

Government indirectly answered the Chinese protest through an editorial in *Izvestiya* on March 24: 'The Soviet Union, having broken finally and irrevocably with the policy of Tsarist expansion and colonial conquest could not attempt by arms to assure the operation of the Chinese Eastern Railway, for such an attempt might have led to participation in the imperialist division of Manchuria. This circumstance dictated the appropriateness of selling the Chinese Eastern Railway to the actual authorities which were established on the territory of Manchuria".

Even after Soviet retreat from Manchuria relations between Japan and the Soviet Union did not improve. Tokyo now conducted a "peace offensive" against the Soviet Union by proposing the "demilitarization" of both the Soviet and Manchurian sides of the border. The Japanese Government repeatedly pointed out Soviet military preparations in eastern Siberia as proof of Soviet aggressive designs. In January 1935 when the Chinese Eastern Railway negotiations were nearing a settlement Hirota told the Japanese Diet: "We hope that now the Soviet Government will pay particular attention to the question of military installations in the Far East". The establishment of a neutral belt along the border proved unacceptable to Moscow as the Trans-Siberian Railway runs close to the Amur. *Izvestiya* wrote in an editorial: "Behind our lines of defense there runs a railroad, which in many places is less than 50 kilometers from the border . . . The Japanese military suggest to us the annihilation of our line of defense. Why don't the Japanese generals demand, as proof of our sincerity, that we build for them a route of approach to our trunk line?"[21]

Litvinov consistently rejected the proposal of "demilitarization" of Japan and repeated his old offer of a non-aggression pact. But the Japanese Government, especially the Japanese militarists, did not want such a pact to limit their freedom of action. There were talks about setting up commissions to settle border disputes but they did not come into existence until 1940. In the meantime the Soviet Union was feverishly building up its strength in the Far East. From 1936 on the Far Eastern Red Army grew rapidly. In July 1938 General Lushkov who had escaped from the Soviet Union to Japan said that the Red forces consisted of 400,000 men with 2,000 planes. According to a Japanese intelligence report there were in the Soviet forces 5 cavalry and 15 infantry divisions, 4 mechanized corps, and 9 air squadrons, totalling 300,000 men.[22] It was this accumulation of military strength which prevented the border incidents from developing into a real war.

It is said that the appetite of an aggressor grows with eating. In the case of Japan this saying is 100 per cent true. After the complete occupation of Manchuria Japanese troops seized Jahol, a part of the former Inner Mongolia, early in 1933 and incorporated it into Manchukuo. In 1935 Japanese forces again invaded Chahar, another part of former Inner Mongolia. The Japanese also instigated their stooge, Yin Ju-keng, to set up a puppet regime in eastern Hopei and another stooge, Mongolian Prince Teh, to set up another puppet regime in northern Suiyuan. It became apparent that Japan intended not only to occupy Manchuria but to conquer all China. These aggressive actions could not fail to arouse an intense hatred toward Japan among the Chinese people, especially among the intellectual class. Professors, teachers, writers, journalists, college students, etc. raised a cry for war against Japan and in looking for an ally in such a war they naturally turned toward the Soviet Union. The Soviet intrigue with the Chinese Communists and the 1929 hostility over the Chinese Eastern Railway were forgotten and pro-Soviet feeling prevailed. The Soviet Union was quite willing to see the Sino-Japanese conflict develop into a full-scale war so that Japan's pressure on Siberia could be lessened. Communist and left-wing writers all encouraged this public sentiment.

At that time Generalissimo Chiang Kai-Shek was not willing to start an all-out war against Japan before China was fully prepared for it. So he made concessions to Japan time and again and tolerated humiliations in his dealings with the Japanese and criticism from Chinese intellectuals. But in the latter part of 1935 he was worried lest Japan might make a sudden thrust against China proper which would nullify his long-range policy. So he also looked to the Soviet Union for help in case of such an emergency. Upon his instructions Chen Li-fu, Director of Organizations in the Central Headquarters of the Kuomintang, approached Bogomolov for a possible secret alliance. Bogomolov told Chen that he personally favored such an alliance and suggested that Chen go to Moscow, as Chiang's personal representative, to negotiate directly with Stalin. Thereupon Chen was sent to Europe via Suez for fear that if he proceeded to Moscow via Vladivostok and Siberia he would surely be discovered by Japanese spies. So Chen under the assumed name of Li Yung-ching sailed to Marseilles on a German steamer at Christmas time and arrived in Berlin in January 1936. He waited there for the final nod of Stalin consenting to the negotiations for a secret alliance before proceeding to Moscow. But that nod never came and Chen returned to Nanking in April without setting foot on Soviet territory.[23] The only explanation for Stalin's attitude seems to be that he was willing to help China fight an all-out war against Japan on the condition that the Soviet Union would not be directly involved in it.

CHAPTER XVI

Evolution of Chinese Communism, 1928-1937

After the failure of the Canton insurrection in December, 1927 it was no longer possible for the Kremlin to speak of a continuing rising wave of the Chinese revolution. Yet it could not admit that the wave had definitely receded because that was the view of the Trotskyists. So in February 1928 the Ninth Plenum of the Executive Committee of the Comintern adopted a resolution, asserting that China was now in "a trough between two waves" and during this the duty of the Chinese Communist Party was to prepare for armed insurrections.

Five months later the Sixth National Congress of the Chinese Communist Party was held in Moscow. It met there for two reasons: first, it was unsafe for a number of leading Chinese Communists to meet in any place under the jurisdiction of the National Government or even in the international settlement or the French concession in Shanghai and secondly, as the Sixth World Congress of the Comintern was being held in Moscow during the same period (July-September) it was easier for the Comintern to supervise the proceedings of the Chinese Congress and to eliminate any possible Trotskyist influence therein. About 170 delegates attended the congress among whom were Chang Kuo-tao, Chou En-lai, Chu Chiu-pai, Hsiang Chung-fa, Hsu Teh-li, Hu Wen-chiang, Li Lih-san, Li Wei-han, Lin Tsu-han, Liu Po-cheng, Wang Chia-hsiang and Yeh Chien-ying. Under the direction of the Comintern the congress condemned the policy of Chen Tu-hsiu as opportunist, rightist deviation and that of Chu Chiu-pai as putschist, leftist deviation. Bukharin, present at the congress as the representative of the Comintern, scolded Chu Chiu-pai: "You are supposed to be a Bolshevik leader, not a playwright. You have led the Chinese revolution as though you were acting in a play." To Chou En-lai he said: "You are in charge of military affairs. You should have estimated your own strength. You are the one most responsible for blind actionism".[1]

The congress, after reviewing the situation since the Fifth National Congress, adopted resolutions on the political question, the peasant movement, the land question, the labor movement, the women's movement, the C.Y. (Communist Youth) movement, propaganda and the organizational question in the Soviet regime.[2] It set up a ten-point program of the Chinese revolution in the present stage as follows: "(a) Overthrow the rule of imperialism; (b) confiscate enterprises and banks of foreign capitalism; (c) unify China and recognize (the principle) of national self-determination; (d) overthrow the warlord-Kuomintang regime; (e) establish the regime of councils of workers', peasants', and soldiers' deputies (Soviets); (f) realize the eight-hour day, higher wages, unemployment relief, and social security; (g) confiscate the land of all landlords—land should belong to the peasants; (h) improve the livelihood of soldiers and allot them land and work; (i) abolish taxes imposed by the (KMT) government warlords and local administration, institute unified progressive taxes, and (j) unite with the proletariat of the world and the Soviet Union".[3] The thesis of the Comintern concerning China also declared: "In China the future growth of the revolution will place before the Party (CCP) as an immediate practical task the preparation for and the carrying through of armed insurrection as the sole path to the completion of the bourgeois-democratic revolution and to the overthrow of the imperialists, landlords, and national bourgeoisie — the Kuomintang".[4]

A revised Constitution of the Chinese Communist Party of 15 chapters and 53 articles was also adopted by the congress in which it was provided that the Chinese Communist Party was a branch of the Comintern and must obey the Comintern's decision.[5]

At the conclusion of the congress in September it elected Hsiang Chung-fa, secretary-general; Chou En-lai, head of Organization Bureau (later replaced by Li Wei-han); Li Lih-san, Propaganda Bureau; Hu Wen-chiang, Military Bureau (later Chou En-lai); Liu Shao-chi, Labor Bureau; and Peng Pai, Peasantry Bureau.[6] Chu Chiu-pai and Chang Kuo-tao were ordered by the Comintern to remain at Moscow for the former was regarded as a putschist and the latter an opportunist. Chu nominally served as the Chinese Communist delegate to the Comintern but actually in exile. The newly elected leaders went back to China to carry out the program and the instructions of the Comintern. As Hsiang Chung-fa had risen from a common boatman his ability and intelligence were not equal to his new task; actual leadership was in the hands of Li Lih-san.

Meanwhile the Chinese Communists were taking advantage of China's internal strife and external trouble to expand their military footing. After the failure of an uprising in southern Hunan early in 1928 Chu Teh retreated to Chingkangshan with a remnant group of peasants, miners and soldiers and joined force with Mao Tse-tung in May. The amalgamated units were reorganized into the Fourth Army of the Chinese Workers' and Peasants' Red Army with a total strength of about 10,000 men but only 2,000 rifles. Chu Teh became the commander of this army while Mao assumed the role of the party commissar. In July Peng Teh-huai led a military uprising at Pingkiang, Hunan and organized the Fifth Red Army. He overran seven districts in the border region of Hunan, Hupei and Kiangsi but was finally crushed by government troops. So Peng also fled to Chingkangshan with 800 remnant troops at the end of 1928.

Besides the forces under Mao at Chingkangshan other Communists were busily forming new Red armies in other parts of China. Thus Hsu Hsiang-chien organized 2,000 peasants into the First Red Army and used Chinchiatsai at Hunan-Hupei-Anhwei border as his base. Ho Lung gathered together 1,000 peasants at the Hunan-Hupei border and formed the Second Red Army. Lo Ping-hui revolted with 400 men of local militia at Kian, Kiangsi and organized the Third Red Army. Chang Yun-yi and Teng Hsiao-ping founded the Seventh and Eighth Red armies in Kwangsi. Fang Chi-min, who staged a revolt with the local militia at Yiyang, Kiangsi, became the commander of the Tenth Red Army. Peng Pai organized the Eleventh Red Army in eastern Kwantung. Liu Tsu-tan and Kao Kang created the Twenty-sixth Red Army in nothern Shensi. Most of these so-called armies had little strength but the Fourth and Fifth armies at Chinkangshan were much stronger and growing.

As the area around Chingkangshan was not fertile and could not produce enough food to feed Mao's growing troops Mao and Chu Teh decided to abandon it. So in January 1929 the Red forces left Chingkangshan, and roved about. As the National Government was busily occupied with other vital matters and did not pay much attention to them they swept over south-eastern Kiangsi, western Fukien, and northern Kwangtung. Wherever they went they seized the arms of the militia, recruited hooligans and poor peasants, massacred the gentry and landowners and established district Soviets. A Red terror soon reigned over the towns and villages under their control and their number grew rapidly.

The Central Committee of the Chinese Communist Party held its Second Plenum at Shanghai in June, 1929 and pledged itself to carry out under the guidance of the Comintern, the resolutions of the Sixth Congress, to conquer the enemy and win over the masses and to accelerate the revolutionary rising tide. It also marked the firm rule of Li Lih-san within the party. When Sino-Soviet hostilities broke out over the Chinese Eastern Railway Li Lih-san put up such slogans as "Support the Soviet Unoin!" and "Defend the Soviet Union with armed force!" In September various Oppositionist groups led by Chen Tu-hsiu, Liu Jen-ching and others met at Shanghai to discuss how to grasp the party power from the hands of Li Lih-san and two months later those so-called Trotskyists were expelled from the party.

In May 1930 the Comintern sent Pavel Mif, director of Sun Yat-sen University at Moscow, to China as its representative and 28 students of the university including Chen Shao-yu, Chang Wen-tien, Chin Pang-hsien, Shen Tse-min and Wang Chia-hsiang accompanied him. These young Chinese Communists had studied in the university since 1926 and felt proud of their mastery of the theory and tactics of Marxism and Leninism. They revolved around Mif as planets around the sun and soon became known as the "Returned Students Clique" or the "Comintern Faction." Mif's patronage won them high positions in the party but they were looked upon with disgust by experienced party veterans. "These fellows," wrote Li Ang, "were all young students who, needless to say, had made no contribution whatsoever to the revolution. . . . These men who were infants in terms of their revolutionary background were now sent back to be leaders of the Chinese revolution."[7]

Meanwhile as a large-scale civil war between government troops and revolting forces under Yen Hsi-san and Feng Yu-hsiang was now in full swing the Communists took advantage to expand. A conference of the delegates from various Soviet areas secretly met in Shanghai in May and passed a political resolution to the effect that there already existed a revolutionary situation and immediate armed uprising should begin. It also proposed that a "Central Soviet Government of China" be established. In the next month the Central Committee of the Chinese Communist Party, acting on Li Lih-san's recommendation, adopted a resolution which became known as the "Li Lih-san line." It asserted that the peak of the revolutionary tide in China had arrived and that "a general strike of a political nature is potent enough to create a nation-wide revolutionary situation favorable to armed revolts and the establishment of a Soviet regime." The Wuhan area was designated as the center of a general uprising, Red troops in the vicinity of the area were to storm the two cities, and Communists in other provinces were to be drafted to Wuhan to help carry out the plan. Guerrilla warfare was to be given up for lacking any practical value in a large-scale armed conflict, while workers were to be heading for political strikes and to suspend economic struggle.[7]

As a consequence of the decisions of the conference and the resolution of the Central Committee, the Revolutionary Military Committee of the Chinese Communist Patry, under the chairmanship of Mao Tse-tung, ordered the Red armies to march on Nanchang and Changsha. The Second Red Army under Lo Ping-hui succeeded in taking the city of Kian but could not proceed to Nanchang. The Fifth Red Army under Peng Teh-huai occupied Changsha towards the end of July, as a first step to seize Wuhan. But his success was short lived and the Communists were driven out of Changsha with heavy casualties after a week's occupation. Then Mao Tse-tung and Chu Teh's main force reached the outskirts of Changsha and attacked the city for a second time but failed to take it. In the field of labor movement the Communists also suffered setbacks in their putschism. By agitating political strikes many hidden Communists exposed themselves and were arrested. In Shanghai alone seven of eight district committees were smashed by local authorities and the party membership in that city dropped from 3,000 to 700.

In the Third Plenum of the Central Committee in August Chu Chiu-pai, who had now been sent back from Moscow, and the Returned Students Clique attacked Li Lih-san for his leftist blind actions but it failed to remove Li from power. In November a letter from the Comintern also condemned the Li Lih-san line and this time Li had to resign from the Politburo. In the next month the Twentieth Red Army under the command of Liu Tieh-chao revolted at Futien against Mao Tse-tung on the basis of the Li Lih-san line but was soon suppressed. Taking this chance Mao liquidated hundreds of anti-Mao Communists who were dubbed members of the A.B. (Anti-Bolshevik) Corps.[9]

Then in January 1931 the Fourth Plenum of the Central Committee, held in Shanghai, formally abandoned the Li Lih-san line. Li publicly admitted his mistakes and was sent to Moscow "to study." Chen Shao-yu, Chang Wen-tien, Chin Pang-hsien, and Shen Tse-min were elected members of the Politburo to replace Li Lih-san, Chu Chiu-pai, Li Wei-han and Ho Chang.

In June Chen Shao-yu was elected acting secretary-general as Hsiang Chung-fa had been arrested and executed in Shanghai, Chang Wen-tien, head of Organization and Shen Tse-min, head of Propaganda. Thereafter the party power was firmly in the hands of the Returned Students Clique.

As the Communist forces in Kiangsi grew larger and larger the National Government had become alarmed. So In December 1930 General Lu Ti-ping, chairman of the Kiangsi Provincial Government, was appointed commander-in-chief to suppress the Red armies and General Chang Hui-tsan, a division-commander, led 30,000 troops into the Soviet area in December 1930. Mao and Chu Teh had about 40,000 men under their command. In terms of training and equipment they were far inferior to the government troops. But at Chingkangshan Mao had adopted four slogans for tactics in guerrilla warfare, viz., "1. When the enemy advances, we retreat! 2. When the enemy halts we trouble them! 3. When the enemy seeks to avoid a battle, we attack! 4. When the enemy retreats, we pursue!"[10] These tactics proved to be very effective and now Mao applied them to General Chang's troops. Unaccustomed to guerrilla warfare Chang soon fell into the trap of the Communists and his forces were almost annihilated. Chang was taken as a prisoner and later executed and almost 10,000 rifles were captured by the Reds.

In February 1931 the National Government launched a second campaign against the Communists with 100,000 troops under the command of General Ho Ying-chin, Minister of War. They advanced cautiously and attempted to encircle the Red forces. Mao and Chu were at first awed by such imposing show of strength and even contemplated to make a dash to Szechuen. But as some of the division-commanders did not coordinate their operations they were defeated by the Communists one by one. After three months of the campaign the Communists succeeded in occupying half a dozen districts, including Juichin, and capturing over 10,000 rifles.

Then Generalissimo Chiang Kai-shek assumed the responsibility of suppressing the Communist forces himself. He went to Nanchang in June 1931 and established his headquarters there.[11] Over 200,000 troops were concentrated in Kiangsi and a third campaign against the Reds started in July. The government forces advanced along three routes and soon penetrated deeply into the Soviet area. Knowing that their strength was far inferior to that under the Generalissimo Mao and Chu adopted the tactics of retreat and avoided battles. District after district was taken by the government forces without fighting. The only fierce battle was forced upon the Red Army near Kian by the troops under the command of General Chen Ming-chu with heavy casualties on both sides. By the middle of September all the districts except Juichin in the Soviet area were recovered and the Reds wer encircled in an ever tightening pocket.

The successful end of the campaign seemed to be in sight when Japan unwittingly saved the Chinese Communists from annihilation. After the Mukden incident of September 18 the Generalissimo had to return to Nanking to cope with Japanese aggression and many divisions had to be withdrawn to North China and the Shanghai-Nanking area to prepare for any emergency. As a consequence the third campaign was abandoned and the Communists re-occupied all the districts which had been taken by the government forces.

Ever since the establishment of a Soviet area in Kiangsi Mao had had troubles with those who controlled the Chinese Communist Party. Mao was dissatisfied with the party leadership under Chu Chiu-pai, Li Lih-san and then Chen Shao-yu; nor were they satisfied with Mao's work in Kiangsi. As Mao grew in strength the struggle between them intensified. But since Mao controlled the Red Army, occupied an area, and contributed funds to the party while the Central Committee could only do underground work in Shanghai, the party leaders had to concede to him to some extent. In November 1931 the First All-Chinese Congress of the Soviets was convened at Juichin to which Chen Shao-yu, Chou En-lai, and other important Communists all went from Shanghai to attend. This congress with 290 delegates adopted a Constitution of the "Chinese Soviet Republic," a Land Law and a Labor Law and elected a 61 member Central Executive Committee with Mao as chairman. A "Provisional Central Government of the Chinese Soviet Republic" was also set up with Mao as chairman and Chang Kuo-tao (who had by now returned from Moscow) and Hsiang Ying as vice-chairmen. Juichin was made the capital. Chu Teh was elected Commander-in Chief of the Red Army.

Having secured his positions as the leader in the Soviet area, Mao now made a clever move to control the party. After Chen Shao-yu's return to Shanghai Mao sent a series of telegrams to the Central Committee asking it to transfer its headquarters to Juichin on the ground that there was a "White terror" in Shanghai and that the "Soviet Government" needed capable leading cadres. As his suggestion was ignored he then threatened that it might henceforth be impossible to supply money to Shanghai because of difficulties of communication. This threat had its immediate effect; the Soviet Union was then sending very little money to the Chinese Communists and most of the party's operating funds were supplied by the Soviet area.[12] So Chen Shao-yu, Chou En-lai, Chu Chiu-pai, Chang Wen-tien, Chin Pang-hsien, Liu Sho-chi, etc., all went to

Juichin and the Central Committee was transferred there in November. Chen Shao-yu was soon sent to Moscow as a delegate to the Comintern and Chin Pang-hsien succeeded him as secretary-general. While Chin Pang-hsien, Chang Wen-tien, Shen Tse-min and some other members of the Central Committee held nominally high positions in the Soviet regime the committee itself became subordinate to Mao who wielded the real power.

The so-called Provisional Central Government of the Chinese Soviet Republic had in February 1932 declared war on Japan and called on all groups and classes in China to resist Japanese aggression. But in fact the Communists were taking advantage of Japanese aggression to expand. When the government withdrew more troops from Kiangsi to fight the Japanese forces in Shanghai the Red forces harassed these troops from the rear and captured prisoners and munitions. As the garrison in Kiangsi was getting thinner the Communists started an offense and occupied Kanchow and Nanhsiung in Kiangsi and Tsangchow in Fukien. Chang Wen-tien at the end of January 1932 even issued a statement to the Communists with the title 'Our Task in the Midst of the Cannon's Roar"; he ordered them to "effect the organization and arming of the masses through propaganda and instigation" and asserted that the slogans of armed uprisings must be translated into action.[18] So instead of fighting the Japanese the Communists were doubling their efforts to overthrow the National Government and were thus helping the Japanese.

As soon as the situation in the Shanghai-Nanking area became stable, the Generalissimo again turned his eyes towards the Communists. There were now loud cries of war against Japan but the Generalissimo, after careful consideration, adopted a policy that in order to resist aggression from without China must first eliminate her enemy within, i.e., the Communists. So in June he set up his headquarters at Hankow and started a fourth campaign against the Reds. In half a year three Soviet areas, one at Hunghu, another at Honan-Hupei-Anhwei border region and a third at Hunan-Hupei-Kiangsi border region, were cleared of Communists whose remnants fled to the border of Shensi and Szechuen and established a new but much smaller Soviet area there. But so far as the so-called Central Soviet area in Kiangsi was concerned the campaign again was not successful. At first government troops had recovered more than ten districts. However, as they marched deep into the Soviet area they could not obtain accurate intelligence for effective coordination and were finally defeated one division after another. The campaign was abandoned in February 1933.

It was at this junction that the Communist strength reached its peak befor the Sino-Japanese War. The Central Soviet area was greatly extended and now embraced some thirty districts in Kiangsi, Fukien and Chekiang. Five army corps of the Red Army were organized and commanded by Chu Teh who also served as commander-in-chief, Ho Lung, Peng Teh-huai, Kwang Chi-hsun and Chi Chang-tung. These five corps were composed of thirteen armies and thirteen independent divisions with a total strength of 300,000 men. The membership of the Chinese Communist Patry also grew to 250,000, consisting mostly of peasants in the Soviet areas.

The National Government, having learned a bitter lesson from the failure of the four campaigns, now began to prepare for another. The Communist tactics was carefully studied and all officers who were going to take part in the forthcoming campaign received special training in ideology and technique. The paochia[14] system was carefully established and a very strict embargo was put on all supplies to the Soviet area. Stone blockhouses were erected at strategic points and highways were constructed to facilitate military transportation. When these preparations had been completed a fifth campaign against the Communists was launched in October.

In the next month Chen Ming-chu revolted in Fukien against the Generalissimo and a so-called People's Government was set up at Foochow. The Generalissimo had to deal with this rebellion first and the Communists again had a breathing spell. The Fifth Plenum of the Central Committee met at Juichin in January, 1934 and elected Chang Wen-tien secretary-general to replace Chin Pang-hsien. The Second All-China Congress of the Soviets was also convened at Juichin about the same time and Mao Tse-tung, Chang Kuo-tao and Hsiang Ying were re-elected chairman and vice-chairmen respectively.

The Fukien rebellion was soon suppressed and troops were transferred back to Kiangsi. Altogether about 300,000 troops took part in the campaign which now began in earnest. They converged on the Soviet area from every direction and advanced slowly but steadily. The tricks which the Communists had used so well in the previous campaigns were no longer effective. Government troops were able to maneuver the Red Army into abandoning the guerrilla tactics for positional warfare and thus afficted heavy casualties on the Reds. As time went on the Soviet area steadily dwindled in size and there was an acute shortage of daily necessities such as salt and edible oils. It became apparent now that the Communists could not hold on indefinitely and something had to be done for the survival. In August Mao, Chou and Chin Pang-hsien began to talk about evacuation and referred the question to Moscow for its instructions. In its reply Moscow advised them to pull out and seek safety somewhere—as far away as Outer Mongolia if necessary. The final decision was then made and the Communists left Juichin and began their Long March in the middle of October 1934. Some 100,000 Red troops broke through the blockade line at night and moved out of Kiangsi and only a small force was left behind to undertake rear guard action. Juichin was soon occupied by government troops and the Central Soviet area was cleared of Red forces.

After almost seven years of Communist rule in part of Kiangsi the population of that province decreased by 8,000,000—from 24,0000,00 in 1927 to 16,000,000 in 1935. Of these 8,000,000 people many were liquidated, others died of starvation or disease and still others fled from their homes to other provinces for good. Within six months after the Communist evacuation the author was sent by the Kuomintang Central Party Headquarters to the former Soviet area. He visited several districts and saw an appalling sight. All able-bodied men had been compelled to leave their homes with the Red Army; only old folks, women and children were left. Rice fields lay barren everywhere due to lack of manpower to plow them. Cities were devastated while villages were burned down to the ground. At one place in Ningtu he saw 10,000 skulls on a hollow ground—a concrete evidence of the Communist cruelty.

After leaving Kiangsi the Red Army under Mao and Chu Teh entered Hunan with government troops in hot pursuit and bombers flying over their heads. So for a week they marched at night to avoid bombing and reconnaissance. Then they marched four hours and rested four hours alternately day and night and made 40 miles in every twenty-four hours. The government troops were not accustomed to such a long march and soon were behind the Reds some distance. Of course they were harassed by provincial troops and local militia and thousands of Reds were killed on their way. But the main force pushed forward from Hunan to Kweichow.

In January 1935 the Red Army reached Tsunyi, Kweichow and halted for a few days of rest. The Politburo held a conference there, and Mao attacked the returned students' leadership for failure in Kiangsi. Mao maintained that Chin Pang-hsien and his group committed two critical errors: failing to ally themselves with the Fukien uprising in 1933 and using improper tactics against government troops in the fifth campaign. These mistakes were Mao's own mistakes but he now held Chin Pang-hsien and others responsible in line with Stalinist tradition. Chang Kuo-tao, who commanded another force in the march and was not present at the conference, presented his ideas in a telegram stating that the Soviets were not effective political instruments for Communist purposes in China but Mao remained indifferent.[15] The conference finally elected Mao chairman of the Central Committee and of the Politburo; thereafter he became the master of the Chinese Communist Party.

After leaving Tsunyi Mao's columns marched through western Kweichow, bisected a corner of Yunnan, crossed the Yangtze and Tatu rivers, pushed northward through eastern Sikang, and in July met with the troops under Chang Kuo-tao and Hsu Hsiang-chien at Mao-erh-kai in western Szechuan. There both forces halted to rest and a conference was held to discuss the party policy. Communications with Moscow were resumed after almost eight months' interruption. Mao realized now that the Chinese Communist Party had no hope to win the struggle with the Kuomintang unless some new and effective tactics were adopted. So the conference, in the name of the Central Soviet Government and the Central Committee of the Chinese Communist Party, issued on August 1 an "Appeal to the Whole People of China to Resist Japan and Save the Country." The proclamation called upon "all sons and daughters of our great motherland, . . . all commanders and soldiers, . . . all parties, groups, and organizations. . . ., all honest young men and women members of the Kuomintang. . . ., all Chinese living abroad. . . . and all our brothers of the oppressed national minorities. . . to unite as one man. . . . for the formation of a United All-Chinese People's Government of National Defense jointly with the Soviet Government and the anti-Japanese local authorities in Manchuria; for the organization of a united All-China Anti-Japanese Army jointly with the Red Army and the anti-Japanese partisan units in Manchuria."[16]

It is apparent that before the adoption of such an important policy the Chinese Communists obtained the approval of Moscow. At that time the Seventh World Congress of the Comintern was in session and on August 2 Georgi Dimitrov, addressing the congress on a world-wide united front policy, said: "We therefore approve the initiative taken by our courageous brother Party of China in the creation of a most extensive anti-imperialist united front against Japanese imperialism and its Chinese agents, jointly with all those organized forces existing on the territory of China who are ready to wage a real struggle for the salvation of their country and their people."[67] Then on August 20 the Comintern Congress adopted a resolution dealing with the new united front policy which referred to China in these words: "In China, the extension of the Soviet movement and the strengthening of the fighting power of the Red Army must be combined with the development of the people's anti-imperialist movement all over the country. This movement must be carried under the slogan of the national-revolutionary struggle of the armed people against the imperialist enslavers, in the first place against Japanese imperialism and its Chinese servitors. The Soviets must become the rallying center for the entire Chinese people in its struggle for emancipation."[68]

With regard to the destination of the Long march a difference of opinion developed among Communist leaders. Mao and Chou En-lai proposed to proceed towards Shensi where they would join force with Liu Tsu-tan and Kao Kang and have access to Inner Mongolia while Chang Kuo-tao and Hsu Hsiang-chien preferred to go to Sinkiang. As no compromise could be reached the two groups were again separated and each pursued its own course.

The main force under Mao some 30,000 strong with Chou En-lai, Peng Teh-huai, and other members of the Central Committee then left Mao-erh-kai early in August and entered the famous Great Grasslands on the border of Szechuan and Sikang, inhabited by Hsifan tribesmen. As the Communists marched through their land the tribesmen "stripped their houses bare, carried off all edibles, drove their cattle and fowl to the plateaus and simply disinhabited the whole area."[69] They attacked and killed the Reds whenever the latter were scattered. Unable to get enough provisions, unable even to get lodgings during the nights, and constantly harassed by the tribesmen, the Communists suffered most during this part of their Long March. Many were killed by the tribesmen or died of starvation, exposure, disease or drowning in the swamps. When they finally came out of the grasslands and reached the border of Kansu almost one-third had perished. After fighting some battles in southern Kansu they finally reached Paoan in northern Shensi in October, 1935, exactly a year after their departure from Juichin. There they merged with the forces under Liu Tsu-tan and Kao Kang.

The other group of the Communist forces now under the command of Chu Teh, Chang Kuo-tao and Hsu Hsiang-chien proceeded from Mao-erh-kai westward in an attempt to enter Sinkiang. They were crossing the Yellow river in Kansu when the Moslem troops under

General Ma Pu-fang interposed them and almost annihilated two Red armies in a fierce battle. Thereupon they had to abandon their plan of going to Sinkiang, turned eastward and entered Ninghsia. It was not until October, 1936 that the two groups again joined force at Huining, Kansu.

When Mao arrived at Paoan his main force had dwindled to a mob of 20,000 men. Added to this figure with the troops under Liu and Kao there were no more than 30,000 Red soldiers in northern Shensi towards the end of 1935. Had a vigorous campaign been started right then Mao and the Red Army would have been doomed. But the troops under General Yang Hu-cheng, Pacification Commissioner at Sian, capital of Shensi, were not strong enough to harass them and the Communists had time to relax and reorganize. Even so the Communists lived a very precarious existence. Paoan, new capital of the Chinese Soviets, was situated in one of the poorest areas in China. There was no industry, no railway, no highway and no working class. The population of the entire Soviet area at that time was less than 1,500,000 of whom more than 85% were illiterate peasants. The region was hilly and food production was hardly enough to support the newly-arrived Red Army

Under such circumstances Mao pushed ahead with the united-front policy. In January 1936 the "Chinese Soviet Government" again sent out a circular telegram, advocating the convocation of an Anti-Japanese and National Salvation Delegates' Conference. In the next month Liu Tsu-tan, commander of the Twenty-sixth Red Army was sent by Mao, under the pretext of "going east to fight the Japanese" to make a sneak attack on western Shansi in order to seize stocks of foodstuff there. Liu's troops were routed in Shansi by government forces and Liu himself was killed in action.

The Communist maneuver failed to affect the determined policy of the National Government, i.e., to suppress the Communist rebellion before fighting the Japanese. In the spring of 1936 the campaign against the Reds was resumed. But this time the Generalissimo committted a big blunder by entrusting Chang Hsueh-liang with the mission of mopping up the remnant Communist forces. The officers and rank and file of the Northeastern Army under Chang all came from Manchuria and regarded themselves as exiles in China proper. They hated the Japanese intensely, had no desire to fight against the Communists, and were easily moved by the Communist propaganda of an anti-Japanese united front. The Communists first approached General Wang Yi-che, an army-commander, and later, through Wang's intermediation, got in touch with Chang

Hsueh-liang himself. A secret understanding was reached and the mopping up operations practically stopped. In October Chang suggested to the Generalissimo at Loyang that the anti-Communist campaign be abandoned and a united front including the Communists be formed to fight a war against Japan and was reprimanded by the latter.

So when the Generalissimo arrived at Sian at the beginning of December 1936 to step up the campaign Chang Hsueh-liang and Yang Hu-cheng—the latter was an old-fashioned, ignorant militarist who was also fooled by the clever Communist propaganda—staged on December 12 a daring military coup, known as the Sian incident and held the Generalissimo in captivity. They presented to him eight demands, viz., (1) reorganize the Nanking Government and admit all parties to share the joint responsibility of national salvation; (2) end civil war immediately and adopt the policy of armed resistance against Japan; (3) release the leaders of the patriotic movement in Shanghai; (4) pardon all political prisoners; (5) guarantee the people's freedom of assembly; (6) safeguard the people's rights of patriotic organization and political liberty; (7) put into effect the will of Dr. Sun Yat-sen; (8) immediately convene a National Salvation Conference. These demands were also sent out to the nation in the form of a circular telegram signed by Chang, Yang and other high commanders of the Northeastern and Northwestern[20] armies who also stated that they tendered their advice to the Generalissimo in order to stimulate his awakening.[21]

With the exception of point 7 all other demands corresponded exactly to the National Salvation Program advocated in a proclamation by the Chinese Communist Party and the "Chinese Soviet Government" on December 1. This fact proves that Chang and the Communists had agreed on such a program. Immediately after the coup Chou En-lai, Chin Pang-hsien, and Yeh Chien-ying went to Sian as Communist delegates to confer with Chang and Yang and on December 14 the formation of a United Anti-Japanese Army consisting of the Northeastern, Northwestern and Red troops was announced.

The attitude of the Chinese Communist Party towards the Sian incident was very interesting. While there had been secret agreement between Chang and the Communists Chang did not tell the latter about his daring plot. The news of the coup surprised them as much as the outside world. At first they saw in it their chance of revenge and the Paoan broadcasts demanded the trial of Chiang by a people's court so as to put him to death. But

Moscow soon intervened and the Communist had to make a complete about-face. The German-Japanese Anti-Comintern Pact had been signed at Berlin in November and Stalin was very much worried that the military might of these two powers might soon be used to crush the Soviet Union. Consequently he was very anxious to see a Sino-Japanese war so that the full force of Japanese aggression would be directed against China, and not the Soviets. He also knew very well that the Generalissimo was the only man who could lead an united China into an all-out war with Japan. So in order to advance the interests of the Soviet Union the Generalissimo must be restored to power and an all-out Japanese war brought about.

The messages exchanged between Moscow and Paoan have never been divulged but the attitude of the Soviet Government was clearly shown in an editorial in *Izvestiya of* December 14 which said in part: "Under whatever slogans and program the Sian insurrection be conducted, this move . . . represents a danger not only to the Nanking Government but to all of China. It is clear that despite Chang Hsueh-liang's anti-Japanese banner, his move can only benefit Japanese imperialism. So long as the Nanking Government conducts a policy of resistance to the Japanese aggressors, the united popular front against Japan is understood by all its participants to mean not a front against Nanking, but a front together with Nanking."[22] The pressure from Moscow left the Chinese Communists no alternative but to persuade Chang to release the Generalissimo. Eight years later when General Hurley talked about the Sian incident with Molotov the latter admitted the following: "Due to the political and moral support of the Soviet Government Chiang had been allowed to return to the seat of his government and the revolutionary leader (Chang Hsueh-liang) had been arrested."[23]

By taking the bold action at Sian Chang Hsueh-liang had expected that Chiang would yield to his demands, that Nanking would compromise with him for Chiang's release, and that his movement would be supported by other military commanders and provincial authorities. But to his great disappointment none of these things happened after the incident. The Generalissimo, with great moral courage, refused to talk terms with him, while the National Government not only refused to compromise with him, but immediately sent out a punitive expedition. The whole nation with the exception of the Communists and fellow-travelers rose as one man to condemn his outrageous action. Chang felt completely isolated and began to regret his adventure. So when the Communists, upon orders from Moscow, changed their mind Chang decided to release the Generalissimo. On December 25 Chang did something as dramatic as the military coup by accompanying the Generalissimo to Loyang and next day to Nanking. He was court-martialed and sentenced to ten years' imprisonment but was pardoned by the National Government at the request of the Generalissimo.[24] The Northeastern Army was transferred from Shensi to Anhwei and Honan while the Northwestern Army was reorganized.

The Sian incident not only saved the Communists from annihilation but gave them a chance to expand. The anti-Communists campaign was thereafter practically abandoned. Within three months the Soviet area was more than doubled in size and the Red forces grew from 30,000 to 90,000 men, including the troops under Chu Teh, Chang Kuo-tao and Hsu Hsiang-chien who had arrived through Kansu and Ninghsia. A Shensi-Kansu-Ninghsia "Soviet Government" was set up in March, 1937 with Chang Kuo-tao as chairman and the Red capital was moved from Paoan to Yenan.

In February, 1937 when the Central Executive Committee of the Kuomintang was holding a plenary session in Nanking the Central Committee of the Chinese Communist Party sent it a telegram in which the Communists formally proposed a united front against Japan. The Chinese Communist Patry demanded (1) cessation of civil war; (2) freedom of speech, assembly, organization, etc.; and release of political prisoners; (3) convocation of a congress for the joint salvation of the country; (4) immediate preparations for war against Japan; and (5) amelioration of the living conditions of the people. It, in turn, pledged (1) to stop all attempts to overthrow the National Government by armed force; (2) to change the "Soviet Government" into the "Special Region Government" under the direction of the National Government and to reorganize the Red Army into the National Revolutionary Army under the direct control of the Military Affairs Commission (of which the Generalissimo was the chairman); (3) to enforce the thorough democratic system of universal suffrage in the areas under the "Special Region Government;" and (4) to put an end to the policy of expropriating the land of landlords and execute persistently the common program of the anti-Japanese united front.[25]

The Kuomintang Central Executive Committee, after careful consideration, adopted a resolution which accepted in principle the Communist request for peace but stipulated that the Chinese Communist Party must agree to (1) the abolition of the Red Army and its incorporation into the national army; (2) unification of government-ment power in the hands of the Central Government and dissolution of the so-called "Chinese Soviet Republic;" (3) absolute cessation of Communist propaganda; and (4) abandonment of class struggle.[26] These conditions were nominally accepted by the Communists as shown in an article by Chen Shao-yu[27] published in *Bolshevik* in April and in the report of Mao Tse-tung to a Communist conference at Yenan in May. Of course what Chen and Mao had in mind was the change of names but not of substance. In his report Mao clearly stated: "There are limits to our concessions. . . We must maintain Communist control in the Soviet region and in the Red Army."[28]

Negotiations soon began between the National Government and the Chinese Communist Patry for the carrying out of these points and establishment of a united front. Before any detailed agreement had been reached the Japanese militarists played into the Soviet hands and brought about the Sino-Japanese War in July.

CHAPTER XVII

The Soviet Union and the Sino-Japanese War

The peaceful settlement of the Sian incident, the spontaneous expression of joy by the Chinese people over the release of the Generalissimo[1], and the rapproachement between the Kuomintang and the Chinese Communist Party after ten years' fighting alarmed Japanese militarists. They now began to think of grasping North China before China was ready to fight against Japan's aggression. In June 1937 Prince Fumimaro Konoye assumed premiership and Hirota became again Foreign Minister. These two politicians connived with the militarists and adopted an even more aggressive policy towards China.

On July 7 a Japanese detachment which was stationed near Peiping and was maneuvering in the vicinity of Lukouchiao (Marco Polo Bridge) suddenly demanded the Chinese garrison at Wanping, a city near the bridge, to evacuate the city on the trumped-up charge that a Japanese soldier was missing. Upon the refusal of the garrison force to comply with this demand the Japanese attacked the city. The garrison force resisted and fighting broke out. Nanking protested to the Japanese embassy and still hoped for a peaceful settlement. But even as negotiations concerning this incident were still going on the Japanese Government sent a part of the Kwantung Army into China proper and attacked Peiping and Tientsin towards the end of the month. The whole nation felt indignant and clamored for a war against the aggressor. The Generalissimo, in a statement issued at Kuling on July 17, declared that China had reached "the limit of endurance" and "cannot do otherwise than be prepared for the supreme sacrifice and the war of resistance."[2] On August 8 the Generalissimo again issued a proclamation to the armed forces, telling them that once war was on it would end either in the annihilation of the enemy or the ruin of ourselves and there could never be any turning back.[3] Five days later Japanese naval forces attacked Shanghai and the all-out Sino-Japanese War which was to last eight years was in full swing.

On August 30 China again brought the case before the Council of the League of Nations, charging that Japan had violated the

League Covenant, the Kellogg-Briand Anti-War Pact and the Nine Power Treaty. Two weeks later China presented a second statement to the council concerning the extension of the warfare and the wanton destruction of life and property by Japanese air-raids. The council, on September 16, referred the Chinese appeal to the Advisory Committee which had been set up in February, 1933 in consequence of the Manchurian crisis. After careful consideration the Advisory Committee submitted two reports to the League Assembly in October, recognizing that the action taken by Japan was a breach of Japan's treaty obligations and recommending that, since Japan was no longer a member of the League, the assembly should invite those members of the League who were parties to the Nine Power Treaty, to initiate consultations for a settlement of the disputes.[4] These reports were adopted by the League Assembly on October 6.

In accordance with this decision the Belgian Government, with the consent of Britain, France and the United States, invited the signatories of the Nine Power Treaty to a conference at Brussels on the Sino-Japanese conflict. Invitations were sent to the original nine powers; to five powers which later adhered to the treaty: Bolivia, Denmark, Mexico, Norway and Sweden; and to Germany and the Soviet Union as major powers. The conference was opened on November 3 and attended by nineteen delegations, including those of Canada, Australia, New Zealand, South Africa and India as members of the British Commonwealth. Germany did not accept the invitation on the ground that she was not a member; while Japan refused to participate, maintaining that the conflict was one purely between Japan and China and in no way concerned other powers. In the conference the British and French delegates adopted a compromising attitude towards Japan, while the small powers had the least desire to offend her. So any strong measure against Japan was out of the question and the conference adjourned after three weeks' meetings without any result.

From the very beginning of the war the sympathy of the American Government and people had been clearly with China. But American economy had not yet wholly recovered from the big depression and isolationism was prevailing in the United States. On October 5 President Roosevelt made his famous "quarantine" speech in Chicago in which he asserted that the epidemic of world lawlessness was spreading and suggested a "quarantine" for those nations infested with it. Mr. Roosevelt did not mention any nation by name, nor specify what he meant by "quarantine", but doubtlessly he referred to Japan and probably had in mind sanctions against her. Public sentiment in the United States was very unfavorable to this idea and Mr. Roosevelt soon dropped it. Consequently in the Brussels Conference the American delegation did not propose economic sanctions against Japan to the great disappointment of China.

On December 12 the American gunboat "Panay" was sunk in the Yangtze river by Japanese planes with two crew members killed and many injured. Such an act of provocation might have resulted in war as the sinking of the "Maine" did in 1898. But the American Government was determined not to be involved in the conflict and the incident was closed after Japan had offered apologies and reparations.

As shown in the previous chapters the Soviet Union was anxious to bring about a Sino-Japanese war in order to lessen Japanese pressure on itself. As early as the spring of 1937 secret talks between Ambassador Bogomolov and Dr. Sun Fo, President of the Legislative Yuan, took place at Shanghai, concerning a non-aggression pact, military loans, etc. In April the conversations had so much progressed that Bogomolov confidentially told Hallett Abend, correspondent of the *New York Times,* that a Sino-Soviet agreement was forthcoming and that: "there will be no more civil wars in China."[6]

Tokyo was well aware of these talks through its intelligence reports and wanted to test the Soviet strength in the Far East. In June 1937 Japanese and Manchukuo troops occupied two islands (Bolshoi and Sennufa) in the Amur near Blagoveshchensk over which the Soviets had claimed sovereignty. The Soviet Government at once protested and sent three gun boats with troops to check Japanese agression. In the encounter that followed one Soviet gunboat was sunk with some casualties. Thereupon the Soviet forces withdrew and the islands remained in the hands of the Japanese. This incident furnished evidence to Japanese militarists that the Soviet Union was not strong enough to intervene in a Sino-Japanese war and stepped up their aggression in China.

On August 21, eight days after fighting had broken out in Shanghai a Sino-Soviet Non-Aggression Pact was signed at Nanking between Bogomolov and Chinese Foreign Minister Wang Chung-hui. In this treaty it was provided, besides the renunciation of war as an instrument of national policy, that "In the event that either of the two High Contracting Parties should be subjected to aggression on the part of one or more third Powers, the other High Contracting Party obliges itself not to render assistance of any kind, directly or indirectly, to such third Power or Powers at any time during the entire conflict, and also to refrain from taking any action or entering into any agreement, which may be used by the aggressor or aggressors to the disadvantage of the Party subjected to aggression."[7]

In letter this treaty was negative in character but in spirit it gave the Chinese Government and people much encouragement. In fact in the early stage of the Sino-Japanese War the Soviet Union was the only power which gave China both moral and material support. From the beginning of the war the Soviet press had condemned Japanese militarists for their aggressive action in China. In both the League of Nations and the Brussels Conference Litvinov spoke frankly against Japan. For instance on October 5 he told the League Assembly: "The Soviet delegation has taken part in the work of the Advisory Committee, of the Sub-committee, and of the Drafting Committee. The Committees have impartially examined all the facts brought before them by the Chinese delegation, and have found these facts correct. We found in the action of the Japanese Government all the elements that constitute aggression, but still we did not use the word 'aggression.' We have not drawn the necessary conclusions from the statements we have made, out of deference to the opinions of some members of the League."[8]

Again in his speech in the Brussels Conference on November 3 Litvinov said: "When it is a question of an aggressive attack by one state against another and if that attack has been in some measure successful, there is nothing easier than for an international organization, in order to gain a momentary success, to say to the aggressor: 'Take your plunder, take what you have seized by force, and peace be with you,' and to say to the victim of aggression: 'Love your aggressor; resist no evil.' But while that may constitute a superficial success of the conference, it does not represent the victory of the peace-loving countries. Such success can only provoke new cases of aggression, giving rise to new conferences, and so on without end."[9]

As China was lacking heavy arms and could not produce enough ammunition for a large-scale war she had to get them from other countries; but as China was also financially tight she could not afford to buy them with cash but had to secure them through loans. One of the powers which came forward to meet China's need was the Soviet Union. Large quantities of arms were sent from the Soviet Union during the latter part of 1937 which were used to equip 24 Chinese divisions. These purchases were made on a loan basis but no agreement was signed at that time.

Another source wherefrom China got arms, strange to say, was Germany. Relations between China and Germany had been very friendly since the conclusion of the Sino-German Treaty of 1921 after the First World War. There had been no disputes and trade and cultural relations rapidly developed. Since 1931 German military advisers had been engaged to train the Chinese forces and German arms were bought in large quantities. After the rise in power of Hitler in 1933 and especially after the conclusion of the Anti-Comintern Pact of 1936 there had been a pro-Japanese tendency in the Nazi Party but high government officials, such as Foreign Minister Konstantin von Neurath, Minister of Defense, Marshal von Blomberg and Minister of Economics Hjalmar Schacht, knew very well that interests of Germany and Japan in the Far East were fundamentally opposite to each other and tried their best to keep China's friendship.

In the summer of 1937 when Dr. H. H. Kung, Chinese Deputy Premier and Finance Minister, returning from London where he had participated in the coronation of King George VI, visited Berlin, agreements were signed by which China exchanged her raw materials for German arms and machinery. After the outbreaks of hostilities German military advisers remained in China and German arms continued to be shipped to China. In fact the Shanghai area was successfully defended for three months partly due to the help of German 15 cm. guns which were delivered after the Lukouchiao incident.

Germany was quite anxious to see Japanese military strength reserved for future use against the Soviet Union and therefore viewed the Japanese attack on China unfavorably. A week after the Lukouchiao incident the author, then Chinese ambassador at Berlin, presented to Minister von Neurath the Chinese official version of the incident and asked for his opinion. Von Neurath expressed the concern of the German Government over the incident and its wish that it could be peacefully settled. Then he added: "If the conflict extends in scope China and Japan will be both playing into the Soviet hands."[10] During the Nazi Party Rally at Nuremberg the author again had a lengthy talk with Minister von Neurath on September 10. The author asked the Foreign Minister to do something to help check Japanese aggression in China and the latter said he was thinking of mediating between China and Japan to end the conflict.

Negotiations soon went on between Berlin and Tokyo for the cessation of hostilities in China. At the end of November when Nanking was being threatened by the Japanese, Oskar Trautmann, German ambassador to China, approached the National Government with the conditions of the Japanese Government for ending military operations which included economic cooperation with Japan, adherence of China to the Anti-Comintern Pact, recognition of Manchukuo, independence of Inner Mongolia, etc. The National Government welcomed Germany's good offices but demanded the restoration of the status quo ante and the immediate evacuation of Japanese forces in China. Meanwhile Nanking was occupied by the Japanese in the middle of December and the National Government removed to Chungking. When the Japanese reply was finally received it was couched in vague terms and China rejected the peace offer in January, 1938. It was after the failure of German mediation and after the reshuffle in the German Government in February, von Blomberg being dismissed and von Neurath replaced by Joachim von Ribbentrop, that Hitler recognized the puppet state, Manchukuo, recalled German military advisers, and stopped the shipment of German arms.

In January 1938 Dr. Sun Fo was sent by the National Government to Moscow to see Stalin to ask for more material aid and Soviet participation in the war, if possible. In a lengthy conversation which lasted from midnight to five o'clock in the morning Stalin told Sun Fo that the Soviet Union could not be involved in a war in the Far East owing to the precarious situation in Europe but would do its best to help China with arms. Stalin also asserted that: "If China carries on the war to the bitter end and is not discouraged by temporary setbacks and occupation of territory by the enemy, then the final victory will surely be China's." According to Stalin's estimate Soviet arms including bombers, fighters, tanks, guns, machine guns, rifles and ammunition to the worth of 300,000,000 rubles had already been sent to China. Voroshilov, Soviet Commissar for Defense, suggested that as no agreement had been signed yet the first loan should be cleared before a second loan was concluded. Then Stalin proposed to fix the amount of two loans at U.S. $50,000,000 each, the first to cover arms already shipped and the second to cover those to be shipped in the future. Sun agreed to the proposal in principle but requested that the amount of the second loan be increased to $100,000,000. Stalin promised to grant a third loan when the second was exhausted and the matter was settled.[11] Soon after this conversation agreements for the first and second loans were signed by General Yang Chieh, who had been in Moscow since the autumn of 1937 in charge of military supplies, and Mikoyan, Soviet Commissar for Foreign Trade.

The second loan was practically exhausted by November 1938 and in April 1939 Sun Fo went to Moscow again to seek a third loan. This time he had to wait a few weeks before he was received by Stalin. Sun requested a loan of $150,000,000 and Stalin agreed in principle. Details of the agreement were later worked out with Voroshilov and Mikoyan. In June two agreements were signed at Moscow: one was the loan agreement which was to be reimbursed with Chinese goods, such as tea, wool, tin, tungsten, antimony, etc., in thirteen years with a 3% annual interest; the other was a commercial treaty which regulated importation and exportation of goods, gave both sides the most-favored-nation treatment and fishing rights in common waters and granted Soviet trade representatives diplomatic privileges. Then in December 1940 another agreement was concluded by which China promised to deliver to the Soviets tea, wool and minerals to the worth of $100,000,000 in return for the military supplies obtained through the first and second loans.

At the beginning Soviet arms were shipped to China mostly via the sea-route from Odessa through the Dardanelles Strait, the Suez Canal, the Red Sea, the Indian Ocean and South China Sea to Canton. After the occupation of Canton by the Japanese in October, 1938 the overland route had to be used. Anticipating the blockade of all coast line by the Japanese the National Government had mobilized a labor force of some 800,000 men to construct a military highway starting from Tarbagatai on the Sinkiang-Central Asia border via Sinkiang, Kansu, Szechuan and ending at Chungking, war-time capital. The highway was more than 3,000 miles long and the workmen, under the supervision of 5,000 technical experts and engineers, completed it at the end of the year by working day and night. Hundreds of trucks and thousands of camels and other pack animals were used on this highway to transport military supplies from the railway stations on the border to Chungking and then distributed to the armies at the front. Even so, the amount that could be transported each day was limited and the journey took a long time—about a month for a truck to make a return trip if without mishaps on the way. Consequently when the Soviet Union stopped its deliveries in the summer of 1941 only one-half of the total credit in the third loan had been used up.

Besides giving China material aid the Soviet Union, in the early stage of the war, also rendered China service in the form of military advisers, instructors, aviators and technical experts. Some 400 to 500 fighters and bombers were delivered to China and Soviet aviators and instructors went along with the planes. A Soviet air base was established near Lanchow, capital of Kansu, and aviation schools with Soviet instructors were set up in Urumchi and Chengtu, capital of

Szechuan. Some Soviet advisers were attached to Chinese armies for strategic and technical purposes. Soviet engineers were employed for the construction of the military highway. After the removal of the Generalissimo's headquarters from Nanking to Hankow in December 1937 and before the recall of the German military advisers in the Spring of 1938, the Soviet military mission under General Cherepanov and the German military mission under General von Falkenhausen had their offices close to each other in the former Japanese concession in that city.

During the first three years of the Sino-Japanese War the relations between Japan and the Soviet Union were at their worst. Soviet Government leaders and press openly attacked Japan as the aggressor in the war while Japanese high officials and press condemned the Soviet Union for helping the Chinese against Japan. At the beginning of April 1938 Tokyo lodged a strong protest with Moscow for its military aid to China to which Moscow replied that the sale of arms to China was in complete accordance with the principles of international law.[12] In May Japanese ambassador Shigemitsu again made representations to the Soviet Foreign Commissariat against the sending of Soviet planes, aviators, mechanics, and large quantities or arms to China since the outbreak of the hostilities and pointing out that a lieutenant in the Soviet Air Force had been captured in China by the Japanese. In his reply Litvinov said that many countries were sending arms and volunteers to China. Thereupon the Japanese ambassador asserted that volunteering was impossible in a state like the Soviet Union and that the Soviet Government would be held responsible for any situation arising from its military aid to China. The Soviet Government did not pay any heed to this warning and shipment of arms to China continued.

Two months later, an incident occurred at Changkufeng which almost became a second Lukouchiao. The Changkufeng hills, overlooking Posiet Bay at the south end of the Soviet Far East, had high strategic value. If the Japanese troops occupied these hills they could keep the bay and nearby area under artillery fire. In 1938 the Soviet Government began to construct a submarine and air base at Posiet Bay and sent troops to occupy these hills which were, up to then, no man's land. Both the Japanese Government and Manchukuo regime protested to the Soviets against violating Manchukuo territory and demanded the immediate withdrawal of the Soviet forces. As this demand was rejected by the Soviet Government on the ground that Changkufeng was in Soviet territory, Japanese-Manchukuo forces on July 15 attacked the hills with artillery and air force. Feeling in the Soviet Union ran very high and the press asserted the nation's readiness to fight.

Fighting and negotiations took place intermittently for over three weeks. Litvinov told Shigemitsu that the Japanese Government must compel the Kwantung Army to respect the existing border line so as to put an end to incidents and border conflicts.[13] As Japan was not willing to have an all-out war with the Soviet Union a truce agreement was finally reached on August 11 by which troops of both sides remained in the positions held at midnight, August 10, and a four-member commission, two from each side, was set up to deal with the demarcation of the frontier. Both sides suffered considerable casualties in these border conflicts. Japanese-Manchukuo losses were 158 killed and 723 wounded; while Soviet losses, 236 killed and 611 wounded.

In May 1939 Japan once more wanted to test strength with the Soviet Union and the most serious and bloodiest border clashes took place in the Nomonhan area. Nomonhan is situated on the border of Manchuria and Outer Mongolia and its rich pastures had always been coveted by Mongolian nomads. Mongols on both sides of the frontier now found themselves divided, part of the area being under the Soviet and part under Japanese protection. Under such circumstances border disputes were bound to happen and an armed clash between Japanese-Manchukuo forces on the one hand and Soviet-Mongolian forces on the other occurred on May 11. The incident soon developed into large-scale hostilities and on May 28 fighting broke out in the neighborhood of Lake Buir in which the Japanese claimed to have shot down 39 Soviet planes and killed 150 Mongols. Molotov, then Soviet Premier and Foreign Commissar, reported to the Supreme Council on May 31 that: "Japanese threats against Outer Mongolia are funny and non-sensical. There is a limit to all this non-sense; it is time for the Japanese to cease all provocations. Owing to our pact of mutual assistance with Outer Mongolia, we will defend the Outer Mongolian borders like our own."[14]

Besides skirmishes which occurred frequently there were several serious engagements in the following months. On June 24 another big Soviet-Japanese air battle was fought above the Khalka River which flows into Lake Buir. According to a Soviet report, it lasted more than two hours and 25 Japanese planes were shot down. On July 3, strong Japanese-Manchukuo forces attacked a hill near the Khalka occupied by the Mongols. Japanese press despatches claimed that 4,000 Mongolian troops were wiped out and 30 tanks and 10 planes were captured. But according to the Soviet account the attacks in three days were repulsed and the Japanese-Manchukuo losses amounted to 800 casualties, 45 planes and 50 tanks. On August 20 the Soviet-Mongolian forces staged a counter-attack and inflicted heavy casualties on the Japanese-Manchukuo forces.

Three days after this battle Moscow and Berlin surprised the whole world by concluding a non-aggression pact between them. The Japanese Government was especially startled to learn that its anti-Comintern ally had been seeking a rapprochement with the Soviet Union without even notifying it. Under such circumstances it had to wind up its adventures at Nomonhan and come to terms with the Soviets. So on September 15 a truce was signed at Moscow by Molotov and Japanese Ambassador Shigenori Togo. Thus the fighting around Nomonhan which had been going on for four months was ended and Tokyo later announced that Japanese forces had suffered a total of 18,000 casualties in these battles.[15] The Japanese Ministry of War admitted that the Soviet forces were mechanically superior to the Japanese and that Japan needed a better mechanized army.

After September 1939 the Soviet Union began to play a double diplomatic game in the Far East. On the one hand it continued to support China in her war against Japan; on the other, it tried to improve its relations with Japan. A new ambassador, Smetanin, was sent to Tokyo in October to promote friendly relationship. Japan, angered by Germany's disloyal action, now also wanted to cultivate Soviet friendship. Soon improvement in Soviet-Japanese relations was shown by the release of the fishermen and fishing boats detained by both sides, by the settlement of disputes on payment for the Chinese Eastern Railway, and by the conclusion of an agreement extending the duration of the fisheries convention.

The Nazi victory in the European war in the summer of 1940 gave Japan a chance to realize her ambition of southward expansion as the principal colonial powers in eastern Asia, Britain and France, had been defeated and were unable to effectively defend their colonies. Prince Konoye, Japanese Premier, proclaimed a "New Order for Greater East Asia" and put into the "Greater East Asia Co-prosperity Sphere" such countries as French Indochina, Thailand, British Malaya and Borneo, the Dutch East Indies, Burma, India, Australia and New Zealand" with Japan, Manchukuo and China as the backbone."[16] She tried first to gain control of French Indochina. In September the Japanese Government forced Vichy to permit the establishment of Japanese air bases in northern Indochina and in October Japanese troops were landed at Haiphong and occupied 22 key centers in the Tongking area. By this stroke Japan not only extended her influence to Southeast Asia but also cut supplies to China via the Kunming-Hanoi Railway, thus hoping to beat China to her knees.

As Japan now decided to push southward her enemy No. 1 was no longer the Soviet Union but the United States, because she knew if not for the United States she could easily seize all Southeast Asia and even Australia. From then on Japan wished to see the Soviet Union keep its neutrality in case of a Japanese-American war. On September 26, 1940 Japan concluded at Berlin a Tripartite Treaty of Alliance with Germany and Italy in which the three powers agreed: "to assist one another with all political, economic and military means when one of the three contracting powers is attacked by a power at present not involved in the European war or in the Chinese-Japanese conflict." By another article it was stipulated that: "the aforesaid terms do not in any way affect the political status which exists at present as between each contracting party and Soviet Russia." [17] It was crystal clear that the pact was designed against the United States.

At the same time when Japan was changing her policy towards the Soviet Union from provoking hostilities to seeking for Soviet neutrality the Soviet Union was also changing its policy in the Far East, from condemning to appeasing Japan and from aiding to deserting China. Stalin was then very much impressed by the military might of Nazi Germany which overran half Europe in such a short time, and was uneasy about a possible German-Japanese thrust against the Soviet Union. So he tried hard to keep good relations with both powers. In October 1940 Moscow declared that the Soviet Government was not excluding the possibility of rapprochement with Japan while Yosuke Matsuoka, Japanese Foreign Minister, said in Tokyo, "after the stormy period in Russo-Japanese relations, the time has come now for cooperation." [18] Negotiations concerning a non-aggression or neutrality pact soon started.

Meanwhile von Ribbentrop wrote to Stalin on October, saying that: "in the opinion of the Fuhrer, also, it appears to be the historical mission of the Four Powers—the Soviet Union, Italy, Japan, and Germany—to adopt a long range policy and to direct the future development of their peoples into the right channels by delimitation of their interests on a world-wide scale." [19] To this letter Stalin replied that he was not opposed to it in principle. Then on November 13, when Molotov paid a visit to Berlin, Hitler and von Ribbentrop proposed to him a draft pact by which the four powers would "undertake to respect each other's natural sphere of influence" and would "undertake to join no combination of powers and to support no combination of powers which is directed against one of the Four Powers."[20] The treaty was to be made public but a secret protocol was to fix Germany's territorial aspirations as to "center in the territories of Central Africa"; those of Italy as to "center in the territories of North and Northeast Africa"; those of Japan, as to "center in the area of Eastern Asia to the south of the Island Empire of Japan"; and those of the Soviet Union in the direction of the Indian Ocean."[21]

Molotov was not satisfied with the sphere assigned to the Soviet Union and did not go into any detailed discussion of the German scheme. After returning to Moscow he handed the German ambassador on November 25 the Soviet outline of a four power pact by which the Soviet sphere was to include not only India and Afghanistan but also Iran and Iraq in Asia and Turkey and Bulgaria in Europe.[22] As Hitler was now determined to invade the Soviet Union no definite answer was given to the Soviet proposal.

By the spring of 1941 Stalin must have sensed the impending German attack on the Soviet Union and was anxious to have its rear secure by keeping Japan neutral in the coming German-Soviet war. Japan, on the other hand, was just as anxious to keep the Soviet Union out of a Pacific war which her policy of southward expansion would eventually bring about. So in March when Matsuoka visited Berlin and Rome he stopped at Moscow and presented Stalin and Molotov with precious gifts. He brought out the question of a Japanese-Soviet treaty in his talk with Stalin who promised him an answer when he returned from Berlin. At Berlin Hitler urged Matsuoka to enter the war against Britain in Southeast Asia and above all at Singapore and advised him to come to an agreement with the Soviet Government. Von Ribbentrop also assured Matsuoka that should the Soviet Union ever attack Japan, Germany would immediately strike.[23]

Upon his return to Moscow in April Matsuoka resumed negotiations with Stalin and Molotov. Matsuoka proposed a comprehensive non-aggression pact but Stalin only wanted a neutrality agreement and demanded the cancellation of Japanese coal and oil concessions on northern Sakhalin as its condition. After six conversations, in two of which Stalin took part, a compromise was reached: Matsuoka agreed to a neutrality pact and Stalin was willing to accept Matsuoka's promise in a secret letter that he would do his best to bring about the cancellation of Japanese concessions not later than six months after signing of the pact. Thereupon a five-year Japanese-Soviet Neutrality Pact was signed on April 13 which provided that "both contracting parties undertake to maintain peaceful and friendly relations between them and mutually respect the territorial integrity and inviolability of the other contracting party" and that "should one of the contracting parties become the object of hostilities on the part of one or several third powers, the other contracting party will observe neutrality throughout the duration of the conflict." By a joint statement attached to the pact the Soviet Union pledged to respect the territorial integrity and inviolability of Manchukuo while Japan, those of the Mongolian People's Republic.[24]

Stalin was so satisfied with the treaty that a celebration was arranged, with the highest Soviet officials and Japanese diplomats attending. A few hours later Matsuoka resumed his homeward journey and Stalin went to the railway station to see him off. On the platform Stalin embraced Matsuoka three times and said: "We shall remain friends." [25]

The Japanese-Soviet Neutrality Pact gave the Chinese Government and people a great shock. Although Sino-Soviet relations had been deteriorating with the increasing conflicts between government troops and Chinese Communist forces since 1940, nobody expected that the Soviet Union would make a complete about-face to appease Japan, even to the extent of recognizing Manchukuo, fruit of Japanese aggression. Such a pact could not fail to help Japan by enabling her to shift a part of the Kwantung Army in Manchuria to China proper for further active campaign. The National Government strongly protested against the joint statement concerning Manchuria and Outer Mongolia and declared that: "The Chinese Government and people cannot recognize any engagements entered into between third powers which are derogatory to Chinese territorial and administrative integrity . . ." [26] In reply Moscow assured Chungking that Soviet policy toward China has not been changed, especially in regard to material aid.[27] This assurance was no more than lip service. The delivery of Soviet arms had been cut down to a minimum since the New Fourth Army incident in January 1941 and was to be completely stopped after the outbreak of the German-Soviet War in June.

After the conclusion of the pact other pending issues between Japan and the Soviet Union were soon settled. Since 1937 Japanese-Soviet trade had dwindled to zero mark but now on June 11 a five-year commercial agreement was signed, providing for the exchange of goods to the value of 30,000,000 yen a year.[28] For the first time after the Russian revolution this agreement defined both tariff and commercial procedures between the two powers. On June 17 a final agreement concerning the demarcation of Mongolian-Manchurian frontier was signed at Moscow. Seaborne traffic between Vladivostok and Shanghai, which since the end of 1937 had been under Japanese control, was resumed after an interruption of more than three years. The fisheries convention was thereafter renewed year after year. But the cancellation of the Japanese coal and oil concessions in northern Sakhalin, as promised by Matsuoka in his letter, was not carried out until March 30, 1944 when by an agreement Japan undertook to surrender these concessions while the Soviet Union undertook to renew the fisheries convention for five years, to pay Japan 5,000,000 rubles, and to deliver to Japan annually 50,000 metric tons of oil on ordinary commercial terms for five years "after the cessation of the present war." [29]

On June 20, 1941, when there were persistent rumors about a German-Soviet war, the Japanese Government made inquiries at Berlin and the German Government flatly denied any warlike intentions. Two days later the Wehrmacht struck. The Japanese Government now felt that it was fooled for a second time by its ally. So when von Ribbentrop sent a message to Matsuoka on July 1, inviting Japan to occupy Vladivostok and push westward in Siberia, an imperial conference decided on the next day to reject the German request. When the United States inquired about the Japanese policy towards the Soviets, the Japanese Government replied that it had "not so far considered the possibility of joining the hostilities against the Soviet Union." [30]

Instead of attacking the Soviet Union, Japan took advantage of the German-Soviet War to intensify her expansion in Southeast Asia. The first move in that direction was the occupation of southern Indochina by Japanese forces on July 21. The United States, Britain, and the Netherlands froze Japanese assets in these countries as a retaliation and the American Government placed an embargo on the export of aviation gasoline and scrap iron and steel to Japan. The situation in the Pacific thus became tense, but the Japanese Government was still hoping to avoid a war with the United States if the latter would not hinder her southward expansion.

Negotiations between Secretary of State Cordell Hull and the Japanese Ambassador had begun in April. The Japanese Government asked the United States to resume normal trade with Japan and to press Generalissimo Chiang to accept Japan's peace terms; and, in return, would promise not to use force in seeking its aims in Southeast Asia and would decide independently whether it would assist Germany in case of a German-American war. The American Government, on the other hand, proposed to Japan a mutual declaration of policy based on four principles, viz., (1) respect for the sovereignty and territorial integrity of all nations; (2) non-interference in the internal affairs of other countries; (3) the open door, or equality of commercial opportunity; and (4) no disturbance of the status quo in the Pacific except by peaceful means. As conditions of both sides were far apart, an impasse was reached in June.

Premier Konoye then proposed in August a meeting between President Roosevelt and himself to settle controversies. President Roosevelt was inclined to have such a Pacific conference but Secretary of State Cordell Hull doubted the ability of Konoye to get the consent of the Japanese militarists to a program acceptable to the United States. Therefore Konoye was informed that the general lines of an agreement be sketched out before the meeting of the two leaders. An imperial conference on September 6 decided that if by the beginning of October the negotiations did not show promise of a satisfactory result Japan would go to war with the United States, Britain and the Netherlands.

As negotiations between Secretary Hull and Japanese Ambassador Nomura dragged on in Washington without much progress, Konoye resigned on October 16 and General Hideki Tojo, Minister of War, became Premier. Togo, known for his friendly attitude towards the Soviet Union, was appointed Foreign Minister. The composition of the new cabinet clearly showed that Japan was bent upon continuing her peaceful relations with the Soviet Union and waging war against the Anglo-Saxon powers. Early in November the Japanese Government sent Saburo Kurusu as a special envoy to assist Nomura in his negotiations with Hull. On November 20 the Japanese envoys presented a modus vivendi which they regarded as representing the greatest concessions Japan was willing to make. Japan and the United States would agree to make no armed advance into Southeast Asia and the Southwest Pacific area; Japan was to remove her troops from southern to northern Indochina upon the conclusion of the present agreement and to withdraw them completely when peace was restored between Japan and China; and the United States was to restore its commercial relations with Japan before the freezing of assets, to supply Japan with oil and to refrain from actions which would prejudice endeavors for the restoration of peace between Japan and China (i.e. not to assist the National Government). Hull rejected these proposals because acceptance of them "would have placed her in a commanding position later to acquire control of the entire western Pacific area"[31] and handed, in turn, to the Japanese envoys on November 26 a ten-point program which called for among other things, withdrawal of all Japanese forces from China and Indochina and a virtual disavowal of the Tripartite Treaty of Alliance in exchange for a multilateral non-aggression pact among the Pacific powers and a trade agreement between Japan and the United States.[32]

Thereupon Japan decided to take immediate action and launched the "sneak attack" on Pearl Harbor on December 7. The United States and Britain immediately declared war on Japan and the United States three days later, on Germany. China, after four and a half year's fighting also officially declared war on Japan. Thus the two wars in Asia and Europe were now linked and the Second World War assumed its full stature. Japan and the Soviet Union, strange to say, observed neutrality towards each other for another three and a half years.

After Pearl Harbor Stalin no longer cared whether China would continue her war against Japan and the Soviet relations with China became exceedingly cool. With the return of Sinkiang to Chinese rule in 1943 the Soviet Union began to adopt a hostile attitude towards China. The Soviet press, friendly to the Chinese Government and upholding the leadership of the Generalissimo since 1937, now shifted to a stand of severely criticizing and condemning Chungking. When the Moscow Declaration was agreed upon by the foreign ministers of the big three on October 30, 1943 Molotov opposed including the sponsorship of China and it was due to the insistence of Secretary Hull that Chinese Ambassador Fu Ping-chang was invited to attach his signature to the document. When the leaders of the four major allies were to get together to discuss military and political questions Stalin refused to participate in any conference to which China was a party. So two conferences were held in November-December, 1943, one at Cairo attended by President Roosevelt, Prime Minister Churchill and Generalissimo Chiang; and the other at Teheran by Roosevelt, Churchill and Stalin. Again, for the same reason the Dumbarton Oaks Conference of 1944 which discussed the formation of a world peace organization had to be held in two sessions: one for the Soviet Union, Britain and the United States; and another for China, Britain and the United States.

CHAPTER XVIII

Role of the Chinese Communists in the Sino-Japanese War

The thunder of guns of Lukouchiao brought about the united front advocated by the Chinese Communists. Soon after the incident Generalissimo Chiang appealed to the Chinese Communists to cease their armed revolt and join the government in its fighting against Japan. On August 15, two days after fighting began in Shankhai, the Central Committee of the Chinese Communist Party issued a "Proclamation of Ten Great Policies for Anti-Japanese Resistance and National Salvation." It called for (1) overthrow of Japanese imperialism (2) military mobilization, (3) total mobilization of the nation, (4) reform of political mechanism, (5) anti-Japanese foreign policy, (6) war-time financial and economic policy, (7) improvement of the welfare of the people (8) anti-Japanese educational policy, (9) elimination of traitors, puppets and pro-Japanese groups, and (10) national solidarity against Japan. Under the last heading it declared: "On the cornerstone of all-out cooperation between the Kuomintang and the Chinese Communist Party, built an anti-Japanese front of all parties, groups, classes, and armies in the country to lead the fight against Japan and to cope with the national crisis by sincere unity."[1]

On September 22 the Chinese Communist Party, through the Central News Agency, published a manifesto to the Chinese nation on the united front. In this manifesto the Chinese Communist Party proposed to the people three general objectives: (1) "Struggle for the independence, liberty, and emancipation of the Chinese nation by sincerely and swiftly preparing and launching the national revolutionary campaign of resistance . . . (2) Realize democracy based on people's rights, convoke the National Assembly in order to enact the Constitution and decide upon the plans of national salvation. (3) Realize the happiness and comfortable livelihood of the Chinese people". On its part the Chinese Communist Party solemnly pledged: (1) to strive for the thorough realization of Dr. Sun Yat-sen's Three People's Principles which are the paramount needs of China today; (2) to abandon all its policy of overthrowing the Kuomintang regime by force and the movement of sovietization, and discontinue its policy of forcible confiscation of land from landlords; (3) to abolish the present Soviet Government and practice democracy based on the people's rights in order to unify the national political power; and (4) to abolish the designation of the Red Army, reorganize it into the National Revolutionary Army, place it under the control of the Military Affairs Commission of the National Government and await orders for mobilization to shoulder the responsibility of resisting Japanese aggression at the front.[2]

On the next day the Generalissimo issued a statement, expressing his satisfaction with the cooperation of the Chinese Communist Party. Immediately the Soviet regime was renamed the "Special Area Government" and later changed to the "Shensi-Kansu-Ningsha Border Region Government". The Red Army was reorganized into the Eighth Route Army consisting of 45,000 men with Chu Teh as commander and Peng Teh- huai as deputy commander and Lin Piao, Ho Lung and Liu Po-cheng as division commanders. Chu Teh was also appointed deputy commander of the Second War Zone under General Yen Hsi-san. In October the scattered Communist forces in Kiangsi and Fukien, about 10,000 men, were reorganized into the New Fourth Army with Yeh Ting as commander and Hsiang Ying, deputy commander. The Generalissimo now stated that the civil war was a thing of the past and would never occur again, while Mao Tse-tung wrote in *Chieh Fang Jih Pao* (Liberation Daily News) in September, "Comrades of the Kuomintang! Together we are carrying out the duty of saving the country . . . Let the Kuomintang and the Communist Party close ranks".[4] The Chinese people were jubilant that China was at last united and could resist Japanese aggression as one man.

But to Chinese Communists who believe that the end justifies the means there is no such thing as keeping a solemn pledge. Two documents issued at that time clearly showed the real intention of the Chinese Communists in advocating the united front. One was a secret document with the title "The Strategic Lines of the Party" which was distributed to party cadres, explaining why the Chinese Communist Party cooperated with the Kuomintang for a second time. It said in part: "At the present juncture when revolutionary sentiments are weak and low and our strength is limited and small, we must compromise with the Kuomintang in order that we may conserve and expand our power to strike . . . Doubtless, the united front is a compromise and is reformist in character. But it is only a temporary departure from the policy of overthrowing the existing institutions by revolutionary means . . . The revolutionary makes use of reformist methods to engage in revolutionary work in the open, to camouflage clandestine activities, and to foster the fighting strength of the masses, so that the bourgeoisie may be overthrown".[5]

The other document was a secret order issued by Mao Tse-tung to political officials in the Communist forces as follows: "The Sino-Japanese War affords our party an excellent opportunity for expansion. Our fixed policy should be 70 per cent expansion, 20 per cent dealing with the Kuomintang and 10 per cent resisting Japan. There are three stages in carrying out this fixed policy: the first is a compromising stage, in which self-sacrifice should be made to show our outward obedience to the Central Government and adherence to the Three People's Principles, but in reality this will serve as a camouflage for the existence and development of our party.

"The second is a contending stage, in which two or three years should be spent in laying the foundation of our party's political and military powers, and developing these until we can match and break the Kuomintang, and eliminate the influence of the latter north of the Yellow river. While waiting for an unusual turn of events, we should give the Japanese invader certain concessions.

"The third is an offensive stage, in which our forces should penetrate deeply into Central China, sever the communications of the Central Government troops in various sectors, isolate and disperse them until we are ready for the counter-offensive and wrest the leadership from the hands of the Kuomintang."[6]

Of course these secret documents were unknown to the Kuomintang and the National Government until a much later date and on their part the united front policy was faithfully carried out. The Military Affairs Commission supplied the Eighth Route and the New Fourth armies with funds and munitions according to their designated strength. Chou En-lai was appointed deputy director of the Political Department of the Military Affairs Commission and many lesser Communists were allowed to join civil and military services in the war zones. A Communist mouthpiece, *Hsin Hua Daily News,* was permitted to be published first at Hankow and later at Chungking. In 1937 a People's Defense Council was formed as an advisory body to the National Government and the Chinese Communist Party was represented by three members in that council. In June 1938 the People's Defense Council was reorganized into the People's Political Council with a greater membership and more definite authority. Seven Communists, Mao Tse-tung, Chen Shao Yu, Chin Pang-hsien, Lin Tsu-han, Wu Yu-chang, Tung Pi-wu, and Teng Ying-chao were appointed by the National Government members of the council and all of them except Mao Tse-tung attended the first session at Hankow. The council adopted a "Program for Armed Resistance and National Reconstruction" with the consent of the Chinese Communist Party.

On the other hand, from the very beginning the Communists were carrying out Mao's secret directive in extending areas under their control and expanding their military strength. Knowing that Communist forces were no match for the Japanese in regular warfare Mao instructed Red Commanders to observe the "principle of four 'Dont's' ": (1) Don't fight when you are not clear about the enemy's movements; (2) don't fight when you are not familiar with the terrain; (3) don't fight when you do not have support of the masses; and (4) don't fight when you are not cocksure of victory. Mao also fixed a threefold responsibility for the Communist forces: fighting, doing productive work, and winning the support of the masses. "The Red Army", declared Mao, "does not fight for the sake of fighting. It fights in order that it may carry on propaganda among the masses, organize them, arm them, and set up Communist regimes for them. Without these objectives fighting would be meaningless and the Red Army would have no justification for its existence."[7]

In September 1937 when the Japanese had penetrated into northern Shansi, the Eighth Route Army was ordered by the Military Affairs Commission to go eastward to engage the enemy. Nieh Jung-chen, deputy commander of the 115th Division, then crossed the Yellow river with 5,000 men and entered Shansi. At Pinghsinkwan Nieh's troops succeeded in making a surprise attack on a Japanese brigade and infiltrated behind the enemy's rear to engage in guerrilla warfare. From northern Shansi they soon penetrated into southern Chahar and western Hopei. The government forces, being far inferior to the Japanese in equipment, were adopting the tactics of "trading space for time" and resisted and retreated alternately. The Japanese, pressing ever forward, left large areas behind them without adequate garrison. Local peasants rose against the Japanese and the Communists soon recruited them into the Communist fold. In less than three months Nieh established a strong base in this area and set up the "Shansi-Chahar-Hopei Border Region Government" which was later approved by the national Government as a conciliatory gesture towards the Communists.

In March 1938 the 120th Division, under the command of Ho Lung, infiltrated into northwestern Shansi, controlled seven districts and set up the "Northwestern Shansi Administration". At the same time the 129th Division, commanded by Liu Po-cheng, was dispatched to southern Shansi, carried on guerrilla activities in the Taihang Mountains, and established the "Southeastern Shansi Administration". Later Liu extended his sphere of influence to the adjacent plains of Hopei, Honan and Shantung and the "Southeastern Shansi Administration" was organized into the "Shansi-Hopei-Honan-Shantung Border Region Government". In July a detachment of Nieh's troops under the command of Teng Hua penetrated into eastern Hopei and set up the "Eastern Hopei Administration". The New Fourth Army which was ordered by the Military Affairs Commission to fight the Japanese in Anhwei and Kiangsu in the summer of 1938 also extended its sphere of influence and established local Communist regimes.

In the early stage of the war not only the Communist avoided battles with Japanese forces, the latter also did not take the Communists seriously and concentrated their attack on government troops. Even a pro-Communist writer as Theodore H. White admitted in his book that: "The Communists fought when they had an opportunity to surprise a very small group of the enemy . . . But during the significant campaigns it was the weary soldiers of the Central Government who took the shock, gnawed at the enemy, and died".[8] When these government forces retreated tens of thousands of rifles were left by them on the battlefield in Shansi, Hopei, Chahar and Suiyuan. "The Chinese Communists", according to American intelligence reports, "collected vast quantities of these abandoned arms and munitions and used them to replenish their own supplies and to arm guerrilla units and local self-defense corps which they organized among the peasants."[9]

During the first two years of the war there were some 250,000 local guerrillas in Hopei and Shangtung besides those in other war areas. Although numerous, they were scattered units and no cooperation, nor coordination existed among them. The National Government also neglected to give them either active assistance or positive directions. Consequently these guerrilla units were gradually absorbed by the Communist forces. Some guerrilla leaders who refused to be incorporated into the Red troops were then crushed one by one. The most widely-known case was that of Chao Tung who was a native of Liaoning and had engaged in guerrilla warfare against the Japanese first in Manchuria and later in the outskirts of Peiping for nearly seven years. Chao was ardently anti-Communist and refused to take their orders. In 1939 he went to Chungking to ask for assistance in military supplies from the Military Affairs Commission and was appointed commander of the Seventh Guerrilla Column. When he was on his way back to his guerrilla base with 120 university students from the rear who all wanted to participate in the guerrilla warfare, they were treacherously attacked by Communist forces at Linsou, Hopei and cruelly put to death.

As the Communists grew stronger and stronger and the areas under their control became larger and larger they began to give up the pretense of cooperation with the government and to conduct active hostilities against government troops. They now adopted the tactics of attacking, defeating and absorbing government units which had become isolated in the rear of the enemy or which were fighting against the enemy desperately. From the spring of 1939 to the end of 1940 many central government troops or provincial forces in Hopei and Shantung were treacherously attacked by the Communists and suffered heavy casualties.

To give an illustration, in March 1940, when the troops under General Kao Shu-hsun and General Sun Liang-cheng were desperately fighting against the Japanese in southern Hopei, Liu Po-cheng's 129th Division suddenly attacked them from the rear. Consequently these troops were routed by the Japanese and had to retreat to the south of the Yellow river. In the meantime the 97th Army under General Chu Huai-ping and Governor Lu Chung-lin's headquarters in another part of Hopei were also attacked by the Communists and practically annihilated. Thus Hopei was cleared of government forces through the joint operations of the Japanese and Communists.

Besides attacking government troops from without the Communists also resorted to infiltration and instigated revolt from within. General Yen Hsi-san, for almost thirty years Governor of Shansi, had had illusions about the Communists and cooperated with them even before the outbreak of the war. When Yen organized the Self-Sacrifice for National Salvation Alliance in 1937 many Communists infiltrated into it. Later Yen organized the New Army and appointed a number of these alliance members who were Communists as political officers. In the fall of 1939 when Yen's other armies were dispatched to the front the Communists instigated twelve regiments of the New Army to revolt and crossed the Yellow river to join the Communist forces.

In the Communist official history of the revolution the military expansion during this period was summed up in the following words: "The first fifteen months of the Sino-Japanese War (July 1937-October 1938) saw the infiltration of the Eighth Route Army and the New Fourth Army behind the enemy lines and the opening up there of areas of liberation. The next two years of military stalemate (from November 1938 to the winter of 1940) saw the development and expansion of the people's armed forces in the liberated areas; the Eighth

Route Army increased from 45,000 to 400,000 and the New Fourth Army, from 15,000 to 100,000".[10] Of course these figures were exaggerated but we can easily infer from the statement that the Communist forces expanded enormously at the expense of government troops and other guerrilla units.

Such things could not be tolerated in peaceful times, and far less so when a nation was engaged in a life or death struggle against foreign aggression. Consequently the National Government had to take a strong attitude vis-a-vis the Communists and the so-called New Fourth Army incident occurred in January 1941. Ever since 1938 the New Fourth Army had created troubles in the Yangtze Valley. It absorbed local militia, attacked government forces, and occupied towns and cities. The most treacherous action took place in October 1940 when ten regiments of that army made a surprise attack at Taihsin on the forces under the command of Governor Han Teh-chin of Kiangsu. As a result General Li Sou-wei, an army commander, was drowned while retreating and General Sun Chi-jen, a division commander, was taken prisoner. Several regiment commanders were killed in action while thousands of soldies were killed and wounded. Thereupon the Military Affairs Commission in November transferred the New Fourth Army to the north of the Yellow river to fight the enemy. But instead of obeying this order it crossed the Yangtze, proceeded southward and attacked the 40th Division at Chinhsien in southern Anhwei. General Ku Chu-tung, Commander-in-Chief of the Third War Zone, then despatched other troops to encircle and disarm these disloyal troops. After five days' bloody fighting (January 7-January 12, 1941) Commander Yeh Ting was captured, Deputy Commander Hsiang Ying was killed in action and the New Fourth Army was disbanded. The government forces also suffered heavy casualties.[11]

This episode naturally caused both the Soviet and Chinese Communist press to raise an outcry against the National Government. The next day after the news had reached Moscow the Chinese embassy was scheduled to give a reception in the evening. Many Soviet high officials who had accepted the invitation suddenly notified the embassy that they could not come by giving any pretext they could think of.[12] Soviet military supples which had been regularly transported to Chungking via the Sinkiang-Kansu-Shensi-Szechuan Highway were soon reduced to a minimum. On the part of the Chinese Communists Mao Tse-tung, in a telegram to Chungking, demanded that General Ho Ying-chin, Chief-of-Staff, and General Ku Chu-tung be punished, that Yeh Ting be released and restored as commander of the New Fourth Army, and that all officers, soldiers and arms taken from the New Fourth Army be given back. Upon the refusal of the Military Affairs Commission all military cooperation between the Communists and the National Government was ended. The Eighth Route Army no longer pretended to take orders from the Military Affairs Commission while the commission in turn stopped sending funds and munitions to the Communists.

After January, 1941 the united front became an armed truce at best. Government troops stationed in the neighborhood of Communist forces had to be on the alert all the time lest they might be surprisingly attacked. Even before the incident Generalissimo Chiang had been severely condemned for using his forces to blockade the Communists instead of fighting the Japanese. It is true that from the fall of Hankow and Canton in October 1938 until the spring of 1944 there had been a stalemate in the Sino-Japanese War except local and indecisive battles but this stalemate was due to Japanese inaction and not to understanding between China and Japan. Chinese armies, being inferior to the Japanese in equipment and training, could not launch an offensive campaign when the Japanese advance halted and the war resulted in a stalemate.

It is also true that many government troops were stationed on the border of the Shensi-Kansu-Ningshia Border Region and were thus not taking active part in the war against the Japanese. In the spring of 1942 the author spent three months in China's vast Northwest, Chinghai, Kansu, Ningshia, Shensi, and a corner of Shansi, as the head of a mission to comfort the troops. He inspected and gave speeches to the officers and rank and file of more than thirty armies and divisions. More than half of these troops, some 200,000 strong, were stationed along the border line of the Communist area and their strength was neutralized so far as the war against the Japanese was concerned. But such a deployment was an absolute necessity because if these troops were not there to check the Communists, the latter would surely march southward to occupy Sian and Hanchung, invade Szechuan from the north and threaten the very existence of the National Government at Chungking.

On the other hand the rapid military expansion of the Communists could not fail to attract the attention of the Japanese. So in the summer of 1940 the Japanese High Command in China decided to take offensive action to remove the Communist menace. The Communists, intoxicated with their successes in absorbing government forces and guerrillas, also abandoned their guerrilla warfare and resorted to mobile warfare. The "Battle of 100 Regiments" started on August 21, lasted three and a half months and raged over a vast area, including Shansi, Hopei, Honan and Shantung. The Communists claimed to have sent 115 regiments totalling some 400,000 men into the battlefield and admitted that the battle resulted in the "death of more than 22,000 Communist troops and an even greater number of men wounded and captured, owing to the poverty of the battle areas, the lack of adequate means of communication, and the difficulty of obtaining necessary supplies".[13]

During 1941 and 1942 the Japanese forces in North China continued their anti-Communist campaign. In August, 1941 more than 100,000 Japanese troops encircled the Shansi-Chahar-Hopei Border Region and inflicted heavy losses on the Communists. In 1942 the Japanese again launched large-scale mopping up operations in Shansi with three divisions and two brigades. The Eighth Route Army once more suffered serious losses and its deputy chief of staff, Tso Chuan, was killed in action in the Taihang mountains. On July 7, the fifth anniversary of the Sino-Japanese War, the Chinese Communist Party admitted in its manifesto that, "this is the most cruel year of the war in which we have sustained the heaviest sacrifices".[14] The result of two years' Japanese anti-Communist campaign was the reduction of the Eighth Route Army's strength from 400,000 to 300,000 and of the population under its control from 40,000,000 to 25,000,000.

At the beginning of 1942 a large part of Japanese forces in North China was transferred to another theatre of war and the anti-Communist campaign was abandoned. The Communists then again had a chance to consolidate. In 1944 the Japanese were losing air and naval battles in the Pacific and, sensing that communications by sea route would soon be cut, they made a desperate attempt to make railway connections on the Asian mainland between the forces in Manchuria and those in Indochina. So in March the Japanese launched an offensive in Central China, occupied a greater part of Honan, and restored through traffic on the Peiping-Hankow Railway. In May another offensive started in Hunan and Changsha was occupied in the next month. After taking Hengyang in August the Japanese pushed westward into Kwangsi. Kweilin was occupied in the middle of November and the Japanese now made an attempt to march northward on Chungking. They were finally stopped at Tushan, Kweichow and retreated to Kwangsi. But Japanese forces from Central China and those from northern Indochina joined hands at Nanning, Kwangsi in September and their purpose of securing railway communications was achieved.

In this last Japanese campaign many government forces fought bravely and suffered heavy losses. Communist troops, taking advantage of this situation, wiped out isolated government units, increased their strength and extended the areas under their control. In April 1945, four months before Japanese surrender, Chu Teh reported to the party congress that they had 910,000 regular troops, 2,200,000 militiamen and controlled 19 "liberated" areas in 16 provinces with a population of about 95,500,000. His data seemed exaggerated but even according to American sources the Communist-controlled area had expanded to 300,000 square miles with a population of 85,000,000[15] while Chinese government sources placed the Communist strength at 500,000.

During the war the political organization in the Communist-controlled area put up a deceptive appearance of democracy to fool the outside world. In 1938 "laws" concerning governmental system in the Shensi-Kansu-Ninghsia Border Region were promulgated by the Chinese Communist Party which provided a pyramidal frame work of various graded people's councils from hsiang (subdistrict) through hsien (district) to the region to be elected by "direct, universal and secret suffrage". Accordingly, the First People's Council of the Border Region was convened in January 1939 and elected Lin Tsuhan, chairman of the border region government. Then in July 1940 the Chinese Communist Party introduced the so-called "three thirds" system into all administrations in the Communist areas to "enable all parties and groups and non-partisan people to participate in the activities of the people's representative organs and in the direction of the border region administrative affairs."[16] By this system in all elections only one third of the representatives could be Communists, another third was reserved for Kuomintang members and the remaining third for non-Chinese Communist Party or Kuomintang people. In case a Communist was elected as head of a certain administrative institution, he must see to it that his staff members were divided in the same way. The "law" even directed the Communists in such positions to cooperate "in a democratic manner", with non-Communists under them and "refrain from disregarding their opinion, domineering them and monopolizing everything".[17]

In practice this "democratic" system is nothing but a farce. The so-called Kuomintang in the Communist regions was a sham party consisting of persons who had been Kuomintang members but were perfectly willing to serve as Communist tools. The so-called non-party people were chosen by the Communists and none of them would dare oppose Communist policies. Any way all persons who did not approve Communism must have all been liquidated and no opposition could have still remained in the Communist regions.

During the war years Mao Tse-tung also consolidated his position in the Chinese Communist Party. Mao wrote in 1937 an essay titled *Concerning Practice*[18] which emphasized the inseparability of knowledge and practice in Bolshevik doctrine and attacked two groups of past Chinese Communist leadership: the "dogmatists" who relied on theory rather than on action, and the "empiricists" who worked zealously but blindly and refused to understand the importance of the theory. The first group clearly refers to Chen Shao-yu and others of the Returned Student Clique; the second refers to men like Ho Meng-hsiung and Lo Chang-lung. In another essay, *On Contradiction*,[89] Mao maintained that contradiction was inherent to the whole universe, even within the Communist party itself. Inner party contradictions would result in the triumph of correct ideology (Lenin-Stalin-Mao) over erroneous ideologies (Trotsky-Bukharin-Chen Tu-hsiu-Chen Shao-yu and others. When Chen Shao-yu returned to Yenan from Moscow in the spring of 1938 he was not given any important position in the party or the border government.

The only possible rival of Mao in the party was Chang Kuo-tao who in the early period of the party had exercised greater influence than Mao himself and had been elected a member of the Executive Committee of the Comintern. As vice-chairman of the Soviet regime in Juichin and during the Long March, Chang had frequently opposed Mao's policy. After the outbreak of the war Chang advocated sincere cooperation with the Kuomintang and the incorporation of the Red Army into the national forces. Such opinion naturally angered Mao and Chang was put under close surveillance in the latter part of 1937. Chang then pretended to repent his wrong way of thinking and expressed his obedience to Mao. In April 1938, when Chang was sent by Mao to participate in a ceremony at the tomb of Huang Ti[20] in Chungpu, Shensi, he took advantage of this trip to flee to Sian and seek for government protection. Thereupon the Chinese Communist Party declared Chang a traitor and expelled him from the party.[21] Later the Presidium of the Comintern confirmed the expulsion of Chang "who has betrayed the cause of Communism and the united anti-Japanese front and who has gone over to the enemies of the people."[22]

In January 1940 Mao published his *On the New Democracy*[23] in which he asserted that since the nature of the present Chinese society was colonial, semi-colonial and semi-feudal, the progress of the Chinese revolution must be in two steps. "The first step is to turn the colonial, semi-colonial and semi-feudal society into an independent democratic society; the second step is to push the revolution forward to build up a socialist society." Prior to the First World War the Chinese revolution was a part of the old bourgeois-democratic world revolution. But since the establishment of the Soviet Union a change took place in the Chinese revolution and it came within the orbit of bourgeois-democratic revolution and had been an ally of the proletarian-socialist revolution of the newest type. Consequently the aim of the Chinese revolution in the present stage was "no democracy in the general sense, but a new and specific kind, of a Chinese type—i.e., new democracy."

Mao then went on to define the politics of the new democracy as the joint dictatorship of several revolutionary classes in a united front in the form of the state, and democratic centralism in the governmental form. Economically the new democracy would adopt neither capitalism nor socialism but a new economy in which private, cooperative and state enterprises would exist side by side, with the first under strict control and the third dominant. The culture of the new democracy would be national, scientific and popular in character. It would stand for the dignity and independence of the Chinese nation, oppose all forms of feudal and superstitious thought, and serve the toiling masses of the workers and peasants. Since its publication Chinese Communists have been taught to regard this essay as their "Bible."

As the Communist forces were now rapidly growing in strength, Mao paid attention to party reconstruction. A Party Academy was established in Yenan and on its opening day, February 1, 1942, Mao delivered a lecture which initiated the Cheng-feng, or "ideological remolding" movement.[24] In his lecture Mao pointed out that there were shortcomings in the party due to the fact that some members still had unorthodox tendencies in learning, in party relations and in literature. The "incorrect" spirit in learning was due to subjectivism; in the party sectarianism was to blame and in literature party formalism was at fault." "These, then, are our duties: anti-subjectivism to reform the tendencies in education, anti-sectarianism to reform the tendencies in the Party, and anti-formalism to reform the tendencies in literature."[25] In the following months he gave two other lectures on party formalism and on literature and art.

An Ideological Purge soon took place. On April 30, the Propaganda Department issued the purge order and designated twenty-two key documents for study by party members. Purge committees were established in all party, political and military organizations under the chairmanship of their respective heads and purge meetings were held after party members had read these documents. In these meetings each Communist was required to expose his own errors both in ideology and in daily life in accordance with the instructions of the documents. Every member stood trembling in front of his comrades and tried to paint as black a picture of himself as possible. At the end of the purge everyone was condemned by his own evidence and his fate was left to be decided by his superiors and ultimately by Mao.

Within a year more than 30,000 party cadres were thus trained and many whom Mao did not like were dislodged from party positions or liquidated. This movement, in short, succeeded in (1) condemning liberalism in order to preserve the 100 per cent purity of the Chinese Communist Party, (2) condemning national consciousness which arose out of the war against Japan in order to assert the supremacy of internationalism (i.e., obedience to the directions of the Soviet Union), and (3) condemning those Communists who aspired to leadership in the party and confirming the unquestioned leadership of Mao.

When Mao was perfectly sure that there could not be the slightest opposition to his leadership in the party he convoked the Seventh National Congress of the Chinese Communist Party on April 23, 1945, seventeen years after the Sixth Congress in Moscow. There were 547 delegates and 208 alternate delegates who claimed to represent 1,210,000 party members, an increase of over one hundred times the membership just before the outbreak of the Sino-Japanese War. The session lasted fifty days and the most important items on the agenda were the political report by Mao Tse-tung, the military report by Chu Teh,[26] the revision of the party constitution, and the election of the Central Committee.

In his report Mao attacked the failures of the Kuomintang and boasted the achievements of the Chinese Communist Party. He demanded the immediate abolition of the one-party rule of the Kuomintang and establishment of a democratic coalition government. In the present stage a provisional coalition government was to be formed after consultations among the representatives of various parties and non-party leaders; in the future a National Assembly chosen in free and unfettered election was to be convened to establish a regular coalition government. This, according to Mao, was the only solution of the present problem in China.

Without any sense of shame Chu bragged in his report that from September 1937 to March 1945 the Eighth Route Army, the New

Fourth Army, and other people's forces fought about 115,000 battles, killed and wounded 960,000 Japanese and puppet troops under Wang Ching-wei regime,[27] took 280,000 prisoners of war, and, together with more than 100,000 Japanese and puppet troops who had turned over to the Communist side, inflicted a total loss of more than 1,340,000 on the Japanese and puppets. He also gave the figures of the Communist war booty as 1028 guns, 7,700 machine guns and 430,000 rifles.[28] But General Okamura, Commander-in-Chief of the Japanese Forces in China, made his report to the Allies after V-J Day that less than 50,000 Japanese had been lost to the guerrillas.[29]

A revised Constitution of the Chinese Communist Party with 11 chapters and 70 articles was adopted on June 11.[30] In its preamble it declared: "The Chinese Communist Party takes the theories of Marxism-Leninsm and the combined principles derived from the practical experience of the Chinese revolution—the ideals of Mao Tse-tung—as the guiding principles of all its work; it denounces any one-side tendencies towards dogmatism and empiricism." It defined the Chinese revolution in the present stage as a new bourgeois-democratic revolution and set the tasks of the Chinese Communist Party as "to struggle for the emancipation of the Chinese nation from foreign imperialist aggression, the liquidation of the feudal oppression of the masses, the establishment of an independent, free, democratic, united, prosperous and strong new democratic federated republic based on the alliance of all revolutionary classes and free union of all races, and to struggle for the realization of world peace and progress". But, "after the complete victory of the national and democratic revolution in China, the task of the Chinese Communist Party will be to struggle, by necessary steps, according to the requirements of China's social and economic development and the will of her people, for the realization of socialism and Communism in China."[31] Mao's important ideas were thus embodied in the constitution and Mao, from then on, became the formally recognized leader of the party. As the Comintern had been dissolved by Stalin in June 1943 it was not mentioned in the new constitution. This omission, however, did not indicate any change in relations between the Chinese Communist Party and the Soviet Union.

The Congress elected a new Central Committee with forty-four members and thirty-three reserve members. Mao was elected by the Central Committee to be its chairman and by the provision of Article 34 of the party constitution served concurrently as chairman of the Central Political Bureau.

CHAPTER XIX

Communist Tactics and American Response

As told in a previous chapter due to the prevailing trend of isolationism in the United States the American Government adopted a strict neutral policy in the early stage of the Sino-Japanese War. But there was no question that American sympathy was with the Chinese side. After the fall of Hankow and Canton in October 1938 as all signs indicated that the war would last for a long time and there could be no early settlement the American Government began to give China economic aid in the form of general commodity credits. In December 1938 a credit of $25,000,000 and in March 1940 another credit of $20,000,000 were given to the Universal Trading Corporation, a private corporation but closely associated with the Chinese Government, for the purpose of purchasing American industrial and agricultural products and services. In October and November 1940 two credits, one of $25,000,000 and the other of $50,000,000, were granted to the Central Bank of China for the same purpose. These credits, totaling $120,000,000, were to be paid back with Chinese wood oil and strategic minerals.[1]

Meanwhile, after the French surrender to Hitler in June 1940 internationalism began to raise its voice in the American public opinion, as the United States was now threatened with a distinct possibility of German occupation of Britain and invasion of America in the future. So in January 1941, after his re-election for a third term, President Roosevelt proposed his lend-lease program to Congress which passed the Lend-Lease Act on March 11. As the United States was now doing everything short of war to help the Allies win the war against Germany, so it also tried to do more to help China win her war against Japan. On March 15 President Roosevelt declared in a speech: "China likewise expresses the magnificent will of millions of plain people to resist the dismemberment of their nation. China, through the Generalissimo, Chiang Kai-shek, asks our help. America has said that China shall have our help".[2] On April 1 an agreement was concluded between the American Department of the Treasury and the Chinese Ministry of Finance and the Central Bank of China by which the department agreed to purchase Chinese Yuan up to an amount equivalent to $50,000,000 "to further the monetary and financial cooperation of the two governments and the stabilization of the United States dollar-Chinese Yuan rate of exchange".[3] After consultations between the Chinese and American Government a lend-lease program to meet the emergency needs of China was agreed upon and President Roosevelt, on May 6, declared China was eligible for lend-lease assistance on the ground that the defense of China was vital to the defense of the United States.

After Pearl Harbor China and the United States became full-pledged allies and from then on American policy towards China assumed two purposes: (1) to secure China's full cooperation in waging war against Japan effectively; and (2) to help China serve as a stabilizing factor in the post war Far East.[4] At the beginning of 1942 a Declaration of the United Nations was signed in Washington by representatives of 26 powers each of which pledged to employ its full resources, military and economic, to carry on the war and not to make a separate armistice or peace with the enemy.[5] It was with a view to raising China's position among the Allies that President Roosevelt invited Mr. T. V. Soong, Chinese Foreign Minister, who was then in Washington, to sign the document with Roosevelt, Churchill and Litvinov on New Year's Day at the White House while representatives of the other 22 nations signed it the next day at the Department of State. After the signing Mr. Roosevelt congratulated Soong for the fact that China now became one of the "big four".

In March 1942 China and the United States concluded an agreement by which the American Government gave financial aid to China to the amount of $500,000,000. This huge credit enabled the Chinese Government to purchase gold for sale in China an as anti-inflationary measure and to redeem Chinese Government securities issued in United States dollars.[6] By a treaty with China signed on January 11, 1943, the United States relinquished the extraterritorial rights which it had enjoyed in China for a century and other privileges granted in the unequal treaties.[7] Upon the insistence of the United States China signed the Moscow Declaration on October 30, 1943, which envisaged the creation of a general international organization based upon the "sovereign equality" of all peace-loving states and open to membership of all such states, large or small.[8] As a signatory of this declaration China later was one of the sponsors for the United Nations Conference on International Organization at San Francisco in 1945 and became one of the five permanent members of the United Nations Security Council. The declaration after the Cairo Conference of November 1943 provided, among other things, "that all the territory Japan has stolen from the Chinese, such as Manchuria, Formosa, and the Pescadores, shall be restored to the Republic of China."[9] All these facts show that Mr. Roosevelt was sincerely helping China not only win the war but become a major power on an equal footing with the United States, Britain, and the Soviet Union.

But this American policy towards China was completely opposed to the aim of Moscow and Yenan for if China actually became a strong power after the war under the leadership of the Generalissimo their plot of overthrowing the National Government and sovietizing China would be completely frustrated. When the tide of the war had been turned in favor of the Allies and an eventual victory was assured in the middle of 1943 Stalin began to pay attention to the ever improving Sino-American friendship. He knew very well that China depended on the United States for the successful conduct of the war and the post-war rehabilitation and reconstruction and consequently to drive a wedge between China and the United States became to him an absolute necessity.

So in the summer of 1943 a double-edged propaganda campaign was started by Communists and their fellow travellers: to discredit the Kuomintang and the National Government on the one hand and to praise the Chinese Communists on the other. It was very easy to paint as black a picture of the Kuomintang and the National Government as possible but it was rather hard to sell the Chinese Communists to the American people who were opposed to Communism. So they resorted to the "big-lie" tactics of German Propaganda Minister Joseph Goebbels and created the myth that the Chinese Communists were not real Communists but "agrarian reformers" and had no relations with the Soviet Union at all.

The first shot seems to have been fired by T. A. Bisson, a member of the International Secretariat of the Institute of Pacific Relations which was closely associated with Communist activities in the United States at that time. In an article, "China's Part in a Coalition War", which appeared in the July 14 issue of *Far Eastern Survey*, official organ of the American Council, Institute of Pacific Relations, Bisson stated that there were two Chinas: one, Kuomintang China, might be called feudal China; the other, Communist China, might be called democratic China. After claiming economic and political reforms for Communist China he wrote: "Over wide areas of this new China, elected councils—village, town and district—and elected executive officials have completely supplanted the old autocratic system of feudal agrarian China . . . It is this democratic process, finally, which permits a large measure of free competition to operate over the whole of the economy. Bureaucratic price controls are not attempted . . . No landlord or merchant, with the watchful eyes of his neighbors upon him, can engage in hoarding or speculation. Within limits set mainly by local democratic checks, the individual landlord or entrepreneur is free, and is even encouraged, to expand his operations, and many are doing so. By no stretch of the imagination can this be termed Communism; it is, in fact, the essence of *bourgeois* democracy, applied mainly to agrarian conditions".

In the early stage of the Sino-Japanese War the Soviet press was friendly towards China and even after the New Fourth Army incident its attitude had been cool but not hostile. Now according to the new party line *War and the Working Class,* official Soviet trade-union journal, published on August 6 an article by Vladimir Rogov, former head of the Tass Agency in Chungking, which threw mud at the National Government and showered bouquets on the Chinese Communists. Rogov condemned some of the important Kuomintang leaders as "appeasers, defeatists and capitulators" who wished to make peace with Japan to break the united front, to undermine the Communist-Kuomintang collaboration, and to incite the persecution of the Eighth Route Army. He charged that Chinese financial and industrial leaders preferred engagement in profiteering to investment in the arms industry. On the other hand he asserted that the Eighth Route and the New Fourth armies had won much glory in the war and the Chinese Communist Party which led those armies enjoyed high prestige among the Chinese masses as their leader for national freedom and independence. Rogov's severely critical words were soon quoted and amplified by Communist spokesmen elsewhere and by American left-wing writers.[10]

These initial attacks were immediately followed by an organized effort to push through this Communist propaganda campaign. Newspapers and periodicals published reports from China and articles on China which attacked the Kuomintang and the National Government and eulogized the Chinese Communists. Among the books which did much to mislead the American public were Agnes Smedley's *Battle Hymn of China,* Maxwell Stewart's *Wartime China,* Lawrence K. Rosinger's *China's Wartime Politics* and *China's Crisis,* Owen Lattimore's *Solution in Asia,* Harrison Forman's *Report from Red China,* Gunther Stein's *The Challenge of Red China,* Theodore White and Annallee Jacoby's *Thunder Out of China,* and Israel Epstein's *Unfinished Revolution in China.*

The limited space of this book permits only a few pertinent quotations from the writings of these authors. Edgar Snow, whose *Red Star Over China* (1938) and *Battle for Asia* (1942) had familiarized American readers with Chinese Communism, wrote in the *Saturday Evening Post* of June 10, 1944: "The fact is there had never been any Communism in China even in Communist areas". On February 17, 1945, he contended that the Chinese Communists "happen to have renounced years ago now any intention of establishing Communism in China in the near future". On May 12, 1945 he wrote: "For the foreign reader it is somewhat confusing that this Chinese agrarian reform movement is called 'Communism' . . . Having built up their armed power long after Moscow had more or less forsaken their struggle as hopeless, the Chinese Red leaders have a strong feeling of independence".

Wrote Owen Lattimore: "The Communists therefore changed their policy [after the outbreak of the Sino-Japanese War]. They cease to expropriate land, unless the landlord went over to the Japanese. They left the landlord on his land, and they defended the land for him against the Japanese; but in return they drastically limited the amount of rent which he was allowed to collect from his tenants . . . A parallel policy was adopted in production and trade." Then he went on to praise the three-thirds election system as "the most positive step yet taken in China by any party away from dictatorship and toward democracy. It confirms the graduation of the Communists from being a perpetual minority opposition party to the status of a party which has good claims to a position within a coalition government".[11]

In *Report from Red China,* Harrison Forman devoted a chapter to these two questions: "First, what is their (Chinese Communists') connection with Soviet Russia? Second, how Communist are these Chinese Communists?" His answers were: "In the five months I spent with the Chinese Communists I saw not the slightest tangible connection with Russia. There were no Russian military and political advisers. The sole Russians in the Border Region were a surgeon . . . and two representatives of the Tass News Agency . . . Occasionally I saw portraits of Marx and Lenin; but these seemed like relics of a revolutionary past. For every portrait of Marx or Lenin I found a hundred of Roosevelt, Churchill, Stalin and Chiang Kai-shek. The portraits of these four hung everywhere . . . Stalin's was there not as the leader of Communism but as the head of one of the United Nations—Allies in the struggle against fascist aggression . . . the Chinese Communists are not Communists—not according to the Russian definition of the term. They do not, at the present time, either advocate or practice Communism . . . Repeated compromises were required (during the past years), until today the Chinese Communists are no more Communistic than we Americans are".[12]

When Mao Tse-tung told Forman that they were no longer Communists in the Russian sense of the word the latter had the naivete to advise Mao to change the name—"change it to 'Neo-Democracy' or 'Democratism' or some such—anything but 'Communism'. Mao shook his head. 'It doesn't matter to us or to our consciences what we or others call our system. And if we were to change suddenly to some other name, there are those in China today—and abroad, too—who would make capital of it, would accuse us of trying to cover up something. No—we cannot, we must not, change the name . . . It is the content and the practice that are important—not the label!' "[13]

Probably the most interesting account of the relationship between the Chinese Communists and the Soviet Union appears in a conversation between Mao Tse-tung and Gunther Stein. Mao's words, as recorded in *The Challenge of Red China,* are quoted here at length:

"China cannot restrict herself to friendly relations with only one power or group of powers. . . It would be just as wrong for China to rely only on the Union of Soviet Socialist Republics and snub the United States of America and Britain as it has been for Chungking, in recent years, to rely only on the United States of America while showing antipathy, suspicion and actual unfriendliness toward the Union of Soviet Socialist Republics and sometimes also toward Britain.

"To count on the aggravation of the differences between the capitalistic countries and the Union of Soviet Socialist Republics and to try to benefit from it, as the National Government in Chungking does, is very dangerous. It is equally against China's own interests and the interests of world peace.

"I do not believe for one moment that conflict between the capitalistic world and the Union of Soviet Socialist Republics is inevitable. On the contrary, we Chinese Communists—who are making a success of the New Democracy which brings all social strata in our areas into close cooperation—are convinced that the capitalistic world and the Union of Soviet Socialist Republics can and will learn to cooperate closely in peace as in war, in spite of occasional difficulties . . .

"China can and must be one of the bridges between the two camps, instead of hoping to win foreign support as one of zones of friction.

"China's progress depends upon real world peace, and the international role of our country can be enhanced only by sincere cooperation with all countries and by helping them overcome their differences."[14]

How reasonable and peaceful these sentences are! But they sound more like the words of Mr. Nehru of India in 1956 than those of Mao in 1944. The reader will amuse himself by comparing these words with what Mao later said in 1949.[15]

When a group of foreign correspondents visited Yenan early in December 1945 Liu Shao-chi, No. 2 man in the Chinese Communist Party, in an interview made the following points: "(1) The Communist Party's program for China at present is one of democratic capitalistic development based on state, private and cooperative enterprise. (2) Russian Communism is not the model for the Chinese Communist policies at present. (3) The program of the Chinese Communists is comparable to the political and economic concepts in the United States at the time of Jefferson and Lincoln. The Chinese Communist Party maintains no liaison with the Russian Communist Party or any other foreign Communist Party. (4) Considering that true Communism is not suited to China in the present stage of political and economic development, the Chinese Communist Party would oppose any party that attempted to introduce Communism of the classical or Russian pattern into China . . ."[16]

This Communist propaganda was highly effective and the American people were soon led to believe that Chungking was corrupt, inefficient, undemocratic and not too anxious to fight against the Japanese; while Yenan was honest, efficient, striving for a democratic rule and sustaining the brunt of the war.

It was understandable that American officials, advisers, technicians, reporters and GI's who spent the last years of the war in Free China had grievances to to complain about. The cities in western China such as Chungking, Chengtu and Kunming, had always been far behind Shanghai, Tientsin or Hankow in comfortable living. Conditions became even more miserable after several years of war and repeated Japanese raids. Streets were unclean, houses were scarce, hotels were bad, means of communications were mainly primitive, while modern conveniences such as running water, flush toilet, gas for cooking, central heating, etc., were simply unobtainable. Even electric light was not available most of the time. There were few amusements to which Americans had been accustomed. In short there was no fun but a monotonous and weary life for the Americans who lived in these cities then. No wonder they had bad impressions of China.

Meanwhile the effect of a several years' full-scale war was telling on the Chinese Government and society. Inflation made the salaried class, government officials, officers, professors, teachers, soldiers, policemen, post-men, etc. suffer most. Due to the rapid rising cost of living they could hardly keep their bodies and souls together. Both efficiency and moral standard naturally dropped. Because of the war some drastic measures limiting individual freedoms, such as censorship of the news and ban on unauthorized public meetings, had to be adopted. All these facts justified legitimate criticism.

But how could the Chinese Communists be accepted as gentle "agrarian reformers" who were establishing a democratic system of government and had no relations with the Soviet Union at all, in the light of their written party constitution, of their more than twenty years' records, and of the behavior of Communists everywhere in the world? Yet it was just what had happened. During an extended tour in the United States in 1947 the author met thousands of Americans, professors, writers, government employees, university students, business men, storekeepers, factory workers, taxi drivers, waiters and waitresses, etc., who wholly or partly believed in this myth. It seemed that the American public swallowed the Communist bait hook, line and sinker. The only explanation for such a phenomenon is that according to Goebbels' principle the bigger a lie is the more easily people are fooled by it. It was not until the loss of the Chinese mainland in 1949 and Mao's participation in the Korean War in October 1950 that the myth concerning the Chinese Communists was completely discarded by the American people.

Of course not all the speeches and writings concerning the Chinese Communists were purposely or unwittingly propagating the party line. There were observers who saw through the Communism game and exposed it. Mr. Rodney Gilberg, an experienced commentator on Far Eastern affairs, wrote in the *New York Herald Tribune* of August 17, 1943: "Their immediate purpose is to undermine the moral credit of China's leadership in this country and to build up the credit of the Chinese Communists, so that when the time comes for the latter to seize the fruits of victory over Japan, after the war, such an achievement, whether by coup or by revolution, will not alienate American sympathy from China, vis-a-vis Japan, or elicit a revulsion of feeling against the Red 'Democrats' and with it armed support for their suppression." After refuting Bisson's article in *Far Eastern Survey* Mr. Gilbert said in conclusion: "But I have yet to be convinced that a Red control of North China, Sinkiang, Manchuria, Korea and Inner Mongolia (which is said to be the minimum objective), affiliated with the Soviet Union to the degree that the Outer Mongolian Red Republic is, would reward China for her sacrifices with the kind of 'democracy' with which the average American would sympathize".

Dr. Lin Yutang, a well known writer who is not a Kuomintang

member and has never been a public official, went back to China in September 1943 and spent six months in Chungking and war areas. In his book, *The Vigil of a Nation,* he wrote:

"The Chinese Communist regime has been able to mobilize manpower and resources more thoroughly than the Chungking government, because its control of the people's lives is more rigid. It has no freedom of speech, no freedom of belief; it rules by regimentation and by terror, by secret agents and local commissars in the army and in civil administrations; it goes through the farce of packed popular elections; it terrorizes the population that dares to dissent or refuses to cooperate; it enforces complete party discipline, the party dominates everything, and party members have exalted privileges; it carries 'purges', 'liquidations', in a drastic and unscrupulous manner; and finally replaces the landlord and employer with the state as the master. Consequently, the people are terrorized.

"In Chungking, people of all classes can criticize the government freely in public places. But in Communist areas, the peasants all 'praise' the regime and have nothing to say against it. The degeneration of the peasantry under Communist rule in occupied areas is, from all report, a clear and certain fact. The final test of a regime is whether the people dare to talk against the regime, and that is a pretty good test of what we mean by 'democracy'. I should like to hear the foreign correspondents returning from Yenan report that they have been able to find one farmer who did not 'praise' the regime as a regime of perfection"[17]

Congressman Walter H. Judd, who had worked ten years in China as a missionary doctor and speaks Chinese fluently, revisited China in the fall of 1954 to see conditions for himself. On March 15, 1955 in a lengthy speech in the House of Representatives on the truth about China he exposed the true character of the Chinese Communists. He came to the conclusion that "the Communists in China and the Communists and fellow-travelers in this country are working primarily in terms of what they believe will best serve Russia's future policies and interests. I am increasingly convinced the Chinese Communists are first Communists and second Chinese, just as we know American Communists are first Communists and second Americans. . . . I, too, was taken in for a time by the talk of their being just agrarian reformers, just Chinese patriots struggling only for freedom of China and for democracy. I am convinced now the primary allegiance of the Chinese Communists is to Russia . . . and their purpose is to make Russia overwhelmingly the strongest power in Asia as well as in Europe . . ."

"By talking about freedom and democracy and unity and so forth," Mr. Judd went on to say, "and by calling all who disagree with them Fascists and dictators, they have succeeded in selling to millions of Americans one of the greatest hoaxes any unsuspecting people ever bought in all history."[18]

In order to investigate the talk about democracy in Communist areas Mr. Judd had a long discussion with Lin Tsu-han, chairman of the Border Region Government. "Since most of the Chinese people still can not read and write,[19] I asked Mr. Lin how the Communists mark their ballots in their so-called elections. 'Well', I was told, 'we have a system of bowls, and the voter who can not read or write drops a bean into the bowl of the man who is his choice.' I said, 'I would like to know whether the voting is in private or out in public, because, if it is done in secret, I can imagine how easy it would be for some people I have read about in some cities in America to stuff that ballot box. They could fill the bowl with beans out of the sleeves in one trip into the booth. And if it is out in public so that the ever present Communist police can be sure that the voter drops in only one bean, you do not imagine he would drop his bean into the wrong bowl, do you, if he wanted to retain his head?' All Mr. Lin could do was grin."[2]

Professor O. Briere, a keen scholar who was among the foreign observers that visited Communist areas during the war, had this to say about the conditions he saw: "One of the first impressions to strike a foreign observer who arrives at Yenan is the atmosphere of suspicion which surrounds him; he cannot take a step without being followed by a spy attached to him and who follows all his movements. Mutual surveillance (among the Chinese) is even more surprising; they too are often accompanied by a companion". Again, "As to the tripartite composition of government, there is no greater hoax than this one. The so-called Communist third commands the levers and holds exclusive power. It would do no good for the other two thirds to try any opposition whatever, particularly in the town of Yenan; if at times a modicum of leeway is accorded the non-Communists, it is only on secondary issues . . ." Again, "The army of Red officials probably exceeds in size that of any other regime; it is one of the mainstays of the state. Never before has any people known such a formidable army of parasites: soldiers, popular militia, officials—they are legion. It is the peasant who pays for this gigantic array of officialdom, and the exactions disgust him: in certain regions the taxes are literally heavier than the total harvest. But in return what does this flock of parasites produce?"[21]

In his report, *The Chinese Communist Movement*, to the Department of War on July 5, 1945, Brigadier General P. E. Peabody, Chief of the Military Intelligence Division, presented the following conclusions: "(1) The democracy of the Chinese Communists is Soviet democracy. (2) The Chinese Communist Movement is part of the international Communist movement, sponsored and guided by Moscow. (3) There is reason to believe that Soviet Russia plans to create Russian dominated areas in Manchuria, Korea and probably North China. (4) A strong and stable China cannot exist without the natural resources of Manchuria and North China. (5) In order to prevent the separation of Manchuria and North China from China, it is essential that, if Soviet Russia participates in the war, China not be divided (like Europe) into American-Britain and Russian zones of military operations."[22]

But since attacks on the National Government and sympathy with the Chinese Communists were very much in vogue at the time, contrary opinions were ignored or jeered at. What was even more unfortunate was that the Communist propaganda line soon affected American policy towards China through such men as Alger Hiss and Harry Dexter White who held high government positions, and through the connections of pro-Communist organizations with government offices. As pointed out by Miss Freda Utley, "During the war one could point to evidence of a State Department-I.P.R. [Institute of Pacific Relations] axis, so close were the personal relations between them, so identical their points of view and the policies they advocated, and so frequently were Institute of Pacific Relations members recruited to serve in agencies affiliated to the State Department, such as the O.W.I. [Office of War Information] and Foreign Economic Administration. . . . in 1943 Philip Jessup resigned from the Chairmanship of the American Council of the Institute of Pacific Relations to serve in the State Department, while Lawrence Salisbury resigned from the State Department (where he had been assistant to the Chief of the Far Eastern Division), to become editor of the Institute of Pacific Relations' fortnightly publication, Far Eastern Survey."[23] According to Miss Utley, the American Government gave its official blessing to the pro-Communist views of the Institute of Pacific Relations by distributing in the Asiatic and Pacific areas some 750,000 I.P.R. pamphlets.[24]

Early in January 1942, at the request of President Roosevelt, Generalissimo Chiang Kai-shek assumed the post of Supreme Commander of the China Theater, which was to include not only China but such parts of Thailand and Indo-China as might be occupied by United Nations forces. The Generalissimo immediately asked the President to appoint an American officer to serve under him and Lieutenant General Joseph W. Stilwell was chosen by Mr. Roosevelt to undertake this mission. He was instructed to supervise and control all American defense-aid affairs for China; to command under the Generalissimo all American forces in China and such Chinese forces as might be assigned to him, to represent the American Government on any International War Council in China; to act as the Chief of Staff of the Generalissimo; and to improve, maintain and control the Burma Road in China.[25] General Stilwell arrived at Chungking in March.

This appointment was a most unfortunate one; it was to adversely affect the friendship between China and the United States. General Stilwell was a brave soldier and fine commander in the field but lacked knowledge of politics or Communism. While serving as American military attache at Hankow in 1938 he had already been "captivated" by Agnes Smedley, a well known Communist writer, and regarded the Chinese Communists as the "white hope" of China. John P. Davis, who had been American consul at Hankow in 1938 and was also a great admirer of Agnes Smedley, was now appointed political adviser to Stilwell. Davis, in turn, brought with him to Chungking such men as John Stewart Service, Raymond Paul Ludden and John Emerson who had pro-Communist leanings.[26]

Immediately after his arrival General Stilwell was given the command of the Chinese forces in Burma and went there to conduct the campaign. But his divisions were quickly beaten by the Japanese with superior equipment and he trudged, with a handful of men, 140 miles through tropical jungle to safety in India. He returned to Chungking in June and soon got into trouble with the Generalissimo. Stilwell wanted to erase the humiliation of defeat and advocated the reopening of the Burma Road with 30 divisions. The Generalissimo rejected his plan on the ground that 30 divisions could not be spared from other war zones in China and that without coordination of the American and British navies, Chinese forces would meet with another disaster in Burma. This difference of strategy together with Communist instigation made Stilwell hate the Generalissimo.

His diary and letters to his wife were now full of name-calling for the Generalissimo and warm praises for the Communists. Two short quotations will suffice to show his bias: "(1) I judge Kuomintang and Kungchantang (Communist Party) by what I saw: (KMT) Corruption, neglect, chaos, economy, taxes, words and deeds. Hoarding, black market, trading with enemy. Communist program . . . reduce taxes, rents, interest, raise production, and standard living. Participate in government. Practice what they preach." (2) "Chiang Kai-shek is confronted with an idea, and that defeats him. He is bewildered by the spread of Communist influence. He can't see that the mass of Chinese people welcome the Reds as being the only visible hope of relief from crushing taxation, the abuses of the army and (the terror of) Tai Li's Gestapo. Under Chiang Kai-shek they now begin to see what they may expect. Greed, corruption, favoritism, more taxes, a ruined currency, terrible waste of life, callous disregard of the rights of men."[27] This unreasonable and arrogant attitude on the part of General Stilwell did a great deal to strain the relations between China and the United States.

After more than two years' deadlock in the relationship between the National Government and the Chinese Communist Party the Generalissimo announced in a speech to a plenary session of the Central Executive Committee of the Kuomintang on September 13, 1943, that the Communist problem was a purely political one and should be solved by political means.[28] Two months later Lin Piao, a Communist division commander, came to Chungking and proposed four points to the government: (1) a legitimate status for the Chinese Communist Party, (2) reorganization of the Communist troops into four armies with twelve divisions, (3) turning the Northern Shensi Border Region (the Shensi-Kansu-Ninghsia Border Region) into an administrative area and reorganization of other areas, and (4) postponement of the dispatch of the Communist troops to the north of the Yellow River until the end of the war.[29] No conclusion was reached in the discussions.

Then in April 1944 Mao Tse-tung sent Lin Tsu-han as representative of the Chinese Communist Party to conduct negotiations with the National Government and the latter, upon receiving the information, delegated General Chang Chih-chung, head of the Political Training Department of the Military Affairs Commission, and Dr. Wang Shih-chieh, secretary-general of the People's Political Council, to Sian to have preliminary conversations with Lin. During these conversations Lin raised many points, of which the most important were: (1) the Communist troops should be reorganized into four armies with twelve divisions; (2) the Shensi-Kansu-Ninghsia Border Region should be changed to the Northern Shensi Administrative Region under the direct jurisdiction of the Executive Yuan and its boundaries should be jointly fixed by representatives of the National Government and the Chinese Communist Party; (3) the Chinese Communist Party should be granted legal status and all its imprisoned members should be immediately released; and (4) the military blockade of the border region should be lifted.

In the middle of May, Chang, Wang and Lin all went to Chungking and on June 5 the government representatives handed to Lin a memorandum prepared by the National Government concerning the solution of the Communist problem. In this memorandum the government agreed to reorganize the Communist troops into four armies with ten divisions, and to change the name of the border region and set up a North Shensi Administrative Office under the direct control of the Executive Yuan. With regard to party affairs they should be conducted during the war in accordance with the *Program of Armed Resistance and National Reconstruction*, while after the war a National Assembly should be convened to adopt a constitution and enforce constitutional government. The Chinese Communist Party should obey the laws of the National Government and enjoy the same treatment as other political parties. When an agreement was reached the government would consider the lift of blockade and the release of Communists on bail who had been arrested on charges of violating the law.

The concessions made by the National Government were quite close to the demands of the Communists, and had the Communists really intended to come to terms with the government a solution would have been reached right then. But the talk of unity, democracy, etc., was merely the camouflage of their purpose to overthrow the government and had no real meaning. So Lin produced a document entitled "Suggestions for the Solution of Some Current Urgent Problems made by the Central Committee of the Chinese Communist Party to the Central Executive Committee of the Kuomintang." These suggestions embodied twelve points which greatly exceeded the demands made either by Lin Piao or by Lin Tsu-han. The National Government was now requested to organize the Communist troops into 16 armies consisting of 47 divisions to accommodate the 475,000 regulars claimed by the Communists. As a compromise the government should at least approve the organization of 5 armies with 16 divisions. Fifteen so-called popularly-elected anti-Japanese local governments in Hopei, Shantung and Suiyuan should be recognized by the National Government. Military supplies furnished by the Allied powers should be equitably distributed to the Communist troops. The Chinese Communist Party should be permitted to conduct party activities and publish party papers in various places in the entire country. As the National Government could not accept these expanded demands the negotiations soon broke off without any result.[80]

In the spring of 1944 reports concerning China's unwillingness to wage any war against the Japanese were so numerous that President Roosevelt became alarmed. Consequently he sent Vice President Henry A. Wallace on a trip to Chungking "to see what he could do toward consolidating the Chinese war effort against Japan". Accompanied by John C. Vincent who had served as counselor of the American Embassy in Chungking and was then chief of the Division of Chinese Affairs of the Department of State, Mr. Wallace made a brief visit to Soviet Central Asia to inspect its agricultural developments and arrived at Chungking in the latter part of June.

The relations between the Chinese Communists and the National Government and between China and the Soviet Union became the main topics of his conversations with the Generalissimo. Mr. Wallace told the Generalissimo that President Roosevelt "had indicated to him if the Kuomintang and the Communists could not get together they 'might call in a friend' and the President might be that friend." The Generalissimo asserted that the Chinese Communists were not "agrarian reformers"; that they followed the orders of the Comintern; that they "hoped for the collapse of the Kuomintang prior to the end of the war because such a collapse would enable them to seize power"; and that he desired a political solution of the Communist problem and urged that the United States maintain an attitude of "aloofness" towards the Communists which would make them more willing to reach a settlement with the Kuomintang.

Not convinced by these remarks, Mr. Wallace declared that "if the Chinese Communists were linked with the Union of Soviet Socialist Republics, then there was even greater need for settlement." He added that "there should be no situation in China which might lead to conflict with the Union of Soviet Socialist Republics." The Generalissimo then asked Mr. Wallace to convey a message to President Roosevelt to the effect that if the United States could bring about a meeting between Chinese and Soviet representatives, he would very much welcome such friendly assistance and "would go more than half way to reach an understanding with the Union of Soviet Socialist Republics."[81] Upon the request of Mr. Wallace an American military observer mission was permitted to go to Yenan and stay there for the purpose of obtaining intelligence. Its reports later highly praised the Communists and urged that they be equipped with better arms.

Since the Korean War Mr. Wallace has changed his attitude towards

Communism and the Soviet Union, but at that time he was in sympathy with the Communists and could not fail to be influenced by the views of Vincent. So in his brief report on this trip to President Roosevelt which was submitted in July 1944 but was not made public until January 1950, he painted a very pessimistic picture of the Chinese situation and severely criticized the Generalissimo. While advocating support for Chiang as a short-term investment he concluded: "It is not believed that he has the intelligence or political strength to run post-war China. The leaders of the post-war China will be brought forward by evolution or revolution, and it now seems more likely the latter."[32]

As Japanese forces were pushing into Hunan in the summer with the intention of invading Kwangsi, the American Communists took their chance to publish a three-quarter page advertisement in many newspapers saying "The time is more than ripe for the United States to insist that the Chungking Government shall put its house in order with a real, not a formal, unification of all Chinese fighting forces."[33] President Roosevelt was also worried about the critical military situation and recommended in early July to the Generalissimo the delegation to General Stilwell of "the powers to co-ordinate all Allied military resources in China, including the Communist forces." The Generalissimo agreed to this proposal in principle but requested that a high ranking American official well acquainted with political as well as military matters and having the complete confidence of the President be sent to Chungking to discuss the problem first. Consequently President Roosevelt, on August 18, appointed Major General Patrick J. Hurley his personal representative to the Generalissimo "with the mission of promoting harmonious relations between Generalissimo Chiang and General Stilwell, and of performing certain other duties in connection with military supplies."

Accompanied by Mr. Donald Nelson, chairman of the War Production Board, General Hurley flew to Chungking by way of Moscow in order to get Soviet opinion on the Chinese situation. In their conversations Soviet Foreign Commissar Molotov spoke to General Hurley and Mr. Nelson of "the very impoverished conditions of the people in parts of China, some of whom called themselves Communists but were related to Communism in no way at all. It was merely a way of expressing dissatisfaction with their economic condition and they would forget this political inclination when their economic condition improved. The Soviet Government should not be associated with these 'Communist elements,' nor could it be blamed for this situation. The solution of the entire situation was to make the Chinese Government work in the common interest and cope with the tasks before it and to make life more normal in China. . . . the Soviets would be glad if the United States aided the Chinese in unifying their country, in improving their military and economic condition and in choosing for this task their best people." [34] Being an honest man himself, General Hurley took Molotov's words at their face value and frequently referred to them as expressing Soviet policy towards China.

General Hurley's arrival at Chungking in September, 1944 was very timely for the clash between General Stilwell and the Generalissimo soon developed into a crisis. As Japanese troops penetrated further and further into China's Southwest in August and September, President Roosevelt urged the Generalissimo to place General Stilwell in command of the Chinese forces under the Generalissimo's direction. The Generalissimo was willing to do that on the condition that the power of distributing lend-lease supplies must remain in the Chinese hands and that Communist forces should not be put directly under the American command but through the channels of the Military Affairs Commission. Then on September 19 a message of President Roosevelt was delivered to the Generalissimo in which the Generalissimo was asked (1) to reinforce the Chinese armies in the Salween area in Burma and press their offensive in conjunction with the British and (2) to place Stilwell in "unrestricted command" of all Chinese forces. If he failed to do these things all efforts, both Chinese and American, to save China would be lost and the Generalissimo must "be prepared to accept the consequences and assume the personal responsibility." [35]

It was hardly proper for the head of one state to send such a reproving and stern message to that of another and Stilwell's personal delivery made the Generalissimo feel more furious. On October 2 he made a lengthy report on the whole affair to the Standing Committee of the Central Executive Committee of the Kuomintang and expressed his strong resentment against Stilwell.[36] He told the committee, in a voice full of emotion, that Stilwell wished not only to command the Chinese forces but to have a free hand in their reorganization and to control all the lend-lease military supplies which Stilwell would allocate to the Communists. According to the Generalissimo, Stilwell disobeyed his orders during the Burma campaign in 1942 and, therefore, was not a man to be entrusted with the command of all the Chinese forces. Consequently, on September 25 the Generalissimo handed General Hurley his answer to President Roosevelt, saying that he was willing to place an American in command of all Chinese armies and air force and to make such changes in the Chinese army staff and personnel as might be necessary to bring harmony in the relations with the American field commander, but could not "confer this heavy responsibility upon General Stilwell, and will have to ask for his resignation as Chief of Staff of the China Theatre and his relief from duty in this area."[37] The Generalissimo also declared that even without American aid he would still fight the war against Japan to the bitter end.

General Hurley now held the view that the break between the Generalissimo and Stilwell was beyond repair and told the President: ". . . if you sustain Stilwell in this controversy, you will lose Chiang Kai-shek and possibly you will lose China with him."[38] President Roosevelt accepted his view, Stilwell was recalled and Lieutenant General Albert C. Wedemeyer was designated to serve as the Generalissimo's chief of staff and the commanding general of the American forces in the China Theater. The question of commanding Chinese forces was dropped.

When the news of the Stilwell crisis leaked out at the end of October it created a sensation in the American press. Reports from Brooks Atkinson, Thobum Wiant and Preston Groves in the *New York Times* severely attacked the Generalissimo and regretted the recall of Stilwell. In an editorial the newspaper wrote: "The facts are that China's war against the Japanese, since the December day nearly three years ago when it became of vital importance to ourselves, has been handicapped by internal discord between the Chungking Government and the so-called Chinese Communists . . . and by Chiang's reluctance to entrust General Stilwell with full command of a unified and enhanced effort, by land and by air, against the Japanese. The United States lost a battle, and the Chinese people may be said to have lost one, too, when Chiang forced Stilwell's recall". After stating that the United States had no more right to demand the replacement of Chiang than to ask Britain to drop Churchill and the Soviet Union to drop Stalin it went on to say, "our government should make clear to Chiang that his prestige should be enhanced, not diminished, if he take certain steps . . . if he make a genuine truce with the Chinese Communists who are, in fact, peasant agrarians. . ."

These sentences show that even an independent and leading newspaper like the *New York Times* did not escape from being influenced by propaganda at that time. To do it justice, however, the conclusion of editorials should also be quoted here: "No matter what happens we cannot fail in our friendship for the Chinese pople. We cannot fail in gratitude to Generalissimo Chiang Kai-shek who has met the supreme test and refuses to surrender. Peace in the Orient without a stable and prosperous China is unthinkable".[39]

Soon after the Stilwell crisis American Ambassador Clarence E. Gauss, who was opposed to the Chinese Communists but by no means friendly towards the National Government, resigned and General Hurley was appointed to succeed Gauss at the end of November, 1944. With General Hurley as the ambassador and General Wedemeyer as the chief of staff, the relations between the National Government and the political and military representatives of the United States soon became very cordial and smooth. But American foreign service men in Chungking like Davies, Service, Ludden, Atcheson, etc. were still following the Communist propaganda line. Their reports to the Department of State were full of condemnations of the National Government and praises for the Chinese Communists.

For instance, Service in his report of October 9, 1944 on the conditions in the Communist areas said: "The Japanese are being actively opposed. This opposition is possible and successful because it is total guerrilla warfare aggressively waged by a totally mobilized population. . . . This total mobilization is based upon and has been made possible by what amounts to an economic, political and social revolution. This revolution has been moderate and democratic. It has improved the economic condition of the peasants by rent and interest reduction, tax reform, and good government. It has given them democratic self-government, political consciousness and a sense of their rights".[40]

On November 7, to cite another example, Davies stated as a conclusion of his report: "The Communists are in China to stay. And China's destiny is not Chiang's but theirs".[41] Again, on November 15 he wrote: "We must not indefinitely underwrite a politically bankrupt regime... A coalition Chinese Government in which the Communist finds a satisfactory place is the solution of this impasse most desirable to us . . . If Chiang and the Communists are irreconcilable, then we shall have to decide which faction we are going to support. In seeking to determine which faction we should support we must keep in mind these basic considerations: Power in China is on the verge of shifting from Chiang to the Communists".[42] These career men even advised the Communists that Ambassador Hurley's "efforts in preventing the collapse of the National Government did not represent the policy of the United States".[43]

George Atcheson who was counselor and in charge of the American embassy during Hurley's trip to Washington drafted a memorandum with Service and Ludden and sent it in the form of a telegram to the

Department of State on February 28, 1945. In this memorandum Atcheson suggested that the President "inform Chiang Kai-shek in definite terms that we are required by military necessity to cooperate with and supply the Communists and other suitable groups who can aid in this war against the Japanese, and that to accomplish this end we are taking direct steps . . ."[44] The Generalissimo was to be made clearly to understand that if he refused to accept this proposal the American Government would then publicly express its policy such as that made by Churchill with reference to Yugoslavia. When General Hurley was shown this telegram he was furious and regarded its sending as an act of disloyalty towards him on the part of his subordinates. The Department of State, especially the Division of Chinese Affairs under Vincent, seemed to favor such a plan but Hurley had the support of President Roosevelt and it was decided that the United States would not arm the Chinese Communists unless with the consent of the Generalissimo. Hurley demanded the dismissal of these pro-Communist and disloyal staff members, but the department merely transferred them to other posts.

When the Stilwell crisis was over General Hurley took up the task of mediating between the National Government and the Chinese Communists. On November 7 he flew to Yenan to talk with the Communist leaders and after two day's discussions returned to Chungking with a five-point draft agreement signed by Mao Tse-tung and considered as a "practical plan" for a settlement with the Communists. This draft agreement called for the reorganization of the National Government into a coalition government "embracing representatives of all anti-Japanese parties and non-partisan bodies" and of the reorganization of the Military Affairs Commission into a United Military Affairs Commission consisting of all anti-Japanese armies. Military supplies acquired from foreign aid would be equitably distributed. The legality of the Kuomintang, the Chinese Communist Party and all anti-Japanese parties would be recognized by the coalition government. The National Government regarded the Communist plan as unacceptable and made a three-point counter-proposal which agreed to recognize the Chinese Communist Party as a legal party and to designate high ranking Communist officers to membership in the Military Affairs Commission on the condition that the Communist forces be reorganized and incorporated in the National Army. This plan was brought to Yenan for consideration by Chou En-lai who had flown to Chungking with Hurley and was soon rejected by the Chinese Communist Party.

In January 1945, after General Hurley had assumed the ambassadorship Chou En-lai, at Hurley's request, again came to Chungking to hold a series of conferences with Foreign Minister T. V. Soong, Dr. Wang Shih-chieh and General Chang Chih-chung with General Hurley attending the meetings. The National Government proposed in addition to the previous three-point plan, to set up, in the Executive Yuan, an organ, resembling a war cabinet with representatives of the Chinese Communist Party and other parties; to appoint one national army officer, one Communist officer, and one American army officer to make recommendations regarding the reorganization, equipment and supplies of the Chinese Communist troops; and to appoint one American army officer as the immediate commander of Chinese Communist troops for the duration of the war against Japan. These proposals were also rejected by Chou.

Then early in February Wang Shih-chieh and Chou En-lai jointly drafted a proposal asking the National Government to call a Political Consultative Conference consisting of representatives of the Kuomingtang and other parties, and non-partisan leaders to consider (1) the establishment of constitutional government, (2) the common political program in the future and the unification of armed forces, and (3) the form in which members of parties outside the Kuomintang would take part in the National Government. This draft was agreed to in a meeting and the Generalissimo also gave his consent. Chou En-lai, in the middle of February, left for Yenan to consult with Mao while Hurley returned to the United States to report to the American Government.

In April General Hurley flew back to Chungking by way of London and Moscow in order to discuss American policy in China with British and Soviet leaders. On the night of April 15 he had a lengthy conversation with Stalin and Molotov in which American Ambassador Averell Harriman also participated. General Hurley reiterated what Molotov told him seven months ago that the Soviet Union was not supporting the Chinese Communist Party and did not desire internal dissension or civil war in China but wanted closer and more harmonious relations with China and Molotov agreed to his analysis. Hurley then told Stalin and Molotov that Prime Minister Churchill and Foreign Secretary Eden had completely concurred in the policy of establishing a united, free and democratic government and uniting all armed forces in China under the leadership of Chiang Kai-shek and Stalin stated that the Soviet Government would support this policy. Stalin even spoke of the Generalissimo as "selfless" and "a patriot" whom the Soviet Union had befriended in times past. General Hurley was very much pleased with Stalin's unqualified agreement to American policy in China and reported it to the Department of State.

General Hurley's naive view of Soviet policy was not shared by American diplomats on the spot. On April 23 George Kennan, American Charge d'Affaires in Moscow, in a telegram to Harriman, who was then in Washington, said: "Stalin is of course prepared to affirm the principle of unifying the armed forces of China. He knows that unification is feasible in a practical sense only on conditions which are acceptable to the Chinese Communist Party . . . " Kennan asserted that in the future Soviet policy respecting China would aim at: (1) re-acquiring all the diplomatic and territorial assets possessed under the Tsars, (2) dominating Chinese provinces in Central Asia contiguous to the Soviet frontier, and (3) acquiring sufficient control in all areas of North China now dominated by the Japanese to prevent other foreign powers from repeating the Japanese incursion.

Ambassador Harriman, who had been present at the Yalta Conference in February 1945, also felt that General Hurley's report, while factually accurate, gave a "too optimistic impression of Marshall Stalin's reaction." He was sure that Stalin would not cooperate indefinitely with Chiang Kai-shek and that if and when the Soviet Union entered the war against Japan, Stalin "would make full use of and support the Chinese Communists even to the extent of setting up a puppet government in Manchuria and possibly in North China if Kuomintang-Communist differences had not been resolved by that time."[45]

In the spring of 1945 victory over Germany was near at hand and victory over Japan not too far off. The American Government and people were anxious that China establish a united, free and democratic government lest civil war would occur right after the Second World War. Knowing this psychology Mao Tse-tung told one of the American military observers in Yenan in two interviews on March 31 and April 1 that China needed American aid both during and after the war; that the Chinese Communists would extend cooperation to the United States regardless of American action; that the Kuomintang could not develop China into a stabilizing power in the Far East, that the Kuomintang was unable to maintain friendly relations with the Soviet Union and other neighbors; and that the Chinese Communist Party represented the interest of the Chinese people and only under Communist leadership could democracy be established in China, therefore it would be to the best interest to the United States to support the Chinese Communists.[46]

Following General Hurley's return to Chungking in May the negotiations between the National Government and the Chinese Communist Party were resumed. Early in July the Communists made two new proposals: (1) the National Assembly scheduled to be convened on November 12 be called off; and (2) a political conference composed of three members each of the Kuomintang, the Chinese Communist Party, the Democratic League[47] and independent political organizations be convened. Negotiations were still dragging on when Japan suddenly announced her unconditional surrender on August 10 and the war was brought to an end earlier than the Allies had expected.

Soon afterwards the Generalissimo sent three telegrams to Mao Tse-tung inviting him to come to Chungking to discuss peaceful unification of China and General Hurley flew to Yenan to fetch him. Mao arrived at Chungking on August 28 and negotiations between government representatives and Communist leaders immediately started. In the middle of September Hurley reported to the Department of State that both sides had agreed to establish a democratic government in China for China's reconstruction and the prevention of civil war; and to support the leadership of Chiang Kai-shek as president of the republic;[48] and the Communists had agreed to recognize the Kuomintang as the dominant party in control of the government and would cooperate with the Kuomintang during the period of transition from the present form of government to a democratic regime. Other questions such as the release of political prisoners; freedom of person, speech, press, belief, assembly and association; etc., were also agreed upon. Only two important points remained to be settled: (1) The Communists claimed the right to appoint or elect governors and mayors in certain provinces and cities, while the government representatives contended that until a constitution was adopted the prerogative of appointing officials should be in the hands of the president. (2) The Communists demanded that their troops should be organized into 48 divisions while the government representatives offered them 20 divisions which formed one-fifth of the peacetime army planned by the government.[49]

Negotiations continued in Chungking following General Hurley's departure for Washington for consultations on September 22. The Communists finally accepted the organization of their troops into 20 divisions and both sides agreed that prior to the establishment of constitutional government a Political Consultative Conference, with 37 members and representing all parties and independents, be convened to exchange views on national affairs and discuss questions relating to national reconstruction and the convocation of the National Assembly. The only principal point on which no agreement had been reached was the question of local government in the so-called "liberated" areas which were then under the control of the Communists.[50]

Mao Tse-tung then returned to Yenan on October 11 and left the unsettled questions to Chou En-lai. During Mao's six weeks' stay in Chungking he pretended to have great admiration and respect for the Generalissimo. In several receptions for him Mao led the gathering in shouting "Long live President Chiang Kai-shek!" The Chinese people were jubilant that peaceful unification would soon be brought about, but their joy was bound to be short-lived.

CHAPTER XX

Yalta Secret Agreement and Sino-Soviet Treaty of Friendship and Alliance

Immediately after Japan's treacherous attack on Pearl Harbor Generalissimo Chiang requested Stalin to participate in the war against Japan and proposed that all the powers fighting in Asia and the Pacific–China, Britain, Canada, Australia, New Zealand, the Netherlands, the Soviet Union and the United States—establish a joint war council to plan and coordinate the strategy of the war under American leadership. In his answer of December 12, 1941 Stalin said that the Soviet Union ought not to divert its struggle to the Far East and concluded: "Soviet Russia must fight Japan, for Japan will surely unconditionally break the neutrality pact. We are preparing to meet that situation, but it takes time to prepare. Therefore, I again implore you not to take the lead in demanding that Soviet Russia at once declare war on Japan."[1]

While President Roosevelt did not make such a request to Stalin the American Government was also anxious to have the Soviet Union join the war against Japan. On December 10 Secretary of State Hull and Soviet Ambassador Litvinov, in a long conversation at the Department of State, touched on this question. Litvinov told Hull that the Soviet Government had decided that because of the strain of the struggle against Germany it could not at that time enter the war in the Far East. Secretary Hull did not argue with Litvinov but hinted that the Soviet Union might have made a wrong decision. He then asked for air bases around Vladivostok and on the Kamchatka Peninsula so that American bombers could strike at Japanese naval bases and cities but Litvinov could not even agree to this demand. Then Hull said to Litvinov: "If Russia should refrain from cooperation with us in the Far East while we continued to aid her in Europe, there would be constant flow of criticism as to why we were aiding Russia against a world movement involving all alike when Russia was not cooperating with us in the Orient."[2]

As Japan was the historical enemy of the Soviet Union Stalin was naturally interested in her defeat in the war. Besides, Stalin saw clearly that the war against Japan offered him a golden opportunity to realize his ambitions in the Far East. But he wanted to choose a most advantageous moment to enter the war so that the Soviet Union would get the maximum benefit at the minimum sacrifice. So on occasions he showed his determination eventually to participate in the war but always refused to make any specific commitment.

It was not until the Big Three Foreign Ministers' Conference at Moscow in October 1943 that Stalin promised Hull once Germany was finally defeated the Soviet Union would enter the war against Japan.[3] A month later at the Teheran Conference Stalin repeated the same promise to Roosevelt and Churchill.[4] Stalin did not demand any price for Soviet participation in the war because he knew that time was not yet ripe. But the question of Soviet need for warm water ports was brought up by Churchill at a luncheon party and Roosevelt mentioned the possibility that the Soviet Union might have access to the port of Dairen in Manchuria. "Stalin immediately expressed the opinion that the Chinese would object to this proposal, but Roosevelt said he thought they would agree to having Dairen made a free port under international guarantee." According to Robert E. Sherwood, Roosevelt was not merely guessing about this but had discussed this very point with Generalissimo Chiang at Cairo a few days previously.[5]

In the latter part of 1944, when the defeat of Germany was assured and when the United States had the control of the air and the sea in the western Pacific American forces were planning an invasion of Manchuria and the home islands of Japan as the last step in defeating that nation. Due to inaccurate intelligence reports, however, American leaders overestimated Japanese strength and were exceedingly anxious to get the Soviet Union into the war against Japan so as to shorten the duration of the war and to save many American lives. So in October 1944, when Churchill paid a visit to Moscow, U.S. Ambassador Harriman took part in their talks and pressed Stalin for specific commitments concerning the war. Stalin promised to enter the war within three months after the collapse of Germany but insisted supplies be accumulated beforehand for sixty divisions of Soviet forces needed to fight the Japanese.

A list of the supplies—computed to provide food, fuel, transport equipment, and other materials for 1,500,000 men, 3,000 tanks, 75,000 motor vehicles, and 5000 planes for a period of two months—was later handed to Major General John R. Deane, head of United States Military Mission in Moscow. The total tonnage of what was asked of the United States, in addition to huge shipments being made under the Lend-Lease program, mounted to more than 860,000 tons of dry and 206,000 tons of liquid cargo. The list was revised but it was not much reduced in total. By the end of June 1945, forty days before Soviet entry into the war the United States had delivered about 80 per cent of these supplies to the Soviet authorities.

Besides securing large quantities of supplies by promising to attack Japan, Stalin also took the chance to demand even a higher price. Stalin told Harriman that the Soviet people would have to know what they were fighting for, so there were also certain political aspects which would have to be taken into account. At that meeting on October 15 Stalin did not elaborate on that subject. On December 14 Harriman told Stalin that President Roosevelt wanted to know more about the political aspects he had mentioned and Stalin enumerated his wishes as follows: (1) the return of the Kurile Islands and southern Sakhalin to the Soviet Union, (2) lease of Port Arthur and Dairen, (3) lease of the Chinese Eastern and the South Manchurian railways and (4) recognition of the status quo in Outer Mongolia.[7] Thus Stalin's price for entering the war against Japan was known to Roosevelt almost two months before the Yalta Conference.

At the beginning of 1945 it became clear that Germany could not hold on much longer and the Big Three must meet again. In choosing a meeting spot Roosevelt and Churchill had suggested places ranging all the way from northern Scotland to Jerusalem but Stalin insisted that it must be within the Soviet Union. So Roosevelt and Churcill finally agreed to go to the Crimea and the Yalta Conference took place early in February.

Roosevelt, Churchill and Stalin gathered at Yalta primarily to discuss European problems, such as, Germany, Poland, Yugoslavia, etc., and problems related to the organization of the United Nations. It was not until some agreements concerning these problems had been reached that the political questions of the Far East were dealt with. From the beginning Roosevelt was prepared to give concessions to the Soviet Union. The policy of the American Government can best be shown in a memo prepared by the Department of State and outlining various proposals which Roosevelt might put before Churchill and Stalin. It said in conclusion: "We must have the cooperation of the Soviet Union to defeat Germany. We sorely need the Soviet Union in the war against Japan when the war in Europe is over. The importance of those two things can be reckoned in terms of American lives. We must have the cooperation of the Soviet Union to organize the peace. There are certain things in connection with the foregoing proposals which are repugnant to me personally, but I am prepared to urge their adoption to obtain the cooperation of the Soviet Union in winning the war and organizing the peace."[8] Consequently Roosevelt gave in to Stalin on many points: Germany, Poland, reparations, membership of Ukraine and White Russia in the United Nations and the Far East.

The Political problem concerning Soviet entry into the war was never discussed in the formal sessions of the conference but only in private talks among the Big Three, especially between Roosevelt and Stalin with Molotov and Harriman acting as aides. On the afternoon of February 8, the fifth day of the conference, Roosevelt and Stalin talked about the Soviet claims in the Far East. Stalin told Roosevelt, "if these conditions were not met, it would be difficult to explain to the Russian people why they must go to war against Japan."[9] Roosevelt was quite lenient and remarked that he saw no difficulty in turning over to the Soviet Union at the end of the war the Kurile Islands and southern Sakhalin. With regard to Dairen he preferred the free-port arrangement, while the Chinese Eastern Railway might be leased by the Soviet authorities or placed under a joint Chinese-Russian commission.[10]

Two days later Molotov handed Harriman a memo with the heading, "Draft of Marshal Stalin's political conditions for Russia's entry in the war against Japan," which embodied in detail all the demands which Stalin had told Harriman in December with the provision that the heads of the three powers agreed that these claims would be unquestionably satisfied after the defeat of Japan. On its part the Soviet Union offered to conclude with China a pact of friendship and alliance. Harriman at once said President Roosevelt would wish (1) to change Soviet leasehold of Port Arthur and Dairen to international free ports; (2) to put the Manchurian railways under the joint operation of a Chinese-Soviet commission; and (3) not to dispose finally of these two matters in which China was interested without the concurrence of the Generalissimo. That afternoon after the formal meeting of the conference Stalin took up the matter with Roosevelt. He agreed to make Dairen a free port, and to put the railways under joint operation; but insisted that since Port Arthur was to be a Soviet naval base, a lease was required. He also agreed on the need for getting the Generalissimo's concurrence in regard to the ports, railways and the status quo of Outer Mongolia but asked the President to break the news to the Generalissimo. Roosevelt in turn agreed to the leasehold of Port Arthur. The problem was thus settled and the Yalta Secret Agreement, bearing the title "Agreement Regarding

Japan" was signed on the next day, February 11, just before Roosevelt's departure.[11]

Owing to its importance and the interest aroused by it the document is here reproduced in full:

"The leaders of the three Great Powers—the Soviet Union, the United States of America and Great Britain—have agreed that in two or three months after Germany has surrendered and the war in Europe has terminated the Soviet Union shall enter into the war against Japan on the side of the Allies on condition that:

"1. The status quo in Outer Mongolia (The Mongolian People's Republic) shall be preserved;

"2. The former rights of Russia violated by the treacherous attack of Japan in 1904 shall be restored, viz.:

(a) The southern part of Sakhalin as well as all the islands adjacent to it shall be returned to the Soviet Union,

(b) the commercial port of Dairen shall be internationalized, the pre-eminent interests of the Soviet Union in this port being safeguarded and the lease of Port Arthur as a naval base of the Union of Soviet Socialist Republics restored,

(c) the Chinese Eastern Railroad and the South Manchurian Railroad which provides an outlet to Dairen shall be jointly operated by the establishment of a joint Soviet-Chinese Company, it being understood that the pre-eminent interests of the Soviet Union shall be safeguarded and that China shall retain full sovereignty in Manchuria;

"3. The Kurile Islands shall be handed over to the Soviet Union.

"It is understood, that the agreement concerning Outer Mongolia and the ports and railroads referred above will require concurrence of Generalissimo Chiang Kai-shek. The President will take measures in order to obtain this concurrence on advice from Marshal Stalin.

"The Heads of the three Great Powers have agreed that these claims of the Soviet Union shall unquestionably be fulfilled after Japan has been defeated.

"For its part the Soviet Union expresses its readiness to conclude with the National Government of China a pact of friendship and alliance between the Union of Soviet Socialist Republics and China in order to render assistance to China with its armed forces for the purpose of liberating China from the Japanese yoke."[12]

It was President Roosevelt who declared in a broadcast to the nation two days after Pearl Harbor: "We are going to win the war and we are going to win the peace that follows."[13] It was the same

Roosevelt who, by committing a major blunder at Yalta, made that peace extremely precarious. Many concessions made to Stalin by Roosevelt were unjustifiable. "These [Yalta] Agreements," wrote William H. Chamberlin, "grossly violated the Atlantic Charter by assigning Polish territory to the Soviet Union and German territory to Poland without plebiscites. They violated the most elementary rules of humanity and civilized warfare by sanctioning slave labor as 'reparations.' And the whole historic basis of American foreign policy in the Far East was upset by the virtual invitation to Stalin to take over Japan's former exclusive and dominant role in Manchuria."[14]

Of all the agreements made at Yalta the least excusable was the so-called Agreement Regarding Japan. By a secret pact the interests of a nation which was not an enemy, nor a "liberated country" as in the case of Poland, but a principal ally which had fought Japan for eight long years, were sacrificed in order to secure Soviet entry into the war. And this was done without that ally's knowing it. A similar case could hardly be found in the history of diplomacy. Of course it is unfair to accuse President Roosevelt for intentionally betraying China; judging by what he had said of and done for China we must say that Roosevelt was a true friend of the Chinese people. But the fact remains that he played unwittingly into Stalin's hands and did great harm to China and to world peace.

Two arguments have been put forward in defense of the Yalta Secret Agreement: one is that it merely restored to the Soviet Union rights which were violated by the treacherous attack of Japan; the other is that had there been no agreement the Soviet Union would have attacked Japan anyway and taken what it wished in Manchuria. Neither of these arguments can hold water. Answering the first argument we will say that Russia's leasehold of Dairen and Port Arthur was forced upon the Manchu Government in 1898, the result of an aggressive action; that the Soviet Government had renounced these Tsarist privileges in its declarations of 1919 and 1920; that the Soviet Government had sold the Chinese Eastern Railway to the puppet state, Manchukuo; and that the Russo-Japanese War of 1904-1905 was not a treacherous attack on Japan's part as in the case of Pearl Harbor. The Soviet Union had no more right to hold these ports and railways in Manchuria than Japan.

With regard to the second argument it is quite possible that even if Roosevelt rejected Stalin's terms the latter might have entered the war against Japan and grasped what he wanted in Manchuria just the same. But in that case the Soviet Union would have committed an overt act of aggression and would have been condemned by the public opinion all over the world except the Communists. As it was, the Soviet march into Manchuria with all its consequences had perfect legality according to international treaties and even had the moral support of the United States.

The tragic irony of the story is that the United States could have beaten Japan without Soviet entry into the war. While the atomic bomb was still an uncertainty, there were intelligence reports showing Japan near collapse as a result of American naval blockade and air attack. American warships were already able to bombard any point on the shores of Japan at will. The Kwantung Army in Manchuria had been diminished both in number and in quality. These reports either did not reach the Joint Chiefs of Staff and President Roosevelt or were simply ignored by them. The mistaken view that Japan still possessed powerful strength and Soviet participation in the war was necessary prevailed and Roosevelt accepted it.

The reason why Roosevelt was willing to undertake to obtain the concurrence of the Generalissimo in this agreement is most likely that he regarded it as something beneficial to China; it would bring about an alliance between the Soviet Union and the National Government and save China the plight of a civil war, as the Chinese Communists, unsupported by the Soviet Union, would come to terms with the government. This kind of reasoning showed that Roosevelt had a mistaken conception of the Chinese Communists and a naive trust of Stalin's pledges. In discussing the internal situation in China Roosevelt told Stalin at Yalta that the blame for the breach between the Communists and the Chungking Government lay more with the Kuomintang than with "the rank and file of the so-called Communists".[15] The word "so-called" proves that Roosevelt was also influenced by the propaganda that the Chinese Communists were agrarian reformers. How much did Roosevelt believe the words of Stalin can be shown by what Harry Hopkins, Roosevelt's most trusted adviser, told Sherwood later: "We were absolutely certain that we had won the first great victory of the peace . . . The Russians had proved that they could be reasonable and farseeing and there wasn't any doubt in the minds of the President or any of us that we could live with them and get along with them peacefully for as far into the future as any of us could imagine . . . We felt sure we could count on him [Stalin] to be reasonable and sensible and understanding . . ."[16]

After the conference the Agreement Regarding Japan was made a closely guarded secret. Its text was kept by Admiral William D. Leahy, Roosevelt's personal chief of staff, in a special file in the White House and probably only half a dozen men in the United States knew its existence. When President Roosevelt made a report on the conference to Congress he did not mention it. Even Vice President Harry S. Truman knew nothing of the pact until after succession to the presidency on April 12 and then he had to make a search for the text. But Roosevelt did show General Hurley the text when the latter returned to Washington at the end of February 1945. Hurley protested that the United States had surrendered the territorial integrity and political independence of China and Roosevelt denied that. But some days later Roosevelt admitted to Hurley that there were some features in the agreement which justified his fears and would like him to go and talk with Churchill and Stalin and see if he could ameliorate it or set it aside.[17] But when Hurley saw Churchill and Stalin in April the question of amelioration of the agreement was not brought up.

The Generalissimo was anxious to have a rapprochement with the Soviet Union and was eager to know what talks concerning China had taken place between Roosevelt and Stalin at Yalta before he sent Acting Premier and Foreign Minister T. V. Soong to Moscow to negotiate. But Roosevelt did not tell Chiang anything about the secret agreement. Even during the San Francisco Conference when T. V. Soong visited President Truman at Washington on May 14 the latter did not mention Yalta. It was not until Stalin told Hopkins and Harriman at Moscow at the beginning of June that the Soviet troops would begin to attack the Japanese forces in early August if China had by then accepted the terms of the agreement, that Truman divulged the secret pact to Soong on June 9. Six days later Hurley officially informed the Generalissimo of the agreement and the latter expressed his disappointment. The Generalissimo also made suggestions that the United States and Britain should become parties to any agreement between China and the Soviet Union and that Port Arthur should be designated as a joint naval base for four powers: China, the Soviet Union, the United States and Britain; but these proposals were not accepted by the American Government.[18]

Soong arrived at Moscow early in July to start negotiations with the Soviet Government. Stalin submitted to Soong drafts of three pacts: a treaty of friendship and alliance, an agreement regarding Dairen and Port Arthur, and another agreement concerning the Manchurian railways. By the draft agreement concerning the ports the Soviet Government proposed the creation of a military zone which was to include not only Dairen and Port Arthur but adjacent land and sea areas and in which the Soviet Government was to have the right to maintain naval and air forces. The Manchurian railways and connected enterprises (factories, workshops, lands, mines, timber tracts, etc.) were to be exclusively owned and operated by the Soviet Union. These demands went well beyond the terms in the secret agreement.

On the other hand, the Generalissimo set down the maximum concessions China could make in return for full Soviet recognition of China's sovereignty in Manchuria and a definite agreement to withdraw moral and material aid from the Chinese Communists and rebellious groups in Sinkiang as follows: (1) Port Arthur to be used as a base by the Soviet navy; (2) Dairen to be made a free port, the Soviet Union being given a lease on docks for merchant shipping; (3) the Manchurian railways to be put under Sino-Soviet joint management. As the terms of the two sides were far apart, no agreement was reached in the talks. Finally Soong told Stalin that he must seek instructions in Chungking but would be ready to return to Moscow when Stalin wished. Soong left Moscow on July 14 while Stalin also departed for the Potsdam Conference.

At the time of the Potsdam Conference (July 16-August 1) Germany had surrendered, the first atomic bomb had just been successfully detonated and Japan was near exhaustion. It became very clear then that the war against Japan could not last much longer. Some of the American high officials began to doubt the desirability of Soviet entry into the war. For instance, Secretary of State James F. Byrnes wrote: "in view of what we knew of Soviet actions in Poland, Rumania and Bulgaria, I would have been satisfied had the Russians determined not to enter the war".[19] But the Combined Chiefs of Staff of the United States and Britain recommended on July 24 "to encourage Russian entry into the war against Japan". So President Truman was anxious to have the Soviet Union in the war and, due to the clever maneuver of Stalin, even wrote a letter inviting Stalin to join the war "on behalf of community of nations to maintain peace and security".[20] Later Truman found out that; "we didn't need Russia there and that the Russians have been a headache to us ever since".[21]

As early as February 1945 Japanese Foreign Minister Hirota approached Soviet Ambassador Jacob Malik with the proposal that the Soviet Union offer its good offices to bring about peace between Japan and the Allies but Moscow never forwarded the request to the Allies. On April 5 the Soviet Government had notified Japan that the Soviet-Japanese Neutrality Pact "has lost its meaning and the continuance of this pact has become impossible". By its terms the pact would remain in effect for another year but the Soviet Government did not intend to observe this stipulation. On July 12 Japanese Ambassador Sato had informed Molotov that the Emperor wished peace and was willing to send Prince Konoye to Moscow to arrange it: this offer had been ignored by the Soviet Government. On July 27 President Truman, Prime Minister Clement R. Attlee, (who had just succeeded Churchill) and Generalissimo Chiang issued a declaration, calling upon the Government of Japan "to proclaim now the unconditional surrender of all Japanese armed forces. . . . The alternative for Japan is prompt and utter destruction".[22] Upon the refusal of the Japanese Government to comply with the ultimatum the first atomic bomb was dropped on Hiroshima on August 6. Stalin was now afraid lest Japan might surrender before Soviet entry into the war. So waiting no longer for China's acceptance of the Yalta terms the Soviet Government declared war on Japan on August 8. The next day Soviet troops marched into Manchuria, while the second atomic bomb was dropped on Nagasaki. On August 10 the Japanese Government expressed its willingness to surrender provided the imperial institutions were preserved. Upon the assurance of the Allies that the form of the government of Japan should be established by the freely expressed will of the Japanese people Japan announced her surrender on August 14.

Meanwhile Soong arrived again at Moscow on August 8 to continue his discussions with Stalin. Soong was wise enough to know that the pact with the Soviet Union would be very unpopular in China and had told Hurley in Chungking: "This proposed agreement will be destructive politically to the man responsible for it". Soong was loath to go to Moscow again but Hurley told the Generalissimo that Soong was the only man other than the Generalissimo himself "with the proper hand to negotiate with Stalin". It was arranged that Soong resigned as Foreign Minister; Wang Shih-chieh was appointed to succeed Soong and went along with him to Moscow.[23]

In their early talks Soong, upon the instructions of the Generalissimo, was willing to grant the Soviet Union a military zone on the Kwantung Peninsula, excluding Dairen but Stalin still insisted on the control of Dairen and the Manchurian railways. Then Harriman intervened and wrote to Molotov that President Truman wished that Stalin would not press for further concessions and would respect the principles of open door and territorial integrity. Thereupon Stalin's attitude became less stiff and the views of the two sides were brought closer. After a few more conversations all points of difference were settled and the pacts were signed by Wang Shih-chieh and Molotov on August 14, the day of Japanese surrender.

There were altogether one treaty, four agreements and two exchanges of notes. By the Sino-Soviet Treaty of Friendship and Alliance the two powers undertook to wage war against Japan until final victory was won, not to conclude separate armistice or peace, and to give each other military and other support in case of a repetition of Japanese aggression after the termination of the war. They were to cooperate in time of peace according to the principles of mutual respect for sovereignty and territorial integrity and of non-interference in internal affairs and agreed to render each other economic assistance in post-war reconstruction. The treaty was to remain in force for thirty years, but if neither party gave notice of its desire to terminate it one year before its expiration then it would remain valid until such a notice was given one year in advance.

By the Sino-Soviet Agreement Concerning the Chinese Changchun Railway the main trunk lines of the Chinese Eastern and the South Manchurian railways were to be united into one railway under the name of the Chinese Changchun Railway and put under joint ownership and operation of the two powers. The joint operation of the railway was to be undertaken by a single management under Chinese sovereignty and as a commercial transportation enterprise. The organization of the Sino-Soviet railway company was to be very much similar to that provided in the Agreement for the Provisional Management of the Chinese Eastern Railway concluded in 1924. The term of the agreement was to be thirty years and after its expiration the railway with all its properties would be transferred to China without compensation.

The Sino-Soviet Agreement on Dairen provided that China was to declare Dairen a free port open to the commerce and shipping of all nations; that China was to apportion wharves and warehouses for lease to the Soviet Union by a separate agreement; that the administration in Dairen was to belong to China but the harbor-master (a Soviet citizen) and deputy harbor-master (a Chinese citizen) were to be appointed by the Soviet manager of the Chinese Changchun Railway in agreement with the mayor; and that Dairen was to be subject to the control of the naval base only in case of war against Japan. By the Sino-Soviet Agreement on Port Arthur the port was to be used jointly by the powers as a naval base and its defense was entrusted to the Soviet Government. A Sino-Soviet Military Commission was to be established to handle the matters of joint use of the base with two Chinese and three Soviet representatives, the chairman of the commission being Soviet and the vice-chairman being Chinese. An annex to the agreement determined the area of the base in which the Soviet Government had the right to maintain its army, navy and air forces. The civil administration of the port was to remain Chinese. Both these agreements were to be effective for thirty years.

By a fourth agreement the powers agreed that the supreme authority and responsibility in the zone of military operations would be vested in the Commander-in-Chief of the Soviet Forces in Manchuria to whom a Chinese military mission would be appointed to ensure contact. A National Government representative and staff would also be appointed for the recovered territory to establish an administration for the territory cleared of the enemy and to serve as liaison between Chinese and Soviet forces. As soon as any part of the liberated territory ceased to be a zone of immediate military operations the National Government would assume full authority in the direction of public affairs.

By an exchange of notes the Soviet Government (1) agreed "to render to China its moral support as well as aid in military supplies and other material sources, such support and aid to be entirely given to the National Government as the Central Government of China"; (2) "reaffirmed its respect for China's full sovereignty over the Three Eastern Provinces (Manchuria) and recognized their territorial and administrative integrity"; and (3) declared that as for the recent developments in Sinkiang it had "no intention of interferring in the internal affairs of China".

The question of Outer Mongolia was dealt with in another exchange of notes. During the Moscow discussions Soong at first maintained that Outer Mongolia had always been Chinese territory but Stalin asserted that Outer Mongolia had long been broken away from China and threatened that if China was not willing to recognize Outer Mongolia's independence China might even lose Inner Mongolia.[24] Then Soong, upon the instruction of the Generalissimo, proposed to settle the question of independence by a plebiscite and Stalin agreed. So in the exchange of notes the National Government declared that after the defeat of Japan should a plebiscite of the Outer Mongolian people confirm their desire for independence China would recognize its independence with the existing boundary as its boundary. While the Soviet Government pledged to "respect the political independence and territorial integrity of the People's Republic of Mongolia".

At the meeting between Stalin and Soong on July 11 the question of the withdrawal of Soviet troops from Chinese territory was raised. Stalin declared to Soong that after the capitulation of Japan the Soviet troops would commence to withdraw within three weeks. Soong then asked how long it would take to complete the withdrawal and Stalin said three months would be the maximum for the completion of the withdrawal. Soong wanted to put such a clause in the agreement concerning military operations but Stalin objected, saying that in that case China had no confidence in his words. Consequently the minutes of that meeting were attached to the agreement and initialed by Wang and Molotov.[25]

It seems now meaningless for China to sign agreements with the Soviet Union at great sacrifice of China's territorial and administrative integrity to bring it into the war against Japan at the time of her surrender. But the National Government was willing to make such a sacrifice in order to secure Soviet friendship and to recover Manchuria. Many veteran members of the Kuomintang were opposed to these agreements but they knew they were faced with a fait accompli and did not want to express their opinion in public. So when the pacts came up for discussions at a joint session of the Central Executive Committee of the Kuomintang and the Supreme National Defense Council on August 24, few members made remarks after Wang's report. Only Sun Fo, President of the Legislative Yuan, praised these pacts as an epoch-making event and said they would offer China thirty years' peace to carry out national reconstruction and at the end of that period China should come out as a real major power. Sun also believed that the internal problem of China (meaning the Communist problem) could now be solved once and for all.[26] The agreements were unanimously approved at the joint session and later passed by the Legislative Yuan. The Generalissimo immediately ratified them in his capacity as Chairman of the National Government.

Those Chinese who knew Soviet ambitions in the Far East and the relationship between the Soviet Union and the Chinese Communists doubted from the very beginning that the Soviet Government would honor its pledges to China despite the heavy price she paid for them. Their fear was soon warranted by facts.

Immediately after its declaration of war on Japan 700,000 Soviet troops marched into Manchuria along three routes and within five days Japan surrendered. But the Kwantung Army did not lay down its arms until August 20 and Soviet troops soon occupied the whole region. For eleven days' fighting the Soviet forces captured 594,000 prisoners of war, 925 airplanes, 369 tanks, 35 armed cars, 1,226 pieces of field artillery, 4,836 machine-guns, 300,000 rifles, 2,300 motor vehicles, 126 tractors, 17,497 horses and mules, and 742 depots with munitions and supplies. In addition, at the time of surrender, the Japanese Kwantung Army had on its hands 1,436 pieces of field artillery, 8,989 machine-guns, 11,052 grenade throwers, 3,078 trucks, 21,084 supply cars, 104,777 horses, etc.[27] These captured and surrendered equipment and supplies were not transferred to the National Government but handed over, with the exception of planes, to the Chinese Communists.

According to a report of the American military attaché in China, units of Chinese Communist soldiers wearing armbands with inscriptions "Eighth Route Army" in both Chinese and Russian were first seen in the streets of Mukden on September 10.[28] How did these Communist troops enter Manchuria, get their arms and expand was shown by the testimony of Chin Chun, officer of the Peace Preservation Headquarters of the Northeast as follows: "On September 6, 1945, at 10 a.m., an officer of the Hopei-Jehol-Liaoning War Area, Sixteen Sub-area, Tseng Ke-lin, and his political commissar, Tang Kai, arrived at Mukden from Chingchow by train. The Soviet Commander of Mukden refused to permit them to leave the train, awaiting instructions from his superiors. After consultations, however, they were permitted to disembark at 9 p.m. the same day, and were stationed near the South Gate, known as Hsiaohoyen. The next day, the Soviet Commander ordered all civilians and Peace Preservation units of Mukden placed under the direction of the Chinese Communist forces.

"After the entry of the Chinese Communist forces into Mukden . . . they forthwith began to expand their forces. Equipment and munitions surrendered by the Japanese and puppet (Manchukuo) troops, with the exception of a small quantity which found their way into the hands of general population, were all transferred to the Communists. In Mukden itself, the Communists expanded to some 50,000 men. They used Penchi as their base of operation and fanned out to areas in eastern and southern Liaoning. On September 16, 1945 Chinese Communist Commander Li Yun-cheng of the Hopei-Jehol-Liaoning War Area Headquarters arrived in Mukden with his troops. My unit was reorganized into the 12th Brigade . . . Since we suffered from the lack of supplies because of the expansion, negotiations were conducted with the Soviet Command and we were able to obtain the supplies of the depots under Soviet control".[29]

By the end of September the National Government had arranged with Washington to use the American fleet under Vice Admiral Daniel Barbey to transport government troops to Dairen and Port Arthur for the purpose of taking over Manchuria from Soviet forces. Consequently on October 1 the Waichiaopu notified Soviet Ambassador A. A. Petrov that the Chinese Thirteenth Army was about to be despatched to these ports. On October 6 the Soviet Ambassador told Acting Foreign Minister Kan Nai-kwang that "according to the Sino-

Soviet agreement Dairen is a commercial port, i.e. a port for the transportation of goods, not of troops, and therefore Chinese troops cannot be landed there". Surprised by this Soviet attitude Kan asked Petrov how Russia could send troops there to disarm the Japanese. Petrov answered that Soviet troops were there at the request of the United States and Britain and now the situation was different. Kan then talked about landing at Port Arthur and Petrov said "since Port Arthur is a naval base the Chinese army can also not be landed there". Asked by Kan if Chinese troops were not landed either at Dairen or Port Arthur how were they going to take over Manchuria, Petrov merely answered this should be arranged by the Chinese representative with the Soviet commander at Changchun, capital of Manchuria.[30]

Meanwhile General Hsiung Shih-hui, newly appointed director of the Generalissimo's Northeast Headquarters, went to Changchun to negotiate with General Rodion Y. Malinovsky, Commander-in-Chief of the Soviet Forces in Manchuria. Malinovsky told Hsiung that he did not have authority to allow a landing at Dairen or Port Arthur but would not oppose landings at other ports of Manchuria—Hulutao, Yingkow and Antung. So on October 26 American ships, with Chinese troops aboard, entered the harbor of Hulutao, but to their surprise, found Chinese Communist forces in control of the port. The commanding Communist officer notified Admiral Barbey that they would resist the landing of government troops. The American ships then proceeded to Yingkow but again found Chinese Communists already there, digging trenches and building barricades near the landing points. The American naval task force had to withdraw again and finally landed the Chinese troops at Chinhuangtao inside the Great Wall thence they had to start a long march overland into Manchuria.

With the help of the United States Air Force in the Far East the National Government then tried to despatch troops by air to Mukden and Changchun. Upon hearing of this plan the Soviet ambassador notified the Waichiaopu on November 13 that only security forces and gendarmes could be so transported and only three or five days before the evacuation of Soviet troops; thus the scheme was dropped. A group of 500 Chinese officials, including newly appointed governors of nine provinces,[31] mayors of Harbin and Dairen, commissioners, secretaries, etc. had been flown to Changchun for the taking over of various provinces. They had waited a few weeks there without being able to do any work. Then early in November Communist forces entered Changchun and harassed the Chinese mission in every way possible; even the light and water supply were cut off. General

Hsiung complained to the Soviet commander but nothing was done to protect them. So the Generalissimo withdrew the whole mission from Changchun in November.

It was not until the middle of November that the Chinese troops who had marched from Chinhuangtao and defeated Communist forces at Shanhaikwan, set foot on the soil of Manchuria. Then they pushed on into Manchuria, fighting the Communists on their way until December when they halted within twenty-five miles of Mukden, awaiting negotiations with Malinovsky at Changchun.

According to the pledge made by Stalin to Soong Soviet troops should completely withdraw from Manchuria on December 2 at the latest, three months from the day when the Japanese signed the instrument for surrender on board U.S.S. "Missouri". But the Soviet Government postponed withdrawal of troops time and again. In the middle of December at a meeting of the Council of Foreign Ministers at Moscow Molotov launched an attack on the stationing of American Marines in North China. Molotov knew very well that the Marines were there at the request of the Chinese Government to help disarm and evacuate the Japanese but he brought up the question to embarass Secretary of State Byrnes and to justify the maintenance of Soviet troops in Manchuria. When Byrnes proposed to list an item—the transfer of the control of Manchuria to the Chinese National Government—on the agenda, Molotov introduced another item—the withdrawal of American troops from China—to counter-balance it. As a result both items were dropped. The official communique of the council stated: "The three Foreign Secretaries . . . were in agreement as to the need of a unified and democratic China under the National Government, for broad participation by democratic elements in all branches of the National Government, and for a cessation of civil strife . . . The two Foreign Secretaries (Byrnes and Molotov) were in complete accord as to the desirability of withdrawal of Soviet and American forces from China at the earliest practical moment consistent with the discharge of their obligations and responsibilities."[32] By interweaving the issue of Soviet occupation of Manchuria with that of American marines in North China Molotov certainly won a game of diplomatic maneuver.

Then in February 1946 Chang Hsin-fu, a well-known mining engineer, who was sent to take over Fushun coal mines, met his death at the hands of Chinese Communists while traveling under a Soviet guard. This treacherous atrocity aroused indignation all over China: professors, teachers, students, merchants, workers, etc. staged anti-Soviet demonstrations in Chungking, Peiping, Nanking, Hankow,

Chengtu, Tsinan, Canton and even in newly recovered Taiwan. Although Moscow protested to the National Government, it wanted to do something to pacify this antagonism. So in the middle of March 1946 Soviet troops finally withdrew from Mukden and Chinese forces immediately entered the city. Southern Liaoning, with the exception of the Kwantung Peninsula, was now under government control and, with the help of the American fleet, more troops were soon transported there. But when Soviet troops evacuated Changchun, Harbin and Tsitsihar in April Communist forces at once occupied them. At the middle of May when Moscow advised the National Government that all Soviet forces had withdrawn from Manchuria except some troops at Port Arthur and Dairen 300,000 Chinese Communist troops under Lin Piao held Manchuria firmly under their control except the region along the railway from Shanhaikwan to Mukden. In March 1947 the Soviet ambassador in Nanking asked the Nationalist Government to take over the administration of Dairen and Port Arthur and the government sent a mission to these ports in June to investigate conditions. But as the Soviets refused the admission of Chinese troops the matter was dropped.

As soon as Soviet troops occupied industrial centers of Manchuria the work of dismantling factories and removing machinery began. Soviet engineers arrived in considerable numbers to supervise the work while Japanese prisoners of war were put to do the actual job. Even the NKVD took part in it. According to the report of the Edwin W. Pauley Mission on Japanese Reparations which visited Manchuria in June 1946, the Soviets "concentrated on certain categories of supplies, machinery and equipment. In addition to taking stockpiles and certain complete industrial installations, the Soviets took by far the larger part of all functioning power generating and transforming equipment, electric motors, experimental plants, laboratories and hospitals. In machine tools they took only the newest and best, leaving antiquated tools behind. In the old Mukden Arsenal, for example, about one-third of the tools were taken, while in the new arsenal, virtually everything was taken or demolished". The direct damage was estimated by the mission at $858,000,000, while the total damage, including deterioration and cost of replacement was put at over $2,000,000,000[33] To the protest of the National Government Moscow shamelessly claimed these spoils as "war booty" while the Soviet press set the value of the removed equipment at only $97,000,000.[34]

The Soviet forces also confiscated about $3,000,000 worth of gold bullion stocks and over 500,000,000 Manchurian yuan from Manchukuo banks. Besides, they also issued 10,000,000,000 yuan in occupational currency almost doubling the total Manchukuo note issue. During their nine months' occupation Soviet troops committed murders, rape and looting on a large scale. How much damage was done by these unruly soldiers individually nobody can give an approximate guess.

The Soviets had also demanded excessive economic concessions in Manchuria. On November 24, 1945 Slatekovsky, economic adviser to General Malinovsky, approached Chang Chia-ngau, chairman of the Economic Commission of the Generalissimo's Northeast Headquarters, with the proposal that 90 per cent of all metallurgical works, 85 per cent of the coal output, 95 per cent of electric power, and a large part of chemical and machine building installations were to be put under joint Sino-Soviet operation with Soviet general managers. Upon the instructions from the Generalissimo Chang declined to enter into discussion until the withdrawal of the Soviet troops.

On January 21, 1946 the Soviet Government presented a note to Chungking asserting that all Japanese enterprises in Manchuria were to be regarded as war booty but the Soviet Government was willing to propose to China a joint arrangement for the development of Manchuria as far as the remnants of the Japanese-built industry in Manchuria were concerned. The National Government agreed to hold conversations with Soviet representatives but Washington, hearing the news, sent a note to both the Chinese and Soviet Governments, stating that since the ultimate disposition of Japanese external assets, such as the industries in Manchuria, was a matter of common interest and concern of the Allies, they should not be removed from Manchuria as "war booty" or disposed by agreement between the Soviet and Chinese Governments for joint control or ownerships.[85] The National Government, in its reply to this note, accepted the American concept, but the Soviet Government simply ignored it.

On March 27, 1946 Petrov handed to the Waichiaopu a formal proposal whereby the principal coal mines, iron mines and foundries, steel mills, oil refineries, cement plants, power plants, salt mines, and the airfields of the principal cities were to be under joint Sino-Soviet control. A joint company was to be formed for each enterprise with each side holding 50 per cent of the stock, and with a Chinese board chairman and Soviet vice-chairman, and a Soviet manager and a Chinese deputy manager. After thirty years these enterprises would be returned to China without any compensation. The National Government was in no mood to grant these concessions to the Soviet Union. Stalin even offered to compel the Chinese Communists to accept the

Generalissimo's rule if the latter agreed to these concessions and to the exclusion of American interests in Manchuria, but the Generalissimo stood firm.[36] After long discussions both in Chungking and in Changchun no basis for agreement could be found and the negotiations broke off.[37]

In accordance with the exchange of notes between China and the Soviet Union Outer Mongolia held a so-called plebiscite on October 20, 1945 to determine whether the Mongolian people wished independence. Lei Fa-chang, Chinese Vice Minister of the Interior, was sent to Ulan Bator to observe the plebiscite. The result of the plebiscite was announced the next day. Of 494,960 eligible voters 98.4 per cent had cast votes and of these votes 100 per cent favored independence. It was indeed unbelievable that a nomadic people living scattered over a vast territory and with primitive means of communications could achieve such "unanimity" and such quick counting of the ballots. The National Government, on January 5, 1946, formally recognized the independence of Outer Mongolia. In the next month it even concluded an agreement with Outer Mongolia for the establishment of diplomatic relations. When Outer Mongolia applied for membership in the United Nations China voted for it in the Security Council but it failed to get the necessary seven votes.

But as a matter of fact Mongolia has never had a shred of independence. As Dr. T. F. Tsiang, Chinese permanent delegate to the United Nations, told the Fourth Session of the General Assembly: "the Soviet Government is maintaining advisers and other personnel in all branches of the government of Outer Mongolia. . . . There are Soviet advisers attached to every unit of the army of Outer Mongolia, and Soviet officers are even participating in the operational activities of the army. The Soviet Government maintains a virtual monopoly of its foreign trade . . . thus compelling it to supply the Soviet Union with a great part of its material resources".[38] Two officers of the Mongolian army, who fled to Peiping in March 1948, confirmed that an army of about 100,000 (one tenth of the population) was being maintained after the war; that Soviet advisers and army personnel were running the country; and that some 25,000 political prisoners worked on forced labor projects under Soviet guards.[39] The so-called Tuvinian People's Republic was absorbed in 1944 into the Soviet Union as the Tuva Province of the R.S.F.S.R.

With regard to Sinkiang, the Soviet Government also did not keep its pledge of non-interference in Chinese internal affairs. After Soviet reluctant withdrawal from Sinkiang in 1943 the Soviet Government had changed its tactics and instigated the native tribes, Kazakhs, Kirghiz, Usbeks, etc., to revolt against Chinese rule. At the end of 1943 groups of these tribesmen, armed with rifles, attacked towns and cities, sometimes with the support of Soviet planes.

In March 1944, Usman, a Kazakh chief, led a revolt near the Mongolian border after receiving military supplies from Outer Mongolia. Chinese troops, sent to suppress the rebellion were bombed by planes bearing Soviet insignia and suffered heavy losses. Under Soviet air cover and with the help of Outer Mongolian troops Usman succeeded in wiping out the entire Chinese garrison at Huihoko consisting of three regiments. The commissioner of the Waichiaopu in Sinkiang protested to the Soviet consul-general at Urumchi but the latter denied any complicity. The Tass News Agency, however, stated that "the Soviet Government will be forced to give the Government of the Mongolian People's Republic every necessary help and support".[40] To the Waichiaopu's demand for an explanation Soviet Ambassador Alexander Panyushkin simply did not answer.

Then in November 1944 an Uzbek, Farkhad, entered Sinkiang from Soviet Central Asia and brought with him arms, including trench mortars and machine guns, for the rebelling tribesmen and assumed leadership of the revolt in the Ili-Ining area. The rebels soon occupied the whole area and pushed eastward within 70 miles of Urumchi. A puppet state, "East Turkestan Republic", was set up in the region occupied by them.

After the conclusion of the Sino-Soviet agreements in August 1945 the National Government representatives negotiated with the rebel leaders at Urumchi for a settlement, with the Soviet consul-general playing the role of an "impartial mediator". After three months' negotiations an agreement was reached in January 1946 by which the rebels consented to relinquish "East Turkestan Republic", while the government granted autonomous status to the region and permitted them to keep an army of six regiments. Ahmed Djan, the Kazakh leader, was appointed Deputy Governor of Sinkiang. A provincial council was to be created, consisting of 10 Chinese and 15 Turkis representing the local Moslem population. The agreement also provided for freedom of religion, fair taxation, and an amnesty for political prisoners. In May 1947 for the first time in the history of Sinkiang a Turki, Mazud Sabri, was appointed governor of the province. This act showed how far the National Government was willing to reconcile with the native tribes.

Meanwhile Usman was appointed Special Administrator of the

Altai Mountains Area by the National Government and soon broke away from the Soviets. He informed the National Government of the Soviet activities in exploiting the mines in Fuyun with armed miners. This move on Usman's part agitated the Soviet authorities who attacked Usman in April 1947 and caused him to retreat to Peitashan, about 130 miles away from Sinkiang-Mongolian border. On June 5 Mongolian troops with the help of Soviet planes attacked Peitashan. The National Government protested with Moscow and through Moscow with the Mongolian Government but the Soviet Government maintained that Peitashan was within the territory of Outer Mongolia and the Soviet press condemned China as the aggressor. Intermittent fighting lasted through the summer of 1947.

The provincial council was also not a success. Instigated by the Soviets the Turki representatives from the Ili-Ining area soon quarreled with other representatives. In August these Turki representatives, led by Ahmed Djan and taking with them several Turki delegates from other parts of Sinkiang, left Urumchi by Soviet planes and returned to Ining. Their demand of the removal of Mazud was rejected by Nanking and the rift between the native tribes and the National Government remained wide.

In January 1949 the Soviet Government, through its consul-general at Urumchi, proposed to the Sinkiang authorities a three-year trade agreement by which the Soviet Union, through its state agency, would enjoy the privilege freely to import from and export to Sinkiang, without corresponding privilege being granted to China in any part of Soviet territory. It also proposed to conclude an agreement with Sinkiang, setting up joint Sino-Soviet companies to explore and exploit the mineral and oil resources for 50 years. Preliminary exchange of views was conducted on a local level but as the Chinese Government regarded, from the very beginning, the Soviet proposals as unacceptable no result came out of these conversations.[41]

CHAPTER XXI

American Efforts at Mediation After The Second World War

At the end of the war against Japan the Chinese Communists saw their golden opportunity to expand. Upon hearing the Tokyo broadcast on August 10, 1945 that Japan was willing to surrender Chu Teh immediately ordered his officers to accept the surrender of the Japanese armies in China. Two days later the Generalissimo issued an order to the Communist forces "to remain at their posts and wait for orders" but it was ignored and the Yenan radio attacked Chiang vehemently. On August 16 Chu Teh, using the title "Commander-in-Chief of the Chinese People's Liberation Army" sent a memorandum to the American, British and Soviet embassies in Chungking, demanding for the Chinese Communists the right to participate in accepting the Japanese surrender by the Allies and in the peace conference and the conference of the United Nations.[1] He especially called upon the United States "to stop lend-lease to the Kuomintang Government immediately". In a telegram to the Generalissimo he said: "the Chinese people are dissatisfied with you and your government which cannot represent the broad masses."[2]

The National Government was not quite ready for the sudden surrender of Japan and encountered difficulties in taking over the vast territory which had been occupied by the Japanese. But with the help of the United States forces in China three armies were air-lifted to East and North China and key cities such as Nanking, Shanghai, Peiping and Tientsin were soon taken over. Additional troops were transported by sea in American ships to coastal provinces and in a few months between 400,000 and 500,000 soldiers had been moved to occupied areas. At the request of the National Government over 50,000 American marines were landed in North China and stationed in Tsingtao, Tientsin, Peiping, Chinhuangtao, etc. to assist the government in maintaining control of key areas of North China and in repatriating the Japanese. Thus Chinese government forces were enabled to receive the surrender of the great majority of the 1,200,000 Japanese troops in China proper together with their equipment and stocks of military materials.

On the other hand, Communist forces, although unable to compete with the government on this point, did make a number of the Japanese to surrender to them, owing to the existence of guerrilla units in Central, North and coastal China. While government forces quickly occupied larger cities, Communist units infiltrated into towns and the countryside and severed the communication lines. In order to obtain their logistic supplies from bases government troops had to keep the lines open and skirmishes occurred between government and Communist troops soon after V-J Day. As the Communists made sneak attacks on government troops whenever there was a chance, fighting spread to 11 provinces in October.

What had been feared by the American Government—a civil war in China after the Second World War—was now actually happening and it worried Washington a great deal. General Hurley was then in Washington for consultation and was urged by President Truman and Secretary of State Byrnes to go back to Chungking to continue his mediation between the Chinese Government and the Communists. Towards the end of November General Hurley had decided to fly to Chungking and then suddenly resigned as ambassador to China on the ground that career men in the Department of State were sabotaging American policy towards China and sided with the Chinese Communists.[2]

On November 27 President Truman announced the acceptance of Hurley's resignation and the appointment of General George C. Marshall, retired Chief-of-Staff of the United States Army, his special representative in China to continue the work begun by Hurley. In his statement, issued on December 15, which also served as his instructions to General Marshall, Truman stated that a strong, united and democratic China was of the utmost importance to world peace and asked the Chinese people to "overlook no opportunity to adjust their internal differences promptly by means of peaceful negotiation".

"The Government of the United States", the statement went on, "believes it essential: (1) That a cessation of hostilities be arranged between the armies of the National Government and the Chinese Communists and other dissident Chinese armed forces . . . (2) That a national conference of representatives of major political elements be arranged to develop an early solution to the present internal strife—a solution which will bring about the unification of China". Asserting that the National Government was a "one-party government", Truman advocated that the proposed conference agree upon arrangements which would give the major political elements "a fair and effective representation in the Chinese National Government". Admitting that the existence of autonomous armies made political unity in China impossible, he declared: "With the institution of a broadly representative government, autonomous armies should be eliminated as such and all armed forces in China integrated effectively into the Chinese National Army".

In conclusion President Truman promised: "As China moves toward peace and unity . . . the United States would be prepared to assist the National Government in every reasonable way to rehabilitate the country, improve the agrarian and industrial economy and establish a military organization capable of discharging China's national and international responsibilities for the maintenance of peace and order".[4]

This statement, originally drafted by John C. Vincent, director of the Far Eastern Office of the Department of State, who was under the influence of Owen Lattimore, gave General Marshall a twofold task—to put an end to the fighting between government and Communist forces and to bring about a coalition government including the Communists. Arriving at Chungking on December 20 the Marshall mission seemed to be very successful in its initial stage. On the day of his arrival Chou En-lai announced that the Communists would seek for an immediate truce to end the civil war and negotiations for a coalition government—exactly what the American Government wanted. At the beginning of 1946 a committee was formed with General Marshall as chairman, General Chang Chun, a close friend of the Generalissimo, representing the government, and Chou En-lai, representing the Communists, to discuss the cessation of hostilities. This Committee of Three held its first meeting on January 7 and reached an agreement three days later.

In accordance with this agreement both the Generalissimo and Mao Tse-tung issued an order on January 10 to their respective armed forces to cease fire and halt all troop movement. Destruction of, and interference with, all lines of communications were also to cease and obstructions placed against such lines would be cleared at once. An Executive Headquarters, consisting of three commissioners representing the government, the Chinese Communist Party and the United States, was to be set up in Peiping for the purpose of carrying out these agreements and instructions and orders unanimously agreed upon by these commissioners would be isued in the name of the President of the Republic of China. Movements of the National Army south of the Yangtse River for the continued execution of the plan of military reorganization and into or within Manchuria for the purpose of restoring Chinese sovereignty would not be prejudiced by this order.[5]

With regard to political problems, the Political Consultative Conference, as agreed upon by the government and Communist representatives in 1945 was convened in Chungking also on January 10 and was attended by representatives of the Kuomintang, the Chinese Communist Party, the Democratic League, and the Youth Party and non-party delegates. In three weeks' deliberations four resolutions were adopted by the conference and an agreement by the sub-committee on the National Assembly.

The Resolution on Government Organization provided for an expanded State Council to consist of forty state councillors, half of whom would be Kuomintang members and the other half, members of other political parties and prominent social leaders. This council was to be the highest political authority in the country, pending the formation of constitutional government. General resolutions of the State Council were to be passed by a majority vote of the councillors present but any change in administrative policy must be adopted by a two-thirds vote. The President of the National Government kept the power to submit any decision of the council for its reconsideration but if three-fifths of the councillors upheld the original decision then the decision must be carried out.

By another resolution the Political Consultative Conference adopted a comprehensive Program for Peaceful National Reconstruction. This program regarded the Three People's Principles as the highest guiding principles for national reconstruction; advocated the unification of all forces under the guidance of President Chiang Kai-shek; recognized the democratization of politics, nationalization of troops, and equality and legality of all political parties as necessary paths leading to national reconstruction; and asserted that political disputes must be settled by political means. Besides these general principles it contained detailed stipulations for the rights of the people, political problems, military affairs, foreign relations, economics and finance, education and culture, rehabilitation and relief, and Chinese residents overseas.

Military problems were dealt with in a third resolution which set up the fundamental principles for the creation of a national army and reorganization of the existing army: the army must belong to the state, the army and political parties must be separated, civil and military authorities must also be separated, etc. As to the practical method it called for the early reorganization of the government troops into 90 divisions according to the plan of the Ministry of War, and of the Communist troops according to the agreement of the Military Sub-Committee. When these steps had been taken all roops of the country would be again reorganized into 50 or 60 divisions.

Regarding the 1936 draft constitution a fourth resolution provided that a Committee for the Reviewing of the Draft Constitution be set up with 25 members of whom five would represent each of the five groups composing the Political Consultation Conference. In addition ten technical experts outside of the conference would be invited to take part in the work. The function of the committee was to revise the draft constitution within two months according to the principles laid down by the conference.

A sub-committee was set up by the conference to deal with the problem of the National Assembly. After long discussions an agreement on the following points was reached, vis., (1) the National Assembly should be convened on May 5; (2) the power of the National Assembly was to adopt the constitution; (3) the constitution should be adopted by a three-fourths vote of the delegates present; and (4) in addition to the 1,200 geographical and vocational delegates who had been or were going to be elected 150 more delegates should be allocated to the Northeast provinces and Taiwan and 700 more delegates apportioned among the various parties and social leaders, making a total of 2,050 delegates.[6]

The Military Sub-Committee referred to above had been formed on January 10 by the Committee of Three with General Chang Chih-chung and Chou En-lai representing the government and the Chinese Communist Party respectively and General Marshall as adviser. It held its first meeting on February 14, and eleven days later reached an agreement entitled "Basis for Military Reorganization and for the Integration of the Communist Forces into the National Army". By this agreement government armies were to be reduced to 90 divisions and Communist forces to 18 divisions during twelve months. At the end of the following six months they were to be again reduced to 50 and 10 divisions respectively. These divisions of not more than 14,000 men each would be organized into 20 armies. The process of integration would start after that. The National Government and the Chinese Communist Party were both required to submit to the Military Sub-Committee, within three weeks of the promulgation of the agreement, respective lists of 90 and 18 divisions to be retained and the order of demobilization of units during the first two months[7]

The resolutions adopted by the Political Consultation Conference and the agreements arrived at in the Committee of Three and the Military Sub-Committee showed that the National Government was willing to make important concessions to the Chinese Communists and other political parties. Had they been faithfully carried out China would certainly have made a long stride towards national unification and democratic government. So when these resolutions and agreements were announced Chinese public opinion expressed enthusiastic approval. The Central Executive Committee of the Kuomintang held a plenary session from March 1 to March 17, 1946 to discuss these problems. While the members felt indignant at Soviet obstruction to China's taking over of Manchuria and at the treacherous murder of Chang Hsin-fu and criticized the weak-kneed policy of Foreign Minister Wang Shih-chieh, they unanimously accepted Political Consultation Conference's resolutions in toto. The prospect for the future was so bright that General Marshall left for Washington in the Middle of March to report to President Truman.

To those who knew the Chinese Communists better it was a certainty that they would not honor their pledges concerning the cease-fire and reduction of their troops. Their avowed policy was not only to maintain but to expand their forces and to harass government troops wherever possible in order to extend the areas under their control. They accepted American mediation for two reasons:

(1) Immediately after the victory over Japan both the prestige of the National Government and the morale of the government troops were quite high while the Communist forces, although obtaining large quantities of arms from the Soviets, had neither the training, nor the experience of large-scale warfare. Had an all-out civil war taken place right then, the Communist forces would have stood every chance of being beaten by the government troops. Negotiations with the government would give them the time they needed to consolidate their position in North China and to have their army trained by Soviet officers in Manchuria.

(2) Negotiations with the government would only be beneficial and could do no harm to the Communists. If the negotiations were successful and a coalition government was formed with Communists holding key posts while Communists forces remained autonomous, well and good, they could then expect to drive the Kuomintang out of power by staging a coup d'etat in the near future. If, on the other hand, the negotiations were broken off as they had every reason to expect, a wedge would have been driven between the National Government and the United States to their advantage.

As early as the end of March there were signs pointing to the fact that peaceful unification was merely wishful thinking. On March 26 the National Government submitted to the Military Sub-Committee a list of the divisions to be retained and units to be demobilized, but the Communists never submitted theirs. Without this preliminary step the work of reorganizing Communist forces simply could not proceed. On April 18, the same day Marshall returned to Chungking, Communist forces occupied Changchun after three days' attack in gross violation of the cease-fire order. Thereafter fighting spread in Manchuria. With the help of the American forces in China seven more government armies were transported to Manchuria. After bloody fighting government forces occupied Szepingkai on May 19 and pushed towards Changchun. Four days later the Generalissimo flew to Mukden to personally control the situation while Changchun was captured at the same time.

After seizing Changchun government forces continued to advance towards Harbin to the north and Kirin to the east. General Marshall then asked for a truce and the Generalissimo complied with this request. Orders were issued on June 3 to cease advances, attacks or pursuits in Manchuria first for ten days, then for half a month, then to the end of the month. Christopher Rand, an American correspondent, reported from Mukden in 1947: "Last summer the government had nine armies here, totalling perhaps 200,000 regular troops and including some of the best American-trained and American-equipped units in China. The Communists were no match for them, as had been proved at the pitched battle of Szepingkai in the preceeding spring. . . Most observers think they could easily have taken the Communists' Manchurian capital of Harbin. They were prevented from doing so by the truce imposed during General George C. Marshall's attempt to mediate the civil war."[8]

While government troops halted their advances in Manchuria, Communists forces took offensive actions in North China and occupied many districts. So the Generalissimo demanded through Marshall the evacuation of the Communists from Jehol and Chahar provinces and from Chefoo, Weihaiwei and all other localities in Shantung occupied after June 7. The Communists never complied with these demands. As a consequence, although orders were issued by both sides on July 1 that no action should be taken unless being attacked by the other side, fighting spread to many places in the month. The Soviet press violently attacked American policy towards China for encouraging the civil war and the Chinese Communist Party issued a declaration on July 7 echoing this sentiment. The Communists began to make troubles for American marines in China. In the middle of July seven marines were kidnapped in eastern Hopei and detained for several days before their release. At the end of the month a Communist unit deliberately ambushed a motor convoy of Executive Headquarters and UNRRA[9] supplies from Tientsin to

Peiping escorted by United States Marines. Three of the latter were killed and twelve wounded.

In the same month Dr. John Leighton Stuart, who was born and brought up in China and had served for many years as president of Yenching University at Peiping, was appointed by President Truman, upon the recommendation of General Marshall, as American ambassador to China. During that summer General Marshall, now assisted by Dr. Stuart, accelerated his efforts at mediation by making eight trips to Kuling, a mountain resort near Kiukiang, to confer with the Generalissimo. Many conversations were held, proposals and counter-proposals were made, and statements were issued by the Generalissimo on the one hand, and by Marshall and Stuart on the other. But due to lack of sincerity on the part of the Communists the situation worsened. At the end of August government troops occupied Chengteh, capital of Jehol, cleared the Communists from the Tsinan-Tsingtao Railway and continued their offensive in northern Kiangsu; while Communists forces were attacking the Lunghai Railway and besieging Tatung, a strategic city in northern Shansi.

Meanwhile President Truman had sent a personal message to the Generalissimo on August 10, expressing his concern at the deteriorating situation in China and at the actions of the selfish interests of extreme elements both in the Kuomintang and in the Chinese Communist Party. In its conclusion the message read: "It can not be expected that American opinion will continue in its generous attitude towards your nation unless convincing proof is shortly forthcoming that genuine progress is being made toward a peaceful settlement of China's internal problems." In his reply on August 28 the Generalissimo praised General Marshall for his most unsparing work to achieve peace and democracy in China, blamed the Commuists for the continued fighting and asserted that the aim of Communist policy was to use armed force to overthrow the government and install a totalitarian regime. He reiterated his policy of broadening the basis of the National Government by including all parties and non-party personnel but stated that success must depend upon the sincerity of the Communists. In another message to the Generalissimo at the end of the month President Truman expressed the hope that the prompt end of the threat of wide spread civil war in China would make it "feasible for the United States to plan for assisting in its industrial economy and the rehabilitation of its agrarian reforms." [10]

When an agreement was signed between the Chinese and American governments on August 30 for the sale of American surplus property located in India, China and on 17 Pacific islands with an estimated procurements value of $900,000,000, the Chinese Communists immediately issued a statement attacking the United States for extending large-scale military aid to the National Government. General Marshall took pains to explain to Chou En-lai that the surplus property did not contain military materials but consisted mainly of machinery, vehicles and communications equipment which would be of use to recovery of the Chinese economy but the Communists simply ignored this explanation. In order to prove his impartiality towards both sides General Marshall advised the American Government to stop the issuing of licenses for the export to China of military equipment and shipments of combat items from the Pacific area to China were also suspended.

On September 30 the Central News Agency, an official organ of the Kuomintang, announced that government troops had begun operations to capture Kalgan, capital of Chahar; simultaneously the Chinese Communist Party declared that it would not send its delegates to the forthcoming National Asembly. These two events made the two sides further apart. General Marshall began to realize that a peaceful solution of the disputes between the government and the Chinese Communist Party was hardly possible and expressed his opinion on October 1 to the Generalissimo that the American Government should terminate its efforts of mediation unless a basis for agreement was found to end the fighting immediately. In his reply the next day the Generalissimo offered more concessions which were not satisfactory to General Marshall. In a meeting between the two men on October 4 General Marshall asserted that a campaign of force was in progress and under such circumstances he could no longer participate in the negotiations. The next day General Marshall sent a message to President Truman, recommending his recall from China.

Upon hearing the news of Marshall's action the Generalissimo expressed his willingness to halt advances on Kalgan and have that city negotiated by the Committee of Three as the first issue. But the Chinese Communist Party rejected this proposal and demanded the withdrawal of government troops to their original positions. General Marshall even went to Shanghai to see Chou En-lai in the hope that Chou might persuade Yenan to accept this truce offer but the latter presented to him a three-point proposal which demanded that all troops should resume the positions held in China proper as of January 13 and in Manchuria as of June 7, that the location of all troops until the time of army reorganization should be fixed, and that government troops moved after January 13 should be returned to their original locations. As no agreement concerning a truce could be reached government troops continued their advances and on October 10 occupied Kalgan and Chihfeng, a strategic center in Jehol. The next day the National Government issued a mandate announcing that the National Assembly would be convened on November 12.

On October 16 the Generalissimo issued a statement reiterating the government's desire for a peaceful solution and presenting, as condition for an immediate truce, to the Communists an eight-point proposal including the restoration of communications, re-disposition of troops in Manchuria as agreed by the Committee of Three in June, continuance of occupation of localities in North and Central China by government and Communist troops, etc.[11] Chou, who had by now returned to Nanking, told General Marshall on October 24 that these eight points were not acceptable to the Communists. Consequently military activities continued and government troops moved north along the Peiping-Hankow Railway in southern Hopei and drove on Antung in Manchuria.

Prior to the convening of the National Assembly the Generalissimo issued another statement on November 8 in which he declared: "As a further evidence of the sincere desire of the government to achieve a lasting peace and political stability for the country, orders have been issued for all government troops in China proper and the Northeast (Manchuria) to cease firing except as may be necessary to defend their present positions."[12] But even after this statement the Communists stubbornly refused to participate in the National Assembly. On December 4 Chou En-lai sent a message to General Marshall setting forth the Communist terms for reopening negotiations: (1) the dissolution of the National Assembly and (2) the restoration of troop positions held as of January 13. These terms were, of course, rejected by the government. At the request of minor parties the convening of the National Assembly was postponed for three days in a last-minute attempt to find a solution. When the National Assembly was finally convened on November 15 delegates of the Kuomintang, the Youth Party and the Social Democratic Party attended the meetings but the Chinese Communist Party and the Democratic League, an association closely affiliated with the Communists, refused to send delegates to it. Four days later Chou En-lai departed for Yenan in an American army plane. The National Assembly was in session forty days, adopted the Constitution of the Republic of China, and was adjourned on December 25.

Since the end of October General Marshall had been convinced by the repeated Communist rejection of all government overtures that any further mediation would be futile and had remained in China in the hope that he might be able to use his influence towards the democratization of the Chinese Government. Now a constitution which was regarded by General Marshall as democratic had been adopted he felt that his service was no longer needed in China. Meanwhile, as Secretary of State Byrnes resigned early in January 1947, President Truman decided to appoint General Marshall his successor. So Marshall was recalled and left China on January 8; his mission which lasted more than a year ended in failure despite the untiring efforts of himself and his subordinates.

Prior to his departure General Marshall issued a lengthy statement in which he blamed both sides for the failure of negotiations. "On the side of the National Government, which is in fact the Kuomintang, there is a dominant group of reactionaries who have been opposed, in my opinion, to almost every effort I have made to influence the formation of a genuine coalition government....They were quite frank in publicly stating their belief that cooperation by the Chinese Communist Party in the government was inconceivable and that only a policy of force could definitely settle the issue."

On the Communist side General Marshall believed that there were liberals and radicals.[13] The liberals were those "who have turned to the Communists in disgust at the corruption evident in the local governments—men who would put the interest of the Chinese people above ruthless measures to establish a Communist ideology in the immediate future." It was the dyed-in-the-wool Communists who "do not hesitate at the most drastic measures to gain their end as, for instance, the destruction of communications in order to wreck the economy of China and produce a situation that would facilitate the over-throw or collapse of the government, without any regard to the immediate suffering of the people involved." General Marshall also severely condemned Communist propaganda by saying "in the deliberate misrepresentation and abuse of the action, policies and purposes of our government this propaganda has been without regard for the truth, without any regard whatsoever for the facts, and has given plain evidence of a determined purpose to mislead the Chinese people and the world and to arouse a bitter hatred of Americans".[14]

At a press interview at Honolulu on January 11 General Marshall told the reporters that "he knew of no evidence that the Chinese Communists were being supported by Russia."[15] But either this assertion was made by the Secretary of State-designate in order not to offend the Soviet Union or General Marshall changed his mind later, for in his statement regarding aid to China to the Committee on

Foreign Relations of the Senate and the Committee on Foreign Affairs of the House of Representatives in executive session in February 1948 General Marshall clearly declared: "The Chinese Communists obtained large quantities of Japanese arms in Manchuria, through direct or indirect Soviet connivance; the number of surrendering Japanese troops in Manchuria is estimated at 700,000."[16]

After General Marshall's departure the Generalissimo asked Ambassador Stuart to make another attempt for the resumption of negotiations. The ambassador approached Wang Ping-nan, Communist representative in Nanking, on January 16 to ascertain whether the Communists would invite a government delegation to Yenan for peace discussions. The reply of Wang was that unless the government would agree to the abrogation of the constitution and the restoration of the military status quo of January 13, 1946 nothing could be gained by sending a delegation to Yenan. On January 20 the Department of Information of the Kuomintang issued a lengthy statement outlining the course of the negotiations with the Chinese Communists and announcing that a new appeal had been made to the Communists for a cease-fire and the resumption of discussions of plans for the reorganization of the army, restoration of communications, and political control of disputed areas. The Communists flatly rejected this offer and insisted on the two conditions Wang Ping-nan had told Stuart. Thereupon the National Government realized the futility of further negotiations and notified the Communist delegation on February 11 that its presence in Nanking was no longer desired.

In the meantime the Soviet press and the Chinese Communists had started a propaganda offensive against the United States. On December 8, 1946 *Izvestiya* published an article saying: "American policy in China is inspired by those reactionary circles in the United States who want to turn China into a semi-colony and a military-strategical jumping-off ground in the Far East."[17] On January 4 and 5, 1947, *Chieh Fang Jih Pao* (Liberation Daily), Communist organ in Yenan, published an article by Lu Ting-yi, head of the Department of Information of the Chinese Communist Party, which unmasked the real Communist attitude towards the United States. In this article Lu praised the Soviet Union as "the defender of world peace" and described the United States as the arch-enemy of mankind.

"After the World War II," Lu wrote, "the American imperialists took the place of Fascist Germany, Italy and Japan, becoming a fortress of world reactionary forces. So-called reactionary forces are precisely the American imperialists with addition of reactionaries in various countries (China's Chiang Kai-shek, Great Britain's Churchill, France's De Gaulle, etc.) and other Fascist remnants (Spain's Franco Government, Japan's Yoshida cabinet and Germany's von Papen and Schacht, etc.). The reactionaries of all countries and the Fascist remnants have now all become traitors directly or indirectly supported and protected by the American imperialists selling out the people of all countries."[8] What a contrast with what Mao Tse-tung and Liu Shao-chi had told American reporters before!

On March 10, 1947 at a meeting of the Council of Foreign Ministers at Moscow Molotov proposed that problems relating to the settlement of the civil war be put on the agenda of the council. This proposal was opposed by General Marshall. Upon hearing the news the National Government immediately announced its opposition to the discussions of China's internal affairs by the Council of Foreign Ministers. But the Chinese Communists, echoing the Soviets, issued a statement favoring the inclusion of this problem on the agenda and demanding that they be represented at such discussions. Due to the firm stand taken by General Marshall, the matter was dropped.

After negotiations were broken off by the Communists the National Government then adopted measures to broaden the basis of government without their cooperation. At the beginning of March, 50 members were appointed to the Legislative Yuan, of whom 17 were Kuomintang, 13 Youth Party, 12 Social Democrats, and 8 independents; and 25 new members to the Control Yuan, of whom 9 were Kuomintang, 6 Youth Party, 7 Social Democrats, and 3 independents. To the People's Political Council 44 new members were added—11 from each of the above-mentioned groups.

In April the State Council and the Executive Yuan were also reorganized. The new State Council had 29 members: 5 ex-officio members (presidents of the five Yuan), 12 Kuomintang, 4 Youth Party, 4 Social Democrats and 4 independents. In the new Executive Yuan General Chang Chun was appointed Premier to succeed T.V. Soong who had resigned in March. Mr. Wang Yun-wu, an independent, was made Deputy Premier; two Youth Party members, Chen Chi-tien and Cho Shun-sheng, were appointed Minister of Economic Affairs and Minister of Agriculture respectively; while two Social Democrats, Li Ta-ming and Chiang Yun-tien, became ministers without portfolio. In a broadcast speech on April 23, the day he assumed office, General Chang announced that the Kuomintang was now in the process of concluding its political tutelage and that the government would adopt political and economic reforms and guarantee civil freedoms and rights.

In making governmental reorganization the door was left open for the Communists to join. For instance, in the case of the State Council 11 seats were left vacant for the Communists and the Democratic League. Their members would surely be appointed to the Executive, Legislative and Control Yuan and to the People's Political Council at any time they agreed to serve in these organs. In a statement he made on April 18 the Generalissimo had declared: "If the Chinese Communist Party abandons its policy of seizing power by force and cooperates to achieve the unity of the nation, it still has the opportunity to join the government and participate in the work of national reconstruction. For the sake of China's suffering people, it is hoped that the Communists will change their present attitude of open rebellion".[19] It was only after the Communists had long ignored this offer and extended their military actions far and wide that the State Council, on July 4, adopted a resolution on general mobilization and proclaimed that the resources of the country would be fully used to suppress the Communist rebellion. On July 7, the tenth anniversary of the outbreak of the Sino-Japanese War, the Generalissimo, in a broadcast speech, urged the people to support wholeheartedly the crusade against Communism.[20]

While the Chinese Communists did not succeed, through American mediation, in bringing about a coalition government according to the Communist pattern; they succeeded in driving a wedge between China and the United States. In order to remove the suspicion of the Communists General Marshall tried to keep an impartial attitude towards both sides. As a consequence all military aid to China had been stopped since the summer of 1946 and even purchase of arms had been banned. A credit loan of $500,000,000, earmarked for China in April 1946 by the Export-Import Bank for reconstruction and economic development, had expired at the end of June 1947 without a single penny being appropriated.[21]

On the morning of his departure from China General Marshall had asked Dr. Stuart what form American policy towards China should take in view of the breakdown of peace negotiations. In his reply Dr. Stuart had outlined three possible courses: "to give active assistance, especially in the way of military advice, to the National Government, in the expectation that the needed reforms would be undertaken and to condition further aid at each stage upon evidence; to drift along with no strong program of our own but an opportunistic one of 'wait and see'; and to withdraw entirely from any participation in China's internal affairs".[22]

In giving his advice Dr. Stuart made it plain that he was all for the first of these courses but to General Marshall and President Truman, who were disappointed at the failure of American mediation, it was the third course which was more appealing. Consequently after 1947 there had been a gradual shift, on the part of the United States, towards a hands-off policy in China. The first sign of such a policy shift was shown in the announcement by the Department of State at the end of January of termination of American connection with the Committee of Three and the Executive Headquarters at Peiping. A month later all United States marines in North China were withdrawn, except a ground contingent at Tsingtao, to the great delight of the Chinese Communists.

It had been regretted by many Americans and Chinese that Marshall's untiring efforts did not bring about a coalition government participated in by the Chinese Communists. Considering the problem in retrospect we must say that even if a coalition government with Communists in it had been formed in 1946 the result could not have been any better than what actually has happened. For unless General Marshall could force the Communists to give up their autonomous forces—something which he was not willing to do and the Communists would certainly not comply with—the formation of a coalition government with Communists in it could not solve the problem. It could have only resulted in one of two alternatives: either by a coup d'etat the Communists would have overthrown the National Government and seized the political power without any fighting as what actually happened in Czechoslovakia in February 1948; or if they had failed to stage such a coup they would have broken away from the government and civil war would have taken place just the same. President Truman evidently had this possible development in mind when he told reporters on March 11, 1948, two weeks after the Czech coup, that "we did not want any Communists in the Government of China or anywhere else if we could help it".[23]

On March 12, 1947 President Truman delivered a message before a joint session of Congress, asking for $400,000,000 in military and economic aid to help Greece and Turkey fighting against Communism. After stating that "the very existence of the Greek state is today threatened by terrorist activities of several thousand armed men led by Communists", President Truman declared: "It must be the policy of the United States to support free peoples who are resisting attempted subjugation by armed minorities or by outside pressures".[24] This message, which has become known as the Truman Doctrine, was an epoch-making event in the post-war world. This doctrine, together with the Marshall Plan, the North Atlantic Treaty Organization, and the formation of an Allied defense force in Europe has saved not only Greece and Turkey, but whole western Europe from Soviet domination.

The question naturally arises, why the Truman Doctrine was not applied to China? The situation in China at that time was exactly the same as in Greece only on a larger scale. Why is it then that in 1947 President Truman helped Greece suppress Communist rebellion while fifteen months ago he had sent General Marshall to mediate between the National Government and the Chinese Communists—an armed minority? The only explanation is that in the case of Greece Presidently Truman realized that "totalitarian regimes imposed on free peoples, by direct or indirect aggression, undermine the foundation of international peace and hence the security of the United States"; while in the case of China Truman and Marshall had been influenced by the opinion of Vincent and Lattimore to believe that the Chinese Communists were agrarian reformers and therefore had advocated a coalition government as a solution of the problem.[25] Had President Truman, instead of sending General Marshall on a mission of mediation, assisted the National Government militarily to suppress the Communist forces right after the Second World War, the story would have been quite different. Such is the tragic irony of history!

CHAPTER XXII

Tragedy on the Chinese Mainland

In the initial stage of their military struggle for the control of post-war China, the National Government had every advantage over the Communists. At the time of Japanese surrender government troops comprised 3,000,000 men and the Communists, while claiming a force of over 1,000,000, probably had 600,000 regular soldiers; the ratio of effectives between the government and the Communists was 5 to 1. Of the 3,000,000 government troops 39 divisions had been largely equipped with American arms and partly trained by American officers. After V-J Day the equipment and training of these divisions continued. The National Government obtained the bulk of arms surrendered by the Japanese forces in China proper and Taiwan, a total of about 1,235,000 men. It also had a small navy and air force. The morale of the troops, which had sunk very low in the later stage of the war, surged to a new high when victory was finally achieved. On the other hand, the Communist forces also received the arms of the 700,000-man Japanese Kwantung Army in Manchuria through the Soviet hands and a small portion of Japanese arms in China proper. But due to their guerrilla background they had to be trained for the use of these heavier arms and also for positional warfare on a large scale.

For this reason in the encounters between government and Communist troops after V-J Day and up to the end of 1946 government forces usually emerged victorious. They cleared the Lunghai Railway (connecting Lienyunkang, a harbor on the Yellow Sea, and Paochi in Shensi), greater parts of the Peiping-Hankow, Peiping-Suiyuan, Tientsin-Pukow railways and the railway lines in Manchuria as far as Changchun. They also chased Communist forces out of most of Shensi, Kansu, northern Shansi, southern Chahar, part of northern Hopei and Jehol and nearly all of Kiangsu. They seized such strategic centers, which had been occupied by the Communists, as Shanhaikwan, Huaiyin (in northern Kiangsu), Kalgan, Chengteh, Chihfeng, etc., and lifted the siege of such cities as Paotow, Kweisui, (both in Suiyuan), Tatung (in Shansi), etc. Even in Manchuria where 300,000 crack Communist troops had gathered government forces beat them time and again, the most fierce battle being fought at Szepingkai. The only Communist gains in this period were their minor advances and infiltration in Shantung, Honan and Hupei.

The beginning of 1947 marked the turning point of the military struggle. The signs of such a change were first evident in Manchuria. After intensive training under Soviet officers the Communist forces under Lin Piao had, by the end of 1946, become a formidable army. On the other hand government troops, who were mainly natives of Central and South China, had become disheartened after performing garrison duties for a long time. The exaltation and excitement concerning victory over Japan had by now disappeared and weariness and pessimism prevailed. Carpet-bag officials from China proper alienated the local populace who had only a few months ago welcomed them as men who liberated Manchuria from both the Japanese and Soviets. As a consequence the Communists thought the time was ripe to take the initiative. From January to May the Communists launched five offensives in Manchuria in rapid succession and had the government troops surrounded in Kirin, Changchun and Szepingkai.

"In the past two months," stated the American consul-general at Mukden on May 31, "morale (of) Nationalist forces had deteriorated at rapidly accelerating pace. Present serious state of their demoralization has been confirmed to us by many sources and has become matter of wide public knowledge and talk. It is reflected in jumpy nerves of military garrison, efforts to evade conscription, and reliable information from all sectors of Nationalist territory (including points distant from recent fighting), indicating that Nationalists in a panicky state are feverishly building trench systems everywhere with only 'Maginot' defense strategy in mind. There is good evidence that apathy, resentment, and defeatism are spreading fast in Nationalist ranks causing surrenders and desertions. Main factors contributing to this are Communists' ever mounting numerical superiority (resulting from greater use (of) native recruits, aid from underground and Korean units), National soldiers' discouragement over prospects getting reinforcements, better solidarity and fighting spirit of Communists, losses and exhaustion of Nationalists, their growing indignation over disparity between officers' enrichment and soldiers' low pay, life, and their lack of interest in fighting far from home among 'alien' unfriendly populace (whereas Communists being largely natives are in position of fighting for native soil.)" [1]

Inside the Great Wall government forces continued to take offensive in the first half of the year. In March 75,000 troops advanced on Yenan, Communist capital, and captured it on the 19th. Widely heralded as a great victory, it was rather an empty one, for the Communists evacuated Yenan without a struggle and did not suffer any serious loss, except that of face. In Shantung government troops also occupied a large part of the province and even captured Chefoo. But the Communists in mid-summer started a movement across the Lunghai Railway and towards the Yangtze River. Within a few months they occupied large areas in Honan, Hupei and Anhwei and established a stronghold. While, according to American estimate, government forces still comprised 2,700,000 men facing 1,150,000 Communists, the government line was over extended and had no reserves for mobile operations. Consequently, thereafter the strategic initiative passed to the Communist hands.

It was at this juncture that President Truman sent General Wedemeyer to China on a fact-finding mission. When the mission was announced on July 11 the National Government at once expressed its welcome in the hope that the mission would result in economic and military aid, while Communist reaction was bitterly hostile. Two weeks later General Wedemeyer, with a group of experts, arrived at Nanking and during a month's stay in China visited the principal centers of the country and talked with a very large number of people and with American and other non-Chinese officials and businessmen. On August 22 he was invited by the Generalissimo to address a joint meeting of the State Council and the Executive Yuan. In his speech General Wedemeyer severely critized the National Government for its corruption and inefficiency and asserted that: "the Central Government cannot defeat the Chinese Communists by the employment of force, but can only win the loyal, enthusiastic and realistic support of the masses of people by improving the political and economic situation immediately." In a public statement on August 24, the day of his departure, he made the same kind of remarks but in a milder tone.[2]

Prior to Wedemeyer's departure the National Government had handed him a memorandum in which it enumerated its difficulties and asserted its determination to check inflation, carry out necessary political reform and build up a democratic constitutional government. With regard to the Communist problem it declared: "the Communists as an armed political party must be suppressed . . . The government fully realizes that the success or failure of this fight against the Communist peril will not only decide its own fate but also the life or death of China as a sovereign power."[3]

In an interview on September 2, Premier Chang Chun told the

United Press correspondent at Shanghai that he recognized the good intentions of General Wedemeyer "but as a representative of the President of the United States Wedemeyer's statement caused a lot of criticism among the Chinese people." Chang also said: "General Wedemeyer paid more attention to people outside the government than in it . . . There were many who wanted to see Wedemeyer and could not. And there were many things not known to the general."[4] On the other hand a Communist broadcast on August 28 called General Wedemeyer a "blood-thirsty butcher and hypocrite" and declared: "It is very possible that he will urge Washington for further aid to Chiang to prop up the Kuomintang government from imminent collapse. Chiang Kai-shek will also exact all his effort for a final struggle and American imperialist will rush aid to Chiang."[5]

Upon returning to Washington General Wedemeyer presented on September 19 his report to President Truman which was not made public until almost two years later. In this report, besides analyzing the situation, General Wedemeyer recommeded American military and economic aid to China under a program of assistance over a period of at least five years. He also suggested financial assistance to China for reconstruction projects and eventually for currency stabilization. In order to obtain American aid China must make effective use of her own resources and initiate sound fiscal policies, must give continuing evidence that the urgently required political and military reforms were being implemented, and must accept American advisors in specified military and economic fields to assist China in utilizing this aid. With regard to Manchuria Wedemeyer recommended that China should be advised to request the United Nations to place Manchuria under a five-power guardianship or, failing that, under a trusteeship in accordance with the United Nations Charter.

In conclusion the report said: "Soviet aims in the Far East are diametrically opposed to and jeopardize United States interest in China in that their aims envisage progressive expansion of Soviet control and dominant influence. Realization of their aim in China would threaten United States strategic security. Time works to advantage of the Soviet Union. The Soviet Union, in achieving her aims, is being actively assisted by the Chinese Communist Party, which by its actions and propaganda is proven to be a tool of Soviet foreign policy."[6]

These recommendations by General Wedemeyer, while drastic and even infringing Chinese sovereignty, would have checked Communist advances in China, had they been fully carried out. But as President Truman and Secretary of State Marshall were now inclined towards a hands-off policy, the report was shelfed and no action whatever was taken by the American Government.

From the winter of 1947 on the military situation steadily worsened. In Manchuria the Communists lanched a big offensive in December and by February 1948 had captured all cities near Mukden and severed all railways into it. All government troops in Manchuria were now isolated in a few large cities who had to be supplied with food and munitions by airlift at great cost to the government. In China proper the Communists occupied Shihchiachuang, an important city on the Peiping-Hankow Railway, towards the end of 1947. They recaptured Yenan late in April 1948 and government forces garrisoning Yenan suffered heavy losses. At the same time Communist forces cut the Tsinan-Tsingtao Railway by occupying Weihsien. They also captured Loyang and Kaifeng on the Lunghai Railway in March and May 1948 respectively. While these cities were recaptured by government troops within a few days the Communists obtained considerable stores of food and munitions.

Meanwhile the National Government was undertaking measures for the democratization of China. Elections for delegates of the National Assembly and members of the Legislative Yuan, as provided for in the constitution of 1946, were held in November 1947 and January 1948 respectively. It was extremely difficult to hold nationwide elections when large-scale fighting was going on in many provinces, yet the government was determined to see constitutional political system established. Altogether 2704 delegates and 759 members of the Legislative Yuan were elected, comprising four groups, the Kuomintang, the Youth Party, Social Democrats and independents. The National Assembly was convened on March 29, 1948 and elected Generalissimo Chiang first President of the Republic of China under the constitution by a vote of 2430 out of 2704 on April 19. Ten days later General Li Tsung-jen was elected Vice President. It also approved by two-thirds majority vote temporary provisions in the constitution granting emergency powers to the President during the period of anti-Communist campaign.

The Legislative Yuan held its first plenary meeting of the first session on May 18. Dr. Sun Fo was elected its president and Mr. Chen Li-fu, vice president. Two days later President Chiang Kai-shek and Vice President Li Tsung-jen were inaugurated. President Chiang then appointed, after obtaining the consent of the Legislative Yuan, Dr. Wong Wen-hao, chairman of the National Resources Commission, to be Premier and to form the first Executive Yuan. The other three

Yuan—the Judicial, Examination and Control—were all formed according to the constitution in the following month and a constitutional government[7] was completely organized.

At this junction the American Government made a final effort to save China from Communist domination. In November 1947 Premier Chang Chun had sent an urgent message to Secretary of State Marshall, asking for "both emergency assistance and a long-range aid program."[8] There had also been a constant demand for aid to China expressed by Senators and Congressmen in the United States. As a consequence President Truman submitted to Congress on February 18 a China aid program which called for an appropriation of $570,000,000 to be available for expenditures until June 30, 1949. Of this total $510,000,000 would be used to finance minimum imports of essential civilian types of commodities chiefly foodstuffs and industrial materials, while $60,000,000 for a few selected industrial and transportation reconstruction projects.

After several weeks' deliberations in which different views had developed between the Senate and the House the China Aid Act of 1948 was finally adopted by Congress on April 2. This act authorized $338,000,000 for economic aid and $125,000,000 for specific grants to be used in the discretion of the Chinese Government—presumably for military purposes. But when Congress came to actual appropriations only $275,000,000 were allotted for economic aid—making a total of $400,000,000[9] The Chinese Government was grateful for this aid, although it feared the amount was far from enough to cope with the situation. The Chinese Communists, on the other hand, attacked the American Government violently and intensified their anti-American propaganda campaign.

Had the procurement and shipment of arms obtained by the military aid funds been expedited they might have boosted the morale of the government troops and stemmed the tide of the Communist onrush, at least in China proper. But due to red tape, inter-departmental discussions, etc., China was not permitted to make use of the sums until the end of June and not able to procure munitions from government stocks until the end of July. Then there were more delays in shipping and the first substantial shipment of arms did not leave Seattle until November 9. When the arms arrived at Shanghai, the Communists had already overrun Manchuria and North China and were knocking at the gate of Nanking. "For some reason or other," said Vice Admiral Russell S. Berkey on May 15, 1950, "it took nine months to get specific items to China. Somewhere in the

United States somebody slipped up, bogged down, or was interferred with. It has never been made plain why this material did not arrive in time."[10]

The newly formed constitutional government was confronted with another serious problem besides Communist expansion, i.e., run-away inflation. Ever since the beginning of the Sino-Japanese War the National Government had maintained a "printing-press" finance. With revenues greatly reduced and expenditures greatly increased the only way to keep the government running and the armies fighting was by issuing bank-notes. Due to the fact that inland China was mainly agricultural, for the first two years the effect of inflation was not generally felt. From 1940 on commodity prices went up, first slowly, then rapidly, and then by leaps and bounds. One indication of the devaluation of the Chinese currency—fapi—was its exchange rate with the United States dollar. At the beginning of the war one U.S. dollar was worth 3.50 fapi dollars; at its end one U.S. dollar could change for more than 2,000 fapi dollars in the black market.

Immediately after V-J Day, due to the public exaltation over victory, confidence in the fapi was restored and commodity prices remained steady for a few months. Then the law of supply and demand ran its course and commodity prices soared again. With the spread of the civil war military expenditures greatly increased the burden of the treasury. At the time of the Wedemeyer mission the issue of fapi notes had reached the astronomical figure of 11,460,000,000,000 dollars. Commodity prices had risen thirty times since January 1946 or about 20,000 times since the beginning of the Sino-Japanese War. A U.S. dollar was worth then 50,000 fapi dollars. Government expenditures came to over three trillion fapi dollars a month and 70 per cent of this total had to be met by currency issuance. Thereafter inflation sped up like a run-away wild horse. When the constitutional government was formed in June 1948 commodity prices were two million times those in July 1937 and the black market rate for the U.S. dollar was one for six million fapi dollars. Two months later commodity prices increased by another 50 per cent, i.e. three million times those of pre-war days and the U.S. dollar went up to one for over ten million fapi dollars in the black market.

The Chinese Government then made a desperate move to stem the tide of economic deterioration by introducing drastic reform measures. On August 19, 1948 it announced the adoption of a new gold yuan currency to replace the old fapi currency at a ratio of one gold yuan to three million fapi dollars. The official exchange rate for a U.S. dollar was set at four gold yuan. Although the new currency was inconvertible, it was to be backed by gold, silver and other official foreign exchange holdings valued at U.S. $200,000,000 and by the securities of government owned enterprises worth U.S. $300,000,000. The issue of gold yuan notes was to be limited to two billion. The people were required to sell gold, silver, and foreign currency notes to the government banks at the pegged rates and those who had foreign exchange holdings abroad were instructed to register with the government. Commodity prices were also fixed according to the new currency. Anybody who was found to sell commodities, gold, silver or foreign exchange notes in the black market would be severely punished.

For a time the new currency worked out quite well and commodity prices were kept steady. The morale of the people was boosted and there was general hope that the situation might be salvaged. The government collected over U.S. $200,000,000 in gold and foreign exchange notes which were handed in, not by the rich, but by people of moderate means. But as the government could not curtail its expenditures and therefore could not limit the issue of gold yuan notes to the two billion ceiling the economic law again prevailed. As the issuance increased commodity price began to rise again. The government then tried to hold prices down at the August 19 levels by police enforcement of the regulations, resulting in the depletion of food and other commodity stocks in such large cities as Nanking and Shanghai and an almost complete stagnation of economic activities. Finally the government had to revoke these regulations and the new currency was a failure in less than three months after its adoption. Increase of issuance and rise of commodity prices again continued in a vicious circle.

Taking advantage of this economic collapse suffered by the government the Chinese Communists launched a general offensive both in Manchuria and China proper. In Manchuria the Communists attacked the cities which had been isolated for many months. The government troops, owing to difficulties of obtaining provisions, were half starving and the morale had become extremely low. Chingchow, a city between Shankhaikwan and Mukden, fell into Communist hands on October 15 and Changchun followed suit a week later. The Generalissimo then told General Wei Li-huang, commander-in-chief in Manchuria to evacuate Mukden and withdraw the 150,000 garrison troops to Yingkow to embark for China proper. But it was too late as these troops did not have the will to fight all the way to Yingkow. Mukden was occupied by the Communists on November 2. General Wei fled in a plane and the entire garrison force surrendered. With the loss of these cities the government also lost 300,000 crack troops equipped with American arms.

In China proper Communist troops captured Tsinan, capital of Shantung, on September 26 and the government lost almost 100,000 men there. In October Paotow, a railway city in Suiyuan, and Chengchow, a city at the junction of Peiping-Hankow and Lunghai railways, were occupied by the Communists. In November the Communists marched on Hsuchow, a strategic city north of Nanking, which was defended by more than thirty divisions, including mechanized units. The battle line extended fifty to sixty miles along the Lunghai Railway. The Battle of Hsuchow lasted more than three weeks, but owing to lack of coordination, low morale and poor strategy government troops were defeated and Hsuchow fell on December 3. Government troops retreated to Pengpu and another great battle was fought there. Although with reinforcements from Central China the battle was again lost and Communist forces were only fifty or sixty miles from Nanking on the north side of the Yangtze River. Almost 400,000 troops were lost in these two battles during November and December 1948.

After the complete occupation of Manchuria the crack Communist troops under Lin Piao were sent inside Shanhaikwan to attack the forces of General Fu Tso-yi who was then in charge of the defense of Hopei and Chahar. Although General Fu's troops fought bravely they were outnumbered and time and again defeated. Paoting, Kalgan and other cities in the two provinces had already been lost and government troops held only Peiping and Tientsin.

As the military situation steadily worsened the public in Nanking became panic-stricken and pessimism and defeatism prevailed in the government and military circles. The only hope to turn the situation for better seemed to lie in immediate and large-scale military aid from the United States. So a few days after the American presidential election the Generalissimo sent a personal message to President Truman, saying: "As a co-defender of democracy against the onrush and infiltration of Communism throughout the world, I appeal to you for speedy and increased military assistance and for a firm statement of American policy in support of the cause for which my Government is fighting". The Generalissimo also requested the appointment of a high-ranking American officer "who will work out in consultation with my Government a concrete scheme of military assistance, including the participation of American military advisers in the direction of operations". In his reply President Truman expressed his sympathy with the Chinese Government and promised to exert every effort to expedite the implementation of the program of aid for China but refused to appoint a high-ranking officer "to advise the Chinese Government regarding its courses of action in the present dilemma".[11] Towards the end of November Madame Chiang Kai-shek flew to Washington to make a desperate appeal to the American Government. She was cordially received but her plea was ignored.

As Nanking was now within the striking distance of the Communist forces a cry for peace was raised among military leaders such as General Pai Chung-hsi, commander of the government forces in Central China, and General Cheng Chien,[12] Governor of Hunan, and by the Hunan and Honan provincial legislatures. They even suggested that if the Generalissimo would step down from the presidency the government could come to terms with the Communists and further fighting could be avoided. As the military situation became hopeless and as dissension among his subordinates became apparent the Generalissimo decided to retire. At a New Year's Eve dinner he told high government officials and Kuomintang leaders his intention to step down from the presidency. Some of those who were present advised him not to take such a step which would make the situation worse but he stood firm.[13] On the New Year's Day, 1949 the Generalissimo issued a message to the nation in which he declared that if the Communists were sincerely desirous of peace and gave such indication the government would be too glad to discuss with them the means to end the war. "If a negotiated peace", the message went on, "is not detrimental to the national independence and sovereignty, but will contribute to the welfare of the people; if the constitution is not violated and constitutionalism preserved, the democratic form of government maintained, the entity of armed forces safeguarded; and if the people's free mode of living and their minimum standard are protected; then I shall be satisfied. . . . If peace can be secured I am not at all concerned about my own position."[14]

On January 8 General Wu Tieh-cheng, Foreign Minister in the newly formed Executive Yuan under Dr. Sun Fo, sent an aide-memoire to the American, British, French and Soviet ambassadors in Nanking, asking their governments to act as intermediaries in the initiation of negotiations with the Chinese Communists with a view to obtaining a restoration of peace.[15] In its reply to the Waichiaopu the American Government, after recalling the failure of its efforts at mediation after the war, concluded: "it is not believed that any useful purpose would be served by the United States Government's attempting in accordance with the Chinese Government's suggestion, to act as an intermediary." Britain, France and the Soviet Union also refused to mediate on the ground that the issue should be settled by the Chinese themselves.

Meanwhile the Chinese Communists, intoxicated with military successes, were bent upon occupying all China. Soon after the new year their forces advanced in three columns towards the north bank of the Yangtze across from Nanking practically unopposed. In the middle of January Tientsin fell to Communist hands and a peace movement was going on in Peiping to surrender the city without fighting. Mao-Tse-tung in a broadcast on January 14 enumerated eight points as the basis of a settlement, including strict punishment of "war criminals", abolition of the constitution, reorganization of the government troops and establishment of a democratic coalition government to take over all authority of the "Kuomintang reactionary government". These terms were so harsh that they amounted to unconditional surrender. On January 19 the Executive Yuan formally proposed to the Communists a cease-fire followed by peace negotiations. Two days later the Communists in their reply asserted that negotiation be held first before issuing the cease-fire order. On the same day the Generalissimo announced his retirement from the presidency and Vice President Li Tsung-jen became Acting President to exercise presidential powers according to Article 49 of the Constitution.

The next day General Fu Tso-yi, after signing a truce agreement with Yeh Chien-ying, chief of staff of the so-called People's Liberation Army, surrendered Peiping and his 100,000 troops to the Communists. North China, with the exception of the beseiged city of Taiyuan and the port of Chingtao, was completely under Communist control. In the five months' warfare since September the Government lost 45 per cent of its military strength, including the best equipped and trained divisions and by February 1949, had only 1,500,000 troops left of which one third were service troops, while the Communist strength had increased from 1,150,000 to 1,600,000 combat effectives. Consequently the Communists by now achieved a numerical superiority, were better equipped and had far superior morale. It would take a miracle to turn the fortunes of war in favor of the government again.

According to the report of Ambassador Stuart to the Department of State, two days after assuming the acting presidency General Li Tsung-jen sent a representative to inform the ambassador that General

Li had been in touch with Soviet Ambassador N. V. Roschin and they had agreed on three points: "(1) strict Chinese neutrality in any future international conflict; (2) the elimination of American influence to as great an extent as possible in China; and (3) the establishment of a basis of real cooperation between China and Russia". The Soviet ambassador had taken a draft agreement on these points with him to Moscow a few days earlier. This representative also asked for an American statement in support of these points so as to strengthen General Li's hands in negotiating with the Soviet Union. In its reply the Department of State considered it "incredible that Li Tsung-jen should seek a United States statement indicating support for the purpose of strengthening his position while at the same time arranging a tentative agreement with Russia calling for elimination of American influence from China".[16] In the light of imminent Communist occupation of the mainland it is extremely doubtful that the Soviet ambassador would work out such a draft agreement. It was either General Li's, or more likely his representative's, wishful thinking.

The Acting President did make every effort to negotiate a peace with the Chinese Communists. A "people's delegation", composed of representatives of civil organizations in Shanghai and headed by Dr. W. W. Yen, former Chinese ambassador to the Soviet Union, with Shao Li-tsu representing the government, flew to Peiping on February 14. They were well received by the Communist leaders at Peiping and later Yen and Shao traveled to Shihchiachuang to see Mao Tse-tung and Chou En-lai. No details were taken up on this exploratory mission but they were told that government delegates would be invited to peace talks in Peiping as soon as practicable. The mission returned to Shanghai on February 27 and hopes for a peaceful settlement were high among government officials and the people.

Differences of policy now developed between Acting President Li Tsung-jen and Premier Sun Fo and the latter resigned in March. General Ho Ying-chin was appointed Premier to succeed Sun. Meanwhile the Communists announced that peace negotiations would be started in Peiping on April 1. At the end of March the government appointed a five-man delegation, headed by General Chang Chih-chung and they flew to Peiping on that day. After two weeks' discussions the Communists handed Chang Chih-chung a document titled "Agreement on Internal Peace" with eight sections and twenty-four articles. The sections were based on the eight points enumerated in Mao's broadcast three months ago, while in the articles there were detailed provisions concerning the surrender of government troops and taking over of all government authorities by the newly formed "democratic coalition government". They seem to be modelled after the instrument of surrender signed by General Okamura, Commander-in-Chief of the Japanese Forces in China, in August 1945. The Communists also set April 20 as the deadline for the acceptance of the agreement, otherwise their troops would cross the Yangtze River and occupy Nanking.

The government rejected the Communist proposal on April 19 and Communist troops crossed the Yangtze two days later at two points both east and west of Nanking. The government then issued orders to continue the war against the Communists and General Ho Ying-chin was appointed concurrently Minister of National Defense in charge of all military operations. But as they knew it was now impossible to make a stand at Nanking which would soon be completely encircled, the Acting President, Premier, ministers, legislators and other high officials all flew to Canton and the Communists occupied the city on April 24 practically without any opposition.

After that it was a whirlwind of Communist advances. The complete collapse of the gold yuan which had by now depreciated to a rate of 10,000,000 gold yuan for a U.S. dollar in the black market added to the calamity of the government. Taiyuan, capital of Shansi, was taken by the Communists on the same day as Nanking. Hangchow was lost at the end of April; Hankow, Wuchang and Sian fell in the middle of May. On May 27, after a few days of fighting, the Communists seized Shanghai.

It the hot months of the summer Communist forces halted their advances and government troops had a breathing spell for re-grouping. At this juncture the Department of State published *United States Relations with China* which clearly indicated that the American Government considered China as a hopeless case and was adopting a hands-off policy. Any will to resist which had still been left among the government officials and troops were now almost completely taken away and everybody expected the worst.

Foochow, capital of Fukien, and Lanchow, capital of Kansu, were occupied by Communist forces in August. In September Gen. Tao Chih-yo, commander of the government troops in Sinkiang, upon the inducement of Chang Chih-chung, went over to the Communist side and Sinkiang was lost. Meanwhile the Communists resumed their general offensive and pushed both from the north and from the east towards Canton. On October 12 the government moved to Chungking and two days later the Communists occupied Canton. They lost no time in pursuing government troops into Southwest China. On November 22 Kweilin, capital of Kwangsi, fell into Communist hands and at the end of the month Chungking was occupied. The government then again moved to Chengtu, capital of Szechwan.

Meanwhile many former war-lords like General Lu Han, Governor of Yunnan, and Generals Teng Hsi-hou and Liu Wen-hui of Szechwan, seeing the government as having lost, surrendered to the Communists. This defection coupled with the annihilation of General Hu Tsung-nan's troops, last group of government military strength on the mainland, made the position of Chengtu untenable. So at the beginning of December the government moved to Taipei, Taiwan, while Acting President Li Tsung-jen flew to New York for surgical operations. By the end of 1949 the entire Chinese mainland, with its 500,000,000 people, was under Communist control!

A question naturally arises in the reader's mind: What caused such a tragedy on the Chinese mainland within four and a half years after V-J Day? The fundamental cause of the defeat and collapse of the Chinese Government on the mainland was the eight-year Sino-Japanese War. As expected by Stalin and the Chinese Communists this long war completely ruined China financially, economically and morally. During the war all the industrial centers along the coast and on the lower Yangtze River were occupied by the Japanese; while practically all coastal and inland shipping in its modern sense and more than 90 per cent of railway transportation were interrupted. Public buildings, factories, homes and sometimes entire cities in inland China were destroyed by Japanese air-raids. The government, with nine-tenth of its revenue gone and with its expenditures mounting every year, had to resort to the printing press to solve its financial problems, while the great majority of the people lost their savings and movable property—the middle class which was rather prosperous before the war was simply wiped out.

In the later stage of the war inflation became so bad and commodity prices rose so high that all salaried persons—government officials, officers, professors, teachers, soldiers policemen, postmen, etc.—could hardly keep their bodies and souls together. Under such circumstances is there any wonder that efficiency in public work and moral standard both dropped to a very low level. Squeeze and corruption prevailed which made political and economic conditions ever worse. The worst effect was on the morale: officials lost the incentive to work, officers and rank and file lost the will to fight, while intellectuals, professors, teachers, university students, etc., lost their confidence in the government and began to have illusions about the Communists. Had these things not happened the Communists would never have been able to occupy the mainland.

Besides this main cause there were other contributory causes to the great tragedy. In the first place China did not, either in the later stage of the war or after the war, do enough to expose the true nature of the Chinese Communists and the aggressive policy of the Soviet Union. While American reporters and left-wing writers were spreading the big lie that the Chinese Communists were agrarian reformers the Waichiaopu and government information agencies ignored the rampant falsehood for fear of offending the Soviet Union. When Soviet soldiers committed murders, rape and looting in Manchuria, when Soviet authorities obstructed the landing of Chinese troops at Dairen and Port Arthur, when they handed over the Japanese arms to the Communists, and when they dismantled and removed machinery and equipment from Manchuria no reports appeared in Chinese newspapers and no appeal was made to the public opinion of the world. In this way the Communist propaganda became very effective, while the Chinese people and soldiers did not know that the Communists were tools of the Soviet Union and their national sentiment was not aroused.

In the second place, at the time of Japanese surrender the prestige of the National Government was very high. The people in the Japanese-occupied areas, in Manchuria and in Taiwan looked upon it as their liberator from the Japanese yoke. But the taking-over soon disheartened them and alienated them. There was confusion and corruption. Many dishonest high-ranking officials and officers simply took this opportunity to work for personal gains and grasped houses, cars, gold and other valuables, goods in the factories, etc., which belonged to the Japanese Government, to the puppet regimes in Nanking and Changchun, to enemy nationals, or to Chinese traitors and collaborationists.

Thirdly, at the end of 1945 the National Government had large reserves of gold and U.S. dollar exchange valued at $835,000,000 [17] which were accumulated mainly through the nondisbursement of a greater portion of the $500,000,000 American credit of 1942 and the payments by the American Government of approximately $400,000,000 against Chinese Government expenditures on behalf of the American armed forces in China. If a new currency had been adopted right then and a budget was strictly kept, government finance could have been balanced and commodity prices stabilized. But the chance was not seized and slipped away. In June 1947 these reserves dropped to only $540,000,000. In August 1949 when the gold yuan currency was adopted official gold and foreign exchange holdings had declined to mere $200,000,000. With little reserve and unlimited expenditures the new currency was doomed from the very beginning. The disaster caused by the collapse of the fapi and the gold yuan greatly hastened the loss of the mainland.

Fourthly, American military authorities regarded the attempt to occupy Manchuria and later the defense of the Manchurian cities as a big strategic blunder. General Wedemeyer advised the Generalissimo soon after V-J Day that "he should concentrate his efforts on the recovery of North China and the consolidation of his military and political position there prior to any attempt to occupy Manchuria".[18] Early in 1948 Major General David Barr, head of the Joint United States Military Advisory Group, recommended the withdrawal from the Manchurian cities. After the defeat in Manchuria General Barr reported: 'the Nationalist Army was burdened with an unsound strategy which was conceived by a politically influenced and militarily inept high command. Instead of being content with consolidating North China, the Army was given the concurrent mission of seizing control of Manchuria, a task beyond its logistic capacities. The government, attempting to do too much with too little, found its armies scattered along thousands of miles of railroads, the possession of which was vital in view of the fact that these armies were supplied from bases in Central China. In order to hold the railroads, it was also necessary to hold the large cities through which they passed. As time went on, the troops degenerated from field armies, capable of offensive combat, to garrison and lines of communication troops with an inevitable loss of offensive spirit".[19] To do justice to the government we must say that if Manchuria was abandoned right after V-J Day, the government would have suffered a serious blow to its prestige.

Finally, mistaken policy towards China on the part of the American Government contributed to the loss of the mainland. The Yalta Secret Agreement, the Marshall Mission, the embargo on arms to China, the White Paper at the critical moment, all these played unwittingly into the hands of the Soviet Union and the Chinese Communists. In his "Letter of Transmittal" of the White Paper to President Truman, Secretary of State Dean Acheson tried to put all the blame on the Chinese Government for the defeat on the mainland and to admit no mistake in American policy. "Nothing that this country did or could have done," wrote Acheson, "within the reasonable limits of its capabilities could have changed that result; nothing that was left undone by this country has contributed to it. It was the product of Chinese internal forces, forces which this country tried to influence but could not." But in the same letter he declared: "The Communist leaders have foresworn their Chinese heritage and have publicly announced their subservience to a foreign power, Russia, which during the last fifty years, under czars and Communists alike, has been most assiduous in its efforts to extend its control in the Far East".[20] Are not these two assertions contradictory to each other?

In this connection we may quote the words of Dr. Stuart who lived in China for fifty years and was the last American ambassador on the mainland: "The aberrant and contradictory policies of the United States Government during the period between the end of World War II and the beginning of the Communist attack in Korea in 1950 served to weaken rather than to strengthen the National Government at a time when it desperately needed sympathetic understanding and assistance."[21] Again, "We Americans mainly saw the good things about the Chinese Communists, while not noticing carefully the intolerance, bigotry, deception, disregard for human life and other evils which seem to be inherent in any totalitarian system. We kept Communist meanings for such objectives as progressive, democratic, liberal, also bourgeois, reactionary, imperialist, as they intended we should do. . . . Therefore, we cannot escape a part of the responsibility of the great catastrophe–not only for China but also for America and the free world—the loss of the Chinese mainland."[22]

CHAPTER XXIII

The Communist Regime and the Soviet Union

When their victory on the Chinese mainland seemed to be assured by the beginning of 1949 the Chinese Communists no longer tried to conceal their relationship with the Soviet Union. On April 3, the day before the signing of the North Atlantic Treaty in Washington, Mao Tse-tung and others issued a manifesto denouncing the pact as "a threat to human peace and security" and declaring: "If the imperialist aggressive bloc dares to provoke this reactionary war, endangering the peoples in the world, we will . . . march forward hand in hand with the ally of China, the Soviet Union, and world forces for peace and democracy in determined struggle against the instigators of an aggressive war to defeat the aggressors, overthrow the imperialist system, and realize the liberation of all mankind and permanent peace."[1]

In an article, entitled "On the People's Democratic Dictatorship", published on July 1, twenty-eighth anniversary of the Chinese Communist Party, Mao Tse-tung announced his foreign policy as follows: " 'You lean to one side'. Precisely so. The forty years' experience of Sun Yat-sen and the twenty-eight years' experience of the Chinese Communist Party have taught us to believe that in order to win and to consolidate the victory we must lean to one side. The experiences of forty years and twenty-eight years, respectively, show that, without exception, the Chinese people either lean to the side of imperialism or to the side of socialism. To sit on the fence is impossible; a third road does not exist."[2] Mao asserted that if the Soviet Union did not exist; if there had been no defeat of German, Italian and Japanese imperialism in the Second World War; if the various new democratic (Communistic) countries had not come into being; and "if there had been no struggle of the masses of the people in the United States, Britain, France, Germany, Italy, Japan, and other capitalist countries against the reactionary cliques ruling over them"; the Communist victory in China would have been impossible.

But the Soviet Government, on the other hand, still pretended to have nothing to do with Mao officially. While the Soviet press hailed Communist victories in China, Soviet Ambassador Nikolai V. Roschin moved early in the year to Canton, the only foreign envoy to comply with the request of the Chinese Government; other chiefs of missions all remained in Nanking. It was not until the end of May that Roschin departed for Moscow for consultation. In July a trade delegation of the "Manchurian people's democratic authorities," under the leadership of Kao Kang, secretary of the Northeast Bureau of the Central Committee of the Chinese Communist Party, arrived at Moscow and concluded a one-year trade agreement with the Soviet Government by which the Manchurian authorities were to deliver agricultural products in exchange for industrial equipment and manufactured goods. When it became known, the Chinese Government protested strongly to Moscow, charging it with violating the Sino-Soviet Treaty of 1945.

In September the so-called Chinese People's Political Consultative Conference met at Peiping to establish a Communist regime. In eight days it adopted a Common Program and an Organic Law of the "Central People's Government of the People's Republic of China."[3] Article 11 of the Common Program provided that "The People's Republic of China shall unite with all free and peace-loving countries and peoples in the world, above all, with the Soviet Union . . . to oppose imperialist aggression and safeguard lasting peace." Then it elected 56 members of "The Central People's Government" with Mao Tse-tung as the chairman and six vice-chairmen. On October 1 the so-called Chinese People's Republic was formally proclaimed, and the Communist regime inaugurated. The following day the Soviet Union discarded its diplomatic mask and recognized the newly-established regime. On October 3, the Chinese Government in Canton broke off its diplomatic relations with the Soviet Union. Soviet satellites immediately followed suit in recognizing the Communist regime.

In December Mao Tse-tung headed a delegation to Moscow which included Chou En-lai, "Premier and Foreign Minister", Li Fu-chun, "vice-chairman of the Northeast People's Government", and Seyfuddin, "vice-chairman of Sinkiang People's Government," ostensibly for the purpose of attending the celebration of Stalin's seventieth birthday but actually to negotiate with the Soviet Government. The result of Mao's two months' stay in Moscow was the conclusion on February 14, 1950 of three pacts, viz., (1) a Sino-Soviet Treaty of Friendship Alliance and Mutual Assistance; (2) an Agreement on the Chinese Changchun Railway, Port Arthur and Dairen; and (3) an Agreement on the Granting of a Long-Term Credit to the "People's Republic of China".[4]

The Treaty of Friendship, Alliance and Mutual Assistance is similar to the Sino-Soviet Treaty of 1945 but has a wider scope. Instead of providing for joint measures to prevent the resumption of aggression by Japan only, the 1950 treaty stipulates cooperation against aggression by Japan or "any other state that may collaborate with Japan directly or indirectly in acts of aggression". This difference clearly shows that the new alliance is aimed at the United States as much as, or even more than, Japan because both the Soviet Government and the Chinese Communists have condemned the United States for rearming Japan. This anti-American purpose was made plain in an editorial of the *Jen Min Jih Pao* (People's Daily), official organ of the Communist regime, on February 26, which declared: "This alliance will effectively prevent Japan and other countries allied directly or indirectly with Japan from renewing aggression and breaking world peace. For this reason, it is a heavy blow against American imperialism which is now fostering the re-emergence of Japanese aggression". The new treaty also provides for "sincere cooperation" in all international actions at ensuing peace and security throughout the world" and for diplomatic consultation "in regard to all important problems affecting the common interests of China and the Soviet Union".

By the Agreement on the Chinese Changchun Railway, Port Arthur and Dairen, the Soviet Government agreed to return the railway to China and to withdraw from Port Arthur "not later than the end of 1952", instead of the term of thirty years as provided in the agreements of 1945. With regard to Dairen it seems that no definite agreement concerning the question of the harbor had been reached because both sides agreed to further consider the question on the conclusion of a peace treaty with Japan. The Soviet Government, however, pledged to hand over to the Peiping regime without any compensation "all the property in Dairen now temporarily administered by or leased to the Soviet Union".

By the Agreement on the Granting of Credit the Soviet Government agreed to grant the Peking regime a credit of $300,000,000 to be apportioned in five equal annual installments starting from January 1950 and to be paid back in ten equal annual installments starting from the end of 1954. The credit was to be used for purchasing industrial and engineering equipment in the Soviet Union. It is rather surprising that Soviet economic assistance to the Peiping regime should be so inadequate—$60,000,000 a year for China's reconstruction—and it is amusing to see the Soviet Union and Peiping regime doing business transactions in terms of U.S. dollars, the currency of their avowed arch-enemy!

By an exchange of notes on the same day Chou En-lai and Soviet

Foreign Minister, A. Y. Vyshinsky, declared that the Sino-Soviet Treaty and agreements of 1945 were now null and void and affirmed the independence of the "Mongolian People's Republic". By another exchange of notes the Soviet Government promised to transfer without compensation to the Peiping regime "the property acquired in Manchuria from Japanese owners by Soviet economic organizations" and also "all the buildings in the former military compound in Peking".[5]

To all appearances these pacts seemed to be quite favorable to the Peiping regime. An American writer asserted that the Soviet Union had by these pacts made considerable concessions to Communist China while Communist China had conceded nothing except the independence of the "Mongolian People's Republic".[6] But it must be remembered that the relationship between the Soviet Union and the Peiping regime is fundamentally different from that between the Soviet Union and the Chinese Government on the mainland. In former days the Soviet Union wanted to grasp as many rights and privileges as it could from the Chinese Government because it regarded the latter as at best an unfriendly power; while with a Communist regime in control the Soviet Union wished to exercise its dominating influence in China rather than to get specific concessions.

Besides, as soon as the pacts were made public there were reports that secret agreements might exist. Taipei suspected that the Communist regime had granted important economic concessions in Manchuria and Sinkiang as well as military, naval and air bases to the Soviet Union; while a *New York Times* correspondent reported from Paris that Mao and Chou had reluctantly agreed to furnish a large force of laborers to Siberia on a contract basis and to accord key positions in the army, secret police, and party organizations to Soviet "adviser".[7] How much of these reports is true can only be judged by subsequent events.

One thing we do know now is that on March 27 three agreements of an economic character were signed between the Soviet Government and the Peiping regime. These agreements were never made public but their contents were divulged in an announcement by both sides.[8] According to this announcement one of the agreements provided for the organization of a Sino-Soviet civil aviation company which was to fly the Peiping-Chita, Peiping-Irkutsk and Peiping-Alma Ata lines and in which the two countries would be on an equal basis. The other two agreements provided for the establishment of a Sino-Soviet petroleum company and a Sino-Soviet nonferrous metal company respectively; the former to prospect for and develop petroleum, while the latter to search for and open up nonferrous metal mines. The products as well as expenses and profits were to be equally shared by the two sides.

Besides these treaties and agreements the Soviet authorities and the Peiping regime have concluded a number of other agreements. There were two agreements signed on February 7, 1950: one concerning telegraphic and telephonic communications and the other dealing with exchange of mails and parcels. To implement the credit agreement a Peiping trade delegation signed two agreements in April 1950 with the Soviet Commissariat of Foreign Trade: a barter agreement and a trade agreement. These agreements were renewed and signed year by year. In March 1951 an agreement was signed between the Peiping "Ministry of Railway" and the Soviet Commissariat of Communications by which through rail traffic would be established as from April 1, 1951.

In August 1952 Chou En-lai, accompanied by Chen Yun, a "Deputy Premier", Li Fu-chun, now a "deputy chief of the Commission on Financial and Economic Affairs", and Su Yu, a "deputy chief of the Army General Staff," went to Moscow where they carried on negotiations with Stalin, Vyshinsky and Trade Minister P. N. Kumykin. Following the conversations a joint communique was issued on September 15 to the effect that a Sino-Soviet commission was to be formed to take immediate steps for the transfer of the Chinese Changchun Railway. At the end of the year a ceremony took place at Harbin with Chou En-lai and Soviet Ambassador A. S. Panyushkin present to solemnize the transfer. After that the name has been changed to the Harbin Railway. With regard to Port Arthur by an exchange of notes between Chou and Vyshinsky the period for joint use of the naval base was to be extended until the conclusion of peace with Japan and consequently Soviet forces in Port Arthur were not withdrawn at the end of the year as provided in the agreement of February 14, 1950.[9]

Ever since the establishment of the Peiping regime some of the columnists, writers, scholars and even political leaders have pinned their hope on the assumption that Mao Tse-tung would someday become a second Tito and break away from the Soviet Union. Judging by subsequent events we must say that this assumption is based on wishful thinking and not on facts. After October 1949, just as prior to that time, the Chinese Communists have echoed every Soviet policy or action in international affairs. The best illustration of the close relationship between Moscow and Peiping is the Korean War. That war was brought about by mistakes rather than by intention. In his speech before the National Press Club on January 12, 1950, Secretary of State Dean Acheson declared by implication that neither Taiwan nor Korea was included inside the American line of defense.[10] As late as May 1950 Senator Tom Connally, chairman of the Senate Foreign Relations Committee, in an interview in the *U.S. News and World Report* said that Korea was not an essential part of American defense strategy and that Russia could overrun it "whenever she takes a notion".[11] Such statements by responsible American political leaders undoubtedly encouraged Stalin to make his decision to invade Korea shortly thereafter.

But when the North Korean Communists actually invaded South Korea on June 25, President Truman suddenly decided to intervene and requested the United Nations Security Council to take action. Because of the absence of the Soviet delegate, Yakov A. Malik, due to Soviet boycott of the Security Council and other U.N. agencies as a protest to the presence of the representatives of the Chinese Government–a big mistake on the part of the Soviet Union — the council unanimously adopted a resolution on June 25 demanding the Korean Communist to withdraw north of the 38th parallel, and another resolution on June 27 calling upon all U.N. members to "furnish such assistance to the Republic of Korea as may be necessary to repel the armed attack and to restore international peace and security in the area".[12] On the same day President Truman ordered American air and sea forces "to give the Korean Government troops cover and support" and three days later authorized the use of American ground troops in Korea. Thus the war was on and later fifteen other nations sent armed forces to participate in the fighting.

In November, when the Korean Communists were on the verge of collapse, the Peiping regime launched a massive attack with hundreds of thousands of so-called "volunteers" under the command of Peng Teh-huai, a "vice-chairman of the People's Revolutionary Military Affairs Commission", and inflicted heavy losses on the U.N. forces. The American, Korean, and other troops were driven from the Yalu River southward until well below the 38th parallel. It was not until the spring of 1951 that the U.N. forces started a counter-offensive and pushed the Chinese and Korean Communists again beyond the 38th parallel. But due to the determined policy of the American Government only to fight a limited war and not to carry it to the Communist bases in Manchuria despite the repeated request of General Douglas MacArthur, commander of the U.N. forces, victory was impossible and the war soon came to a stalemate.[13] On February 1, 1951 the U.N. General Assembly, in a resolution, condemned the Peiping regime as an aggressor and on May 18, in another resolution, recommended member states to immediately prohibit the shipment to Communist China and North Korea of arms, ammunition, strategic materials, etc.

In a broadcast, on June 23, 1951, Malik declared in New York that the Korean conflict could be settled by peace talks if both sides so desired. This statement showed that due to their heavy casualties the Chinese Communists were willing to have a cease-fire; while the U.N., especially the United States which had borne the brunt of the war, was also weary of it. As a consequence armistice negotiations were opened at Kaesong on July 10. From then on, although fighting continued, no major battles took place. But early in 1952 both the North Korean and Peiping regimes announced to the world that American forces in Korea were engaged in germ warfare which was, of course, a complete hoax. After nine or ten months' negotiations a cease-fire and withdrawal of both forces two kilometers from the existing battle-line were agreed upon and a neutral commission consisted of representatives of Sweden, Switzerland, Czechoslovakia and Poland was to supervise the armistice terms. But the question of repatriation of prisoners-of-war remained unsettled: the U.N. representatives would not agree to compulsory repatriation as insisted by the Communists. It was not until June 1953 that the Communists gave in on this point and the armistice agreement was finally signed on July 27.

Why should the newly-formed Peiping regime engage in a war against the United States, the most powerful nation in the world? In the first place, Mao must have participated in the war in compliance with the wish of Stalin. Since Stalin did not want to be involved in this conflict the only way to save the Korean Communist forces from annihilation was to use the military strength of the Peiping regime. Secondly, from 1946 to 1948, 100,000 Korean Communists took part in the fighting in Manchuria between Chinese Government troops and Communist forces. So now when the Korean Communists were in grave danger Mao would have lost his prestige, not only among the Koreans but among the Communists in all Asian nations, had he stood idly aside and seen the Korean Communist regime fall to pieces. Thirdly, in 1950 Mao was having internal troubles, both political and economic. A foreign war, coupled with clever propaganda, would divert the Chinese people's attention and arouse their national sentiment and would surely be advantageous to the regime. For these reasons Mao decided to take the risk of a war.

Despite their numerical superiority and initial success the Communist troops were no match for the United States forces in equipment and training. Had the American Government made the decision to carry on the war wholeheartedly, had the American air force in Korea been permitted to bomb military bases and supply lines in Manchuria the war would have ended in a U.N. victory,[14] and not only the North Korean regime but even the Peiping regime could have collapsed. As it was, the war ended almost exactly where it started three years ago. The Peiping regime, although suffering hundreds of thousands of casualties, boasted the war as a great victory and its prestige on the mainland and among the Asian nations was enhanced. Due to the large quantities of heavy arms, including planes, obtained from the Soviet Union during the war, the Chinese Communist forces actually became much stronger in 1953 than in 1950.

Ever since 1946 the French Government had fought a war in Indo-China against Viet Minh forces under Ho Chi Minh, the Communist leader. After the armistice in Korea it was feared that the Peiping regime would now use its military strength to help Ho Chi Minh. So in September 1953 Secretary of State John Foster Dulles told the American Legion that Peiping might send its own army into Indo-china and warned: "The Chinese Communist regime should realize that such a second aggression could not occur without grave consequences which might not be confined to Indo-china".[15] On January 12, 1953, in an address to the Council on Foreign Relations, Secretary Dulles declared that local defense must be reinforced by massive retaliatory power and again warned the Peiping regime that hereafter the United States would rely "upon a great capacity to retaliate, instantly, by means and places of our choosing".[16] These clear warnings prevented the Peiping regime from sending troops to Indo-china, but did not stop the flow of military supplies from the Chinese mainland to Ho Chi Minh. With these supplies the Viet Minh forces scored a big victory by capturing Dienbienphu in May 1954.

In April 1954 an international conference, attended by the United States, Britain, France, the Soviet Union, the Peiping regime and other nations taking part in the Korean War, was held in Geneva to discuss peace and unification in Korea and a cease-fire in Indo-china. There Moscow and Peiping presented a united front vis-a-vis the Western world. They refused to accept the U.N. proposal for free elections in Korea under U.N. supervision while the Soviet Union presented a counter-proposal for elections supervised by representatives of North and South Korean authorities and for withdrawal of foreign troops from Korea within six months. No agreement was reached on this point. They also attacked the peace treaty with Japan concluded in San Francisco in 1951 and charged that the United States was re-arming Japan and strengthening Japan as a base for aggression. In July the Geneva Conference, with the United States observing but not participating, arrived at a cease-fire agreement concerning Vietnam by which the country was divided at the 17th parallel with Viet Minh taking the north and the Vietnamese Government keeping the south—a diplomatic victory for Moscow and Peiping.

The aggressive actions of the Peiping regime have not been confined to Korea and Indo-china. In his speech at the Eighth National Congress of the Chinese Communist Party in September 1956 Mao declared that Red China must support "national independence and liberal movements" in Latin America, Africa and Asia. While the Peiping regime has little influence in Latin America or Africa, like an octopus its arms have reached into every country in Asia, not so much in armed interference but in infiltration and subversion. According to Chinese intelligence reports an "International University" has been set up in Harbin to train cadres for Asian and Pacific countries. The first group of 700 students, consisting of Communist youths from Taiwan, Japan, the Philippines, Malaya, Indo-china, Australia, New Zealand, Indonesia, India, Burma and Thailand, were graduated at the end of 1954 and have presumably been sent back to their native lands to do subversive work.

In April 1955 a semi-official conference of Asian nations took place in New Delhi, capital of India, for five days. Fourteen Asian nations, including three Communist regimes, Peiping, North Korea and Outer Mongolia, sent delegates while the Soviet Union and Egypt sent observers. The conference adopted resolutions, calling for economic, cultural and social cooperations among the Asian nations and strongly opposed colonialism existing in Asia. It advocated that Taiwan should be handed over to the Peiping regime, Goa to India, West Irian (West New Guinea) to Indo-China, and Ryukiu Islands to Japan, and supported the struggle for independence in Malaya, Arabia and North Africa.[17]

Immediately after the closing of this conference an Afro-Asian Conference was held in Bandung, Indonesia from April 18 to April 24. Among the 29 Asian and African nations attending the conference only Peiping and Viet Minh were Communist regimes. Chou En-lai headed Red China's delegation and tried to fan hatred against colonialism and Western imperialism. But this time he was not successful. Due to the presence of anti-Communist leaders from a number of nations such as Iraq's Fadhil Jamali, Pakistan's Mohammed Ali, the Philippines' Carlos Romulo, Thailand's Prince Wan, Ceylon's Sir John Kotelawala, etc., Chou's plot was frustrated. These leaders told Chou that "Communism confronts the world with a new form of colonialism much deadlier than the old one"; and that: "We (must not be) misled into opening our doors to a more insidious form of imperialism that masquerades in the guise of liberation".

The most outspoken words were those of Kotelawala, Prime Minister of Ceylon, who said: "Colonialism takes many forms. Think, for example, of those satellite states under Communist domination in central and eastern Europe . . . Are these not colonies as much as any of the colonial territories in Africa? If we are united in an opposition to colonialism, should it not be our duty to declare our opposition to Soviet colonialism as much as to Western imperialism? It has been the experience of most countries in this part of the world that the local Communist parties regard themselves as the agent of the great Communist powers of Russia and China . . . In my country, for example, the local Communist Party has been so bold as to declare openly that, if there were a war in which Ceylon found herself on one side and Russia and China on the other, the Communists in Ceylon would do everything in their power including fighting, to promote the victory of Russia and China and the defeat of Ceylon".[18]

The conference adopted resolutions on economic and cultural cooperations, on human rights and self-determination, on peoples in dependent territories and on the promotion of world peace. It denounced "colonialism in all its manifestations," but there was no mention of Western or American imperialism.

The Chinese Communists invited Communist parties of 56 countries to send representatives to their Eighth National Congress and practically most of the top Asian Reds were there. Through their speeches we learn how the Communist movement is getting on in various countries. In Burma an autonomous Communist state was said to have been established in its northern borderland occupied by Chinese Communist forces which included young Kachin graduates from Peiping's "National Academy of Minorities". This invasion force is not likely to withdraw until the so-called autonomous Communist state is in firm control of the overrun territory with some 100,000 aboriginal mountaineers. In Thailand, there is a so-called Free Thai movement under Communist leader Nye Beri who is reported to have 30,000 troops based in Yunnan, China, and in the extreme south of the country the Communists control a border area of some 9,000 square miles. In Ceylon the Communist Party has achieved in pressing the Ceylon Government into signing two trade agreements with Peiping in 1952 and 1956. In North Korea the Chinese "volunteers" and a great number of Chinese technicians are participating in the post-war rehabilitation and construction.

Hoang Quoc Viet of Vietnam's Lao Dong (Communist) Party declared that: "the China of today is the Vietnam of tomorrow". The Indian delegate, E. M. S. Namboodiripad, emphasized that the unity of the Soviet Union, China and India would be a decisive blow to world imperialism. A message from the Central Committee of the Indonesian Communist Party claimed its membership had grown from one million to six million after the elections of 1955. In Japan there are 30,000 thoroughly brainwashed Japanese repatriates from the Chinese mainland and have received from Peiping no less than 2,231,000,000 Japanese yen between 1952 and 1956 to do subversive work. As Japanese delegates to the congress were denied passports by the Japanese Government a message was sent by the Japanese Communist Party saying: "The struggle of the Japanese people, headed by the working class, against control by United States imperialism and the Japanese reactionary clique, for peace and independence, for preventing the revival of militarism and for extending freedom and democracy, is progressing".[19]

In Malaya and Singapore thousands of Chinese Communists have used the jungle as their base and carried on guerrilla warfare since 1948. The Communists are exercising increasing influence over Chinese youth through their infiltration into the schools. The Philippines seems to be the only nation in Southeast Asia in which Communist influence has been waning since President Ramon Magsaysay assumed his office at the end of 1953.

In October 1956 a secret Regional Conference of Communists in Asia and the Pacific was held in Peiping. The proceedings and resolutions were not made public, but stepped up subversive work in Asian and Pacific non-Communist countries was reportedly a major topic.

A month later, significantly, Chou En-lai was busily visiting North Vietnam, Cambodia, Laos, India, Pakistan, Nepal and Afghanistan for the purpose of forming a sort of united front in supporting Egypt and opposing Western imperialism. While in Hanoi, Chou En-lai told a big reception for him that Red China would support North Vietnam in its struggle for Vietnam's unification and that Red China and North Vietnam were members of the same family headed by the Soviet Union.[20] Later, in New Delhi, Chou and Prime Minister Jawaharlal Nehru conferred for several days and it was reported that Nehru wished to serve as a "link" between the American Government and the Peiping regime.[21]

The close relationship between Moscow and Peiping has continued even after the death of Stalin in March 1953. The Kremlin leaders, Nikita S. Khrushchev, Nikolai A. Bulganin, Georgi M. Malenkov, etc., knowing that they do not have the same prestige in Red China as Stalin had, have tried to please the Chinese Communists. In September 1954 Khrushchev, Bulganin and Mikoyan went to Peiping to participate in the celebration of the fifth anniversary of the establishment of the Communist regime on October 1 and presented to "the Chinese people" the machinery and equipment needed for running a state farm of about 50,000 acres, including 98 tractors, 100 combine harvesters, and 120 tractor-drawn grain sowers.[22] Eleven days later Moscow and Peiping jointly announced that the Soviet Government had agreed to transfer, as of January 1, 1955, the Soviet shares in the Sino-Soviet civil aviation, petroleum and nonferrous metal companies to the Peiping regime. On the fixed date the transfer was affected.[23] On May 25, 1955 by a joint communique Moscow and Peiping declared that the Soviet Union had withdrawn its armed forces from Port Arthur and that all installations in that area had been transferred to the Peiping regime.[24]

Those who have hoped that the breach between Moscow and Peiping would occur after the death of Stalin are bound to be disillusioned. Not only did they present a united front at Geneva, but they showed signs of close cooperation on every occasion. In the "Constitution of the People's Republic of China", adopted by the "National Congress of People's Delegates" in September, 1954, the preamble reads in part: "Our country has built up an indestructible friendship with the great Union of Soviet Socialist Republics and the people's democracies . . . This friendship will be continuously developed and consolidated".[25]

Even the post-mortem purge of Stalin by Khrushchev at the Twentieth Congress of the Soviet Communist Party in February 1956 seems to have affected the Moscow-Peiping relationship very slightly. While Khrushchev and other Soviet leaders' denunciation of Stalin shocked Communists in European satellites and Western nations, the Chinese Communists took it very coolly and in a matter-of-fact way. Mao Tse-tung, Chu Teh, Chou En-lai, etc., never said anything publicly concerning this episode while the Communist press only commented on Stalin's mistakes very mildly. When Mikoyan, a Deputy Premier of the Soviet Government who headed the Soviet delegation to the Eighth National Congress of the Chinese Communist Party, told the congress on September 17 how the Soviet Union had dealt with the cult of individual there was no enthusiasm among the delegates and the question was not discussed. The only indirect response was the emphasis on collective leadership in the party, government and army in the speeches of Mao Tse-tung and others.[26]

In the same speech Mikoyan declared: "The enemy very much desired to create a breach—however small—in Chinese-Soviet relations and friendship. But they viewed this relationship in the light of capitalist relations. There has never been a friendship in the world comparable with that between the great peoples of our two nations and our two powerful parties. . . . Our solidarity can never be shaken". He praised Mao as "a creative adaptor of the Marxist-Leninist theory". Then he went on to promise Soviet economic aid: "The Chinese can draw from our experience and proceed with their reconstruction without going through a preparatory stage, when they construct their country with the cooperation of the Soviet Union and other socialist countries. They can skip the intermediate stage and pass from backwardness directly to the highest technical level up to the zenith of the highest scientific and technical advancement".[27] On the other hand Mao pledged his support for "the camp of peace, democracy and socialism headed by the Soviet Union".[28]

Latest developments in the European satellites clearly show that Mao is supporting every move of the Soviet Union. In the middle of October 1956 it was reported from Warsaw that Mao had told Edward Ochab, first secretary of the Polish United Workers (Communist) Party, who was in Peiping for the Eighth National Congress, that "the Poles should go ahead in their efforts to obtain internal independence and develop their own socialist system as the Yugoslavs have done." [29] Judging by the condemnation of Tito by the Chinese Communists from 1948 until the Kremlin's rapprochement with him in 1955 and by subsequent events we are doubtful about the accuracy of this report.

When the Soviet Government announced its willingness to withdraw its troops from Hungary the Peiping regime also advocated non-interference of other nations' internal affairs. But when a day or two later Moscow changed policy and massacred the Hungarian people by the thousands with guns and tanks, Peiping also changed its attitude and its official organ, *Jen Min Jih Pao* (People's Daily) blamed the Hungarian revolution as being instigated by Western imperialism in order to restore capitalism in Hungary.[30] On November 21 in a broadcast based on an editorial of *Jen Min Jih Pao*, the Peiping radio said: "The Hungarian people can see that Soviet policy toward the people's democracies is truly one of equality, friendship and mutual assistance, not one of conquest, aggression and plunder, and that the outpourings of imperialist propaganda machines are nothing but lies and slanders . . . As soon as the subversive forces of imperialism there are wiped out and social order is fully restored, the Soviet and Hungarian governments will undoubtedly hold talks on an absolutely equal footing, as in the Soviet-Polish talks, and will make arrangements concerning Soviet forces in Hungary that fully conform to Hungarian independence and sovereignty".[31]

With regard to the Middle East crisis Peiping has also echoed the voice of Moscow. On September 15 at the opening meeting of the Eighth National Congress Mao declared: "We resolutely oppose any attempt to encroach on the sovereignty of Egypt and to start armed intervention. We must completely frustrate the schemes of imperialism to create tension and prepare for war".[32] In the middle of November after the landing of British and French troops at the mouth of the Suez Canal, Chou En-lai sent a message to the Egyptian President, Col. Gamal Abdul Nasser, offering 20,000,000 Swiss francs as Peiping regime's financial aid to Egypt against British and French aggression. Peiping also announced that 250,000 "volunteers" were ready to go at any moment to Cairo to fight for world peace.[33] At the time of this writing the crisis is not yet over and what will result from it only time can tell.

Besides presenting a united front in their diplomacy there are other ties which bind together Moscow and Peiping. One of these ties is the so-called world peace movement. As a Communist counterpart of the United Nations a World Peace Congress was formed in Paris in April 1949 and claimed a membership of 72 countries. When the Chinese Communist representatives returned to Peiping a Chinese Peace Congress was organized as the national unit of the World Peace Congress. In October 1952 a Peace Conference of Asia and the Pacific Region was held at Peiping to which 22 Asian and 13 North and South American nations, New Zealand and Australia sent delegates with British, French, Brazilian and Algerian observers. In its resolutions the conference pointed out that American preparations for war presented a great threat to world peace and strongly opposed the re-armament of Japan.

Two months later a World People's Peace Conference opened at Vienna attended by 1880 delegates representing 85 nations. After eight days' discussions the conference issued a manifesto, asking among other things the conclusion of a five-power peace pact by the

United States, Britain, France, the Soviet Union and Red China, admission of the Peiping regime and other 14 nations to the United Nations, and prohibition of germ warfare and atomic weapons. In the meetings the United States was condemned as the chief warmonger while the Soviet Union and Red China were praised as peace-loving nations. It goes without saying that this peace movement is a part of the cold war and the Kremlin has exercised a dominating influence in the congress and conferences.

There is also a tie of economic character. Ever since its establishment the Peiping regime has depended upon Soviet economic aid for the reconstruction and industrialization of the Chinese mainland. But this aid has been disappointing to the Chinese Communists. It has been rendered more in the form of technical assistance than in the form of money or capital goods. Since the occupation of the mainland Soviet advisers, political, military and technical, have come to China by the thousands. Soviet engineers have helped the Peiping regime in repairing existing railway lines and building new ones, harnessing the Huai and other rivers, putting up new factories and increasing coal, oil and steel production. State farms have engaged the service of Soviet agriculturists and public hospitals have employed Soviet doctors. Yet during Stalin's life the Peiping regime received little assistance in the form of industrial and agricultural machinery or equipment, and it had to pay heavily for what it did receive with food and other products. Some of the Soviet coal-mining machines sent to China were poor in quality when compared with the Japanese.[34] Some of the light industry machinery taken away from Manchuria by Soviet authorities in 1945 was handed back to the Peiping regime in 1950 but none of the vast amount of installations for heavy industries has been returned.[35]

After the death of Stalin Peiping appealed to Moscow for more economic and technical aid to carry out its first Five Year Plan to a success. In September 1953 a message was sent by Mao to Malenkov to express his thanks for the latter's promise to extend aid "in the construction and reconstruction of 91 new enterprises and to the 50 enterprises now being built or reconstructed in China".[36] Three months later it was reported that three new projects of the Anshan Iron and Steel Company in Manchuria were being constructed with Soviet help. But even this promise was not fully performed. In January 1954 the Soviet Government told the Peiping regime that it could not fulfill all of Peiping's demands for machinery, nor could it use all the agricultural products from Red China.[37] At the Eighth National Congress of the Chinese Communist Party Mikoyan again promised increased aid. How much of this promise will be put into effect remains to be seen.

In foreign trade the Peiping regime has also limited itself to dealings with the Soviet Union and satellite countries. In 1954 imports from and exports to these countries formed over 80 per cent of the total; the remaining 20 per cent were mainly with other Asian and African nations, trade with Western nations being practically negligible. In 1955 trade with the Communist bloc increased by 30 per cent while that with the non-Communist world increased by only one per cent.[38]

In the field of education and culture the Peiping regime also leans completely to the Soviet side. Four days after the establishment of the regime a Sino-Soviet Friendship Association was organized with Liu Shao-chi, No. 2 Chinese Communist, as its president. By the end of 1952 its membership reached the astounding total of 38,900,000 due to the fact that all members of the Red armed services and public security forces had collectively joined the association. It had then 1896 regional associations at the provincial, city, and hsien levels and 119,978 branch associations.[39]

The main functions of this association are to introduce Soviet culture to the Chinese people and to influence them with pro-Soviet propaganda by publishing books, newspapers and periodicals and by using other media of mass propagation such as lantern slides, movie films, broadcasts, etc. It has sent many Chinese delegations to the Soviet Union and invited several Soviet cultural missions to China to give lectures, concerts and theatrical performances. A Soviet Exhibition Center was built in the suburb of Peiping in 1954 in which exhibits of Soviet economic and cultural achievements take place constantly while exhibits on a smaller scale have been held all over the country.

In schools and universities on the mainland today both China's traditional culture and philosophy and Western learnings are being discarded and only Communist ideology and Soviet thought are being injected into the students. Professors and scholars who had absorbed Chinese classical or Western learnings have all undergone the process of "brainwashing". The new educational system is modeled after that of the Soviet Union. Russian has taken the place of English in high schools and universities. Some newly established universities have engaged Soviet professors and used Russian books. A "mass translation" of Soviet text books has been going on since 1953 and these translated texts are used in schools. History is re-written to suit Communist purposes. Chinese sages, philosophers, statesmen, and heroes are now downgraded while bandit chiefs such as Huang Chao,

Li Tze-cheng and Chang Hsien-chung are now praised as revolutionary leaders. The United States is described as the arch-enemy of China, while the Soviet Union becomes China's best friend. The historical fact that Russia took the Amur and Ussuri regions from China is completely deleted. College graduates have been sent to the Soviet Union to pursue advanced studies but none of them are permitted to go for the same purpose, not only to the United States, but even to Britain which has recognized the Peiping regime.

With such political connections with, and economic and cultural dependency on, the Soviet Union it is simply inconceivable that the Peiping regime will some day break away from Moscow. It is true that Moscow and Peiping have had differences of opinion from time to time and Peiping may be dissatisfied with Moscow as in the case of economic aid. Their interests may even conflict with each other as in the case of Sinkiang and Manchuria. But these differences and conflicts are overshadowed by the fact that they work for a common program—to sovietize the whole world, and have a common enemy—the United States. As pointed out by Mr. Harry Schwarz: "to both sides the alliance is a political necessity and to Communist China it is also a vital economic necessity".[40]

At the Bandung Conference, in order to cover up his aggressive intention and to please anti-Communist delegates, Chou En-lai dedeclared: "The Chinese people do not want to have war with the United States. The Chinese Government is willing to sit down and enter into negotiations with the United States Government to discuss the question of relaxing tension in the Far East and especially the question of relaxing tension in the Taiwan area".[41] On the other hand the American Government was advised by London and New Delhi to have direct talks with the Communist regime. So on July 25, 1955 Washington and Peiping announced forthcoming talks on an ambassadorial level. The talks between American Ambassador to Czechoslovakia, U. A. Johnson, and Communist "Ambassador" to Poland, Wang Ping-nan, started at Geneva on August 1. At first they talked about the freedom of movement of Americans on the Chinese mainland and of Chinese in the United States and some agreement was reached. Then Wang Ping-nan brought up the question of raising the embargo on strategic materials to Red China and that of higher level negotiations presumably between Secretary of State Dulles and Chou En-lai. Ambassador Johnson told Wang that the American Government would not discuss any other question until the Peiping regime had set free all Americans on the mainland and renounced the use of force in the Taiwan Strait. As of November 1956 talks had dragged on for sixteen months without much result. There are a dozen or so American citizens still detained on the mainland and the Peiping regime has stubbornly refused to renounce the use of force. On the other hand Chinese citizens in the United States are free to leave the country any time they wish but few have chosen to go back to the mainland.

It is not within the scope of this book to describe the conditions of the Chinese mainland under Communist rule. But a few words about its character seem to be necessary. Before the occupation of the mainland in 1949 many Chinese, especially the intellectuals, had illusions about the Communists. Dissatisfied with the government they were misled to believe that the Communists were liberal and democratic and that Communist rule could only be better and not worse. Since then they have been completely disillusioned. Communist rule has been a combination of modern dictatorship and ancient tyranny. Its foundation is built upon armed force, secret police and firing squad. There is no freedom of speech, no freedom of press, no freedom of worship, no freedom of association, no freedom of movement; in short, all political and civil liberties and human dignity have disappeared. Today the Chinese people on the mainland live not as individuals but as tools of the Communist state.

Furthermore, they live under a reign of terror. No one has any sense of security; no one knows how long he is going to live because he can be liquidated at any time under any pretext. Some generals and high government officials who were captured by the Communists have been spared their lives to serve as examples of Communist leniency, but otherwise there has been a genocide on a gigantic scale. Government officials, military officers, Kuomintang party workers and persons with influence on the mass have been shot or tortured to death. Landlords, rich peasants, and even middle peasants have been liquidated in the "land reforms", while the Three Anti Campaign of 1951 against corruption, waste and bureaucratism, and the Five Anti Campaign of 1952 against bribery, tax evasion, fraud, theft of state properties, and revelations of state secrets, killed many industrialists, businessmen, officials in the regime and even Communist Party cadres. Frank Moraes, an Indian writer who visited the mainland in April-June, 1952, heard that about two million persons had been executed, and Mark Tennien, a Catholic priest, estimated that by 1953 the figure had risen to seven millions or even more.[42] According to Chinese government estimates at least nineteen millon persons had been liquidated up to November 1956.[43] Besides, in 1952 some ten to sixteen million persons were held in labor camps.[44] There must have been many more million people who died of exhaustion from slave labor or starvation!

Some foreign observers who have visited the mainland have praised the Communist regime for its efficiency and its accomplishment in economic reconstruction. No doubt due to its dictatorial character the Communist regime can do things or can enforce its orders more efficiently than the Chinese Government on the mainland; no doubt the Communist regime has built more railways, roads, airfields, etc., and has increased the production of heavy industries in the past seven years. But the crucial question is, are the Chinese people on the mainland happier than before, or has their standard of living been raised? The answer is, NO. The peasants, of whom 56 per cent have been forced to join advanced cooperatives (collective farms), are not happy because the land has been taken away from them and they are now mere farm workers.[45] Even the factory workers, who are praised as the leading class, pioneers in revolution, etc., are required to work more hours but less wages because as they are now the "owners" of the factories they should not haggle over the pay. There is, of course, no more freedom to strike. The national capitalist class and the petite bourgeoisie are, of course, even more suppressed. Intellectuals, besides hard living conditions, suffer also from spiritual suffocation. The only groups which enjoy luxurious living on the mainland are party elite and high-ranking officers.

That the great majority of the Chinese people on the mainland are opposed to Communist rule is clearly shown by the following facts. In the early stage of the rule there were simultaneous uprisings in many provinces in the form of guerrilla warfare against the Peiping regime. Without coordination and without outside assistance these guerrillas were gradually wiped out by Communist forces. But the anti-Communist movement has kept on and individual or small-group actions take place almost anytime, anywhere. Lo Jui-chin, Communist "Minister of Public Security", admitted in his report to the "National Congress of People's Delegates" on June 22, 1956 that from October 1949 to May 1956 there were 5,548,000 cases of anti-revolutionary (anti-Communist) activities.[47] This statement proves how widespread has been the anti-Communist movement.

In 1956 armed uprisings have occurred among the peasants in Manchuria and Southwest China, and the Kawa tribesmen on the Yunnan-Burmese borderland. The Tibetans, who had enjoyed autonomy for hundreds of years but were conquered by Communist forces in 1951, have also risen in arms against the Communists.[48] On October 10, National Celebration Day, there were large-scale anti-Communist riots in Canton and many railway tracks, bridges, theatres, public buildings were wholly or partly destroyed by bombs.[49]

At the end of the Korean War there were about 20,000 prisoners of war taken from Chinese Communist forces. Out of these 20,000 more than 70 per cent refused to return to the Chinese mainland when the armistice talks were in progress. At first Communist representatives insisted on compulsory repatriation but the United Nations Command would not agree. It was finally agreed that they were to be placed in the custody of a neutral commission and to be visited by Communist representatives for the purpose of persuading them to accept repatriation. So for 90 days these prisoners of war were lured, induced and threatened by Chinese Communists to return to the mainland, yet only a handful changed their mind. In January 1954 14,209 anti-Communist prisoners were set free by the United Nations Command and they all went to Taiwan in American transports. Most of them have joined the Chinese Army and are willing to fight back to their homes on the mainland.

After the loss of the mainland over a million Chinese have fled to Hongkong to escape Communist tyranny. Some of them may be rich men or landlords but most of them are small traders, workers, peasants and students. Hundreds of thousands of them live in shacks and take up manual work to earn a few Hongkong dollars[50] a day to keep their bodies and souls together. Yet they prefer this kind of life to returning to Communism. Another significant fact is that the labor organizations in Hongkong repudiate the Communist regime and support the Chinese Government in Taiwan. Each year on October 1, anniversary of the establishment of the Peiping regime, few Communist flags can be seen in Hongkong; while on October 10, National Celebration Day, the whole city is bedecked by tens of thousands of the Blue-Sky-and-White-Sun flags. On October 10, 1956 riots broke out in Kowloon, caused by the fact that a British police officer took down some Chinese flags flying from a building, and lasted two days.[51]

These facts prove to us that Communist rule has been forced on the Chinese people and not accepted by them through their free choice. If a free election can be held on the mainland under supervision of the United Nations we are sure that the Communist regime will be overthrown by a great majority vote of the people.

CHAPTER XXIV

Free China Fights On

The period immediately after the loss of the mainland was indeed the darkest hour for China. Although the Chinese Government was established in Taiwan and was determined to carry on the struggle against the Soviet Union and the Communist regime, it had both internal and external troubles. Internally the government was disintegrating. Acting President Li was recuperating in the United States, while Premier Yen Hsi-san and ministers of the Executive Yuan had resigned en bloc. But there was no authority either to accept or to reject their resignation and the administration simply dragged on. The government finance was so tight that it covered its expenditures by using its meagre gold holding in the treasury. The troops who had just retreated from the mainland were still in a disorganized state. A Communist invasion seemed to be imminent and the populace was panic-stricken.

Externally China's allies in the Second World War now deserted her. At the beginning of 1950 Britain recognized the Communist regime and Norway, Denmark, Finland, Sweden, Switzerland and the Netherlands soon followed suit. Some non-Communist Asian nations, Burma, India, Pakistan, Israel, Indonesia and Ceylon, also recognized the Peiping regime. Even the United States, long regarded by the Chinese Government and people as their best friend, was now seriously considering recognition. As early as October 1949, before the complete loss of the mainland, the Department of State convened a conference attended by "experts" on Far Eastern problems and some department officials. During the discussions the majority of the participants held the view that the Chinese Government was "finished" and they were no longer interested in its fate. When the question of recognizing the Communist regime was brought up by the chairman, Philip Jessup, several participants strongly advocated recognition and even assistance and only a few were opposed to hasty action.[1]

The Department of State would have openly advocated recognition of the Peiping regime, if not for the humiliation suffered by the American Government at the hands of the Chinese Communists. The intrusion of Red soldiers into Ambassador Stuart's bedroom in the

American Embassy at Nanking, the physical violence inflicted upon William Olive, a consular official at Shanghai, the arrest and maltreatment of Consul-General Angus Ward at Mukden, and the seizure of consular offices at Peiping, all these events "produced in the United States such waves of popular resentment that official action affirmatively favorable to the Communists was precluded."[2] On January 14, the day following the seizure of Peiping offices, Secretary of State Acheson had to recall all American consular personnel from the Chinese mainland.[3]

But even though Secretary Acheson did not propose an out-right recognition he was determined to abandon China to her own fate and President Truman approved this policy. Taiwan then became an important issue in American foreign policy and many American leaders, both political and military, such as ex-President Herbert Hoover, Secretary of Defense Louis Johnson, General Douglas MacArthur, Supreme Commander of Allied Forces in Japan, Senators Robert A. Taft, William F. Knowland and H. Alexander Smith, Congressman Walter Judd, etc., advocated the protection of Taiwan against Communist invasion. On December 22, 1949 the Joint Chiefs of Staff under the chairmanship of General Omar Bradley decided to help the Chinese Government defend Taiwan and advised the despatch of a military mission there. A week later at a meeting of the National Security Council, President Truman, after hearing the opposite view of Acheson, overruled the Joint Chiefs of Staff and upheld the hands-off policy.[4]

The day following the decision made by the Joint Chiefs of Staff, Secretary Acheson sent a secret directive, which later leaked out from Tokyo, to American diplomatic and consular representatives in the Far East, telling them of the abandonment of Taiwan by the American Government. This message said in part: "Formosa (Taiwan) has no military significance . . . we should occasionally make clear that seeking United States bases on Formosa, sending troops, supplying arms, dispatching naval units, or taking similar action would (a) accomplish no material good for China or its Nationalist regime; (b) involve the United States in a long-term venture, producing at best a new era of bristling stalemate and at worst possible involvement in open warfare".[5] Pressed by Senator Knowland, Acheson admitted to the Senate Committee on Foreign Relations on January 10, 1950 that he was responsible for this secret directive.[6]

To clarify the situation, President Truman, at his press conference on January 5, 1950, read a statement on Taiwan which said in part: "The United States has no desire to obtain special rights or privileges or to establish military bases on Formosa at this time. Nor does it have intention of utilizing its armed force to interfere in the present situation. The United States Government will not pursue a course which will lead to involvement in the civil conflict in China". The United States would not "provide military aid or advice to Chinese forces on Formosa" but would continue the program of economic assistance of which $100,000,000 was unspent from the appropriations of 1948.[7] There was much opposition to this policy in Congress. But being in a minority they could not affect the policy of the administration. Senator Knowland, who had just come from a visit to Taiwan, declared: "Munich should have taught us that appeasement of aggression, then as now, is but surrender on the installment plan".[8]

It was against such domestic and international background that Free China took its shape. As Acting President Li repeatedly refused the request of the Chinese Government to return to Taiwan even after his complete recovery from illness, delegates of the National Assembly, the Taiwan Provisional Legislature, the Kuomintang Central Headquarters, and many civic organizations requested Generalissimo Chiang Kai-shek to resume the presidency as the only way to save the situation. In compliance with this popular request, President Chiang resumed office on March 1. With the consent of the Legislative Yuan, General Chen Cheng was appointed Premier to succeed General Yen Hsi-san and a new Executive Yuan assumed work on March 15.

With the establishment of a new Central Government reforms immediately began. Government expenditures were drastically cut and revenue was increased. Armed services were reorganized, paper soldiers were eliminated, and their pay was raised. With living conditions improved, the morale of the officers and rank and file began to rise. The confidence of the people in the government was gradually restored as they knew that there were now responsible men at the helm.

The resumption of office by President Chiang and the establishment of a new Central Government were very timely, for in the middle of April the Communist invasion of Hainan Island began. As Hainan is only about twenty miles off the shore of Kwangtung it was easy for the Communists to land troops on the island and to reinforce them. Consequently, after several days' fighting, government forces began to evacuate Hainan and by the end of the month the evacuation was completed. In the middle of May, anticipating an attack from the Communists, the government withdrew its troops on the Chusan Islands off the shore of Chekiang. All the 150,000 effectives on the islands retreated to Taiwan without a single casualty. While the government abandoned two areas, the withdrawal was orderly and the defense of Taiwan was strengthened. Had there been no responsible government Free China might have collapsed at that time.

Then came the Korean War and the American Government once more changed its policy towards China. In his statement on June 27, 1950 President Truman, after declaring that he had ordered American air and sea forces "to give the Korean Government troops cover and support", went on to say: "The attack upon Korea makes it plain beyond all doubt that Communism has passed beyond the use of subversion to conquer independent nations and will now use armed invasion and war. . . . In these circumstances the occupation of Formosa by Communist forces would be a direct threat to the security of the Pacific area and to United States forces performing their lawful and necessary functions in that area. Accordingly I have ordered the Seventh Fleet to prevent an attack on Formosa. As a corollary of this action I am calling upon the Chinese Government on Formosa to cease all air and sea operations against the mainland". The Seventh Fleet was also instructed to "see that this is done".[9]

An aide memoire of the Department of State to this effect was presented to President Chiang on that night by American Charge d'Affaires Robert Strong in the presence of Foreign Minister George Yeh. At an Executive Yuan meeting the next day it was decided to accept in principle the proposal of American Government and orders were immediately issued to Chinese naval and air forces to suspend operations against the mainland.

With the exception of the United States, China was the first country to offer military assistance to the Republic of Korea. On June 29 in compliance with the resolution of the United Nations Security Council on June 27, the Chinese Government notified the Department of State that China was willing to send troops to Korea to assist in operations against North Korean Communist aggressors. The next day in another aide memoire the Chinese Government declared that it was ready to send three divisions, 33,000 men, to Korea. This offer was turned down by the American Government ostensibly on the ground that these forces were needed for the defense of Taiwan but actually the American Government was afraid that the presence of Chinese Government troops on the battlefield might give the Chinese Communists a pretext to get into the Korean War.

As American policy towards China changed from hands-off to assistance, close relationship between the two countries which had existed during and immediately after the Second World War was soon resumed. On July 31 General MacArthur with top-ranking staff officers paid a visit to Taipei to confer with the Generalissimo concerning the defense of Taiwan and a week later Major General Alonzo Fox, deputy chief of staff to General MacArthur, and Major General Howard Turner, commander of the 13th United States Air Force, set up liaison offices in Taipei. Since the loss of the mainland, the American embassy at Taipei had been taken care of by a secretary, and now Mr. Karl Rankin arrived as minister and chargé d'affaires. In March 1953 Minister Rankin was appointed ambassador by President Eisenhower to succeed Dr. Stuart who had resigned in 1952.

In order to help defend Free China the American Government has rendered her both economic and military assistance. During the five fiscal years, 1951-1955, $539,000,000,000 were appropriated for China which were grouped into four categories: (1) the commodity program, to procure essential commodities for Taiwan such as cotton, wheat and barley, soyabeans, etc., (2) the industrial program, to help develop industries in Taiwan such as electric power and tele-communication, food processing, ceramics, fertilizer, chemical products, lumber and wood products, metals and metal fabricating, shipbuilding, railroads, fisheries, paper and pulp, etc.; (3) the technical assistance program, to send technicians, scholars, and government employees mainly to the United States but a few to Japan and Hongkong, for in-service or academic training and also to invite American experts and technicians to Taiwan; and (4) the common use program, to supplement the military aid.[10] For the fiscal year 1956 (July 1955-June 1956) in the foregn aid program passed by Congress on July 29, 1955, $100,000,000 were allotted to Free China.[11] This economic assistance has enabled the Chinese Government to maintain a comparably stable currency, to improve production in both agriculture and industry, and to carry out a Four Year Plan for the achievement of economic self-sufficiency.

Military assistance began with the establishment of the Military Assistance Advisory Group (MAAG) in May 1951, whose mission was "to help the Chinese armed forces strengthen the island of Taiwan and the Pescadores (Peng-hu) and help them maintain internal security".[12] Starting with eleven officers and men the group has steadily grown until at present (November, 1956) it has well over a thousand. In the first two years most of the military supplies received by Free China were small arms. After President Eisenhower assumed office heavier arms began to arrive and on June 19, 1953 the Chinese Air Force received its first allocation of jet aircraft. On July 27, 1953

Major General William C. Chase, testifying before the Senate Appropriations Committee and the Far Eastern Sub-Committee of the House Foreign Affairs Committee, asserted the great strategic importance of Taiwan and the necessity of giving large military aid to Free China. He said that the Chinese armed forces on Taiwan were a very definite asset as a strategic reserve and also acted as a deterrent to the Chinese Communists in any move they might make in great force into Southeast Asia.[13] Thereafter more appropriations were made for military aid but the figure for each year, being a military secret, has never been made public.

Even after the participation of the Peiping regime in the Korean War in November 1950 President Truman's order to the Seventh Fleet to prevent Taiwan from attacking the mainland was not rescinded. Consequently a ridiculous situation developed in which Chinese Communist troops were fighting American forces in Korea on the one hand, while the United States Navy was defending the mainland on the other. So, in his first State of the Union message to Congress on February 2, 1953, President Eisenhower declared: "There is no longer any logic or sense in a condition that required the United States Navy to assume defensive responsibilities on behalf of the Chinese Communists. This permitted those Communists, with greater impunity, to kill our soldiers and those of our United Nations allies in Korea. I am, therefore, issuing instructions that the Seventh Fleet no longer be employed to shield Communist China. Permit me to make crystal clear—this order implies no aggressive intent on our part."[14] This decision was viewed with great satisfaction in Free China. On the following day Generalissimo Chiang Kai-shek issued a statement hailing President Eisenhower's move to deneutralize Taiwan as not only judicious but morally and militarily sound.

As the 100-mile-wide Taiwan Strait makes invasion from either side extremely hazardous there have been no large-scale engagements between government and Communist forces since the evacuation of Hainan in April 1950. But even after abandoning the Chusan Islands Free China held several groups of off-shore islands which stretched from the Tachen Islands in the Taichow Bay to Quemoy. Quemoy is only a few miles away from the shore of Amoy and has been an immediate objective of the Communists. As early as November 1949 Communist forces crossed the narrow channel and tried to occupy Quemoy but were repulsed with heavy losses. Since then artillery duels have been going on between Quemoy and Amoy from time to time. The fiercest exchange of shells took place in September 1954. A large army and a great number of vessels were gathered in the neighborhood of Amoy evidently for a second attempt of invasion. Communist gunfire started on September 3 and in a single day sent 6,000 rounds across the sea. But all guns of the defenders immediately fired back and the Chinese Navy and Air Force also took action. A combined air-sea assault on the Communist military build-up destroyed their gun positions and sank a number of gunboats and many motor junks. The Communist plot was frustrated. This was the first time that the Chinese Air Force put jet fighters into action.

There have also been occasional air and sea battles. In July 1954 Lieutenant Liang Tien-chia, captain of Warship No. 106, won a sea battle with a Communist flotilla off the Chekiang coast and was recommended by the Generalissimo for his brilliant performance. At the end of October another sea battle occurred near the Chekiang coast and nine Communist vessels were damaged. On November 4 Chinese Air Force planes engaged in a dog-fight with Communist planes north of the Tachen Islands for the first time. Ten days later the Chinese destroyer-escort, "Taiping" was sunk by four Communist PT boats near the Tachens. On June 27, 1955 two Communist MIG-15 fighters attacked two Chinese Air Force jet trainers and a Chinese commercial airliner over the Taiwan Strait, damaging the commercial plane and downing one trainer. In a communique the Chinese Air Force announced that the attacking MIGs were directed from the ground in Russian.[15]

As early as June 1949 the Chinese Government announced the closure of Communist-held seaports such as Shanghai, Tientsin, Tsingtao, etc. After the loss of the mainland the closure was extended to the whole coast line. While the Chinese Navy is not strong enough to make this closure effective, ships which carry arms or strategic materials to some mainland port and pass through the Taiwan Strait have been searched and intercepted. As most of the ships belonged to foreign companies they were set free after the seizure of the strategic goods. In September 1954 a Soviet tanker "Tuapse" which intended to go to Shanghai was seized in the waters near Taiwan. Later the French Government offered its good offices to mediate in the dispute and the tanker was released after the confiscation of its oil. But some members of its crew refused to go back to the Soviet Union and stayed on in Taiwan or obtained asylum in the United States.

Besides government forces Chinese guerrillas have also been active along the mainland coast. In August 1952 they landed at Kingchenwei in Pingyang district on the Chekiang coast and captured 125

Communist prisoners. In September they occupied two islands south of Amoy but later had to give up. In October a three-day battle was fought between Communist forces and guerrillas on Nanjih Island 60 miles from Foochow, and the latter killed about 2,000 and captured 810 Communists. In June 1953 sea-borne guerrillas staged assaults on four Communist-held islands in the Wenchow Bay, killing and wounding 1,200 Communists. On July 16 the guerrillas in the Quemoy area, after receiving special training, conducted a successful commando raid against Tungshan Island off the southern Fukien coast. They inflicted over 2,000 casualties on the Communists and brought back 485 prisoners, but also suffered heavy losses themselves.

Since 1953 negotiations had been going on between Washington and Taipei for the conclusion of a treaty of mutual defense. After concluding treaties of the same character with the Philippines, Australia and New Zealand, Japan, Korea and the formation of the South-East Asia Treaty Organization,[16] the United States also needed a treaty with Free China to complete the collective defense system of the free world against Communist aggression in the Pacific area. Consequently the Sino-American Mutual Defense Treaty was signed in Washington on December 2, 1954 by which "each party recognizes that an armed attack in the West Pacific area directed against the territories of either of the parties would be dangerous to its own peace and safety and declares that it would act to meet the common danger in accordance with its constitutional processes. Any such armed attack and all measures taken as a result thereof shall be immediately reported to the Security Council of the United Nations. Such measures shall be terminated when the Security Council has taken the measures necessary to restore and maintain international peace and security".

The application of this treaty is limited to Taiwan and the Pescadores, and the islands in the West Pacific under American jurisdiction; but may be extended to other territories by mutual agreement. By this treaty the United States is granted the right to "dispose such land, air and sea forces in and about Taiwan and the Pescadores as may be required for their defense as determined by mutual agreement". The ratifications of the treaty were exchanged at Taipei on March 3, 1955 and it came into force immediately. It is to remain in force indefinitely but either party may terminate it by giving notice one year ahead.

This treaty was viewed with satisfaction by both sides. Secretary of State John Foster Dulles declared after the ceremony: "the signing of this defense treaty will put to rest once and for all rumors and reports that the United States will in any manner agree to the abandonment of Formosa and the Pescadores to Communist control"; while Foreign Minister George Yeh responded: "this treaty will serve to promote the common cause of freedom, particularly at this juncture of the world situation". In a message to Secretary Dulles congratulating him on his contribution to world security, Generalissimo Chiang stated that "a necessary link in the chain of Far Eastern defense has now been forged". The Chinese press in Taiwan lauded the treaty, while the *New York Times* said in an editorial: "We believe that free Chinese throughout the world will be heartened by this pact. We believe also that Americans will be heartened by an action that is clearly defined and that makes formal a position that most Americans strongly support".[17]

To the Chinese Communists this treaty serves as another evidence of "American imperialism" in China. As the treaty did not cover the off-shore islands held by Free China the Peiping regime wanted to put American policy to test. It chose the Tachen Islands which are about 250 miles northwest of Taiwan as its immediate objective and built up military strength on the Chekiang coast. On January 10 and 19, 1955 large groups of Communist planes raided the islands and dropped hundreds of bombs. On January 18 the Communists succeeded in landing on Yikiangshan, a small islet of less than half a square mile and 8 miles away from the Tachens, after an air and amphibious assault with scores of planes, several gunboats, and many motor junks. Yikiangshan, being only a small outpost of the Tachen group, was garrisoned by 720 guerrillas who defended the islet heroically. But as no outside help could reach them with the Communists enjoying overwhelming local air superiority they were practically all killed in action in more than 56 hours' fighting and the islet was occupied by the Communists who paid a heavy price for it—1,200 dead and several hundred wounded in the battle.[18]

With the loss of Yikiangshan the Communists intensified their attack on the Tachens. There were daily air-raids and guns mounted on Yikiangshan shelled the islands across the sea. It was at this juncture that the American Government advised Free China to withdraw from the Tachens on the ground that without air superiority it would be impracticable to send naval support and food and munitions to the defenders. To make a stand on the Tachens without regard to its cost would be to play into the Communist hands. In case the Chinese Government decided to evacuate, the United States Seventh Fleet would provide the necessary protection and assistance.

Meanwhile, to show his determination to resist Communist aggression in the Far East, President Eisenhower, in a message to Congress on January 24, 1955, declared that "Formosa and the Pescadores should not fall into the control of aggressive Communist forces" and asked for a congressional resolution authorizing the President to employ the armed forces promptly and effectively for this purpose. The message also spoke of "taking into account closely related localities and actions" which might determine the failure or success of an attack on Formosa and the Pescadores. The President expressed his wish that "we would welcome any action by the United Nations which might, in fact, bring an end to the active hostilities in the area".[19]

An identical resolution was promptly introduced both in the Senate and House of Representatives to authorize the President "to employ the armed forces of the United States as he deems necessary for the specific purpose of securing and protecting Formosa and the Pescadores against armed attack, this authority to include the securing and protection of such related positions and territories of that area now in friendly hands . . .". Congress adopted this resolution almost unanimously: the House, by a vote of 409-3 on January 25, and the Senate by a vote of 85-3 three days later. It was promptly signed by President Eisenhower on January 30 and thus given the force of law.[20]

The Chinese Government was reluctant to withdraw its forces from the Tachens without a fight as such an evacuation might affect the morale of both the troops and civilians. But as the American advice was militarily sound it finally decided to comply. On February 5 the Department of State announced that the Seventh Fleet had been ordered to assist and protect the evacuation from the Tachens and that it had informed the Chinese Government of American policy to "extend assistance to the Republic of China in defending such relative positions and territories now in its hands as the United States deems to be essential in the defense of Formosa and the Pescadores". The next day the Chinese Government issued orders for the evacuation of the islands. Besides 15,000 troops there were 17,132 civilians who were given free choice, to leave or to stay, and who without a single exception decided to evacuate to Taiwan. So 32,132 persons with 40,000 tons of military materials and personal property were evacuated between February 8 and 12. A total of 132 American ships, including a 45,000-ton aircraft carrier with 3,400 men on board, and 27 Chinese ships took part in the evacuating work. Due to the presence of the powerful Seventh Fleet, the Communists did not interfere and there was not a single incident. Shortly after this pull-out the Chinese Government also evacuated Nanchi Island, 140 miles from

Taiwan. Some 5,000 regulars and guerrillas and 2,000 civilians were moved to Taiwan.

After the evacuation of the Tachens the question of other off-shore islands, Quemoy and Matsus, came to the fore. On January 31, the United Nations Security Council had passed by a vote of 9-1 a New Zealand resolution, calling on the council to bring about a cessation of fighting "in a number of islands close to the Chinese coast" and thereby remove a potential threat to international peace and security. The only negative vote came from the Soviet Union while China abstained. On the same day it also adopted a resolution to extend an invitation to the Peiping regime to send a representative to join the discussions; this time China opposed the resolution with the Soviet Union abstaining.[21] But as Peiping promptly rejected the invitation, the whole matter was dropped by the Security Council.

There were talks among political leaders in Britain and India that these off-shore islands should be handed over to the Chinese Communists as a price for a cease-fire. Even some influential Americans seemed to hold the opinion that these islands were not worth fighting for. To clarify China's position Generalissimo Chiang Kai-shek told C. L. Sulzberger of the *New York Times* on March 22: "It would not be fair to try and force us to give up the off-shore islands without a fight . . . The United States should not accede to the British idea on this . . . It is a mistake to think that because we evacuated the Tachens we will evacuate Matsus and Kinmen (Quemoy). We shall certainly fight for them".[22]

As the joint resolution of Congress did not mention by name Quemoy and Matsus the question now arose, in case of a Communist attack on these islands, would the United States help Free China defend them? The official American attitude was that the decision whether to help defend them or not could only come from the President. After a visit to Taiwan early in March, Secretary Dulles said in a press conference on March 15 that the President presumably would order United States air and sea forces into action if there was an attack on the off-shore islands as a part of the larger assault on Taiwan and that his recent discussions with the Generalissimo took account of the possibility that the United States might have to help defend these islands.[23] Up to the present the Peiping regime has not been able to carry out its threats to invade these islands or Taiwan itself.

Besides military engagements between government and Communist forces there is another front in which battles have been fought between Free China on the one hand and the Soviet Union and Communist regime on the other—the diplomatic front. These battles have taken place in the United Nations and its specialized agencies. They started with China's accusation of the Soviet Union in the United Nations. As early as May 1948, when the Legislative Yuan held its first session, a number of legislators raised the cry of accusing the Soviet Union in the United Nations for its violation of the Sino-Soviet Treaty of Friendship and Alliance of 1945. But the Waichiapou hesitated, fearing that such an action would offend the Soviet Union and make it extend greater help to the Communists. It was not until September 1949 that the Executive Yuan at Canton decided to make such an appeal to the United Nations.

On September 27 the Chinese delegation to the Fourth Session of the United Nations General Assembly wrote to the president of the assembly requesting that an item, "Threats to the political independence and territorial integrity of China and to the peace of the Far East, resulting from Soviet violations of the Sino-Soviet Treaty of Friendship and Alliance of 14 August, 1945 and Soviet violations of the Charter of the United Nations", be added to the agenda. But as the agenda of the session had already been adopted a new item had to be passed by the General Assembly before it could be put on the agenda. On September 29 the assembly, despite Soviet strong opposition, resolved by a vote of 45-6 to put this item on the agenda and referred it to the First Committee for discussions.

As there were other important items ahead of China's proposal, such as the question of Greece, the question of former Italian colonies, and the "Peace Plan" proposed by the Soviet Union, the First Committee did not take up China's accusation of the Soviet Union until November 25. On that day Dr. T. F. Tsiang, China's chief delegate, made an eloquent presentation of the case, enumerating Soviet aggressive actions in Manchuria, Outer Mongolia, and Sinkiang and how the Soviet Union had used the Chinese Communist Party to undermine the independence and integrity of China and the peace of the Far East. Later he introduced a draft resolution requesting the General Assembly to determine that the Soviet Union by obstructing the Chinese Government in re-establishing its authority in Manchuria and by giving economic and military aid to the Chinese Communists had violated the United Nations Charter and the Sino-Soviet Treaty; to urge all Member States to desist and refrain from giving any military and economic aid to the Chinese Communists; to recommend to all Member States not to accord diplomatic recognition to any regime organized by the Chinese Communists; and to call upon all Member States to refrain from taking advantage of the present situation in China for any purpose that is incompatible with the political independence and territorial and administrative integrity of China.[24]

The delay of almost two months in taking up this item for discussion was very unfortunate for China as the situation had greatly worsened. In September the Chinese Government was in Canton, controlled the southwestern provinces and had over a million soldiers under its command. By November 25 not only Canton had been lost but the government was already evacuating Chungking and the complete loss of the mainland was merely a matter of days. The Peiping regime had been established and recognized by the Soviet Union and its satellites; even Britain and some other Asian and European countries had already made up their minds to give the Peiping regime recognition in the near future.

Consequently the Soviet chief delegate, A. Y. Vyshinsky, refused to participate in the discussions on the ground that Tsiang no longer represented China. Britain was strongly opposed to the Chinese proposal while the French representative kept silence. China had counted upon the support of the United States delegation, yet Philip Jessup, American representative in the First Committee, while criticizing the Soviet action in Manchuria mildly, introduced, together with the delegates of Australia, Mexico, Pakistan and the Philippines, a joint resolution which said nothing about the Soviet Union but was merely a reiteration of the open-door policy.[25]

It was the representatives of smaller nations, such as Ecuador, Peru, Cuba, El Salvador, Lebanon, Belgium and New Zealand who upheld international justice and condemned the Soviet Union. Strong words against appeasement to aggression were uttered by Martinez Moreno, delegate of El Salvador, who criticized the attitude of the great powers as lacking in foresight and responsibility and reminded the assembly of the story of Munich. He expressed his full support for the Chinese draft resolution and could not understand why the various delegations took one attitude towards Communist aggression against Greece and an entirely different attitude towards Communist aggression against China.[26]

Finally on December 8 the General Assembly adopted the five-nation joint resolution presented by Jessup and also another sponsored by the delegations of Cuba, Ecuador and Peru and amended by those of Lebanon and Uruguay which referred China's accusation of the Soviet Union "to the Interim Committee of the General Assembly for continuous examination and study . . . and to report to the next session of the General Assembly with recommendations, or to bring it to the attention of the Secretary-General in order to report to the Security Council if it deems it necessary to do so . . . ."[27]

The Interim Committee held its meetings in February and September 1950 and Tsiang repeated his accusations against the Soviet Union. But there were no discussions and the committee did not report either to the secretary-general or to the General Assembly. During the Fifth Session of the General Assembly the question was again brought up in the First Committee. On November 21, 1950 Tsiang, besides reiterating the charges made in 1949, enumerated the crimes committed by the Communist regime and asserted that through this regime "the sovereign rights of the Chinese people are being robbed by the Soviet imperialists".[28] He submitted a draft resolution calling for the appointment of a "United Nations Commission of Enquiry to gather information and facts relating to this item from Member States of the United Nations".[29]

This time Soviet Delegate Malik took part in the debate, answered the Chinese charges and objected to the establishment of a commission of enquiry. Although the American delegation under Secretary Dulles supported the Chinese draft resolution, the British and other delegations opposed it. As a result the assembly adopted a Syrian proposal to instruct the Interim Committee to continue inquiry on this question.[30]

In 1951 the question lay buried in the Interim Committee. On January 26, 1952 it was again brought up before the First Committee in the Sixth Session of the General Assembly. After an exchange of sharp words between Tsiang and Malik the debate went on for several days. The delegations of the United States, Colombia, and the Philippines strongly supported the Chinese position. Finally the committee adopted China's draft resolution whose essential portion read: "The General Assembly . . . finding that the Union of Soviet Socialist Republics obstructed the efforts of the National Government of China in re-establishing Chinese national authority in the three Eastern Provinces (Manchuria) after the surrender of Japan and gave military and economic aid to the Chinese Communists against the National Government of China, determines that the Union of Soviet Socialist Republics, in its relations since the surrender of Japan, has failed to carry out the Treaty of Friendship and Alliance between China and the Union of Soviet Socialist Republics of 14 August, 1945".[31] On February 1 the resolution finally passed the General Assembly by a vote of 25-9 with 24 abstentions.[32] While the Chinese appeal to the United Nations had some kind of result, the resolution in its final form was very mild in language and did not in any sense condemn Soviet aggression.

Towards the end of 1955 another diplomatic duel between China and the Soviet Union took place in the United Nations over the so-called package deal. After the admission of Indonesia in 1950 no new members were admitted to the United Nations because the Soviet Union had vetoed all applicants until its satellites, Albania, Bulgaria, Hungary, Romania and the so-called Mongolian People's Republic were also admitted. For several years there was a deadlock on the question. Then in the Tenth Session of the General Assembly, Canada and 27 other member states submitted a draft resolution, known as the package deal, which provided that the General Assembly request the Security Council to consider "the pending applications for membership of all those eighteen countries about which no problem of unification arises".[33] The eighteen countries referred to were, according to the order of their applications, Albania, "the Mongolian People's Republic", Jordan, Ireland, Portugal, Hungary, Italy, Austria, Romania, Bulgaria, Finland, Ceylon, Nepal, Libya, Cambodia, Japan, Laos and Spain.

When the question came up for discussion in the Ad Hoc Political Committee on December 2, Dr. Tsiang raised his objection to the package deal as in violation of Article 4 of the Charter which provides for admission only of peace-loving nations. Tsiang specifically regretted the exclusion of the Republic of Korea and opposed the inclusion of Outer Mongolia which was not an independent state and which had committed aggression against China in 1947 and against Korea in 1950.[34] But as the great majority of member states wished to have the issue settled, the Ad Hoc Political Committee adopted the resolution on December 7 and the General Assembly approved it on the following day.

The only thing the Chinese delegation could do to defeat the admission of Outer Mongolia was to use the veto in the Security Council, but the Soviet representative, Arkady A. Sobolev, threatened to veto all other applicants if Outer Mongolia was not admitted. The situation became very grave and many delegations, friendly towards China, advised Tsiang not to use the veto power. Pressure was brought upon the Chinese Government to change its policy by friendly powers including the United States, but Generalissimo Chiang stood firm. On December 13 the package deal came to a vote in the Security Council. In addition to the eighteen applicants the Chinese delegation proposed the admission of the Republic of Korea and Republic of Viet Nam. The Soviet Union vetoed these two countries, China vetoed Outer

Mongolia and then the Soviet Union vetoed all the other thirteen non-Communist countries. Only Albania, Hungary, Romania, and Bulgaria were passed.[35] The next day, upon the request of the Soviet delegation, another meeting of the Security Council was held in which another vote was taken for these thirteen countries and all except Japan were admitted.[36] The Soviet Union now wanted to admit Outer Mongolia and Japan in another package but China refused to accept it. So altogether sixteen nations were accepted by the General Assembly in the evening of December 14. Thus China used the veto power for the first time to defeat the admission of Outer Mongolia to the U.N.

During the past seven years Free China has also put up a fight with the Soviet Union over China's representation in international organizations. The question was first brought up by Malik in the Security Council. On January 10, 1950 Malik introduced a resolution which read in its operative part: "The Security Council considers illegal the maintenance in the Security Council of the United Nations of the representative of the Kuomintang group and insists upon his exclusion from the Security Council". In his statement before the council two days later, he threatened that unless his resolution was adopted he would not participate further in the work of the council. In his reply Tsiang emphasized the fact that he represented a government which was based on a constitution and elected by the Chinese people while the puppet regime of Peiping was the result of Soviet aggression. As his resolution failed to get seven votes which were required for its adoption Malik walked out of the council meeting and remained out until after the Korean War.

Since then the Soviet Union has tried for more than a hundred times to oust the Chinese Government and to give China's representation to the Peiping regime in the United Nations General Assembly, Social and Economic Council, Trusteeship Council and various specialized agencies such as the International Labor Organization, United Nations Educational, Scientific and Cultural Organization, Food and Agricultural Organization, World Health Organization, etc. Although it has been supported by its satellites and by some other countries which have recognized the Peiping regime, Moscow has not yet succeeded once in its attempt. The only time a representative of the Communist regime ever participated in a United Nations meeting was in November 1950 when Wu Hsiu-chuan was invited to speak before the Security Council in connection with the question of "Complaint of Armed Invasion of Taiwan", brought up by the Soviet Union. In some cases when there was no Soviet representative some of the so-called neutralist nations served as Soviet spokesmen. For instance in the Sixth Session of the General Conference of UNESCO held at Paris in June 1951, as the Soviet Union was not yet a member, it was India's representative, Sarvepalli Radhakrishnan, who attacked the Chinese Government and asked for the invitation of the Peiping regime to the conference.[38] In the Twelfth Session of the United Nations General Assembly it was again the Indian representative, Krishna Menon, who brought up the question of China's representation in the General Committee on November 14, 1956.

The attitude of the United States towards this question is all important because it is with the support of the United States that Free China has won diplomatic battles in the United Nations and other international organizations. The question of admitting the Peiping regime to the United Nations and the related question of recognizing it by the United States have raised a great controversy in the United States. Many articles have been written, speeches given and debates held on these questions.[39] While there are prominent individuals, professors, writers, businessmen, etc., who are in favor of admission and recognition, there is no doubt that the great majority of the American people are opposed to them. Powerful labor and veteran organizations have adopted resolutions in opposition to the admission of the Peiping regime to the United Nations. A Committee for One Million Against the Admission of Communist China was organized in 1953 under the sponsorship of such men as ex-President Herbert Hoover, General Marshall, Senators Knowland, Smith, John J. Sparkman and Hubert H. Humphrey, Congressman Judd, Charles Edison, former Governor of New Jersey, Joseph C. Grew, former Under-Secretary of State, George Meany, President of the American Federation of Labor, etc.[40] This committee actually got a million signatures for its petition to the American Government.

The American Government, especially the Department of State, which was wavering at the beginning of 1950, changed to a firm policy after the Peiping regime's participation in the Korean War. In December of that year British Prime Minister Clement R. Attlee came over to Washington to discuss with President Truman the Korean situation. Attlee proposed to compromise with the Chinese Communists by offering them the seat in the United Nations so that a cease-fire could be obtained. American participants in the talks, President Truman, General Marshall, Secretary of State Acheson and Assistant Secretary of State Dean Rusk who was in charge of Far Eastern Affairs, were all opposed to such an idea. Truman declared that "the Chinese Communists were Russian satellites";[41] Acheson said, "we could not buy the friendship of the Chinese Communists";[42] while

Marshall pointed out, "we could not afford to let Formosa go".[43] Thus the British suggestion was rejected. Five months later Rusk declared at a China Institute banquet in New York: "We do not recognize the authorities in Peiping for what they pretend to be. The Peiping regime may be a colonial Russian government—a slavic Manchukuo on a larger scale. It is not the government of China . . . It is not Chinese. It is not entitled to speak for China in the community of nations".[44]

President Eisenhower and Secretary of State Dulles have been firm on this point. On many occasions they have made it plain that they are opposed to recognize the Peiping regime or to let it enter the United Nations. On June 20, 1956 President Eisenhower signed into law a joint resolution by Congress which read: "It is the sense of the Congress that the Communist China Government should not be admitted to membership in the United Nations as the representative of China". Visiting Taipei early in July Vice President Richard M. Nixon delivered a personal message from President Eisenhower to Generalissimo Chiang which, besides paying tribute to the Generalissimo's leadership and courage, asserted: "Let there be no misapprehension about our own steadfastness in continuing to support the Republic of China". At a press conference on July 8 Nixon declared that he had never seen President Eisenhower soften on the United States position of non-recognition of the puppet Peiping regime and on the opposition to the admission of Communist China to the United Nations.[45] In his reply to President Eisenhower on July 20 the Generalissimo expressed his sense of appreciation for reassurance of continued support and said: "the greatest danger confronting Asia today is the effect already evident in Asia of the 'smile' tactics and economic penetration waged by Russia and the Chinese Communists, with opportunist collaboration of the so-called neutralist countries".[46]

In August 1956 when the Democratic and Republican National Conventions were held in Chicago and San Francisco respectively, they both adopted a plank in their platforms pledging their continued opposition to the seating of the Peiping regime in the United Nations.[47]

During the last seven years (1950-1956) Free China has not only fought military and diplomatic battles against the Soviet Union and the Peiping regime, but made sweeping reforms in its internal affairs. It is beyond the scope of this book to enumerate the achievements of the Chinese Government in a detailed way. Suffice it to give a sketch of what progress has been made along the political, military, economic and educational lines.[48] With the help of American supplies and the service of the MAAG the shattered divisions of 1950 have been built up into a powerful army. Incompetent officers and over-age soldiers have been retired from service and paper soldiers no longer exist. The Chinese Navy and Air Force are small but are well trained and efficient. With better pay and consequently better living conditions the morale of the armed services has been restored to a high degree.

With the help of American economic aid industry and agriculture in Taiwan have made long strides. For instance the production of rice increased from 894,000 metric tons in 1946 to 1,610,000 metric tons in 1955, that of sugar from 86,000 tons to 803,000 tons, that of cotton goods from 2,493,000 yards to 160,000,000 yards, that of coal from 1,040,000 tons to 2,350,000 tons and electric power from 472,000,000 kwh to 1,966,000,000 kwh.

During Japanese rule from 1895 to 1945 the opportunity of the Taiwanese people, being regarded as colonial subjects, to receive secondary and higher education was very much limited. When the Chinese Government took over Taiwan in 1945 there were only 29,005 high school students (of whom 16,104 were Japanese) and 2,346 college students, (of whom 1,807 were Japanese). So out of a population of six million only 539 youths were studying in the colleges. Since then the Chinese Government, despite its financial difficulties, has done everything possible to spread and improve education. In the spring semester of 1955 there were 125,808 high school students and 13,778 college students. The number of primary school students also grew from 877,551 to 1,237,904; 92 per cent of the school age children were actually attending school. Added with those in the normal and technical schools there were over a million and a half students in 1955 out of a population of ten million.

What is even more important is that the government has regained the confidence of the Taiwanese people by land reform and democratization of the political system. In 1945 the Taiwanese people felt jubilant in returning to the lap of China after 50 years' foreign rule. But the carpet-baggers from the mainland and the harsh rule of Governor Chen Yi soon alienated them and there occurred the February 28 riots in 1947. In 1949, when General Chen Cheng was Governor, he introduced a land reform program which reduced the farm rental from 50 to 55 per cent of the total annual yield of the main crop to 37.5 per cent. The living conditions of 300,000 tenant farming families have been improved. In 1953 another step in land reform was taken. It was called the "land to the tiller" program by which 143,000 chia, or about 345,500 acres, of privately owned land had been transferred to the ownership of 195,000 tenants and part-tenants. Local self-governing system, as provided in the Constitution of 1946, was first put into practice in 1950. Today provincial assemblymen, hsien and municipal councilors, city mayors and hsien magistrates are all elected by universal suffrage and secret ballot; only the governor and members of the provincial government are still appointed by the Central Government. The people have shown keen interest in these elections and in some localities those who actually went to the polls on the election day constituted over 84 per cent of the qualified voters. These reforms have changed the attitude of the Taiwanese, who form 80 per cent of the population of Free China, towards the government from resentment to support.

The relationship between Free China and the thirteen million overseas Chinese scattered all over the world is worthwhile noting. Despite the loss of the mainland the great majority of these overseas Chinese are still loyal to the Chinese Government. From 1950 down to the present hundreds of overseas Chinese groups have paid visits to Taiwan. Since 1951 thousands of overseas Chinese students have come to Taiwan to continue their studies. Between 1950 and 1952 286 anti-Communist organizations were established among the overseas Chinese. In October 1952 an Overseas Chinese Conference was held at Taipei, with 223 delegates representing Chinese in 26 countries. It passed two most important resolutions, one was to organize an Overseas Chinese United National-Salvation Association and the other was to call on the overseas Chinese to intensify economic warfare against the Communist regime. It also adopted an Overseas Chinese Anti-Communist Pact which has since then been signed by 565 groups in 30 countries.[49]

Free China is small in size (about 14,000 square miles) and population, but exercises great moral influence and is of great importance to the free world. "It provides," reported the special study mission of 1955 of the House Foreign Affairs Committee, "to the 600 million Chinese on the mainland a symbol of hope and encouragement to resist their Communist conquerors. It serves as a center of loyalty to the 12 million overseas Chinese occupying such strategic positions in at least 8 countries in southeast Asia; without a Free Chinese Government to which to turn, these Chinese communities could hardly resist the pressure to become powerful fifth columns for Communist China".[50] In conclusion we may say in Free China today the government, the armed forces and the people are all pledged to carry on the fight against Soviet and Communist aggression to the bitter end and are convinced that an un-Chinese, un-democratic and tyrannical rule as the Peiping regime will ultimately collapse.

References

CHAPTER I

1. In its wider sense the name Tartars include the Mongols. Here it denotes a separate tribe.
2. It is also rendered Chenghiz Khan, Jenghis Khan or Genghis Khan by different writers.
3. Quoted in *Encyclopaedia Britainnica,* 14th edition, Vol. 12, p. 1000.
4. Quoted in *ibid,* Vol. 12, p. 1001.
5. See map in Wells, *The Outline of History,* Vol. 2, p. 704.
6. Well, *op. cit.,* Vol. 2, p. 708.
7. Pares, *History of Russia,* p. 53.
8. Quoted in Wells, *op. cit.,* Vol. 2, pp. 706, 707.
9. See map in Wells, *op. cit.,* Vol. 2., p. 709.
10. Pares, *op. cit.,* p. 76.
11. Vernadsky, *A History of Russia,* p. 47.
12. Pavlovsky, *Chinese Russian Relations,* pp. 1, 2.

CHAPTER II

1. Yakhontoff, *Russia and the Soviet Union in the Far East,* p. 5.
2. Ho Han-wen, *Chung O Wai Chiao Hsih* (History of Sino-Russian Diplomatic Relations), p. 59.
3. Yakhontoff, *op. cit.,* p. 7
4. See Dallin, *Th Rise of Russia in Asia,* pp. 1-6.
5. Yakhontoff, *op. cit.,* p. 18.

CHAPTER III

1. Ravenstein, *Russians on the Amur,* p. 19.
2. *Ibid,* p. 83.
3. Ho Chiu-tao, *Ping Ting Lo Chah Fang Lueh* (The Strategy of Conquering the Russians), Vol. 1, p. 1.
5. Ho Chiu-tao, *So Fang Pei Cheng,* (Studies on Northern Frontier), Vol. 36, p. 7a.
6. According to Yakhontoff's *Russia and the Soviet Union in the Far East* Peng Chun's forces consisted of 10,000 soldiers, 5,000 sailrs, 200 pieces of artillary and 100 transports (p. 11). This account seems to be an exaggeration.
7. See Kang-hsi's letter to the Tsar in Ravenstein, *op. cit.,* pp. 54-56.
8. Baddeley, *Russia, Mongolia, China,* Vol. 2, p. 134.
9. *Ibid.,* Vol. 2, pp. 167, 168.
10. See the letter in *ibid* Vol. 2, p. 196.
11. Liu, "Russo-Chinese Relations up to the Treaty of Nerchinsk" in *Chinese Social and Political Scienc Review,* Vol. 23, No. 4, p. 407.
12. For Sparthary's mission see Baddeley, *op. cit.,* Vol. 2, pp. 242-422.
13. See Chinese text in *Ping Ting Lo Cha Fang Lueh,* p. 27b. English translation is from Liu, *op. cit.,* pp. 413-414.

14. Quoted in Liu, *op. cit.,* p. 418.
15. *Ping Ting Lo Cha Fang Lueh,* pp. 28b, 29a.
16. See map in Liu, *op. cit.,* facing p. 422.
17. See explanation in Liu, *op. cit.,* pp. 438-439. English translation of the Manchu text can be found in Liu, *op. cit.,* p. 423; while that of the Russian text, in Yakhontoff, *op. cit.,* pp. 351, 352. Chinese text appears in *Chung O Wai Chiao Hsih,* pp. 74, 75.
17. See Lange, *Journal of Residence at the Court of Peking,* Vol. 2., p. 300.
19. Quoted in Pavlovsky, *op. cit., pp.* 31, 32.
20. See Chinese text in Ho Han-wen, *op. cit.,* pp. 79-81.
21. Quted in Pavlovsky, *op. cit.,* p. 29.
22. Cahen, *Histoire des Relations de la Russie avec la Chine sons Pierre le Grand* (1689-1730), p. 224.
23. See Chinese text in Ho Han-wen, *op. cit.,* pp. 83, 84.

CHAPTER IV

1. Quoted in Yakhontoff, *op. cit.,* pp 20, 21.
2. Vladimir (Pseudonym), *Russia on the Pacific and the Siberian Railway,* p. 185.
3. Ho Han-wen, *op. cit.,* p. 99.
4. See English version of the memorial of the Military Governor of Kirin to the Manch Government in Wu, *China and the Soviet Union,* pp. 63, 64.
5. Ho Han-wen, *op. cit.,* p. 103.
6. *Ibid,* pp. 104, 105.
7. See English version of the text in Yakhontoff, *op. cit.,* pp. 352, 353.
8. See English version of the text in *ibid. pp.* 353-357.
9. *Ibid,* p. 23.
10. The last two cities are in Sinkiang. See Chapter V.
11. Morse, *International Relations of the Chinese Empire,* Vol. 1, pp. 613, 614.
12. See English version of the text in Yakhontoff, *op. cit.,* pp. 357-365.

CHAPTER V

1. See the chapter on Hsi-yu in *Han-sou* (History of Han).
2. See text in *Treaties, Conventions, etc. Between China and Foreign States,* Vol. 1, pp. 70-75.
3. See text in *ibid* Vol. 1, pp. 127-143.
4. See Lansdell, *Chinese Central Asia,* Vol. 2, Ch. 31.
5. Boulger, *Life of Sir Halliday Macartney,* p. 334.
6. See Morse, *op. cit.,* Vol. 2, pp. 270-275.
7. Ching Han-tsai, *Tso Wen Hsiang Kung Tsai Hsi Pei* (Tso Chung-tang in the Northwest), pp. 110-111.
8. According to Kuropatkin, Yakub was killed in a fight with his treasurer, Sabir Akhoon. See Lansdell, *Chinese Central Asia,* Vol. 2, p. 62.
9. Tso Tsung-tang, *Tsou Kao* (Compiled Petitions to the Throne), Vol. 51, p. 18.
10. The most important pass was the Musart pass traversed by Emperor Chien-lung's military road from Ili to Aksu.
11. Hu Chiu-yuan, *O Ti Ching Hwa Shih Kang* (A Short History of Russian Aggression in China), p. 90.

12. A pound sterling was worth about four taels of silver at that time.
13. Quoted in Wu, *op. cit.*, pp.104-105.
14. Tso Tsung-tang, *op. cit.*, Vol. 55, p. 35.
15. During the early part of the reign of Emperor Kwang-hsu there were two Emperesses Dowager, Tse-an and Tse-hsi, who made important decision on policies together. Later Tse-an died and Tse-hsi ruled alone who became well known to foreigners.
16. Boulger, *op. cit.*, p. 347.
17. Quoted in Wu, *op. cit.*, pp. 108, 109.
18. See "Yamen's General Observation in Seven Points" in Boulger, *op cit.*, pp. 345, 346.
19. Sir Halliday Macartney was for thirty years councilor to the Chinese legation in London and had much to do with the kidnapping of Dr. Sun Yat-sen in 1896. Prosper Giquel had served as the director of the Foochow arsenal.
20. See Wu, *op. cit.*, pp. 112, 113.
21. See text in *Treaties, Conventions, etc. Between China and Foreign States,* Vol. 1, pp. 168-178.
22. Boulger, *op. cit.*, p. 351.
23. Tseng Chi-tse was known to foreigners as Marquis Tseng, a title he inherited from his father.
24. Morse, *op. cit.*, Vol. 2, p. 338.
25. See Curzon, *Russia in Central Asia,* pp. 343-370.

CHAPTER VI

1. Manchuria was formerly called by the Chinese "Three Eastern Provinces" because these three provinces were all situated northeast of Shanhaikwan.
2. Quoted in Dallin, *op. cit.*, pp. 24, 25.
3. See text in *Treaties, Conventions, etc., Between China and Foreign States,* Vol. 2, pp. 588, 589.
4. See Wang Yun-shen, *Liu Shih Nien Lai Chung Kuo Yu Jih Pen* (China and Japan in Sixty Years), Vol. 1, Ch. 10.
5. See the letter from the King, record of conversation between Li Hung-chang and Hsu Hsiang-yu and the reply of Li Hung-chang to the King in *Ching Chi Wai Chiao Hsih Liao* (Documents Concerning Foreign Relations During the Reign of Kuang-hsu and Hsuan-Tung) Vol. 68, pp. 29-35.
6. The title signifies that the members of this society were opposed to westernization or modernization of Korea.
7. *Foreign Relations of the United States,* 1894, Appendix I, p. 30.
8. See Ho Han-wen, *op. cit.*, pp. 142, 143.
9. *Ching Kwang Hsu Tsao Chung Jih Chiao Hse Hsih Liao* (Documents Concerning Sino-Japanese Negotiations during the Reign of Kwang-hsu), Vol. 13, pp. 20-24 and Vol. 14, p. 14.
10. *Ibid,* Vol. 13, p. 31 and Vol. 14, pp. 28-30.
11. See Morse, *op. cit.*, Vol. 3, pp. 29, 30.
12. See *Foreign Relations of the UUnited States,* 1894, p. 81.
13. See text in *Treaties, Convention, etc. Between China and Foreign States,* Vol. 2, pp. 590-596.
14. See Witte, *The Memoirs of Count Witte,* p. 84.
15. The loan was raised by six French and four Russian banks but was guaranteed by the Russian Government. See Morse, *op. cit.*, Vol. 3, p. 53.

16. *Ching Chih Wai Chiao Hsih Liao* , Vol. 116, p. 35.
17. See Li's telegram to the Tsungli Yamen on May 8, in *ibid.*, Vol. 121, pp. 5, 6.
18. See Chinese text in *Chung Wai Tiao Yueh Hui Pien* (Collection of Treaties and Agreements Between China and Foreign States), Vol. 7, p. 356.
19. See Morse, *op. cit.*, Vol. 3, p. 104.
20. See text in *Kwang Hsu Tiao Yueh* (Treaties and Agreements during the Reign of Kwang-hsu, No. 45.
21. See text of these agreements in *Tung Ya Kwan Si Teh Tsung Tiao Yueh Hui Chuan* (Collection of Special Treaties Concerning Eastern Asian Relations).
22. See German Foreign Office, *Die Grosse Politik der Europaischen Kabinette,* 14 Band, I. S. 58.
23. See text in *Treaties, Conventions, etc, Between China and Foreign States,* Vol. 2, pp. 208-214.
24. See *Ching Chi Wai Chiao Hsih Liao,* Vol. 119, p. 18.
25. See text of two conventions in *Treaties, Conventions, etc. Between China and Foreign States,* Vol. 1, pp. 219-232.
26. See text in *ibid,* Vol. 1, pp. 233-238.
27. Quoted in *North-China Herald,* March 7, 1898.
28. See text in *Treaties, Conventions, etc., Between China and Foreign States,* Vol. 1, pp. 946-949.
29. See text of the two conventions in *ibid,* Vol. 1, pp. 539-542.
30. Rockhill, *Treaties and Conventions with or Concerning China and Korea,* p. 173.
31. *Ibid,* pp. 174, 175.
32. *Ibid,* pp. 178, 179.
33. *Ibid,* pp. 181, 182.
34. *Ibid,* pp. 183, 184.
35. Italy demanded in February 1899 the lease of Sanmenwan in Chekiang but was rejected by the Manchu Government.
36. See correspondence in *Foreign Relations of the United States,* 1899, pp. 128-142.
37. *Ibid,* p. 142.
38. The Empress Dowager had strong personal ill-feeling against foreigners because she was opposed to reform and would have dethroned or even killed Emperor Kwang-hsu in 1898 if not for the sympathy of the foreign envoys in Peking towards the Emperor for his intended reform.
39. See *Foreign Relations of the United States,* 1900, pp. 304, 316, 317, 324, 328, 344, 345 and 359.
40. See *China,* No. 5, 1900.
41. Belgium, Netherlands and Spain besides the eight powers which sent troops to China.
42. Songiyama, a secretary in the Japanese legation at Peking, was murdered by a mob.
43. See text in *Treaties, Conventions, etc. Between China and Foreign States,* Vol. 1, pp. 306-313.
44. See Fraser, *The Real Siberia,* pp. 177-180.
45. See Witte, *op, cit,* pp. 107-108.
46. See Chow Mien's letter to Li Hung-chang, *China,* No. 6, 1901, pp. 72, 73.

47. 48. See See Yang Yu's telegram to Li Hung-chang in the archives of the Waichiaopu.

49. Yang Yu fell on the ground in front of the legation on March 21 when coming back from the Foreign Office and was seriously wounded. He died in Moscow.

50. See Chinese translation in the archives of the Waichiaopu.

51. See text in *Foreign Relations of the United States,* 1902, p. 514.

52. See text in *Treaties, Conventions, etc. Between China and Foreign States,* Vol. 1, pp. 239-250.

53. See *Foreign Relations of the United States,* 1903, pp. 53-56.

54. See China, No. 2, 1904, pp. 86, 87.

55. See text in *Tung Ya Kwan Si Teh Tsung Tiao Yueh Hui Chuan,* p. 934.

56. See text in *Foreign Relations of the United States,* 1905, p. 814.

57. See text of the two agreements in *Traties, Conventions, etc Between China and Foreign States,* Vol. 2, pp. 636-641.

58. See Witte, *op, cit,* pp. 152-159.

59. See text of the two agreements in Yakhontoff, *op. cit.,* pp. 376-378.

60. See Kennan, *E. H. Harriman: A Biography,* Vol. 2, p. 14.

61. See *Foreign Relations of the United States,* 1910, pp. 249 et seq.

62. See Dallin, *op. cit.,* pp. 106, 107.

64. See the telegram to various envoys quoted in Wang Yun-sen, *op. cit., Vol.* 5, p. 349.

65. See text in *Treaties, Conventions, etc. Between China and Foreign States,* Vol. 1, pp. 266-273.

66. See text in Ho Han-wen, *op. cit.,* pp. 267, 268.

CHAPTER VII

1. See Dillon, "The Secession of Mongolia from China" in *Contemporary Review,* April 1912, pp. 580, 581.

2. Quoted in *Dallin, op. cit.,* p. 103.

3. Quoted in *ibid,* p. 125.

4. See Chen Chung-tsu, *Wai Meng Ku Chin Hsih Hsih* (Recent History of Outer Mongolia), p. 7.

5. See *China Year Book,* 1919, p. 587.

6. Meaning "Great Venerable Sacred Reincarnated Ruler."

7. Dillon, "Chinese Pale of Settlement" in *English Review,* Vol. 13, p. 291.

8. Under the Manchu rule khanates had been renamed pu or tribes.

9. See Wei Kang, "O Meng Chiao Hseh Hsih Mo" (Russian-Mongolian Negotiations in *Yung Yen Magazine,* Vol. 1, No. 1, pp. 10, 11.

10. Quoted in Weigh, *Russo-Chinese Diplomacy,* pp. 166-167.

11. Quoted in *ibid,* p. 168.

12. See translation of the telegrams in *ibid,* pp. 168-169.

13. Chinese Ministry for Foreign Affairs since 1912.

14. See Wei Kang, *op. cit.,* pp. 11, 12.

15. Siebert, *Entente Diplomacy and the World,* p. 35.

16. See Chen Chung-tsu, *op. cit.,* p. 29.

17. See Siebert, *op. cit.,* pp. 25, 39, 42.

18. See text in Yakhontoff, *op. cit.,* p. 379.

19. See text of the agreement and protocol in MacMurray, *op. cit.,* Vol. 2, pp. 992-996.

20. See telegram from Liu Chin-jen to the Waichiaopu quoted in *China Times,* November 14, 1912.
21. See Pavlovsky, *op. cit.,* p. 54
22. See Hu Chiu-yuan, *op. cit.,* pp. 150, 151.
23. See text in Chang Chung-fo, *Chung Hua Min Kuo Wai Chiao Hsih* (Diplomatic History of the Republic of China), Vol. 1, pp. 134, 135.
24. See text of the declaration and notes in MacMurray, *op. cit.,* Vol. 2, pp. 1066, 1067.
25. See Weigh, *op. cit.,* p. 180 and Pavlovsky, *op. cit.,* p. 58
26. Sazonov's letter to Miller, Russian consul-general in Urga on January 30, 1914, quoted in Pavlovsky, *op. cit.,* pp. 59, 60.
27. See text in MacMurray, *op. cit.,* Vol. 2, pp. 1239-1243. See also Pi Kuei-fang, *Wai Meng Chiao She Hsih Mo Chi* (An Account of Negotiations Concerning Outer Mongolia).
28. See text in MacMurray, *op. cit.,* Vol. 2, pp. 1243-1244.
29. See Chinese text in Ho Han-wen, *op. cit.,* p. 293. English text in MacMurray, *op. cit.,* pp. 1247-1249, is somewhat different.
30. Dallin, *op. cit.,* p. 141.
31. Khoshuns were Mongolian administrative units.
32. Dallin, *op. cit.,* p. 142.
33. *Ibid,* p. 142.
34. Pavlovsky, *op. cit.,* p. 62.
35. See text in Ho Han-wen, *op. cit.,* pp. 281, 282.
36. See text in MacMurray, *op. cit.,* Vol. 2, pp. 1178-1179.
37. See text of the agreements in MacMurray, *op. cit.,* Vol. 2, pp. 1035, 1039, 1179, 1180.

CHAPTER VIII

1. See text in MacMurray, *op. cit.,* Vol. 2, pp. 1327, 1328.
2. See text in Yakhontoff, *op. cit.,* pp. 380, 381.
3. See Morse and MacNair, *Far Eastern International Relations,* pp. 588, 589.
4. See Dallin, *op. cit.,* p. 153.
5. Vernadsky, *A History of Russia,* p. 258.
6. See text of the agreements and supplement in MacMurray, *op. cit.,* Vol. 2, pp. 1411-1414.
7. Morse and MacNair, *op. cit.,* p. 672.
8. See text of the mandate in Ho Han-wen, *op. cit.,* p. 312.
9. See *China Year Book,* 1923, p. 618.
10. See Chinese text in Ho Han-wen, *op. cit.,* pp. 306-308.
11. See text in Yakhontoff, *op. cit.,* pp. 352, 353,
12. Later, under the Soviet Government, it was extended to Alma Ata and Chemkent.
13. See text in *Treaties and Agreement With and Concerning China,* 1919-1929, pp. 23-25.
14. Quoted in Wu, *op. cit.,* p. 133.
15. See Pasvolsky, "Present Status of Mongolia" in *Baltimore Sun,* November 28, 1921.
16. See Chu, *Tsui Chin Hse Nien Chung O Tse Chiao Hse* (The Last ten years in Sino-Russian Relations), p. 159.

17. See text of the mandate in Chang Chung-fo, *op. cit.*, pp. 497-499. Five nations refer to Chinese, Manchurians, Mongolians, Mohammedans and Tibetans.

18. Quoted in Pavlovsky, *op. cit.*, p. 80.

19. See *Letters Captured from Baron Ungern* published by the Special Delegation of the Far Eastern Republic to the United States during the Washington Conference. See also Pavlovsky, *op. cit.*, pp. 76-81.

20. See Tan, *Political Status of Mongolia*, pp. 65, 66. See also Pasvolsky, *Russia in the Far East*, p. 117.

21. See the letter from the Mongolian Ministry of Internal Affairs to the Provisional Revolutionary Government published at Chita on September 1 in *Nation* October 26, 1921, p. 486.

22. Pasvolsky, *op. cit.*, p. 176.

23. *Ibid*, pp. 177-179.

24. See text in *Treaties and Agreements with and Concerning China*, 1919-1929, pp. 53-55.

CHAPTER IX

1. See *Izvestiya*, No. 138 (402) July 5, 1918, p. 7.

2. *China Year Book*, 1924, p. 868. English translation of the Russian text in *Russian and the Soviet Union in the Far East* is somewhat different in language and without the clause concerning the Chinese Eastern Railway.

3. Dennis, *Foreign Policies of Soviet Russia*, p. 316.

4. See text in *China Year Book*, 1924, pp. 870-872.

5. See text in Dallin, *op. cit.*, p. 192.

6. *China Year Book*, 1924, p. 859.

7. *North China Herald*, November 14, 1922.

8. See *China Year Book*, 1924, pp. 873-876.

9. See Wu, *op. cit.*, pp. 148-151.

10. See text of the agreements and declarations in Yakhontoff, *op. cit.* pp. 387-398.

11. See text in *ibid*, pp. 398-404.

CHAPTER X

1. See under "Russia," *Encyclopaedia Britannica*, 14th Edition, Vol. 19, p. 742.

2. See Voitinsky's account of this meeting in *Pravda*, March 15, 1925.

3. Quoted in Creel, *Russia's Race for Asia*, p. 18.

4. Payne, *Mao Tse-tung*, p. 72.

5. See Chen Pan-tsu (Chen Tan-chiu), "Reminiscences of the First Congress of the Communist Party of China" in *Communist International*, October, 1936. pp. 1361-1366. The spelling of the names was different because they were not translated by Chen according to Mandarin pronunciation.

6. *Ibid*, p. 1363.

7. *Ibid*, p. 1364.

8. *The First Congress of the Toilers of the Far East*, published by the Comintern (Petrograd, 1922), p. 1.

9. *Ibid*, Second Session, pp. 21-39.

10. See Kisseleff, *The China Illustrated Review*, III, No. 369, January 21, 1928.

11. Quoted in North, *Moscow and Chinese Communists,* p. 63.

12. See Hatano, "Chung Kuo Kung Tsan Tang Hsih" (History of the Chinese Communist Patry) in *Ajia Mondai Koza,* Vol. 2, p. 31.

13. Quoted in Wan, *The Rise of Communism in China,* p. 3.

14. *China Year Book,* 1924, p. 863.

15. See Dr. Sun's letter of September 17, 1923 to Karakhan in the Louis Fischer file of Sun-Karakhan correspondence.

16. See Karakhan's letter in the same file.

17. Quoted in Wan, *op. cit.,* p. 4.

18. See English translation of the platform in Hsu, *Sun Yat-sen, His Political and Social Ideals,* pp. 134-139.

19. See *San Min Chu I* translated by Price, p. 364.

20. See English translation of Dr. Sun's first lecture on *Min-sheng-chu-i* in Hsu, *op. cit.,* pp. 389-415.

21. Told to the author by Mr. Tsou Lu who was then President of Kwangtung Normal College

22, 23. This inside story, told to the author by Mr. Chen Li-fu, has never been published before.

24. See Voitinsky, "The Situation in China and the Plans of the Imperialists," *International Press Correspondence,* May 6, 1926, pp. 600, 601.

25-27. See Tsou Lu, *Chung Kuo Kuo Min Tang Hsih Lueh* (A Short History of the Kuomintang), pp. 159, 160.

CHAPTER XI

1. *International Press Correspondence,* December 1, 1926, p. 1429.

2. *Ibid,* p. 1430.

3. Quoted in North, *op. cit.,* p. 92.

4. See text in *International Press Correspondence,* April 14, 1927, p. 493.

5. The author, as member of the provincial executive committee and concurrently Commissioner of Education in the provincial government, was arrested by Communist students on the street and was detained with other Kuomintang members. A so-called people's court sentenced them to death in May but fortunately they all escaped.

6. Chinese police and soldiers were forbidden to enter the Legation Quarter by the Protocol of 1901.

7. Oudendyk, *Ways and By-ways of Diplomacy,* p. 349.

8. See *Su Lien Yin Mou Wen Chen Hui Pien* (Collection of Documents on the Soviet Conspiracy), Peking, 1928. An English translation of this work has been made by the East Asian Institute of Columbia University; it has been published under the title *Documents on Communism, Nationalism, and Soviet Advisers in China, 1918-1927*

9. See "Resolution of the Chinese Question," *International Press Correspondence,* June 16, 1927.

10. This sentence appears in a version of the telegram recorded in Chen Tuhsiu's *Letter to the Comrades* but not in Stalin's book.

11. Stalin, *Marxism and the National and Colonial Question,* p. 249.

12. Tang, *Suppressing Communist Banditry in China,* p. 29. Tang was a confidant of Wang Ching-wei.

13. English translation of the resolution in Yakhontoff, *op. cit.,* pp. 410-417.

14. *International Press Correspondence,* October 6, 1927, p. 1236.

15. See the letter in *A Documentary History of Chinese Communism,* pp. 102-118.

16. *The Autobiography of Mao Tse-tung* (as told to Edgar Snow), p. 35.

17. *Ibid,* p. 37.

18. *Report of the 15th Congress of the Communist Party of the Soviet Union,* pp. 291-295.

19. Trotsky, *Problems of the Chinese Revolution,* pp. 291, 292.

20. See Li Ang, *Hung Se Wu Tai* (The Red Stage), Ch. 4.

21. See "Resolution on the Chinese Question," *International Press Correspondence,* March 15, 1928, pp. 321, 322.

CHAPTER XII

1. Dallin, *op. cit.,* p. 254.

2. See Article V and IX of the Agreement in Yakhontoff, *op. cit.,* p. 397.

3. See Far Eastern Information Bureau, *Documents with Reference to the Sino-Russian Dispute,* 1929.

4. Quoted in Wu, *op. cit.,* pp. 200, 201.

5. See text in *China Year Book,* 1929-1930, p. 1221

6. See text in Ho Han-wen, *op. cit.,* pp. 402-404.

7. Quoted in Dallin, *op. cit,* p 265.

8. This article provided that the two governments pledged themselves not to engage in propaganda directed against the political and social systems of either contracting party.

See Ho Han-wen, *op. cit.,* pp. 406-408.

10. Quoted in Dallin, *op. cit.,* p 262.

11. For the details of these engagements see Ho Han-wen, *op. cit.,* pp. 408-412.

12. See Department of State, *Foreign Relations of the United States,* 1929, Vol. 2, pp. 404-406.

13. See Dallin, *op. cit.,* p. 269.

14 See text in Ho Han-wen, *op. cit.,* pp. 414, 415.

CHAPTER XIII

1. Quoted in Dallin: *op. cit.,* p. 194.

2. Quoted in *ibid,* p. 193.

3. According to Beloff, Bodo and fifteen other officials were shot at that time but there is not enough evidence to support this statement. Other sources simply say Bodo was ousted from power. See Beloff's *The Foreign Policy of Soviet Russia.* Vol. I, p. 242.

4. *Ibid.* p. 244.

5. See text of the constitution in *British and Foreign State Papers,* Vol. CXXXIV, 1931 pp. 1224-1232.

6. *China Year Book,* 1925, p. 428.

7. See Wu: *op. cit.,* pp. 168, 169; and Ho Han-wen: *op. cit.,* pp. 300, 301

8. Quoted in Beloff; *op. cit.,* Vol. I, p. 243.

9. Quoted in Beloff; *op. cit.,* Vol. I, p. 243.

10. Quoted in *ibid,* p. 246.

11. Quoted in *Tikki Okean* (1936) No. 3, p. 77

12. Stalin, Molotov and others, *The Soviet Union and the Cause of Peace,* p. 33.

13. See text in *China Year Book* 1936, p. 21.
14. See text of the notes in *Ibid,* pp. 21-23.
15. See Dallin: *Soviet Russia and the Far East,* p. 81.

CHAPTER XIV

1. Quoted in Dallin: *Soviet Russia and the Far East,* p. 91
2. See the story in Wu: *Turkistan Tumult,* Ch. 3.
3. See text of the agreement and annexes in Wu: *China and the Soviet Union,* pp. 376-379.
4. See the story in *Turkistan Tumult,* Ch. 8.
5. *Ibid,* p. 169.
6. See Hsu Chung-hao: *Hsin Chiang Chih Lueh* (General Description of Sinkiang), pp. 266-272.
7. Barmine: *One Who Survived,* p. 231.
8. See Wu: *China and the Soviet Union,* pp. 257, 258.
9. See the Waichiaopu: *Su Lien Tui Sinkiang Tse Ching Chih Ching Lueh* (The Economic Aggression of the Soviet Union in Sinkiang), Ch. 4.
10. Quoted in Beloff: *op. cit.* Vol. I, pp. 237, 238.
11. Hedin: *The Silk Road,* p. 166. Tupan was Sheng's official title. Apresoff was the Soviet consul-general.
12. Barmine: *op. cit.* pp. 231, 232.
13. *Moslem World,* 1936, p. 415.
14. See *The Times,* March 25, 1939.
15. See *ibid,* June 1, 1939.
16. See Novins, *Gateway to Asia: Sinkiang,* pp. 58, 74.
17. See English version of Sheng's letter to Generalissimo Chiang Kai-shek in the Waichiaopu, *op. cit.* pp. 59-69.
18. See English text of the agreement in *ibid.* pp. 45-53.
19. See Sheng's letter in *ibid,* pp. 59-69.
20. See *ibid,* Ch. 6.
21. See *New York Times,* August 30, 1944.
22. See *New York Herald Tribune,* July 31, 1945.

CHAPTER XV

1. Peking was renamed Peiping after the National Revolutionary Army occupied it in June 1928.
2. See text of the resolutions and notes in *China Year Book,* 1931-32, pp. 614, 617, 621, 622.
3. Quoted in Pratt: *A History of United States Foreign Policy,* pp. 582, 583.
4. See *Report of the Commission of Inquiry,* Series of League Publications: VII, Political, 1932, VII 12.
5. Quoted in Wu: *China and the Soviet Union,* pp. 217, 218.
6. There was no truth in the information that China turned down an Soviet offer of a non-aggression pact or even a mutual defense pact in 1933, as reprted in Edgar Snow's *Battle for Asia,* P. 296.
7. Quoted in Dallin: *Soviet Russia and the Far East,* footnote, p. 3.
8. See Potiemkine and others: *Histoire de la Diplomatie,* Vol. III, pp. 442, 443.

9. See *Soviet Union Review,* March 1932, p. 56 and February 1933, pp. 46, 47.
10. See text in Archives of the Waichiaopu, quoted in Wu: *op. cit.* pp. 218, 219.
11. Quoted in Dallin: *op. cit.,* p. 11.
12. *Ibid.,* p 14.
13. *Shih Shih Yu Pao* (Current Affairs Monthly) Vol. XI, No. 5, p. 305.
14. See Article 9 of the agreement in *Treaties and Agreements with and Concerning China, 1919-1929,* p. 136.
15. See Wu: *op. cit.,* p. 239.
16. *Soviet Union Review,* June 1933, p. 135.
17. See C. C. Wang: "The Sale of the Chinese Eastern Railway," in *Foreign Affairs,* October 1933, p. 65.
18. See Dallin: *op. cit.,* p. 19, footnote 15.
19. See *Contemporary Japan,* June 1935, pp. 142-157.
20. See text in *China Year Book,* 1935, p. 139.
21. Quoted in Dallins *op. cit.* p. 23.
22. Hidaka: *Manchukuo-Soviet Border Issues,* p. 260
23. Chen's mission was kept a top-secret but the author went to Europe on the same steamer and as Chinese ambassador in Berlin served as a liaison between Chen and the Generalissimo.

CHAPTER XVI

1. See Li Ang, *op. cit.,* Ch. 6.
2. See *Chung Kuo Kung Chan Tang Ti Liu Tzu Tai Piao Ta Hui Chueh I An* (Resolutions of the Sixth National Congress of the Chinese Communist Party).
3. See *A Documentary History of Chinese Communism,* p. 132.
4. *Thesis and Resolutions of the VI World Congress of the Communist International,* p. 1672.
5. See text in Peabody, *The Chinese Communist Movement,* (in U.S. Senate McCarran Hearings, Part 7A, App. II) pp. 2406-2412.
6. *A Documentary History,* pp. 34, 35.
7. Li Ang, *op. cit.,* p. 139.
8. See Wan, *op. cit.,* p. 21.
9. See Chang Kuo-tao, "Mao—A New Portrait by an Old Colleague" in *New York Times Magazine,* August 2, 1953, p. 46.
10. See Snow, *Red Star Over China,* p. 159.
11. The author served as a member of the Committee on Party and Political Affairs in the Generalissimo's headquarters and had personal experience in the third campaign.
12. See Li Ang, *op. cit.,* pp. 155-157.
13. Wan, *op. cit,* p. 29.
14. A kind of civilian organization; ten families were organized into a chia, and ten chias into a pao, to help police suppress subversive Communist activities.
15. See North, *op. cit.,* p. 166.
16. *International Press Correspondence,* December 21, 1935, p. 1729.
17. *Ibid,* December 2, 1935, p. 972.
18. *Ibid,* September 19, 1935, p. 1181.
19. Snow, *op. cit.,* p. 192.

20. The Northwestern Army was under the command of Yang Hu-cheng.

21. See the story of the Sian incident in Mme. Chaign Kai-shek, *Sian, A Coup D'Etat, and* Snow, *op. cit.*, pp. 395-429.

22. Quoted in Dallin, *Soviet Russia and the Far East,* p. 69.

23. Department of State, *U.S. Relations with China,* p. 72.

24. Chang Hsueh-liang now lives quietly in a mountain resort in Hsinchuh, Taiwan.

25. Se *China Weekly Review,* February 27, 1937, pp. 433-436.

26. *China Year Book,* 1938, p. 532.

27. Chen Shao-yu, "The Only Road for the Salvation of the Chinese People," *Bolshevik,* April 15, 1937, pp. 69-81.

28. Quoted in Dallin, *op. cit.*, p. 133.

CHAPTER XVII

1. See *China Weekly Review*, January 2, 1937, p. 153.

2. See text of the statement in *China Year Book* 1938, pp. 353-355.

3. See Tsou Lu, *op. cit.*, p. 197.

4. See text of the reports in *China Year Book* 1938, pp. 374, 375.

5. For the story of the conference see Department of State conference series 37, *The Conference of Brussels.*

6. See Abend, *My Life in China*, pp. 237-239.

7. See text of the treaty in Wu, *op. cit.*, pp. 394, 395.

8. League of Nations, *Official Journal*, Special Supplement, No. 177, p. 31.

9. *The Conference of Brussels*, p. 34.

10. From the author's diary on July 14, 1937.

11. When Dr. Sun Fo was on his way back to China the author spent four days with him at Prague. This account is from the author's diary at that time (February 28-March 4, 1938).

12. *Bulletin of International News*, April 23, 1938, p. 381.

13. See *Pravda*, August 8, 1938.

14. The *Times*, June 1, 1939.

15. *Ibid.*, October 4, 1939.

16. See Feis, *The Road to Pearl Harbor*, pp. 114, 120.

17. See *Tokyo Gazette*, November 1940, pp. 193-194.

18. Quoted in Dallin, *Soviet Russia and the Far East*, p. 156.

19. Department of State, *Nazi-Soviet Relations, 1939-1941*, p. 213.

20. *Ibid.*, p. 249.

21. *Ibid.*, p. 257.

22. *Ibid.*, pp. 258, 259.

23. Office of the United States, Chief of Counsel for Prosecution of Axis Criminality, *Nazi Conspiracy and Aggression*, Vol. IV, p. 520.

24. See text of the treaty and statement in *New York Times*, April 14, 1941.

25. See Dallin, *op. cit.*, pp. 164, 165.

26. *China Weekly Review*, April 19, 1941, p. 214.

27. *Bulletin of International News*, May 3, 1941, p. 587.

28. *Ibid.*, June 28, 1941, p. 860.

29. *New York Times*, April 1, 1944.

30. Grew, *Ten Years in Japan*, p. 400.

31. Hull, *Memoirs of Cordell Hull*, Vol. 2, p. 1070.

32. *Ibid.*, Vol. 2, p. 1083. For the Japanese-American negotiations see *Ibid.*, Vol. 2, pp. 71, 77, 78 and 79.

CHAPTER XVIII

1. See text in *A Documentary History of Chinese Communism*, pp. 242-245.
2. See text in *Ibid.*, pp. 245-247.
3. The designation was later changed to the Eighteenth Group Army but it remained to be known as the Eighth Route Army.
4. Quoted in Dallin, *Soviet Russia and the Far East*, p. 139.
5. Quoted in Wan, *op. cit.*, pp. 48, 49.
6. *Chung Kuo Kung Chan Tang Wen Ti Wen Chien* (Documents on the Problem of the Chinese Communist Party), presented to the People's Political Council in March 1941 and published by the Supreme National Defense Council in 1944.
7. Quoted in Wan, *op. cit.*, p. 57.
8. White and Jacoby, *Thunder Out of China*, pp. 209, 210.
9. Peabody, *The Chinese Communist Movement* (published as United States Senate, McCarran Hearings, Part 7A, App. II), p. 2333.
10. Quoted in Wan, *op. cit.*, p. 56.
11. For a detailed account of Communist clashes with government forces see Li Chiu-sze, *Chung Kuo Kung Chan Tang Yu Kang Chan Chun Hsih* (The Chinese Communist Party and Operations of the War of Resistance).
12. Told to the author by Shao Lih-tsu, who was then Chinese ambassador at Moscow.
13. Quoted in Wan, *op. cit.*, p. 60.
14. *Ibid.*, p. 61.
15. Peabody, *op. cit.*, p. 2355.
16. *Laws and Regulations of the Shensi-Kansu-Ninghsia Border Region* (n.p., n.d.), p. 7.
17. *Ibid.*

18, 19. See the essays in *Mao Tse-tung Hsuan Chi* (Selected Works of Mao Tse-tung).

20. The legendary first emperor of the Chinese nation.
21. See Li Ang, *op. cit.*, pp. 177-181.
22. Quoted in Dallin, *op. cit.*, p. 141.
23. See extract in English in *A Documentary History of Chinese Communism*, pp. 263-275.
24. See text of the lecture in *ibid.*, pp. 375-392.
25. *Ibid.*, p. 377.
26. See text of the reports in *Chi Ta Wen Hsien* (Documents of the Seventh National Congress of the Chinese Communist Party).
27. Wang Ching-wei deserted the National Government in December 1938 and established a puppet regime in Nanking in March 1940.
28. *Ibid.*, Chu's report, *On Battlefields in the Liberated Areas*, p. 16.
29. See White and Jacoby, *op. cit.*, p. 210.
30. See text in *A Documentary History of Chinese Communism*, pp. 422-439.
31. *Ibid.*, pp. 422, 423.

CHAPTER XIX

1. See *U.S. Relations with China*, p. 1044.
2. *Ibid.*, p. 26.

3. *Ibid.*, p. 1044.
4. See Hull, *Memoirs of Cordell Hull*, Vol. II, pp. 1583-1587.
5. See text in *New York Times*, January 3, 1942.
6. See *U.S. Relations with China*, pp. 32, 33.
7. See text in *Documents on American Foreign Relations*, Vol. V, pp. 485-501.
8. See text in *Ibid.*, Vol. VI, p. 229.
9. See text in *New York Times*, December 1, 1943.
10. See, for example, "An Appraisal of Conditions in China by Raymond Gram Swing", a portion of a broadcast on August 11, 1943, as reproduced in *Amerasia*, Vol. VII, No. 9, pp. 281-284.
11. Lattimore, *Solution in Asia*, pp. 108, 109.
12. Forman, *Report from Red China*, pp. 176, 177.
13. *Ibid.*, pp. 179, 180.
14. Stein, *The Challenge of Red China*, p. 355.
15. See Chapter XXIII.
16. *New York Times*, December 5, 1945.
17. Lin, *The Vigil of a Nation*, p. 227.
18. Judd, *What is the Truth About China?* reprinted from his speech in the House, pp. 11, 12.
19. In the Border Region the illiterate constituted at least 85 per cent of the people.
20. Judd, *op. cit.*, p. 14.
21. Quoted in Dallin, *op. cit.*, p. 225.
22. Peabody, *op. cit.*, p. 2305.
23. Utley, *The China Story*, pp. 149, 150.
24. *Ibid.*, p. 155.
25. See Feis, *The China Tangle*, p. 16. Burma Road is the highway connecting Kunming and Ledo via Burma, later renamed Stilwell Road.
26. See Utley, *op. cit.*, pp. 105-109.
27. Undated notes in *The Stilwell Papers*, pp. 316, 317.
28. See text of the Generalissimo's speech in *U.S. Relations with China*, p. 530.
29. See text in *Ibid.*, p. 533.
30. See reports to the People's Political Council by Chang Chih-chung and Lin Tsu-han, September 15, 1944 in *U.S. Relations with China*, pp. 531-548.
31. See summary notes of the conversations by Vincent in *U.S. Relations with China*, pp. 549-560.
32. See text in *New York Times*, January 19, 1950.
33. Quoted in Judd, *op. cit.*, p. 12.
34. *U.S. Relations with China*, p. 72.
35. See Feis, *op. cit.*, p. 189.
36. The author was a member of the Standing Committee of the Central Supervisory Committee and was present at the meeting. The account here is from his diary on that day.
37. See text of the aide-memoire in the *Joint Committee on Military Situation in the Far East*, p. 2874 et seq.
38. Feis, *op. cit.*, p. 198.
39. See the reports and editorial in the *New York Times*, October 31, and November 1, 1944.
40. *U.S. Relations with China*, p. 566.
41. *Ibid.*, p. 573.

42. *Ibid.*, p. 574.

43. See Hurley's letter of resignation to President Truman in *U.S. Relations with China*, pp. 581-584.

44. Quoted in Feis, *op. cit.*, p. 269.

45. See text of Hurley's report in *U.S. Relations with China*, pp. 94-96, Kennan's telegram, pp. 96, 97, and Harriman's comment on the report, pp. 97, 98.

46. See Peabody, *op. cit.*, pp. 2378, 2379.

47. The league was formed by several small political organizations and was pro-Communist.

48. The official title of the head of China was the Chairman of the National Government, but it was generally referred to as the president.

49. See *U.S. Relations with China*, pp. 105-107.

50. *Ibid.*, pp. 107-110.

CHAPTER XX

1. Quoted in Feis, *op. cit.*, p. 8.

2. Hull, *op. cit.*, Vol. II, p. 1112.

3. *Ibid.*, p. 1309.

4. See *U.S. Relations with China*, p. 113, footnote 1.

5. Sherwood, *Roosevelt and Hopkins; an Intimate History*, pp. 791, 792.

6. Deane, *The Strange Alliance*, pp. 248, 249.

7. See Feis, *op. cit.*, pp. 232, 233.

8. *Ibid.*, p. 235, footnote 10.

9. Sherwood, *op. cit.*, p. 867.

10. See Feis, *op. cit.*, pp. 242, 243.

11. *Ibid.*, pp. 244-248.

12. *U.S. Relations with China*, pp. 113, 114.

13. *Rendezvous with Destiny*, p. 193.

14. Chamberlin, *America's Second Crusade*, p. 220.

15. Sherwood, *op. cit.*, p. 868. Sherwood referred to Roosevelt as saying "the blame lay more with the Comintern and the Kuomintang . . .". It may be assumed that the word "Comintern" is an error.

16. *Ibid.*, p. 870.

17. See Hurley testimony, *Joint Committee on Military Situation in the Far East*, pp. 2883-2888.

18. See Feis, *op. cit.*, pp. 314, 315.

19. Byrnes, *Sepaking Frankly*, p. 208.

20. *Ibid.*, p. 209.

21. Hillman, *Mr. President*, p. 123.

22. See text in *Documents on American Foreign Relations*, Vol. VIII, pp. 105, 106.

23. See Feis, *op. cit.*, p. 330.

24. Wang's verbal report to the joint session of the Central Executive Committee of the Kuomintang and the Supreme National Defense Council on August 24, 1945 as recorded in the author's diary.

25. See English texts of the treaty, agreements and notes in *U.S. Relations with China*, pp. 585-596. The minutes of the meeting can be found in Wu, *op. cit.*, pp. 413, 414.

26. As recorded in the author's diary on August 24, 1945.

27. Chinese Delegation to the United Nations, *China Presents Her Case to the*

United Nations, pp. 15, 16.

28. See Feis, *op. cit.*, p. 382, footnote 13.

29. Chinese Delegation to the United Nations, *op. cit.*, p. 17.

30. Kan's verbal report at the meeting of the Supreme National Defense Council, on October 8, 1945, as recorded in the author's diary.

31. Manchuria was divided into nine provinces by the National Government after the war instead of three as before.

32. See text in R11A, *United Nations Documents* (1946), pp. 263, 264.

33. Department of State, *Bulletin*, 1946, p. 1154.

34. See *Izvestiya*, January 29, 1947.

35. See Department of State release, March 5, 1946.

36. See Marguerite Higgins' article in *New York Herald Tribune*, October 16, 1951.

37. See Chinese Delegation to the United Nations, *op. cit.*, pp. 26-28.

38. *Ibid.*, p. 30.

39. See *United Press* despatch, March 10, 1948.

40. *New York Times*, April 3, 1944.

41. For the story in Sinkiang see Chinese Delegation to the United Nations, *op. cit.*, pp. 30-32; Dallin, *op. cit.*, pp. 361-368; Beloff, *Soviet Policy in the Far East 1944-1951*, pp. 97-101.

CHAPTER XXI

1. At the request of General Hurley the National Government had appointed Tung Pi-wu one of the Chinese delegates to the San Francisco Conference.

2. Dallin, *op. cit.*, pp. 233, 234.

3. See Hurley's letter of resignation to President Truman, November 26, 1945, in *U.S. Relations with China*, pp. 581-584.

4. See text, *ibid.*, pp. 607-609.

5. See press release on this order in *U.S. Relations with China*, pp. 609, 610.

6. See texts of the resolutions and agreement in *Ibid.*, pp. 610-622.

7. See text, *ibid.*, pp. 622-627.

8. See Rand's article in *New York Herald Tribune*, June 13, 1947.

9. The United Nations Rehabilitation and Relief Administration.

10. See text of the three messages in *U.S. Relations with China*, pp. 652-654.

11. See text, *Ibid.*, pp. 674, 675.

12. See text, *ibid.*, pp. 677, 678.

13. In this respect General Marshall was evidently influenced by Communist clever propaganda. Any Communist, whether Russian, Chinese, American, British, French, Yugoslavian, etc., by virtue of being such, believes in proletarian dictatorship and the suppression of all fundamental freedoms. So a liberal-Communist is a self-contradictory term.

14. See text, *ibid.*, pp. 686, 689.

15. *New York Times*, January 12, 1947.

16. *U.S. Relations with China*, p. 381.

17. Quoted in Beloff, *Soviet Policy in the Far East 1944-1951*, p. 53.

18. See English version of the article in *U.S. Relations with China*, pp. 710-719.

19. See text, *ibid.*, pp. 739, 740.

20. See *China Magazine*, August, 1947, pp. 5 et seq.

21. See *U.S. Relations with China*, pp. 364-367.

22. Stuart, *Fifty Years in China*, pp. 178, 179.

23. *U.S. Relations with China*, p. 273.
24. *New York Times*, March 13, 1947.
25. See U.S. Senate, *Report of the Committee on Judiciary* (McCarran Hearings), p. 198 et seq.

CHAPTER XXII

1. *U.S. Relations with China*, pp. 315, 316.
2. See summary of remarks at the meeting and text of the statement in *U.S. Relations with China*, pp. 758-764.
3. See text, *ibid.*, pp. 817-822.
4. *Ibid.*, p. 815.
5. *Ibid.*, p. 817.
6. See text, *ibid.*, pp. 764-814.
7. The National Government no longer existed after May 1948. The official title of the present government is the Central Government of the Republic of China.
8. See his letter to General Marshall on November 17, 1947 in *U.S. Relations with China*, pp. 372, 373.
9. See *Ibid.*, pp. 387-390.
10. Quoted in Utley, *The China Story*, p. 45.
11. See text of the Generalissimo's letter and President Truman's reply in *U.S. Relations with China*, pp. 888-890.
12. General Cheng Chien, although a veteran Kuomintang member, later deserted the cause and went over the Communist side; while General Pai Chung-hsi is now in Taiwan, serving as vice chairman of the Strategic Advisory Committee to the President.
13. From the author's diary on January 1, 1949.
14. See English version of the text in *U.S. Relations with China*, pp. 920-922.
15. See text in *Ibid.*, pp. 922-923.
16. *Ibid.*, p. 293.
17. See *ibid.*, pp. 783, 784.
18. *Ibid.*, p. 131.
19. *Ibid.*, p. 336.
20. *Ibid.*, p. 16.
21. Stuart, *Fifty Years in China*, p. 272.
22. *Ibid.*, p. 237, 238.

CHAPTER XXIII

1. *New York Times*, April 4, 1949.
2. *A Documentary History*, p. 453.
3. See text of these documents in Ta Kung Pao *Jen Min Shou Tse* (People's Handbook), 1951, pp. C1-C15.
4. See English version of the text of these pacts in *The Sino-Soviet Treaty and Agreements, Peking*, Foreign Language Press, 1950.
5. See text of these exchanges of notes in *Ibid.*
6. See North, "The Sino-Soviet Agreements of 1950", *Far Eastern Survey*, July 12, 1950.
7. See *New York Times*, February 16, 1950.
8. See *Hsin Hua Yueh Pao* (New China Monthly), Vol. II, p. 134.
9. See text of the communiqué in *New York Times*, September 16, 1952.

10. *Ibid.*, January 13, 1950.
11. *U.S. News and World Report*, May 5, 1950, p. 30.
12. These resolutions and other documents concerning the Korean War can be found in U.S. Senate, *The United States and the Korean Problem Documents, 1943-1953.*
13. See U.S. Senate, *Military Situation in the Far East* (Hearings before the Committee on Armed Services and the Committee on Foreign Relations, 1951.)
14. See *Ibid.*
15. *New York Times*, September 3, 1953.
16. *Ibid.*, January 13, 1954.
17. See *Jin Min Shou Tse*, 1956, pp. 383-385.
18. See *Time*, May 2, 1955, pp. 26-28.
19. See Chinese News Service, New York, press release, October 24, 1956.
20. See Associated Press despatch from Hongkong, November 19, 1956.
21. *New York Times*, November 29, 1956.
22. *People's China*, November 1, 1954, p. 40.
23. *Ibid.*, February 16, 1955, p. 7.
24. *Ibid.*, June 16, 1955.
25. *Jen Min Shou Tse*, 1956, p. 2.
26. *New York Times*, September 22, 1956.
27. *Ibid.*, September 18, 1956.
28. *Ibid.*, September 23, 1956.
29. See Sydney Gruson's despatch from Warsaw in *Ibid.*, October 16, 1956.
30. See editorials in *Jen Min Jih Pao*, November 3 and 4, 1956.
31. *New York Times*, November 22, 1956.
32. See Associated Press despatch from Hongkong, September 15, 1956.
33. See United Press despatch from Tokyo, November 14, 1956.
34. See *Chung Su Yu Hao* (Sino-Soviet Friendship), August 10, 1951, p. 9.
35. See *Hsin Hua Yueh Pao*, Vol. 3 (1951), p. 826.
36. *People's China*, October 1, 1953, p. 3.
37. See Associated Press despatch from London, January 24, 1954.
38. *Jim Min Shou Tse*, 1956, p. 528.
39. *People's China*, November 16, 1952, p. 23.
40. See Schwarz, "Sino-Russian Friendship is Useful to Both Sides", in *New York Times*, September 23, 1956.
41. *Time*, May 2, 1955, p. 28.
42. See Wittfogel, *Mao Tse-tung, Liberator or Destroyer of the Chinese Peasants?* p. 11.
43. Quoted in President Chiang's Message to the Nation, November 12, 1956.
44. For details see Deverall, *People's China, Sweat Shop Arsenal*, pp. 118-130.
45. See Reuter's despatch from Peiping in *New York Times*, June 10, 1956.
46. The working class, the peasant class, the petite bourgeoisie, and the national capitalist class are the four classes represented by the four small stars in the Communist flag; the big star indicates the Communist Party.
47. Quoted in President Chiang's message, *op. cit.*
48. See Chinese News Service, *Free China Weekly*, July 3, 1956.
49. See Hsin Hwa News Agency despatch from Canton, October 16, 1956.
50. A Hongkong dollar is worth about 16 cents in U.S. money.
51. *New York Times*, October 12, 1956.

CHAPTER XXIV

1. See Stuart, *op. cit.*, p. 271.
2. *Ibid.*, p. 274.
3. *New York Times*, January 15, 1950.
4. See *Time*, January 2, 1950, pp. 11, 12; and January 9, 1950, pp. 9, 10.
5. *New York Times*, January 4, 1950.
6. *Ibid.*, January 11, 1950.
7. *Ibid.*, January 6, 1950.
8. *Time*, January 16, 1950, p. 15.
9. See text of the statement in *New York Times*, June 28, 1950.
10. For details see *China Handbook* 1955-56, Ch. XVI.
11. See *New York Tmes*, July 30, 1955.
12. *China Handbook* 1955-56, p. 315.
13. *Ibid.*, p. 643.
14. *New York Times*, February 3, 1956.
15. *China Handbook* 1955-56, p. 698.
16. This organization, formed in September 1954, includes eight countries, viz: The United States, Britain, France, Australia, New Zealand, the Philippines, Thailand and Pakistan.
17. See text of the treaty and other quotations concerning it in *New York Times*, December 3, 1954.
18. See an account of the battle in *China Handbook* 1955-56, pp. 6, 7.
19. *New York Times*, January 25, 1955.
20. *Ibid.*, January 25, 26, 29 and 31, 1955.
21. *Ibid.*, February 1, 1955.
22. *Ibid.*, March 23, 1955.
23. *Ibid.*, March 16, 1955.
24. Chinese Delegation to the United Nations, *China Presents Her Case to the United Nations*, pp. 49, 50.
25. See text, *ibid.*, pp. 50, 51.
26. The author was one of the Chinese delegates to the Fourth Session of the General Assembly. This account is from his diary on December 2, 1949. See also United Nations, *Official Records of the Fourth Session of the General Assembly, First Committee*, 1949, pp. 355-357.
27. See text in Chinese Delegation to the United Nations, *op. cit.*, p. 50.
28. See Chinese Delegation to the United Nations, *China Fights for Peace and Freedom*, pp. 63-78.
29. United Nations, *Official Records of the General Assembly, Fifth Session, First Committee*, 1950, p. 349.
30. *Ibid.*, pp. 365-373.
31. United Nations, *Official Records of the General Assembly*, Supplement No. 20, p. 4.
32. *Ibid.*, *Plenary Meetings, 1951-1952*, pp. 452-453.
33. Chinese Delegation to the United Nations, *The Charter of the United Nations and the Package Deal*, p. 35.
34. See Tsiang's statement, *ibid.*, pp. 5-13.
35. See *New York Times*, December 14, 1955.
36. *Ibid.*, December 15, 1955.
37. *China Fights for Peace and Freedom*, p. 3.

38. The author was China's chief delegate to that conference.

39. See Walch, *Complete Handbook on Recognition of Communist China*, for a list of articles and opinions on both sides up to the end of 1954.

40. *New York Times*, October 24, 1953.

41. Truman, *Memoirs*, Vol. II, p. 399.

42. *Ibid.*, p. 403.

43. *Ibid.*, p. 408.

44. *New York Times*, May 19, 1951.

45. *Free China Weekly*, July 10, 1956.

46. *Ibid.*, August 14, 1956.

47. See text in *New York Times*, August 12 and 22, 1956.

48. For detailed information see *China Handbook* 1955-1956.

49. See *China Handbook* 1955-1956, Ch. 21.

50. U.S. House, 84th Congress, 2nd Session, *Report of the Special Study Mission to the Middle East, South and Southeast Asia, and the Western Pacific*, p. 171.

Select Bibliography

Abend, Hallett, *My Life in China,* New York, 1943.

Autobiography of Mao Tse-tung as Told to Edgar Snow, Hongkong, 1949.

Baddeley, John F., *Russia Mongolia and China,* 2 vols., London, 1919.

Ballantine, J. W., *Formosa: A Problem for the United States Foreign Policy,* Washington, 1952.

Band, William and Claire, *Two Years With the Chinese Communists,* New Haven, 1948.

Barmine, Alexander, *One Who Survived,* New York, 1945.

Bates, Ernest S., *Soviet Asia,* London, 1942.

Bau, M. J., *The Foreign Relations of China,* New York, 1921.

Belden, Jack, *China Shakes the World,* London, 1950.

Bell, John, *Travels From St. Petersburg in Russia to Diverse Parts of China,* 2 vols., London, 1763.

Beloff, Max, *The Foreign Policy of Soviet Russia,* 2 vols., London, 1947, 1949.

Soviet Policy in the Far East, 1944-1951, London, 1953.

Bienstock, Gregory, *The Struggle for the Pacific,* London, 1937.

Borowitz, Albert, *Fiction in Communist China,* Cambridge, Mass., 1954.

Boulger, D. C., *Life of Yakub Beg,* London, 1878.

England and Russia in Central Asia, 2 vols., London, 1879.

Central Asian Question, London, 1885.

Life of Sir Halliday McCartney, London, 1908.

Brandt, C., Schwarz, B., and Fairbank, John K., *A Documentary History of Chinese Communism,* Harvard, 1952.

Buell, P. L., *International Relations,* New York, 1929.

Buss, Claude A., *War and Diplomacy in Eastern Asia,* New York, 1941.

Byrnes, James F., *Speaking Frankly,* New York, 1947.

Cameron, James, *Mandarin Red,* London, 1955.

Carnegie Endowment for International Peace, *Treaties and Agreements With and Concerning China, 1919-1929,* Washington, 1929.

Chamberlin, William H., *America's Second Crusade,* Chicago, 1950.

Beyond Containment, Chicago, 1950.

Chang Chung-fo, *Chung Hua Min Kuo Wai Chiao Shih* (Diplomatic History of the Republic of China), Vol. 1, Peiping, 1936.

Chapman, H. O., *The Chinese Revolution, 1926-1927,* London, 1928.

Chen Chung-tzu, *Wai Meng Ku Chin Shih Shih* (Recent History of Outer Mongolia) Shanghai, 1926.

Chen Po-wen, *Chung O Wai Chiao Shih* (Sino-Russian Diplomatic History) Shankhai, 1928.

Chen Tu-hsiu, *Kao Chuan Tang Tung Chih Shu* (Letter to Comrades of the Whole Party) mimeographed, available in Hoover Library, Stanford.

Chiang, Kai-shek, *Resistance and Reconstruction,* New York, 1943.
Chiang Soong Mei-ling, Madame, *Sian: a Coup d'Etat,* Shanghai, 1937.
Chieh Fang She, *Chi Ta Wen Hsien* (Documents of the Seventh National Congress of the Chinese Communist Party) Yenan, 1945.
Chin Han-tsai, *Tso Wen Hsiang Kung Tsai Hsi Pei* (Tso Tsung-tang in the Northwest) Chungking, 1945.
China Handbook, Chungking, 1937-1945; New York, 1950; Taipei, 1951-1956
China Year Book, New York, 1912-1919; Tientsin, 1921-1930; Shanghai, 1931-1939.
Chinese Delegation to the League of Nations, *Japanese Aggression and the Nine Power Conference,* Geneva, 1937.
Chinese Delegation to the United Nations, *China Presents Her Case to the United Nations,* New York, 1949.
China Fights for Peace and Freedom, New York, 1951.
Chung Kuo Hsiang Lien Ho Kuo Kung Su Su Lien (China Accuses the Soviet Union in the United Nations) New York, 1952.
The Charter of the United Nations and the Package Deal, New York, 1955.
Chinese Imperial Maritime Customs, *Treaties, Conventions, etc., Between China and Foreign States,* 2 vols., Shanghai, 1908.
Chu, C. L., *Tsui Chin She Nien Chung O Chih Chiao Hse* (The Last Ten Years of Sino-Russian Relations), Shanghai, 1926.
Clyde, Paul H., *International Rivalries in Manchuria,* Columbus, Ohio, 1928.
United States Policy Toward China, Durham, 1940.
Compton, Boyd, *Mao's China: Party Reform Documents, 1942-1944,* Seattle, 1952.
Council on Foreign Relations, *Documents on American Foreign Relations,* New York.
Creel, George, *Russia's Race for Asia,* New York, 1949.
Curzon, George Lord, *Russia in Central Asia in 1889,* London, 1889.

Dallin, David J., *Soviet Russia's Foreign Policy, 1939-1942,* New Haven, 1942.
Soviet Russia in the Far East, New Haven, 1948.
The Rise of Russia in Asia, New Haven, 1949.
The New Soviet Empire, New Haven, 1951.
Davies, Joseph E., *Mission to Moscow,* New York, 1941.
Dennet, Tyler, *Roosevelt and the Russo-Japanese* War, Garden City, 1925.
Dennis, Alfred L. P., *The Foreign Policy of Soviet Russia,* 2 vols., London, 1924.
Department of State, *Foreign Relations of the United States.* Washington. (Series)
U.S. Foreign Relations: Japan, 1931-1941, Washington, 1942.
Nazi-Soviet Relations, 1939-1941, New York, 1948.
U.S. Relations With China, Washington, 1949.
Foreign Relations of the United States: China, 1942, Washington, 1956.
Deverall, R. L. G., *People's China, Sweat Shop Arsenal,* Tokyo, 1954.
Dewey, Thomas, *Journal to the Far Pacific,* New York, 1952.
Dunlap, A. M., *Behind the Bamboo Curtain,* Washington, 1956.

Endicott, M. A., *Five Stars Over China,* Toronto, 1953.
Epstein, Israel, *The Unfinished Revolution in China,* Boston, 1947.

Fairbank, John K., *The United States and China,* Harvard, 1948.
Far Eastern Information Bureau, *Documents With Reference to the Sino-Russian*

Dispute, 1929, Nanking, 1929.
Feis, Herbert, *The China Tangle,* Princeton, 1953.
Fischer, Louis, *The Soviet in World Affairs,* 2 vols., Princeton, 1930.
Fitch, Geraldine, *Formosa Beachhead,* Chicago, 1953.
Forman, Harrison, *Report from Red China,* London, 1946.
Changing China, New York, 1948.
Friters, George, *The International Position of Outer Mongolia,* Dijon, 1939.

Gelder, Stuart, *The Chinese Communists,* London, 1946.
Gale, George S., *No Flies in China,* New York, 1955.
Golder, Frank, *Russian Expansion in the Pacific,* Cleveland, 1914.
Griswold, A. W., *The Far Eastern Policy of the United States,* New York, 1938.

Hedin, Sven, *Big Horse's Flight,* London, 1936.
The Silk Road, New York, 1938.
Hidaka, Noboru, *Manchukua-Soviet Border Issues,* Dairen, 1938.
The Comintern's Intrigue in Manchukuo, Dairen, 1940.
Ho Chiu-tao, *Ping Ting Lo Chah Fang Luch* (The Strategy of Conquering the Russians).
So Fang Pei Cheng (Studies on the Northern Frontier) 6 vols., Peking, 1865.
Ho Han-wen, *Chung O Wai Chiao Shih* (History of Sino-Russian Diplomatic Relations), Shanghai, 1935.
Hornbeck, Stanley K., *The United States and the Far East,* Boston, 1942.
House of Representatives, Committee on Foreign Affairs, Subcommittee No. 5, *Communism in China,* Washington, 1948.
One Hundred Years of Communism, Washington, 1948.
Hsu Chung-hao, *Hsin Chiang Chih Lueh* (General Description of Sinkiang) Chungking, 1944.
Hsu, Leonard S., *Sun Yat-sen, His Political and Social Ideals,* Los Angeles, 1933.
Hsu, Shu-hsi, *Introduction to Sino-Foreign Relations,* Shanghai, 1941.
Hu Chiao-mu, *Chung Kuo Kung Chan Tang Teh San Shih Nien* (Thirty Years of the Chinese Community Party), Peiping, 1951.
Hu Chiu-yuan, *O Ti Ching Hua Shih Kang* (A Short History of Russian Aggression in China), Taipei, 1952.
Huang Yueh-po, Yu Lun-mu, and Pao Li-jen, *Chung Wai Tiao Yueh Hui Pien* (A Collection of Treaties Between China and Foreign States) Shanghai, 1935.
Hull, Cordell, *Memoirs of Cordell Hull,* 2 vols., New York, 1948.
Hunter, Edward, *Brain-Washing in Red China,* New York, 1951.

Ides, E. Y., *The Three Years' Land Travels of His Excellency E. Ysbrand Ides from Moscow to China,* London, 1705.
Institute of Pacific Relations, *Soviet Source Materials on U.S.S.R. Relations With East Asia, 1945-1950,* New York, 1950.
International Relations Committee, *The Sino-Russian Crisis,* Nanking, 1929.
Isaacs, H. R., *The Tragedy of the Chinese Revolution,* Stanford, 1951.
Draft Survey of Materials Relating to Communism in China, 1927-1934, manuscript available in Hoover Library, Stanford.
Jones, F. C., *Manchuria Since 1931,* London, 1949

Kennan, George, *E. H. Harriman: A Biography,* New York, 1922.
Krausse, Alexis, *Russia in Asia, 1558-1899,* New York, 1899.

Lange, Lorenz, *Journal of Residence at the Court of Peking,* 1763.
Lansdell, H., *Chinese Central Asia,* 2 vols., London, 1893.
Lattimore, Owen, *Situation in Asia,* Boston, 1945.
Li, Ang, *Hung Se Wu Tai* (The Red Stage), Peiping, 1946.
Lin Yutang, *The Vigil of a Nation,* New York, 1945.
Linebarger, Paul M. A., *The China of Chiang Kai-shek,* Boston, 1941.
Liu, F. F., *A Military History of Modern China, 1924-1949,* Princeton, 1956.
Liu Shao-chi, *Internationalism and Nationalism,* Peiping, 1948.
Liu Shaw-tong, *Out of Red China,* New York, 1953.
Liu Yen, *Tsui Chin San Shih Nien Chung Kuo Wai Chiao Shih* (Chinese Diplomatic History of the Last Thirty Years), Shanghai, 1930.
Lobanov- Rostovsky, A., *Russia and Asia,* New York, 1933.

MacMurray, John van A., *Treaties and Agreements With and Concerning China,* 2 vols., Washington, 1921.
Mao Ssu-cheng, *Min Kuo Shih Wu Nien I Chien Chih Chiang Chieh Shih Hsien Sheng* (Mr. Chiang Kai-shek Before 1926) 20 vols. Shanghai, 1937.
Mao Tse-tung, *Lun Lien Ho Cheng Fu* (On Coalition Government), Yenan, 1945.
Hsin Min Chu Chu I Lun, (On the New Democracy), Yenan, 1949.
Lun Jen Min Min Chu Chuan Cheng (On the People's Democratic Dictatorship), Hongkong, 1949.
Mif, P., *Heroic China,* New York, 1937.
Modlhammer, Franz L., *Moscow's Hand in the Far East,* Tokyo, 1938.
Moorad, George, *Behind the Iron Curtain,* Philadelphia, 1946.
Moore, Harriet L., *Soviet Far Eastern Policy, 1931-1945,* Princeton, 1945.
Moraes, Frank, *Report on Mao's China,* New York, 1953.
Morse, H. B., *International Relations of the Chinese Empire,* 3 vols., London.
Morse, H. B., and MacNair H. F., *Far Eastern International Relations,* New York, 1931.

Norins, Martin R., *Gateway to Asia: Sinkiang,* New York, 1944.
North, Robert C., *Kuomintang and Chinese Communists Elites,* Stanford, 1952.
Moscow and the Chinese Communists, Stanford, 1953.
Norton, H. K., *The Far Eastern Republic of Siberia,* New York, 1923.

Oudendyk, William, *Ways and By-Ways of Diplomacy,* New York, 1939.

Pares, Sir Bernard, *A History of Russia,* New York, 1937.
Pasvolsky, Leo, *Russia in the Far East,* New York, 1922.
Pavlovsky, Michel N., *Chinese Russian Relations,* New York, 1949.
Payne, Robert, *Mao Tse-Tung, Ruler of Red China,* New York, 1950.
Philips, G. D. R., *Russia, Japan and Mongolia,* London, 1942.
Pi Kuei-fang, *Wai Meng Chiao She Shih Mo Chi* (An Account of Negotiations Concerning Outer Mongolia) Peiping, 1928.
Powell, John, *My Twenty-five Years in China,* New York, 1945.
Pratt, Julius W., *A History of United States Foreign Policy,* Englewood Cliffs, New Jersey, 1955.

Ravenstein, Ernest G., *The Russians on the Amur,* London, 1861.
Rockhill, William W., *Treaties or Conventions With or Concerning China and Korea, 1894-1904,* Washington, 1945.
Rosinger, Lawrence, *China's Crisis,* New York, 1945.
China's Wartime Politics, Princeton, 1944.
Rostow, W. W., *The Prospects for Communist China,* Cambridge, Mass., 1954.
Roy, M. W., *Revolution and Counter-Revolution in China,* Calcutta, 1946.
Rowe, David N., *China Among the Powers,* New York, 1945.

Schwarz, B. L., *Chinese Communism and the Rise of Mao,* Harvard, 1950.
Senate, *The United States and the Korean Problem Documents, 1943-1953,* Washington, 1954.
Senate Committees on Armed Services and on Foreign Relations, *Hearing on Military Situation in the Far East,* Washington, 1951.
Senate Committee on the Judiciary, *Hearings on the Institution of Pacific Relations* (McCarran Hearings), Washington, 1952.
Senate Committee on the Judiciary, *Hearings on Strategy and Tactics of World Communism,* Washington, 1954.
Seton-Watson, Hugh, *From Lenin to Malenkov,* New York, 1953.
Sherwood, Robert E., *Roosevelt and Hopkins,* New York, 1948.
Siebert, George A. *Entente Diplomacy and the World,* New York, 1921.
Skrine, F. H., *Expansion of Russia, 1815-1900,* Cambridge, 1915.
Smedley, Agnes, *Battle Hymn of China,* New York, 1943.
Smith, Walter Bedell, *Moscow Mission, 1946-1949,* New York, 1949.
Snow, Edgar, *Red Star Over China,* New York, 1938.
Battle for Asia, New York, 1942.
Sokolsky, George E., *Tinder Box of Asia,* New York, 1934.
Stalin, Josef, *Marxism and the National and Colonial Question,* New York.
Stalin, Josef, and Molotov, Vyacheslav, *The Soviet Union and the Cause of Peace,* New York, 1936.
Stein, Guenther, *The Challenge of Red China,* London, 1945.
Stettinius, Edward, *Roosevelt and the Russians: The Yalta Conference,* New York, 1949.
Stilwell, Joseph W., *The Stillwell Papers,* New York, 1946.
Stimson, Henry L., *The Far Eastern Crisis,* New York, 1936.
Stuart, John Leighton, *Fifty Years in China,* New York, 1954.
Su Lien Yin Mou Wen Chen Hui Pien (Collection of Documents on the Soviet Conspiracy), Peiping, 1928.
Sun Yat-sen, *San Min Chu I* (The Three People's Principles), Canton, 1924.
Supreme National Defense Council, *Documents on the Problem of the Chinese Communist Party,* Chungking, 1944.

Ta Kung Pao, *Jen Min Shou Tse* (People's Handbook), Shanghai, 1950-1956.
Tang Leang-li, *The Inner History of Chinese Revolution,* London, 1930.
Teichman, Sir Eric, *Journey to Turkestan,* London, 1937.
Tong, Hollington, *Chiang Kai-shek,* Taipei, 1953.
Toynbee, Arnold J., *Survey of International Affairs,* London. (Series).
Trotsky, Leon, *Problems of the Chinese Revolution,* New York, 1932.
Truman, Harry S., *Memoirs,* 2 vols., Garden City, 1956.

Tseng, Chi-tse, *Tseng Hui Min Kung Chuan Chi* (Collection of Tseng Chi-tse's Writings), Shankhai, 1894.
Tso Tsung-tang, *Tsou Su* (Compiled Petitions) 120 vols., Shanghai, 1890.
Tsou Lu, *Chung Kuo Kuo Min Tang Shih Lueh,* (A Short History of the Kuomintang), Chungking, 1945.

Utley, Freda, *The China Story,* Chicago, 1951.
Last Chance in China, New York, 1947.

Vernadsky, George, *A History of Russia,* London, 1929.
Vladimir (pseudonym), *Russia on the Pacific and the Siberian Railway,* London, 1899.

Waichiaopu, *Kwang Hsu Tiao Yueh* (Treaties and Agreements During the Reign of Kwang-hsu), 16 vols., Peiping, 1925.
Waichiaopu, *Su Lien Tui Sinkiang Chih Chin Chi Ching Lueh* (Soviet Economic Aggression in Sinkiang), Taipei, 1950.
Walch, J. Weston, *Complete Handbook on Recognition of Communist China,* Portland, Maine, 1954.
Wallace, Henry A., *Soviet Asia Mission,* New York, 1946.
Walker, Richard L., *China Under Communism,* New Haven, 1955.
Wan Yah-kang, *The Rise of Communism in China,* Hongkong, 1952.
Wang Liang, *Ching Chih Wai Chiao Shih Liao* (Documents Concerning Foreign Relations During the Reign of Kwang-hsu and Hsuan-tung) Kwang-hsu 218 vols., Hsuan-tung, 24 vols., and appendices, Peiping, 1932.
Wang Yun-sheng, *Liu Shih Nien Lai Chung Kuo Yu Jih Pen* (China and Japan in Sixty Years), Tientsin, 1934.
Wales, Nym, *Red Dust: Autobiographies of Chinese Communists as Told to Nym Wales,* Stanford, 1952.
Wei, Henry, *China and Soviet Russia,* Princeton, 1956.
Weigh, Ken-sheng, *Russo-Chinese Diplomacy,* Shanghai, 1928.
White, Theodore H., and Jacoby, A., *Thunder Out of China,* New York, 1946.
Wilbur, C. Martin, and How, Julie L., *Documents on Communism, Nationalism, and Soviet Advisers in China, 1918-1927,* New York, 1956.
William, Maurice, *Sun Yat-sen Versus Communism,* Baltimore, 1932.
Willkie, Wendell, *One World,* New York, 1943.
Willoughby, W. W., *Foreign Rights and Interests in China,* 2 vols., Baltimore, 1920.
Witte, Count Sergie Y., *The Memoirs of Count Witte,* New York, 1921.
Wittfogel, Karl A., *Mao Tse-tung, Liberator or Destroyer of the Chinese Peasants?* New York, 1955.
Wu, Aitchen K., *Turkistan Tumult,* London, 1940.
China and the Soviet Union, New York, 1950.
Wu Hsiu-chuan, *China Accuses,* Peiping, 1951.

Yakhontoff, Victor A., *Russia and the Soviet Union in the Far East,* London, 1932.
The Chinese Soviets, New York, 1934.
Young, C. Walter, *The International Relations of Manchuria,* Chicago, 1929.

Zacharias, Ellis, *Secret Missions,* New York, 1946.

Index